Lt Gen Faruk Yahaya
COUNTER TERRORISM &
COUNTER INSURGENCY THEORY
MEETS PRACTICE

Adonis & Abbey Publishers Ltd
24 Old Queen Street, London SW1H 9HP United Kingdom
Website: http://www.adonis-abbey.com
E-mail Address: editor@adonis-abbey.com

Nigeria:
Plot 2560, Hassan Musa Katsina Street, Asokoro, Abuja, Nigeria
Tel:+234(0)7058078841/08052035034
Website: http://www.adonis-abbey.com
E-mail Address: editor@adonis-abbey.com

Copyright 2023 © Lt Gen Faruk Yahaya

British Library Cataloguing-in-Publication Data
A catalogue record for this book is available from the British Library

ISBN: 978-1-913976-23-1

The moral right of the author has been asserted

All rights reserved. No part of this book may be reproduced, stored in a retrieval system or transmitted at any time or by any means without the prior permission of the publisher

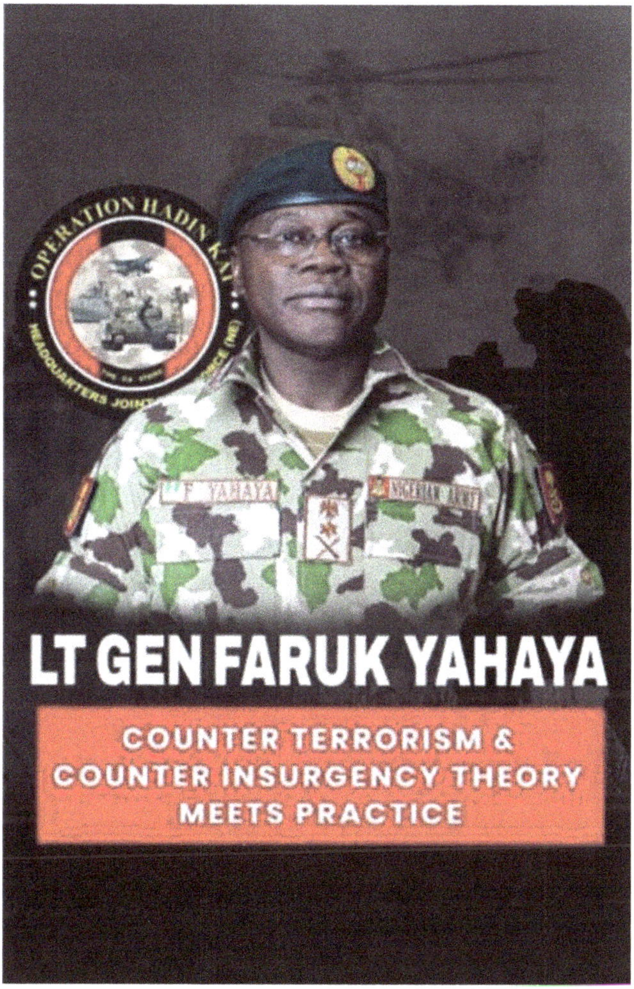

LT GEN FARUK YAHAYA

COUNTER TERRORISM & COUNTER INSURGENCY THEORY MEETS PRACTICE

Edited by
Maj Gen Emeka Onumajuru

Table of Contents

Foreword 7
Preface 9

Section One
Making of a Military Leader
Imprints of Leadership 17
Huffing and Puffing for Tough Times: Military Training at the 49
A Life of Service to the Nation and Humanity 61
Leadership Grooming and Selection 79

Section Two
Nigeria's National Security Problematic
Precedence, Origin and Dynamics of Insecurity in Nigeria:Theoretical and Empirical Notes 105
Factors and Actors of Insecurity in Nigeria: Manifestations and Impacts 129
Terrorism and Insurgency in Nigeria 151

Section Three
CTCOIN: Leading From the Front
Evolution of CTCOIN Operations in the North East Nigeria 175
Commanding the North East Theatre 217
Non-Kinetic Approaches to CTCOIN Operations in Nigeria 239

Section Four
CTCOIN: Operational and Strategic Thoughts
Operational and Strategic Thoughts 263
Leadership in CTCOIN Operations 271
Operational Levels Tactics and Manoeuvre in CTCOIN 281
Fire Support in CTCOIN Operations 297
Utility of Intelligence in CTCOIN Operations 305
Primacy of Politics in CTCOIN 315

Section Five
Nigerian Army of the Future
Vision and Strategic Posturing 339
Final Thoughts 365

Reflections
Gen LEO Irabor 372
Maj Gen IM Yusuf 374
Maj Gen AB Omozoje 375
Notes on the Contributors 395

References 397

Index 417

Foreword

On 27 May 2021, when I appointed Lieutenant General Faruk Yahaya as the 22nd Chief of Army Staff, I knew I was selecting a thoroughbred military leader and strategist. I was clear-headed that I had chosen one of the finest in the Nigerian Army to bring fresh impetus to our counterterrorism and counterinsurgency efforts and to consolidate the gains made in pushing back terrorists and insurgents who have challenged our peace and stability as a nation. Since the mantle of leadership of the Nigerian Army fell on him, he has justified his choice as a patriotic, courageous, honest, and proactive strategic leader with sound understanding of the nuances of counter terrorism and insurgency.

This book on General Faruk Yahaya presents two treatises for the price of one. First is the biographic exposition of a gentle, cerebral, and resolute General. It traces his humble beginnings in Sifawa, Sokoto State, to the steady rise to Generalship in the Nigerian Army. There was no premonition that Faruk would end up with a life in military service. His early days foretold the story of an endowed man under the grace of the Almighty, who took the opportunities offered by the environment, time, and circumstances to rise to the leadership of the Nigerian Army. It gives credence to Nigeria as a land of great and equal opportunities to its citizens.

The second treatise offers an understanding of Nigeria's national security complexity and ongoing efforts to overcome them. This section explores the origins, precedence, and dynamics of insecurity by critically examining the historical, political, environmental, and socio-economic background of terrorism and insurgency in Nigeria. It presents the evolution and diverse mix of the ways and means to achieve the ends of counterterrorism and counterinsurgency. It records the sacrificial contributions by men like General Faruk Yahaya who have served in all echelons of command in the Nigerian Army (including command of the North-East theatre) to bring the military element of power to bear in our aspirations for a safe and secure nation. Most importantly, it points to the enormous progress already made in the fight against terrorism and insurgency. This is a solemn promise I made to the Nigerian people, and a promise being delivered through the instrumentality of men like General Faruk Yahaya.

The book provides in greater detail, the strategic thoughts and insights of a serving Chief of Army Staff fighting and winning the war against terrorism and insurgency in Nigeria. I commend General Faruk Yahaya for his wealth of professional military experience, for his service to the Nigerian nation and for his insights, which he has generously shared in this book. I recommend this book to personnel of the Armed Forces of Nigeria, security operatives, military historians, scholars, and all those who wish to understand the dynamics of counterterrorism and counterinsurgency in Nigeria and beyond.

Muhammadu Buhari *GCFR*
President Commander-in-Chief of the Armed Forces Federal Republic of Nigeria

04th April 2023

Preface

Military leadership, in the modern context, is the multi-disciplinary capability of military personnel to integrate the concepts and practice of military professional values to influence men under authority to attain assigned mission objectives. Military leadership is grounded on a long value chain of typical leadership development activities such as recruitment, selection, orientation, general and special training, career development, mentoring, leadership grooming, strategic dipping and honing, diverse military service, and performance assessment. At the strategic level, the classic nexus between military and political leadership is that the former promotes an amenable environment for the latter to thrive. In other words, the military service is an extension of politics by other means.

In Nigeria, we have had a long experience with military leadership that also doubled as political leaders so the lines between military and political leadership assessment were rather blurred. Nigeria has benefited from the service of its military leaders in traditional security, defence, and military roles since the establishment of the Fourth Republic in 1999. The appointment of Lieutenant General Faruk Yahaya as the 22nd Chief of Army Staff (COAS) in May 2021, in the middle of a Counter Terrorism and Counter Insurgency (CTCOIN) campaign fits this description. It affords the opportunity to x-ray and highlight what Nigeria's top military Generals are really made of.

General Faruk Yahaya has had rich experience in the entire value chain of military leadership training and grooming. As an Infantry officer, he has been thoroughly trained in conventional, non-conventional and evolving hybrid warfare. He has also done staff courses and associated leadership training at various echelons of military command. In particular, he has been schooled in the concepts and principles of CTCOIN. Quite significantly, General Faruk Yahaya has had the unique experience of doing at least 4 tours of duty responsible for CTCOIN at the operational and military strategic levels. These were: Brigade Commander of 4 Brigade Benin; Brigade Commander of 29 Task Force Brigade Borgozo, which was a part of the defunct Operation LAFIA DOLE; General Officer Commanding 1 Division, Kaduna; Theatre Commander Operation HADIN KAI; and now the COAS where the buck stops.

Evidently, General Faruk Yahaya is a highly trained Nigerian military General who has been responsible at various times for executing the Federal Government's efforts to counter the real threats of terrorism and insurgency. How did he perform in the past and how is he performing now? How did he translate the concepts and theories of CTCOIN into practice? This book titled "Lieutenant General Faruk Yahaya: Counter Terrorism and Counter Insurgency Theory Meets Practice", attempts to answer these pertinent questions. The book is written in five Sections, each exploring a sub-theme of the main plot as shown.

Section 1 titled "Making of a Military Leader", is a scholarly account of the Man, General Faruk Yahaya. It explores the development of the subject's life with emphasis on core values, patterns and profiles of character, strengths and weaknesses, points of inflexion as well as notable acts of fame and early achievements that collectively define the Man. It also puts on record the high points of his career in the Nigerian Army and the Armed Forces of Nigeria (AFN). This part covers the "Imprints of Leadership"; "Huffing and Puffing for Tough Times Ahead: Military Training at the Nigerian Defence Academy"; "A Life of Service to the Nation and Humanity"; and lastly, "Leadership Grooming and Selection".

Section 2 titled "Nigeria's National Security Problematic" veer off, albeit temporarily, from the Man and focuses on an academic and evidence-based review of the Problem of the Study, which basically is terrorism and insurgency. It explores the background, evolution, and threats of insecurity. It gives an unbiased review of the historical and immediate causes of insecurity in Nigeria, the manifestations of diverse forms of insecurity, and the theoretical principles for countering them. It covers "Precedencies, Origins and Dynamics of Insecurity in Nigeria: Theoretical and Empirical Notes"; "Factors and Actors of Insecurity in Nigeria: Manifestations and Impacts" and "Terrorism and Insurgency in Nigeria".

Section 3 titled "CTCOIN - Leading from the Front", explores the meeting between the Man and the Problem of the Study under various environments and conditions. Put differently, it presents the meeting of theory and practice in CTCOIN. It x-rays the principles and practices of the various military operations conducted in the operational areas, with particular focus on the experiential narrative of Gen Faruk Yahaya. It is written on "Evolution of CTCOIN Operations in North-East Nigeria"; "Commanding the North-East Theatre" and "Non-Kinetic Approaches to CTCOIN Operations in Nigeria".

Section 4 is on "Operational and Strategic Thoughts". It x-rays thoughts on different aspects of military operation and strategies, especially regarding CTCOIN. It deals with "Leadership in CTCOIN Operations, "Operational Level Tactics and Manoeuvre in CTCOIN", "Fire Support in CTCOIN Operations", "Utility of Intelligence in Operations", and "The Primacy of Politics in CTCOIN".

Section 5 is titled "The Nigerian Army of the Future". It explores the strategic insights and projections for the Nigerian Army in the future and their likely impact on national security. This section is on "Vision and Strategic Posturing" which examines the vision and mission statement of the COAS, and "Final Thoughts on the Future of the Nigerian Army".

Leadership is an eclectic expression that speaks to the fundamental essence and imperative of man to make his environment and life better, more amenable, and more productive. In typical military leadership style, General Faruk Yahaya has led the Nigerian Army to accomplish many missions. The summation of the narrative is that General Faruk Yahaya has served and will continue to serve. The essential value of the book lies in chronicling the life of a simple unassuming Nigerian, destined for greatness, selected through the principle of equal opportunity in the nation, and groomed by a culmination of time, circumstance and fortune to reach the peak of Generalship in Nigeria and more importantly, to change the course of its national security history.

EV Onumajuru
Maj Gen
Editor-in-Chief

Section One

Making of a Military Leader

Lt Gen F Yahaya *NAM CFR*
Chief of Army Staff

Imprints of Leadership

Leadership is one of the major factors contributing to the success of human groups, corporate entities, communities, and nations. For military organizations, leadership is critical in peacetime as well as in times of conflict and war. The Great Man Theory of Leadership postulated by Thomas Carlyle assumes that some people are born with innate attributes that set them apart from others and these qualities are responsible for their assuming positions of power and authority as well as their success. This theory testifies to the lives and leadership of great men such as Mahatma Gandhi, Abraham Lincoln, and Napoleon Bonaparte. However, contemporary wisdom holds that leaders are both born and made. In other words, some leadership qualities are genetic, while others can be developed. The jury is out on the exact proportions of intrinsic and extrinsic leadership qualities. Although recent studies by Leach (2021) suggest that leadership is 30 per cent genetic and 70 per cent learned, the exact boundaries are seemingly blurred, but what is obvious is that the effective development of inbred leadership qualities will offer more impact than unharnessed genetic traits. This chapter focuses on the predisposing conditions for the natural growth, development, and leadership of Lieutenant General Faruk Yahaya. These include, but are not limited to, factors such as family background and history; circumstances of birth; an early physical environment; as well as social environment and institutions.

Faruk Yahaya is a proud native of Sifawa, one of the major districts in the Bodinga Local Government Area of Sokoto State, Nigeria. Sifawa is a modem-day manifestation of ancient cultures and traditions as well as the legacy of the Islamic Jihad. Legend has it that the place was named after the first settler, *a Barebari* hunter named Sifawa who migrated from Kanem Borno Empire in present-day Borno State sometime around the eleventh century AD.

The progenitor of Sifawa came with a rich history as his native people, the *Barebaris* of Bomo trace their own origin all the way to Yemen in the Middle East. Indeed, it is strongly held that the founder of the *Barebaris* was among the descendants of Seif ibn Dhi Yazan, a legendary Yemenite figure who migrated westward and settled around the Lake Chad region where he eventually founded the ancient Kanem Bornu Empire. As the name Sifawa suggests, it was said to have been derived from Seifuwa, the popular Kanembu name for descendants of Seif ibn Dhi Yazan. As a result of possible family or dynastic tussles, he migrated and settled at the place that later became known as Sifawa. This narrative is given credence by ancient accounts of the Kings of Borno, which say that the *Barebari* of Seifuwa proudly saw themselves as the descendants of a family in Yemen and did not lose their Arab identity or fully become Negro until about 1200 AD. When the *Barebaris* arrived in Sifawa, they met other tribes such as the Hausa-speaking elements, Fulanis and perhaps other communities. Gradually but surely, the *Barebaris* were assimilated into the predominant Hausa language, culture, and traditions and indeed, became part of them.

At the turn of the 19th century, while Great Britain and Ireland were being united under King George III, the seeds of discord that would ironically give birth to great and remarkable events in Northern Nigeria were being sown at Gobir, a contiguous Hausa state north of the Kebbi Kingdom. On assumption of the throne of his fathers in 1801, Yunfa the Sarkin Gobir found himself in conflict with his former teacher, Uthrnan ibn Fodiyo, the Fulani Islamic philosopher, scholar, teacher, and reformer. Yunfa logically wanted greater secular control over his domain. However, although Islam had been spread to the Hausa states by Arab merchants since the eleventh century AD, Uthrnan ibn Fodiyo was appalled by the paganism, hypocrisy, and greed of the ruling Hausa elite and sought to impose the tenets of Islamic law, good governance, and cultural refinement. This was a classic conflict between the state and religion. The state won the first encounter as Uthrnan ibn Fodiyo was exiled to Degel by Yunfa in 1802, but this turned out to be a temporary and Cadrnean victory as Uthrnan ibn Fodiyo responded by mobilizing and assembling his disciples who eventually fought the Fulani Islamic Jihad.

The Jihad started in 1804; by 1808, Alkalawa, the capital of Gobir, had been conquered. Uthrnan ibn Fodiyo quickly overran much of the northern Nigeria's Hausa states and established their Caliphate. At the height of its glory, the Sokoto Caliphate as:

Adamawa; Bauchi; Daura; Gobir; Gombe; Gwandu; Kano; Katagum; Katsina; Kebbi; Nupe; and Zaria in Northern Nigeria and extended far a field to present day Burkina Faso, Niger, and Cameroon. As Hill (2009) observed, "with the help of a large Fulani cavalry and Hausa peasants, Uthman ibn Fodiyo overthrew the region's Hausa rulers and replaced them with Emirs who were mostly Fulanis". Sheikh Uthman ibn Fodiyo first visited Sifawa, in 1805 on his way to Magabci around at a critical stage of the Jihad. Additionally, after the fall of Alkalawa the seat of Gobir's political power in 1808, he settled at Sifawa, where he laid the foundation for the administration of the Caliphate from 1809 to 1915. As a result, Sifawa played an important, albeit non- kinetic, role in the Jihad. According to Alhaji Muhammad Buhari Tambari, (MON), the District Head of Sifawa, oral traditional accounts state that Sheikh Uthman ibn Fodiyo, settled firstly at Sifawa after the fall of Gobir before moving to Sokoto. Indeed, most Jihad commanders were said to have obtained their flags from Sheikh Uthman ibn Fodiyo in Sifawa, before embarking on their Holy war campaigns. To this day, the Mosque of Sheikh Uthman ibn Fodiyo, the Sheikh's house, and the tombs of some of his disciples are still present in Sifawa.

Fig 1: Front View of Sheikh Uthman ibn Fodiyo Mosque Sifawa

Fig 2: Inside View of Uthman ibn Fodiyo Mosque, Sifawa

Fig 3: Residence of Sheikh Uthman ibn Fodiyo at Sifawa

Fig 4: Tomb location of popular Disciple of Sheikh Uthman ibn Fodiyo, Suleman Autadu

Within a period of 800 years, Sifawa had experienced cultural assimilation by two patently different socio-cultural forces. The majority Hausa natives first voluntarily assimilate the minority settlers. This was a gradual process of integration that occurred over time, perhaps as a natural response to the cultural pressures of the predominant Hausa population and as an inherent self-preservation mechanism to ensure the safety and security of the settlers. It manifested changes in behaviour, values, beliefs, vocations, and the way of life of the people much in keeping with the postulations of Keefe and Padilla (1987). However, the second experience was the eventual and ironic assimilation of the invading Fulani Jihadists by the supposedly conquered Hausa.

Sifawa is now one of the seven districts of Bodinga, which is one of Sokoto State's 23 Local Government Areas. In alphabetical order, the other six districts of Bodinga LGA are Badau, Bagarawa, Bodinga; Danchadi, Dingyadi, and Tulluwa. Bodinga LGA is bounded: to the North by Wamakko LGA; to the Northeast by Kware LGA; and to the East by Dange-shuni LGA. Furthermore, it is bound: to the South by Shagari and Tureta LGAs; and finally, to the West by Yabo LGA.

Fig 5: Map of Sokoto State showing Bodinga LGA

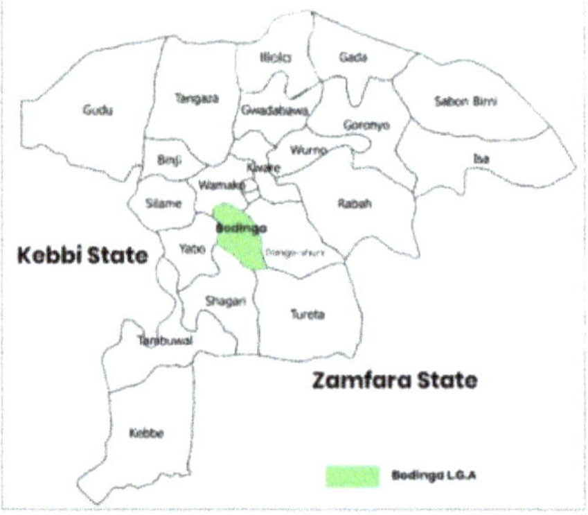

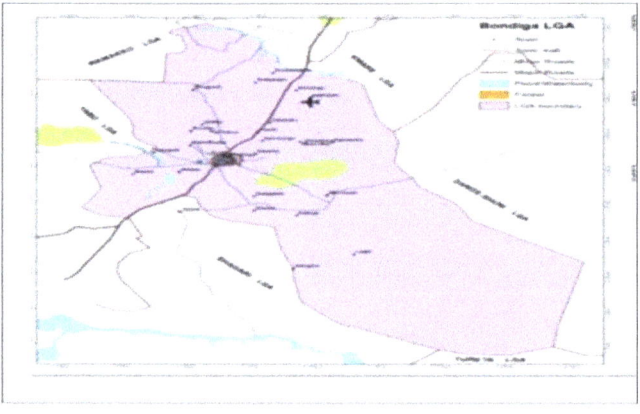

Source: Nigerian Geological Survey Agency

Fig 6: Map of Bodinga LGA

Source: Nigerian Geological Survey Agency

Sifawa is about 35 kilometers southwest of Sokoto, roughly between Latitudes 10°N and 14°N and between Longitudes 3° 3 11E and 7° 15^{1}E. From data obtained at the Nigerian Geological Survey Agency, Sifawa had an estimated population of about 31,165 in 2022. The people are predominantly Hausas. Other major towns in Sokoto State close to Sifawa are Bodinga and Yabo. Indeed, Bodinga and Sifawa seem to have merged. The main approach to Sifawa is through the Sokoto - Jega highway. Along this road and just before Bodinga town, the attraction of Sifawa beckons. It sits on a plateaued high ground surrounded by valleys much like "an elevated nest in the Savannah". Some parts of the high ground average about 300 meters above sea level. From afield, the valleys show a bed-land topography of sandy plains broken by steep-sided iselbergs and ranges. These were the remains of a lost river that served as a southwestern barrier to the settlement, some two hundred years ago and beyond. Lake *Bela,* located west of Sifawa, is a major landmark in the lowlands. The soil types in the valleys are mainly sandy topsoil and clay subsoil. Although these valleys are now generally dry due to climate change, they were once frquently flowing with water, and its banks provided some of the richest and most fertile lands in Sifawa. The valleys fit the description of the Savannah by Trimingham (1962) as "a land of agriculture where basic food crops and cash crops are grown. It is equally a land where sheep, goats and cattle find abundant herbage". The life of a typical Sifawa indigene fits this desciption perfectly. In Sifawa, one was primarily a farmer, a herder or both before anything else.

The climate of the area is subject to the movement of the Inter-Tropical Convergence Zone (ITCZ) or the *Calms* because of its largely windless nature. This is the zone where the Northeast and Southeast trade winds converge. The locations and movements of these two major air masses determine the temperatures and precipitation and indeed, the dry and rainy seasons of the area. The dry season is generally made up of two weather types. The first is *Hunturu* or Harmattan between November and January and sometimes up to February and even March. It is characterized by cold, dry, and hazy weather due to Northeasterly winds. In this period, leaves and stalks dry up and water reservoirs such as Lake *Bela* begin to recede. The next period is the *Bazara* or hot season which occurs generally from March to May, sometimes extending into June. The heat of *Bazara* can become so unbearable that people seek the intervention of Allah subhanahu wa ta'ala (SWT), the most glorified and most high. After *Bazara* comes *Damina* or the rainy season from around June to October. *Damina* extends to *Malka,* the period of heavy rainfall. *Malka* is distinguished by abundant rain, which causes seasonal flooding in water concentration points and reservoirs such as Lake *Bela*. Quite significantly, the fields again bloom with luxuriantly green vegetation during *Malka*.

There are basically two major types of vegetation in Sifawa characterized by their use as fodder for animals or as food and other purposes by man. The most common plants used as fodder are *Burburwa, Gadagi* (also popularly called horse groundnut), *Gamba, Balashiyu, Harkiya, Gemunkusa, Danfarkami, Harwatsi* and *Bagaruwa*. While *Burburwa* (or Eragrostis ciliaris) is an excellent fodder of first choice, *Gamba* (or Andropogon gayanus) is particularly used as animal feed during *Malka* when most other grasses are not palatable. Plants for human use are grouped into two. The first group are consumed as food, drinks, and medicine. The most common trees and shrubs in this group are *Tsamiya*, Locust Beans, *Dunya, Kuka, Sahara, Geza, Kalgo, Bugaruwa* and *Sahara*. Any or all of the parts of these plants such as their leaves, fruits and seeds are consumed raw, cooked, or processed for that purpose. In particular, locust beans (or *Parkia biglobosa)* are used to make *Kalwa* or *Daddawa,* a popular and nutritious condiment for soup and *Dunya* fruits (or *Vztax dominant)* are used to make *Madi and Alewa,* which are tasty sugars good for human health.

The second group are plants used for other human purposes. For instance: *Burburwa* stems are used for ornamental mats and broom; *Gamba* is used for mat-making, local roofing, and fencing; *Dorawa* (or *Arki oliveri)* seed capsules (or *Makuba)* are used as plastering mud and in dye pits; *Dunya* trees are used as mortars, pestles, and as handles of hoes, knives and other implements due to their strength; The common *Bugaruwa* (or *Acacia arabica)* is used as gum in its fresh form, for tanning leather as well as for shade and fencing; *Sahara* (or *Guiera senegalenis)* is used as firewood for cooking; *Geza* leafs are used for maternity baths, whereas the wood is used as firewood and in making roofs; and lastly, *Kaba* (or *Adansonia digi)* is generally used for making local mats, local roofs and ornaments.

In Sifawa, just like in most places in Northern Nigeria, plants are precious and wonderful life-giving gifts from Allah (SWT). Until recent efforts at afforestation to fight desertification, these plants mainly occurred naturally. They sprout, flourish, and fade away in their due seasons. The cycles of life and death of plants are crucial to the existence, survival, wellbeing, and prosperity of the people. It is therefore important that people recognize these plants and at least know their uses. fu addition to these naturally occurring plants, the people of Sifawa cultivate basic food crops such as millet, guinea com, beans, and wheat, as well as cash crops such as ground nuts, tobacco, and cotton. Typically, the people also rear animals such as sheep, goats, and cattle. These are the pristine vocations in Sifawa passed down from generations to generations irrespective of the status or position of the person. Faruk remembers that as a child, he joined his siblings to do farm work during holidays and weekends, after school hours and sometimes even during school break time.

The ancestry of General Faruk Yahaya can be traced to the time of the Islamic Jihad. Between 1809 and 1815, when Sheikh Uthman ibn Fodiyo settled in Sifawa, the town remained the administrative headquarters of the Caliphate. As stated earlier, most of the flagbearers, and subsequent Emirs, in the constituent emirates under the Sokoto Caliphate, either received their flags or frequented Sifawa to pay homage and seek blessings from the Sheikh. From Sifawa, the Sheikh divided the administration of the Caliphate into two. He placed the eastern part under the care of his son Muhammadu Bello, while the western part was under the charge of his brother Abdullahi ibn Fodiyo. Throughout the Sheikh's stay at Sifawa, Abdullahi Fodiyo lived at Bodinga while Muhammadu Bello founded and settled at Sokoto. In 1815, Uthman ibn Fodiyo moved to Sokoto where he died two years later. He left his son Buhari in charge of Sifawa.

Following the emergence of Muhammad Bello as Caliph after the death ofUthman ibn Fodiyo, Abdullahi ibn Fodiyo moved to Gwandu where he finally settled. As a result, Mallam Buhari relocated and joined Abdullahi in Gwandu before settling in Tambuwal. When Mallam Buhari left Sifawa, he left the town in the care of the Ajiya (or caretaker in Hausa language).The first Ajiya was from the great merchant class, the Wangarawa family. Ajiya and the people who succeeded him continued to report to Buhari at Tambuwal. After the death of Buhari, his son Umar succeeded him and remained in charge of Sifawa, through his representative. An important development occurred in 1850 when the then Sultan, Aliyu Babba ibn Muhammad Bello separated Sifawa from Tambuwal and placed it under the leadership of Aliyu, son of Buhari ibn Sheikh Uthman ibn Fodiyo, alongside Dogondaji, which was placed under Bara'u son of Buhari ibn Sheikh Uthman ibn Fodiyo. The appointment of Aliyu as Sarkin Kudun of Sifawa in 1850 was a watershed in the history of Sifawa District.

Clearly, it was no longer administratively convenient to keep the office of Ajiya as it then was. Administratively, the roles of Ajiya were then redefined to be a "caretaker of the treasury" of the town, as it had been in the Caliphate. The new Sarkin Kudu of Sifawa appointed Ajiya Alhamdu, a popular livestock farmer as the new Ajiya of Sifawa in 1850. This was a position of great honour and trust. Ajiya Alhamdu distinguished himself in this position so much so that his name became synonymous with the title and his family became known as the Ajiya family. Indeed, up to this day, the now honorific title of "Ajiya of Sifawa" is still held by members of the Ajiya family.

Ajiya Alhamdu was a polygamous man who had thirteen children - Abdulrahman; Abdullahi Bayaro; Imrana; Haliru; Hauwa'u; and Halidu. Others were Shayau, Buhari, Yusuf, Isah, Fatima, Ahmad, and Sa'idu. Expectedly, given his antecedence, Ajiya Alhamdu was a man of values. He raised his children in the fear of Allah (SWT) and in the timeless values of honesty, integrity, hard work, community service and sacrifice. Not much is known of all of these children except that Sa'idu his last child, sired four children namely: Mallam Yahaya; Malam Audi, Rukayyatu (or Ruke) and Lamso but he died rather early when Mallam Yahaya, his first child, was still young. As was the tradition of the people, Mallam Yahaya was taken in and brought-up by a relative, Liman Muhammadu Mijinyawa who was a teacher and counsellor. Mallam Yahaya studied under Liman Mijinyawa and became known as a hardworking and disciplined Islamic student.

After receiving elementary and secondary Islamic education known as *Makarantar Alla* and *Makarantar Ilimi or Zaure* respectively at Sifawa, Mallam Yahaya travelled to different places in and outside Nigeria in search of knowledge. He was in Zamfara, Katsina, Zaria, Kano, and Barno among other places in Northern Nigeria and parts of some neighbouring countries bordering Nigeria to the North. In these places, he stayed with prominent scholars at various centers of learning receiving tertiary-level Islamic education. He learned from and acquired useful knowledge and experiences from these scholars and specialists in diverse Islamic disciplines. He was exposed to scholarly perspectives, multiple environments, and the diverse lifestyles and cultures of different peoples. According to Ibrahim Muhammad Liman, one of the students of Mallam Yahaya, "these experiences gave Mallam Yahaya broad scholarly insights in interpreting legal texts when handling practical issues".

Arising largely from his diverse and expansive learning experiences, Mallam Yahaya, became a vibrant and dynamic, yet intuitive, flexible, and insightful Islamic teacher, counsellor, and preacher. These values were clear in his teachings and interpretation of legal texts. Significantly, they were manifested in the philosophy of his judgments and verdicts on contentious religious and social issues, as attested by his students and listeners. He was also known for his specialization in Islamic disciplines such as Arabic grammar, pre-Islamic Arabic literature, Islamic law and jurisprudence, Islamic history and biographies, Tafsir, and the science of the Hadith.

A unique and remarkable feature of Mallam Yahaya's scholarship was his deep knowledge of Islamic texts. He memorized and mastered hundreds of poems, including the pre-Islamic collections which were a serious challenge to his students who could hardly read from textbooks while he was reciting, translating, and making commentaries from memory. He was thus an excellent reciter of the Holy Qur'an and was frequently invited to public recitations and entertainment, particularly during religious activities. An associated skill of his vocation was handwriting. Due to the limited access to books and the absence of electronic publications at the time, the only way one could own books was to copy them by hand. This gave Mallam Yahaya the added advantage of being a good hand writer.

After a lengthy sojourn of learning and teaching, Mallam Yahaya settled in Sifawa. He was one of the pioneer teachers at the Jama'atul Nasril Islam (JNI) Primary School Sifawa. The school was established in 1967 as a community school to teach Islamic education, but with time, it expanded its academic curriculum to accommodate Western education. Initially, Mallam Yahaya was a volunteer, but was later employed by the government when community schools were taken over in 1975. He was a Religious Studies Teacher and Discipline Master. His presence and participation in the affairs of the school along with that of his colleagues; Mallam Saidu, who was the first Headmaster, Mallam Bello Muhammed, Mallam Abdullahi, and Liman Muhammadu Balarabe, who later became the Imam of Sifawa, was a major factor that persuaded parents to enroll their children in the novelty known as *Makarantar Baka*.

In honour of the first Headmaster, the school was renamed Mallam Saidu Nizzamiyya Primary School, Sifawa in 2004.

Fig 7: Mallam Saidu Nizzamiyya Primary School, Sifawa

Mallam Yahaya turned out to be one of the best students in the household of Liman Mijinyawa. This was no mean feat for the young man, considering the antecedents of Liman Mijinyawa, His grandfather Muhammed Ibn Muhammed Madaro was a contemporary of Muhammed Bello, the second Sultan of Sokoto, and fought in the Battle of Maru alongside his son Abubakar popularly known as Sahabi. Muhammed died in the battle, but his son Abubakar Sahabi survived and initially settled in Maru. Thereafter, he relocated to Sokoto from where he was appointed as Chief Imam of Sifawa around 1850 at the same time the first Sarkin Kudu of Sifawa was appointed. The Mijinyawa family thus had a reputation for bravery, scholarship and service. They played significant role during the Jihad and in the defence of the Caliphate. To this day, the imams of Sifawa Central Mosque and other imams of mosques in nearby township are appointed from the extended family. Liman Mijinyawa had many children but eight survived. These were Liman Muhammadu Balarabe, who became Chief Imam of Sifawa; Hajiya Fatima (Jabbo), his first daughter; Alkali Ahmadu; Liman Abdullahi; Rabi'atu; Alhaji Shehu; Sa'adatu; and Amamatu. Hajiya Fatima followed the family tradition and became a female Islamic teacher, a remarkable feat for a woman at the time.

Liman Mijinyawa and Mallam Yahaya had a traditional one-on-one mentorship where the older mentor and younger mentee are matched through an informal relationship. With more experience, knowledge, and connections, Liman Minjinyawa was able to pass along all he had learned to the younger Mallam Yahaya. Their relationship was strongly bound by clarity of intent, seamless communication, and commitment. Mallam Yahaya grew in knowledge and character over time, and in appreciation of his good standing and Islamic intellectual exploits, Liman Muhammadu Mijinyawa gave his first daughter Hajiya Fatima to Mallam Yahaya in marriage. This was the greatest reward and honour a student could receive from a teacher in those days.

Mallam Yahaya and Hajiya Fatimah were blessed with ten children namely: Hajiya Hawaw'u (Yar'audi) Hajiya Fatima (Amere); Aisha Mahammadu Lawali; and Hajiya Maryam (Yarlele). Others are Hajia Lubabatu (Luba); Alhaji Abubakar Yahaya; Faruk; Hadiza; and Ummu Kalthum. Five of these children are now late. The surviving siblings of Faruk, in order of birth, are Haiya Fatima (Amare); Hajiya Maryam (Yarlele); Hajiya Lubabatu (Luba), and Alhaji Abubakar Yahaya.

Fig 8: Mallama Fatima Yahaya

Fig 9: Alhaji Abubakar Yahaya

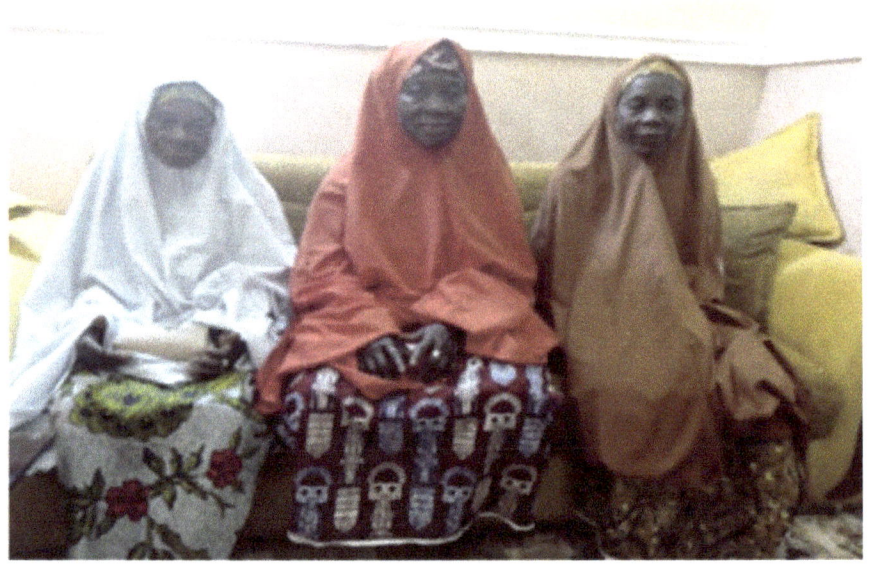

Fig 10: Hajiya Fatima, Hajiya Maryam and Hajiya Lubabatu

In later years, Mallam Yahaya established private *Makarantar Alla* and *Makarantar Ilimi*. His wife Hajiya Fatimah was the *Modibbo* or female teacher and taught girls and women Islamic education in her matrimonial home. The couple had a strict routine of teaching and managing the school. Yet every Thursday and on special occasions, Mallam Yahaya would go to nearby villages and settlements for Qur'anic recitals and public enlightenment along with his students and contemporaries. This was in addition to his regular teaching programmes at the Mosque.

Hajiya Fatimah was well into her pregnancy by early 1966, having become pregnant near the end of the *Hunturu* or Hamattan season of 1965. On Tuesday 4 January 1966, she felt lower abdominal movements and mild pains preceded by vibrant baby kicks. With seven previous deliveries, she had a feeling of *deja vu* for she had felt these sensations many times before. She summoned *Arbiki*, the local midwife. The *Arbiki* was half-expecting such a call. By virtue of her professional calling, she knew most of the women needing her delicate services. In the morning of Wednesday 5 January 1966, Hajiya Fatimah was delivered of a healthy and bouncing baby boy with the help of the *Arbiki* in accordance with Islamic practice. When Yahaya Sa'idu saw his newborn son, he was happy and dutifully whispered the Muslim call to prayer, the *Adhan,* into his right ear. The baby boy was brought before a gathering of male Islamic scholars and family elders on the seventh day, which was 12 January 1966 for the naming ceremony or *Tasmiyah* in accordance with Islamic injunction. Mallam Yahaya reflected deeply. What is in a name? Gladly, this question has long been answered.

Naming a child in Islam has a profound effect because it is believed to exert a defining impact on the child's personality and development as well as his or her interactions with others and the environment. Basically, Islam considers the moment of choosing a name and the *Tasmiyah* as some of the most pivotal events in a person's life. The Tasmiyah prayers allow a baby to be accepted and protected by Allah (SWT). So it must be done with deep reflection. A good Muslim name is a fundamental right of the child and a solemn duty of the father. Indeed, the Holy Prophet says that "it is the responsibility of every father to choose the name of his child" The name must announce the essence of the child and eloquently link the child to the beauty and awesomeness of Allah (SWT). Gladly, Mallam Yahaya did not need to think too long. There are special and peerless names originated by Prophet Muhammad, peace be upon him (PBUH) in Islam and Hausa culture, which include his own name Muhammad and those of his closest companions namely: Abubakar Sadiq; Umar Faruk; Usman; and Aliyu. Therefore, these names are revered. The first name Muhammad is normally given to the first male child in the family. For male children, this is followed by the names: Abubakar Sadiq; Umar Faruk; Usman; and Aliyu in that order. Mallam Yahaya therefore named his new boy child 'Faruk' because he is the third male child after Muhammad Lawal and Abubakar in reverence to Prophet Muhammad (PBUH) and his rightly guided Caliphs. After the *Tasmiyah* ceremony in the morning, the happy family gathered with well-wishers in the afternoon for the *Walimah* celebrations.

According to Majma'ul Luggatul Arabiya (2011), Faruk, also transliterated from the common Arabic given and family name,

Farooq which means "one who distinguishes between right and wrong". Thus, Mallam Yahaya Sa'idu was divinely guided to name his third son Faruk. In a lighter mood, however, Faruk was also called Faru-Faru by his parents and older siblings, when he did a good deed. Faru in Hausa is the lovely harmless tree without thorns that bears edible fruits and is loved by everyone. With hindsight, Faruk, Farooq or the informal Faru, the Almighty Allah (SWT) already knew everything that the young boy would one day justify the significance and multiple goodness of his iconic name. To underscore the rich antecedents of his name, Faruk remembers that as a young person, he liked being called *Farukun Mallam Yahaya* meaning Faruk of Mallam Yahaya. This special attachment to his father symbolized love and affection. Secondly, the association with the prestigious and revered title 'Mallam', which is only conferred on men of great learning in Hausaland, was a thing of great honor, dignity, and personal satisfaction.

The ancestry of General Faruk Yahaya depicted in the figure below shows direct linkages and associations with the Sokoto Caliphate.

Fig 11: Ancestral lineage of Lt Gen Faruk Yahaya

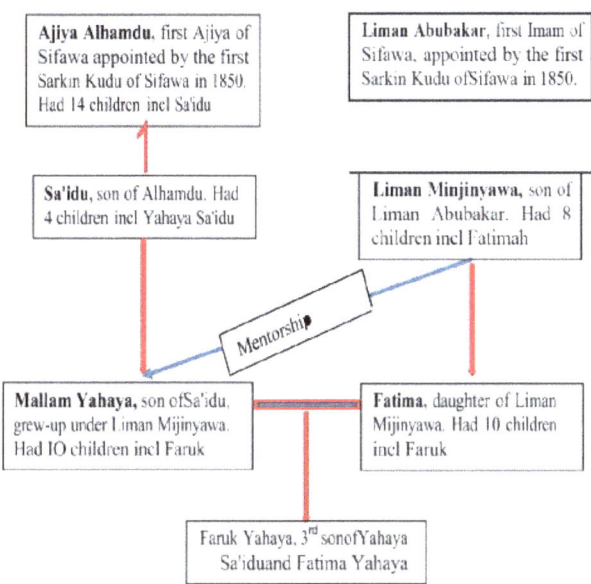

Faruk's paternal and maternal great grandfathers were associated with the Sokoto Caliphate. His paternal great grandfather was the first Ajiya of Sifawa, appointed by the first Sarkin Kudu of Sifawa who was in-turn appointed by Sultan Babba in 1850, and his maternal great grandfather was the first Imam of Sifawa, appointed by the first Sarkin Kudu also in 1850. His father was a distinguished Islamic scholar and preacher as well as an accomplished school teacher, while his mother was an Islamic teacher. Additionally, his maternal uncle Liman Muhammadu Balarabe was the Imam of Sifawa when Faruk was growing up. Beginning with the third Sultan of Sokoto, both families have produced accomplished administrators as well as Islamic scholars and teachers.

Although Faruk was Hajiya Fatimah's eighth child, he was special because he looked much like Liman Mijinyawa her father. Just like his father, Faruk grew up in his grandfather's household. Hajiya Fatimah was fond of Faruk and treated him with much love and affection because she saw her beloved father in him. Faruk's maternal family grew fond of him as a result of the strong bond between mother and son. Having received much motherly love, Faruk grew up to be kind, caring, considerate and helpful. He was very dear to his parents, particularly his mother.

Indeed, he was without doubt, her favourite child and trusted confidant. When she had a discrete or confidential task, Faruk was the first choice and the go-to person. She sold *Bulla* which is a confectionary like *Tuwo*, made of millet and com, and Faruk was her preferred sales assistant. When he was done selling at sunset, he would "advise" his mother, as he had seen her do on numerous occasions, to give the remaining food to the poor, and she would happily oblige him. Such was their understanding and bonding.

Faruk's three surviving sisters Fatima, Maryam and Lubabatu vividly remember some of the experiences and exploits of their younger brother who would later become a foremost general in the Nigerian Army. To Hajiya Fatima, the eldest sister, Faruk was sympathetic and just. He will go to great lengths to reconcile children fighting on the streets, no matter how busy he is. If he is given a portion of food or gifts to divide among his siblings, he will do so in a transparent, fir, and equitable manner. On her part, Maryam still remembers him as a small wise boy. At a time when all his older sisters were married and had settled in their matrimonial homes, one day, all three of them came visiting. After about two hours of visiting, their mother, Hajiya Fatimah, began to remind them to return to their matrimonial homes, as is customary in the North. Faruk saw their presence as a great opportunity to get his household chores done, so he encouraged his mother to let them stay longer. *"Bari su dade kadan"*, he pleaded. In the convivial atmosphere, he had his way. The three sisters stayed longer, they all had quality time together and significantly, Faruk's chores for the day were all quite easily done. Maryam also remembers Faruk as a very determined person. One day, all the children were sent to finish some farm work. Faruk's siblings believed the work could not be finished that day. However, he insisted the work could be finished and motivated by his unyielding and infectious zeal, the work was completed that day, proving that he could succeed at anything for which he had unlimited enthusiasm. To Lubabatu, the youngest of the three sisters, Faruk was dutiful and did his daily household chores unfailingly. After school, he would join other children to fetch water for the home with claypots. However, because he was small, she recalls that when the children returned from the stream with their pots full of water, the adults at home would make sure Faruk was relieved of his weight first, before others, to avoid the mishap of dropping the claypot.

Moreover, Faruk was a well-adjusted child. Though he was a quiet boy, he thoroughly enjoyed playing. At dusk he joined other children in the *Sundu* merry-go-round play and took part in night wrestling, a game that his older brother Abubakar excelled in. He was also decidedly cautious. He would follow his peers to the nearby stream to play but would seldom dive into it to avoid undue risk. With childhood friends such as Aliyu Modi Sifawa and the late Nasiru, they crisscrossed the *elaborate fadama* farms in and around Sifawa, moving from one part of the community to another, either running errands for adults or just exploring the environment and being boys. At this time, Faruk was just a shy, curious and obedient small boy, as attested by his brother, Abubakar Yahaya. He was developing fast, and soon the free time of pre-school was drastically cut short with the beginning of education.

Given the intellectual and scholarly pedigree of his parents and maternal uncle, Faruk started *Makarantar Alla* or Qu'ranic education at a tender age. With the able guidance of his parents and uncle, he was able to master the Qu'ran and graduate from Qu'ranic education at the tender age of nine in early 1975. More importantly, Faruk learned about the Islamic faith, about the five daily prayers, including specific obligatory movements and words to recite in Arabic. He also learned about the Islamic lifestyle, such as dress code, diet, social interaction, and spiritual obligations. While a great deal of this information can be found in books, and tutorials, the most pleasant and effective way to learn the Islamic way of life is with a patient and willing mentor. From his father, mother, and uncle, Faruk was adequately mentored.

While receiving Qu'ranic education, Faruk was enrolled in JNI Primary School (now Mallam Saidu Nizzamiyya Primary School), Sifawa in 1971 at the age of five. He went to school on foot just like the other children. School started at 8:00 in the morning and continued till *Tara*, or breaktime, at 12 noon when pupils were allowed to go home to eat. Sometimes during *Tara*, Faruk recalls doing chores such as going to fetch water either on foot or with the aid of a donkey. At the peak of Bazara or dry season, pupils go to school with water, in water bottles or small locally made clay pots, to stay hydrated.

Faruk's father worked as an Islamic Education Teacher at the school, which helped him to cope. Each class was limited to 24 pupils. Some of his classmates in JNI were: Alhaji Aliyu Modi Sifawa, Alhaji Haliru Muhammad Liman, JusticeAminu Garba Sifawa, Malam Umaru Junaidu, Mallama Inno Umaru, and Mallama Hadi Dandi. The curriculum was a hybrid ofIslamic and Western education and included subjects such as: Arabic, Islamic Studies, and Arithmetic. His favourite subject was grammar, and the subject teacher was Mallam Abubakar Ibrahim Lafiagi from who also doubled as the Headmaster. Some teachers made quite an impression on him and he remembers Ibrahim Aliyu Illo, Mallam Abubakar Tambari also known as Tsoho, who later became the Headmaster and Mallam Yusuf Abdullahi Barade who became the Headmaster when Faruk was in Primary Seven. Barade (2022) happily recalled Faruk's time in school and stated that he was a very intelligent, teachable, diligent, and responsible pupil.

Fig 12: Primary School Classmates

Aliyu Modi Sifawa   Haliru Muhammed Liman   Aminu Garba Sifawa

At school, Faruk showed his adaptability. He was focused on his studies. He hardly forgot what he was taught and indeed, treasured his textbooks and notebooks. According to Abubakar, "when boys of his age would pawn their used notebooks for a handful of groundnuts, Faruk kept all his notebooks from Primary One to Primary Seven". Such was the diligence of this small bookworm. He really enjoyed school and was motivated to do well. Faruk was always first in order of academic merit from Primary One to Seven. In Primary Four, he could read the newspapers, particularly the Today Newspaper and the Hausa language *Gaskiya tafi Kwabo*. In Primary Four, he was appointed class monitor on merit. In Primary Five something remarkable happened to him. In late July 1975, he travelled with family and friends for a wedding in Kontagora. The wedding was postponed and then the military coup that toppled General Yakubu Gowon occurred on Tuesday 29 July 1975. He was trapped in Kontagora with his family and friends for 2 weeks due to obvious *force majeure*. When he returned to school after two weeks, he was suspended from the position of leadership for an unauthorized absence.

However, after investigation, the School authorities reinstated him because his absence was not intentional and to recognise his good standing. Quite significantly, he maintained this good standing and outstanding leadership qualities so much that he was appointed Head Boy in his final year, which was Primary Seven. Faruk remembers two significant events in Primary Seven. First is that, whenever there was a shortage of teachers in the school, he was tasked along with a few other carefully selected pupils in the school to teach the Primary One and Two classes. Secondly, quite often during *Tara* break, Primary Seven pupils were marched to the Sarkin Kudu of Sifawa by the School Headmaster and admonished to be of good character and to be focused in their education.

He eventually passed out in 1977 with excellent grades in all his subjects in the First School Leaving Certificate (FSLC) examinations. After the Common Entrance examinations, he was admitted to three tertiary institutions including the prestigious Arabic Teachers College (ATC)/College of Arts and Arabic Studies (CAAS) now Sheikh Abubakar Gurni Memorial College (SAGMC), Sokoto as well as the Sokoto Teachers College (STC).

He was at STC for about two weeks before moving to CAAS. He chose CAAS primarily because of his Islamic background. At the time, the school was one of the best post-primary schools in Sokoto, with quality teachers from all over the world. It was also one of the best in the North for Islamic education. Students came from far and wide in the North and even from Southern Nigeria in search of top-notch Islamic education. He attended this school between 1977 and 1982, where he trained as a teacher. CAAS had a hybridized curriculum combining Islamic with Western education. Faruk thus took subjects such as Islamic Studies, Islamic History, Arabic Language, English Language, Mathematics, Physical and Health Education, Hausa, Principles and Practice of Education (PPE) as well as Practical Teaching (Teaching Practice).

Fig 13: Front View of Sheikh Abubakar Gumi Memorial College

His classmates include: Ibrahim Gidado, Tafarkin Sokoto, former Sokoto State Commissioner for Information; Shehu Samaila Suleiman, retired School Principal, Director of Quality Assurance and now Galadima Rabah; Alhaji Sule Magaji, a businessman and politician; Ibrahim Sa'idu, who was the Class Monitor; as well as Usman Taju, former Manager of Access Bank; Some other schoolmates were: Bello Mukhtar; Professor Nasiru Aminu Kalgo of Usman Dan Fodiyo University, Sokoto; Late Barrister Innuwa Abdulkadir; Musa Labbo Jega, Registrar, University of Science and Technology, Aliero, Kebbi State; Colonel Garba Moyi Isa (retired), former Sokoto State Commissioner for Security; Tari Usman Rini; Malami Galadima, the Galadima of Talata Mafara; and Yakubu Abubakar, retired School Principal. Faruk has kept in touch with the surviving members of this small group of old friends to this day, demonstrating his value of the importance of friendship. These friends offer him unwavering support and useful advice that can be very uplifting. They are also a great source of inspiration.

Fig 14: Ibrahim Gidado   Fig 15: Shehu Samaila Suleiman   Fig 16: Alhaji Sule

Fig 17: Picture of Faruk with classmates at CAAS, Sokoto
Faruk is seated in the middle row, second from left, followed by Barade, and Sule Magaji is fourth from left

Although CAAS was renowned for world class Islamic education, it was also a very regimented institution for the leadership grooming of young Nigerians. Students were generally managed themselves through the school and house leadership system; indeed, there were junior and senior leaders among the students for the entire school, hostels, and for sports; junior students served older students to instill the values of service and respect for authorities; daily checks were conducted on students before lights-out; and competitive house inspections were conducted weekly by the Duty Master and remarkably, selected students were periodically tasked to research, prepare and make presentations on assigned topics to the entire students at the School Assembly. This was a sure way to improve knowledge, self-confidence, and public speaking skills.

Faruk lived in CAAS with two principals: Late Usman Junaidu, who later became the Waziri of Sokoto; and Sheikh Bello Gusau, who graduated them. He was well known by his teachers. These include Mathematics teachers such as Mrs Toma from Egypt, Mr Ndukurma from India, and Emmanuel Egwaba Enugu fromAbia, State as well as Islamic Studies teachers such as Mallam Sabir, Sheikh Shaddat from Sudan, Sheikh Abu Koshin from Egypt, and Mallam Nasir Kwatarkwashi from Zamfara State. Others were: Sa'idu Muhammad Dansadau; Mr. Bolati from India; Mallam Abubakar Abdulkarim, Mallam Shehu Abdullahi, Mr Girgis, an American, Mallama Gyal-gyale, Mr.Amir from Egypt, Mr. Remon,, Ameliya Guzman, Ibrahim Bagobiri from Zamfara State and Malam Mas'ud. These teachers, individually and collectively, impacted his life in terms of knowledge, discipline, character, and personal conduct.

During Faruk's time in school, Mathematics was the toughest proposition. This was not due to the presumed difficulty of the subject but rather to the personality of one of the Mathematics teachers, the unforgettable Mr Ndukurma from India. He was a short and rigid man, but he was such a disciplined, strict, and professional teacher. He kept strictly to time, took attendance religiously, taught his subject diligently, administered all continuous assessments tests and measurements, set the best examples of character, and expected only the best from his students. Faruk remembers that Mr Ndukurma was so principled that when he spoke in the Assembly, his word was like law because even the Principal would always agree with him. He will say Mr Ndukurma has spoken. During examinations, Mr Ndukurma prepared the examination hall like an impregnable fortress, a strict no- go area. If, by any chance, a student strayed around the prepared Examination Hall, he would most likely feel a sense of guilt without even committing any offence. Such was the maverick nature of Mr Ndukurma that he hardly had a friend, but Faruk was his favourite student. Only Faruk knows how he did it, but could be related to the meeting of like minds.

Faruk's favourite subjects were Mathematics and Islamic Studies. However, he excelled in every subject and won most of the academic prizes and awards on offer every year. At the end of school, he was among the best 12 candidates from CAAS, out of 100, who passed the

Teachers Grade II Certificate at one sitting in 1982.

After 5 years at CAAS, Faruk had become more matured in his set values. Alhaji Sule Magaji, remembered him as being very religious, quiet, time conscious, respectful, and obedient. To Ibrahim Gidado, and Tafarkin Sokoto, Faruk "was a smallish boy with elderly maturity; he was a specially gifted student. Although introverted, he was a special and highly intelligent student who often topped the class. His only known rival for the top spot in class were Muhammad Usman Taju and Ibrahim Sa'idu". Two former classmates, Shehu Samaila Suleiman, Galadima Rabah also agreed that Faruk was a gifted student and he was a kindhearted, patient, humble, and accommodating person who was never involved in any criminal or immoral activity. However, there was another side to Faruk that many may not know. He enjoyed a good laugh. According to Ibrahim Gidado, despite his quiet demeanour, he would burst out laughter whenever Tari Usman Rini, the class clown cracked his rancorous jokes. On a more serious note, Faruk was honest, obedient, and patriotic. Even at an early age, his love for his native land Sifawa was remarkable. He joined other senior students from Sifawa to receive and orient new students from his community. He liked the school and was dedicated to the activities of his schoolhouse the Sardauna House, which he represented in sports.

After graduating from the College of Arts and Arabic Studies in Sokoto in 1982, Faruk proceeded to the University of Sokoto to do the pre-degree programme for Education and Islamic Studies in the Faculty of Education. In this programme, he again showed his academic mettle by topping the class. While he was at the university, his older brother Abubakar enlisted in the Nigerian Army as a soldier. This stirred a latent passion in him. When the publication for admission into the Nigerian Defence Academy (NDA) was made in 1985, he bought an application form and on Saturday 27 April 1985, took the entrance examination. He passed the examination, and commenced Officer Cadet training at the NDA for the 37 Regular Combatant Course on 27 September 1985. Eight years after joining the Nigerian Army, Faruk lost his beloved father Mallam Yahaya Sa'idu on Saturday 20 March 1993 which is equivalent to the 26th Ramadan 1413 AH. His father had transformed him from a child to a boy and then to a man with intentional guidance, education, and good role modeling. Indeed, as Johnson (2013) suggested in his book, Faruk's father had instilled in him the values and character traits he needed to succeed in life. Mallam Yahaya Sa'idu left behind a great legacy through his children and past students of both his public and private schools, some of whom now occupy important religious and public offices in Nigeria. These include personalities such as Dr Ibrahim Muhammad Liman, former Chairman of the State Universal Basic Education Board, Alhaji Abubakar Yahaya, Permanent Secretary in the Sokoto State Civil Service, and Haliru Muhammad Liman, Director of the Ministry of Education, Sokoto and current Deputy Imam of the Sifawa Central Mosque. His father's life, like a good candle, lit many other candles.

On 22 April 1996, Faruk met Salamatu Aliyu (as she then was) was in Abuja while she was doing her National Youth Service (NYSC). After a short courtship in line with Islamic injunction and according to the will of Allah (SWT), they got married on Friday 21 March 1997. Mrs Salamatu Faruk Yahaya had a solid Islamic education and holds a Master of Arts degree in Literature-in-English. She is a member of the prestigious Chartered Institute of Personnel Management (CIPM). She actively participated in the activities of the Nigerian Anny Officers' Wives Association (NAOWA) as her husband's career progressed in the Army. Consequently, she received many awards and recognitions for her outstanding performances in different capacities in the association and by the grace of Allah, she is currently the president of NAOWA. Out of military circles, she is an Assistant Director in the Department of Voter Education and Publicity at the Independent National Electoral Commission (INEC) Headquarters, Abuja.

In all of these years, Mrs Salamatu Faruk Yahaya has proven to be an excellent wife, more precious than a jewel. Faruk and Salamatu are first and foremost good friends, trusting, loving, and caring. In a 2022 interview, Salamatu said: "I make bold to say that there has been no single time I can remember that we had a serious quarrel. I am not saying that my husband and I are perfectionists, but our marital issues are usually resolved amicably. I cannot remember taking any matter to a third party. The most interesting thing is that our children, who are always around us, cannot say that they have witnessed any quarrel between us. He is a good husband and father, and we sincerely thank Allah (SWT) for blessing us with a man after his heart. In a nutshell, Faruk is my best friend, my role model, my teacher, and everything". These values have strengthened their marriage and they are blessed with four lovely children: Al-Ameen; Kareemah; Habeebah; and Fatimah (Ummi). Except the youngest who was born in Abuja, others were born in Sokoto. Faruk's children are endowed with good education and values. His first son, Al- Ameen is a graduate while others are still pursuing their different degrees.

Fig 18: Faruk and Salamatu on Wedding Day

Fig 19: Faruk and Family

On 6 October 2008, Faruk lost his beloved mother Hajiya Fatimah Yahaya, with whom he shared a very special bond. At the time, he was a Colonel serving as Deputy Director Military Secretary, Army Headquarters. On 18 July 2019, the Hajiya Fatima Yahaya Foundation was established in loving memory of his parents and their legacy of learning, teaching, and service to the community and the nation. The goal of the foundation is "to assist the less privileged in society and to cater welfare to their members". In retrospect, the historical, socio-political, environmental, and personal accounts rendered here leave enduring residues in many respects. One of the striking consequences of the Jihad and the establishment of the Sokoto Caliphate was the harmonious coexistence between the diverse elements within the Caliphate. The Fulanis, the conquerors and supposed overlords, gradually lost their distinct identity while leaving significant imprints on the dominant Hausa way of life. This led to the evolution of a homogeneous Hausa-Fulani culture that became a feature of the social landscape of the Sokoto Caliphate. Usman and Bello (1979) argue that the ethnic line between the Hausa and the Fulani has become remarkably blurred as a result of their long coexistence. The consequences of concubinage, inter-marriages among the diverse ethnic groups, social interaction and Islamic values of fraternity and universalism came together to produce the same cultural climate in modem Sifawa and other parts of northern Nigeria.

A major political impact of the Jihad was the dispossession of the political authority of the pre-Jihad Hausa states and other neighbours as well as the establishment of the Sokoto Caliphate. The Jihad led to the emergence of the Hausa-Fulani ethnic group as a strong political factor in Nigeria. This solidarity has been enhanced by a common religion and culture which have collectively affected the political dynamics of Nigeria. The consequences of these religious and socio-political phenomena are strongly manifest in Nigerian politics today. Another distinguishing feature was the establishment and promotion of Islamic education and enlightenment, which fueled the quest for cultural refinement and good governance in the North in general and in Sifawa in particular.

Considering Sifawa as a microcosm of these dynamics, the historic town fits the concept of cultural assimilation as "the economic, social and political integration of an ethnic minority group into mainstream society". It can be likened to a "melting pot" of cultural dialectics that eventually form a more resilient and enduring culture (Maddern, 2013). The residue of the cultural conversations in Sifawa is that today the people are known to be stalwart, hardworking, and industrious. They are farmers much in keeping with their Hausa ancestry and herders in line with their Fulani and Berber heritage. They are predominantly devout Muslims. In keeping with the teachings of Uthman ibn Fodiyo, they actively encourage learning, literacy, education, and scholarship, particularly in Islamic and Arabic studies even for women. An Islamic scholar is thus a man or woman of great importance in Sifawa and is treated with utmost respect. This is because Islam places a high value on education and as the religion spread among diverse peoples, education became an important instrument to create a universal and cohesive social order. By and large, the communal passion and aspiration for enlightenment robbed off on Western education too. Consequently, Sifawa is known throughout Sokoto State as a place for education and enlightenment. The result is that the town has a comparatively high number of graduates, accomplished academics, and successful civil servants in Sokoto State.

The foregoing presents the cultural and socio-political milieu of Sifawa and the family background of General Faruk Yahaya. His ancestors clearly show direct ties to Sheikh Uthman ibn Fodiyo' associates. Indeed, his parentage shows men and women of learning and character who left outstanding legacies of leadership. Faruk was finely honed in strong leadership qualities as a result of his background and bloodline. His early life showed certain inherent qualities that may be characterized by five universal personality traits namely: extraversion; agreeableness; openness; conscientiousness; and neuroticism. As a person, he was quite reserved and thoughtful but trusting and helpful. In terms of openness, he was a mix of both extremes. While he generally gave the impression of an unexciting and pragmatic person, he was also known to be spontaneous and animated in response to appropriate stimuli. He was careful, deep, painstaking, calm, and confident at all times, especially in formal matters.

Growing up for Faruk was a roller coaster of everyday experiences, and continuous learning. He recalled learning from a variety of sources, rom his parents, family elders, his older siblings, his Teachers, Headmaster, and the religious Clerics. He imbibed six core values of character or the so called "character counts". According to Glassman (2008), these six pillars of character, namely; trustworthiness, respect, responsibility, fairness, care, and citizenship, were proposed by a group of nonpartisan and non-sectarian youth development experts in 1992 and transcend cultural, religious, and socio-economic differences. Profiled against these six character counts, Faruk shows a striking personality. As a trustworthy person, he was known to be honest as a young person and would always keep his promise(s). He has the courage to do the right thing, conscious of his good name and reputation. He was loyal to constituted authority and will always stand by his family, friends, and community. He treated others with respect following the Golden Rule that says, "do unto others as you would want others do unto you". Faruk was considerate and tolerant of personal differences of others. He would do the right thing and even more, seeking and accepting responsibilities and standing by his words, actions, and deeds. He liked to set a good example for others. In particular, he would not take advantage of vulnerable people and was fair to others. He was kind, caring and compassionate. He freely expressed gratitude and was forgiving. In terms of citizenship, he showed the desire to make his community and environment better, showing the quality of obedience and the potential for both public and community service.

Looking back, the Yahaya Family of Sifawa and the Sifawa community groomed a young man who was willing, able, and ready for service to the nation. He came from such a rich family heritage and long line of seasoned public servants, administrators, community leaders, and clerics who instilled in him the values of good citizenship, service, and leadership. In the words of the District Head of Sifawa, Muhammad Buhari Tambari "Sifawa is an old historical town and Faruk came from a family of highly learned members of society". He had been imbued with language skills, motor skills, intellectual ability, physical development, as well as moral values and judgement. He was young, educated, and ambitious. He possessed all the qualities desirous of soldiers and soldiering. He was unconscious but sensitive to Kelly Roper's "Ode to Soldiers", as "steady, solid, and strong; optimistic, outstanding, and organized; loyal, logical, and level-headed; diligent, decisive and disciplined; intelligent, idealistic, and, when necessary, immovable; earnest, effective and efficient; rational, resourceful, and resolute; yes, a soldier is many things, but above all, a soldier is a hero"

Early in 1985, Faruk was a student of Education and Islamic Studies at the University of Sokoto, but he wanted more. In April 1985, destiny beckoned on him, and he joined the crowd of young candidates at the entrance examination for the NDA 37 Regular Combatant Course. As is often said, the rest is now history. In retrospect, was Faruk Yahaya simply born to assume strategic leadership in later years? In other words, were all his leadership qualities inbred? On the other hand, were all his military leadership qualities developed from scratch by the institution of the Nigerian Army and the Armed Forces of Nigeria? Considered together, was there a hybrid of inbred leadership qualities finetuned by institutional leadership development of the military? Was Faruk Yahaya prepared for the strategic military leadership positions he assumed in later years? The answers to these probing questions are not blowing in the wind as Bob Dylan sang, but, paraphrasing the cryptic catchphrase of the X-Files, and speaking presciently, "the answers are all in here".

Huffing and Puffing for Tough Times: Military Training at the Nigerian Defence Academy

In no other profession are the penalties for employing untrained personnel so appalling or so irrevocable as in the military.
General Douglas MacArthur (26 January 1880- 5 April 1964)

The above assertion by General MacArthur flags the imperative of personnel training in the profession of arms. Military training is designed to inculcate and improve the capabilities of military personnel in their respective roles. It helps in developing and retaining the knowledge, skills, abilities, values, and attitudes necessary for members of the armed forces to survive and accomplish assigned missions. Military training is the foundation for professionalism, mission accomplishment and operational effectiveness in the armed forces. As warfare and threats to security mutate and evolve from symmetric to asymmetric, military training and education must change and respond to these new realities. It must continually be forward-thinking, innovative and creative, both in understanding how warfare is evolving and in adapting training to meet the challenges (Greer, 2018).

Consequently, the Federal Government of Nigeria (FGN), in giving primacy to the training of its military personnel established the NDA Kaduna on 5 February 1964, in response to Nigeria's defence needs to train officers for the Armed Forces of Nigeria. Before then, the institution was known as the Royal Military Forces Training College (RMFTC). After independence in 1960, it became known as the Nigerian Military Training College (NMTC).

Before the establishment of the NDA, Nigerian military officers were largely trained at the Royal Military Academy (RMA), Sandhurst, England. Some of the notab Nigerian officers trained at RMA Sandhurst include Brigadier Zakariya Abubakar Hassan Maimalari from 1951-1953, and Lawan Umar, both of whom were from then Borno Province in the present North East geo-political zone of Nigeria. It needs to be underlined that Maimalari and Umar were the first four Africans, along with the late King Hassan of Morocco and Charles Buah from Ghana, to ever attend and successfully pass out of the RMA, Sandhurst. Unfortunately, Lawan Umar, it was reported that he was eventually forced to resign his commission from the Army, while Zakariya Maimalari became the first regular combatant Nigerian in the Officer Corps of the Army having been commissioned Second Lieutenant on 16 February 1953 (Poloma, 2014). Other eminent Nigerian officers trained at Sandhurst include General Adeyinka Adebayo, Philip Effiong, Wellington Bassey with Army Number (N1), Aguiyi Ironsi (N2), Samuel A. Ademulegun (N3), and Ralph A. Shodeinde (N4) among many others.

The role of the academy is to provide each officer cadet from the Nigerian Army, Nigerian Navy, and Nigerian Air Force with the knowledge, skills and values necessary to meet the requirements of a military officer through military training, academic excellence, and character development. In essence, the NDA is an institution where selected young, able-bodied men and women are groomed into well-educated, courageous, virile, and erudite subalterns. The NDA in 1981 started bilateral training of foreign militaries from friendly nations in Africa. In its 59 years of existence, the NDA has transformed from a diploma awarding institution into a globally renowned military university. In 1985, the Academy commenced its undergraduate programmes for officer cadets in training and has produced some of the best men and women in boots and gowns, including Lt Gen Faruk Yahaya, whom destiny called to become a cadet in that year. It is salutary to note that the NDA now offers various postgraduate degree programmes up to the doctoral level for both military and civilian students, respectively. The NDA's core mandate remains the training of young officer cadets through its 5 years Regular Combatant Course (RCC), which culminates in the award of a Bachelor's degree and a presidential commissioning into the rank of Second Lieutenant for Nigerian Army cadets or equivalent in the Nigerian Navy and the Nigerian Air Force. Part of the transformation of the NDA was the commencement of training for female cadets in September 2011.

Having completed his secondary school education at the then College of Arts and Arabic Studies, now Sheikh Abubakar Gumi Memorial College, Sokoto, in 1984, Faruk Yahaya gained admission into the University of Sokoto, and now Usman Dan Fodio University of Sokoto to study History and Islamic Studies in the same year. Faruk was among the first to start the pre-degree programme, and he won all the prizes in his first year before he joined the NDA as a cadet. The journey to become an officer cadet in the NDA was divinely orchestrated and not planned by human knowledge or understanding. People in his hometown of Sifawa who knew him as a child never imagined Faruk would pursue a military career because of his pious, humble, and introverted personality as a child. However, what God has destined for any person will surely come to pass because He alone knows what a child will be right from the mother's womb.

Faruk had gone to visit his elder brother Alhaji Abubakar Yahaya who was then a private soldier at the Nigerian Army Depot in Zaria and now a Permanent Secretary in the Sokoto State Civil Service, when he went to the vendor's stand to do 'freelance' reading of the daily newspapers. Habits, it is said, die hard, as a primary school pupil, Faruk had developed the habit of reading newspapers. His primary school classmate, Alhaji Haliru Mohammed Sifawa, the Chief Imam of Sifawa, Bodinga LGA Sokoto State, confirmed this. Alhaji Haliru Sifawa recalled how he and the young Faruk Yahaya started reading newspaper headlines in primary school, precisely in Primary 4, when the English language was introduced in his school by the Headmaster, Alhaji Yusuf Barde. The young Faruk Yahaya started reading the popular Northern Nigeria newspaper titled "Gaskiya Ta fi Kwabo', (which translated as "Truth is Worth More Than Money") which was printed three times a week as the world's first Hausa language paper. The newspaper was founded in 1939 by the British Colonial Administration as a propaganda tool to counter a false rumour that the British Colonial Administration was planning to hand over her West African colonies to Adolf Hitler of Germany. The rumour created a lot of apprehension in the people, and a medium of communication was needed to douse the tension. Consequently, the colonial officials created a vernacular newspaper to reach out to the majority of northerners since there was no major newspaper in northern Nigeria then compared to the southern part of Nigeria (Duyile, 1989).

In the early months of 1985 in Zaria, Faruk visited a newspaper stand and saw the NDA advertisement for prospective cadets. When he came back to his elder brother, Alhaji Abubakar Yahaya, he told him he was going to apply to join the military. Due to their upbringing and trust in each other, his elder brother did not discourage him from enlisting in the military. It was not a common occurrence to see a family blessed with only two boys, both of whom enlisted into the army. For the young Faruk, who was a brilliant student, to think of abandoning his university education to enlist into the army was a matter of destiny calling him. Faruk sat for the NDA entrance examination in Sokoto in April 1985 and was successful. Thereafter, he was invited for interview and in May 1985, he received a letter of admission from NDA and reported on

Friday, 27 September 1985, to begin the degree programme started by NDA in that academic session. As recalled by Faruk "when we passed out from college (secondary school), I was taken to 'Alwasa' to teach; thereafter, I proceeded to the university. I always want things to be done well, and was motivated and inspired to join the army by the then Major General, now President Muhammadu Buhari, when he visited Sokoto State in 1984. In the words of Lt Gen Faruk Yahaya "I didn't know anybody when I joined the Nigerian Army except my brother who was a private soldier, that is what I want to see in the system and that is what I aspire to achieve". It is instructive to note that since he became the Chief of Army Staff, Gen Faruk Yahaya has brought his philosophy of meritocracy to bear in the posting and appointments of key officers to strategic positions. Officers have been appointed to command, instructional and staff positions purely on merit and not on primordial consideration.

The idea of Faruk joining the military did not go down well with his family especially his mother, Hajiya Fatima Yahaya. She didn't dislike the military, but she had two sons, one of whom had already joined and the other who was about to do so. In their time, the impression of any son joining the military was like a child lost to society. Little-wonder, Hajiya Fatima was not settled with the idea that his beloved Faruk had a special relationship with enlisting in the Nigerian military instead of pursuing the academic path he had already chosen at the University of Sokoto. On the part of Alhaji Yahaya, Faruk's father, it was a mixed bag of joy and sadness given the fact that among his children, Faruk was his favourite and most beloved son, in whom he *was well-pleased*. Faruk was loved more than all his siblings by his father because of his amiable character, obedience and moral uprightness. As noted by his primary school classmate, Mallam Aliyu Modi, due to Faruk's deep religious background and commitment, we thought he would never join the military. Some of his school mates in primary and secondary schools thought he would be a doctor, a religious Sheikh or follow any other career path apart from the military. According to Alhaji Ibrahim Gidado, a secondary school mate, "Faruk was a very intelligent, humble and obedient student. He was introverted, and we were surprised that he joined the Army". When a child is destined for greatness, heaven and earth align to bring it to fruition. Indeed, Faruk's enlistment in the military was never envisaged by mortals but was a divinely ordained pathway for the young man.

In September 1985, Faruk sacrificed his 200-level university education at the then University of Sokoto to enrol as a cadet in Regular Combatant Course 37 of the Nigerian Defence Academy heralding the take-off of a rewarding and unblemished military career. A striking point about his joining the military is the fact that he had the temerity and courage to be enlisted despite the fact that his only brother was already a private soldier.

When Faruk reported at the NDA with other cadets the first day, they were ushered in by senior cadets and rigorously subjected to physical drills and exercises that challenged the resolve of many of the first-termers to continue. The drills and puttee (physical training) parades started in earnest, the early morning exercises, endurance tests, and all manner of physically and mentally challenging training. To welcome Faruk to the NDA, a certain senior cadet, Ariyo Mbang, drilled him almost all day from his Mogadishu to Dalet Battalion, and at the end of the day, the senior cadet offered him tea, which he refused to have, not understanding how someone who has been mean and cruel to him all day would suddenly become a friend. However, due to his deeply held religious beliefs and understanding, he thought that perhaps, the senior cadet was not after-all wicked but just keeping to the traditions of the Academy. During Faruk's stay in the NDA, there were arguably very mean and apparently tyrannical senior cadets who inflicted maximum punishments and puttees on junior cadets. Faruk made up his mind to be different and true to his amiable as well as God fearing character, was not in this category of senior cadets in the NDA. Little wonder, he was the darling of both the junior and senior cadets throughout his years as a cadet in the Academy. As recalled by Major General UU Bassey, "senior cadet Faruk Yahaya was not known for malice or being tyrannical. He was a complete gentleman and very focused, if you committed an offence, he would punish you".

It should be noted that in NDA, as a "clown", which is a name given to freshers, the treatment that ushers the first termer (cadet) into the Academy include "Puttee Parades". In NDA, the puttee exercises were organized by the senior cadets who would assemble the first termers at a specific location and share them among themselves. These are designed to de-civilianize the cadet and make him tougher for the military profession. In as much as these drills and exercises were meant to toughen the cadets up for the future challenges of the profession, many cadets saw them as sheer meanness and man's inhumanity to man. Faruk, like most of his course mates, was quite apprehensive of these 'punishment' and puttee parades and often thought they made the wrong choice by coming to the Academy. It is salutary to note that Cadet Faruk Yahaya did not puttee people but was firm when a junior cadet crossed the redline. The junior officers, such as Major Generals UU Bassey and EV Onumajuru, among others, who met him as their senior in the Academy recalled that he was not known as a puttee marshal. He had a cordial relationship with all cadets, instructors, and staff of the NDA.

Faruk was among the first-termers who were given orientation and a briefing about the nature and organization of cadet training in the NDA. They were briefed on how to conduct and comport themselves as "clowns" and divided into four battalions, namely Burma, Mogadishu, Abyssinia and Dalet. These battalions are designated for Regular Combatant cadets in the NDA. There are also the Ashanti and Colito Battalions earmarked for Direct Short Service Cadets. In the NDA, the cadets are divided into battalions for ease of administration, and Faruk was in Mogadishu. While some of his course mates such as Maj Gen IM Yusuf, Commandant NDA; Maj Gen OA Akintade, Chief of Logistics, Army Headquarters; Maj Gen SO Olabanji, Commander Training and Doctrine Command (TRADOC), Nigerian Army; and Maj Gen AB Omozoje, Chief of Policy and Plans (COPP), Army Headquarters, were in other Battalions. They were duly assigned NDA numbers and Faruk's Number was NDA/3833. The fresh cadets were taught and practiced various dimensions of military drills. These drills include coming to attention, marching and turning about, coming to a halt, and saluting, among others. Like many other 'clowns' in the NDA, Faruk got what he did not bargain for. Every fresher at NDA received a treatment, especially from senior cadets, officers and non-commissioned officers that made them think they were in the wrong place. Some of them thought and attempted to abandon the military training. The gruelling physical drills, punishments and other seemingly tough exercises that the NDA cadets are meant to undergo were intentionally designed to afflict maximum pain and toughen them against the challenges of the profession of arms. Faruk Yahaya was not fully prepared for this, but having left his undergraduate programme at the university, he had no other choice but to brace up for the numerous challenges that the cadet training brings to him. No doubt, he also considered leaving the NDA, but having burned his bridges and given his obedient, amiable and humble nature, he did not suffer much from the puttee parades and the other treatments senior cadets meted out to the junior ones, with whom they, for reasons best known to them, did not like their faces or in reality had committed one offence or another.

As a first-termer in NDA, Faruk Yahaya was level-headed and focused, which he maintained through the final year. Cadet Faruk was mentored by several instructors in the NDA who had a great impact on him. Chief among these mentors and instructors, whom he revered for their outstanding influence on him and other cadets, is Col Abba. In his words, General Faruk posited that the Academy laid the foundation of what he has become. He only maintained what was inculcated in him during his training at the Academy. He also recalled his days at the Nigerian Army Depot, where he used to spend some of his holiday time as a cadet. He recalled several instances when he could not go home during the holidays because the allowance was not paid and he did not have money. During this period, he would go to the Depot in Zaria to stay with his elder brother. General Faruk Yahaya recalled that during his time in theAcademy, military instructors and civilian lecturers were highly revered. They were selected as the best for the Academy at that point in time and they gave their best. Little wonder, Faruk and some of his course mates have become high flyers in their various corps and appointments, considering the quality of training.

Cadet Faruk Yahaya due to his brilliance and leadership prowess was the Course Senior for his course in the Academy for 5 years, a feat nobody before and after him has achieved in the NDA. Having passed all the trainings and excelled in all the exercises, Faruk and his other successful course mates were ready to be commissioned as second lieutenants. Unfortunately, some cadets were relegated to next the course for various infractions as charged by the academy's authorities. It is common for some cadets to be relegated and those who were relegated could pass out with their juniors. The event that culminated in the passing out from the Academy is the Passing Out Parade (POP).

Passing out Parade

For every cadet in the Academy, the big picture is the day he will pass out of the NDA, marking the end of the puttees, rigous of training, and other uncertainties.

The POP is a day cadets look forward to as they wipe away all their tears and pains in the Academy. Faruk was not an exception having toiled in the Academy for 5 years as a cadet. The preparation for the POP is a long, tortuous and rigorous one. It usually starts with bush camps in two locations, Kaduna and Jos, for a few weeks. The camp exercises involved a lot of practical military activities, such as firing at dummy enemies and engaging in mock wars. The camp exercise rounds off with a camp-fire. Like other fifth-termers, Faruk Yahaya was eagerly looking forward to his final exit from the Academy. His level-headedness, general aptitude, and academic performance also commended him for cadet leadership as well as leadership after the Academy.

Faruk Yahaya who commenced officer cadet training on 27 September 1985, was granted a Regular Combatant Commission as a member of the 37 Regular Course on 22 September 1990, in the rank of second lieutenant with seniority in the same rank effective 27 September 1985, into the Nigerian Army Infantry Corps. According to General Faruk Yahaya, he elected to join the Infantry Corps because "I felt that I wanted to be where it was happening. Everyone is supporting Infantry". As also corroborated by Maj Gen IM Yusuf, "during our time, it was a sign of valour to go to the fighting arm, which is the Infantry", however, it is the prerogative of the Army to assign Corps based on a cadet's performance in academic and military training activities, as well as other observed personal traits.

The Infantry is one of the teeth arms of the Nigerian Army and the queen of battle. "It is the surest guarantor of peace, which Nigeria needs in addition to carrying out its normal role as the combat arm capable of capturing and holding ground". (army.mil.ng, 2023). To tell the truth, Faruk Yahaya desired to be a combatant officer both in spirit and in letter. He was given the option to choose his Corps while in the NDA, and his first choice was and is still the Infantry. There are several other corps he could have chosen such as the Signals, Finance, Intelligence, Supply and Transport, Military Police, Armoured or Artillery Corps, but he was divinely directed to select the 'Queen of the Battle'. The Corps in the Nigerian Army are broadly categorised into three groups, namely Combat, Combat Support and Combat Services Support. On one hand, the Combat Arms or those regarded as the 'teeth arms', are responsible for fighting and defeating the threats. They are the Infantry and Armoured Corps. The Combat Support Arms are those specialized forces on the frontline that offer vital combat support to the Infantry and Armoured Corps. They include the Artillery, Army Engineers, Signals, Intelligence and Supply and Transport among others.

The Service Support Arms provide essential and necessary services that enable the fighting arm to do its job. During cadet Faruk's time in the Academy, it was fashionable for cadets to settle for Combat and Combat Support Arms, but things have changed now perhaps due to several other extraneous factors such as technology, the nature of threats, the evolving nature of society, and globalisation. It is common these days for many cadets to prefer to join the Infantry Corps unlike some years ago when some would prefer other Corps such as Finance, Intelligence and Supply and Transport. There is absolutely nothing immoral or bad in that, but it is necessary for cadets to note that the essence of the military is to promote the country's national interest and maintain its territorial integrity by land, sea and air at all cost as contained in Section 217 of the Federal Republic of Nigeria 1999 Constitution as amended.

In his final year as a cadet in the NDA, Faruk was an appointment holder. He was the Cadet Senior Under Officer (CSUO), an appointment that was divinely bestowed on him. The appointment of cadet Faruk Yahaya as the CSUO was an eloquent testimony that the authorities of the NDA had observed his performance as a cadet both in terms of academic and other activities as well as his character and leadership traits. Faruk passed out as a leader and was singled out among his peers in the NDA as a leader. He graduated 3rd in order of merit among cadets of the 37 Regular Course. In one of his reports written by the then Col M Abba CBC 1989/1990, it was stated that "he will make a first-class officer, if he continues with such a progress". Indeed, Lt Gen Faruk Yahaya has lived up to that report as he commands the Nigerian Army as Chief of Army Staff. According to Maj Gen IM Yusuf, Commandant NDA, "we unanimously appointed (Cadet Faruk Yahaya) as our course senior. Each year he continued until the final year. There was no rancour in appointing him". He further stated that "he (Faruk Yahaya) was well respected among us and our lecturers. We would always send him to interface with lecturers on our behalf. He was our right choice".

Speaking further on the core attributes of Lt Gen Faruk Yahaya, Maj Gen IM Yusuf observed that, the COAS has three key attributes empathy, patience, and humility. He stated that Lt Gen Faruk Yahaya is gifted with empathy. He recalled that in the North East Theatre, whenever he heard a location had been overrun, he would always speak with the Commander to know who was wounded and who was lost. He will not ask about the equipment first because he believes strongly in the human angle. Anyone who knows him and works with him would notice that Gen Faruk Yahaya is so patient. He has a natural gift of patience and tolerance. In terms of humility, he has it in excess. He is very modest in dealing with superiors, equals, and subordinates. He is highly knowledgeable in every aspect of life. His humility is evident in the way he dresses, always on white clothes and shoes. His taste has not changed even as COAS (IM Yusuf, Personal Communication, 2023). As underlined by Maj Gen OA Akintade, Cadet Faruk Yahaya was our natural course senior. He carried us along with ease. I have never seen him quarrel with anyone. He never separated from us. We are still intact. Our relationship has not in any way been strained. Everyone speaks freely with him as COAS and he has an uncommon way of easing tension. He is humble, easygoing, intelligent, fair and highly humourous, he said. It is salutary to underscore the fact that 38 years down the line, Lt Gen Faruk Yahaya has remained humble, easy-going and maintained all the positive attributes he exhibited at NDA as a cadet. Maj Gen AB Omozoje, COPP Army Headquarters, recalled that cadet Faruk Yahaya liked to follow the rules, was always present at every parade and did the right thing. He was a disciplined cadet and had a way of telling the truth to power. He stayed within the accepted norms.

It is also underlined that Gen Faruk Yahaya's professional accomplishments have not in any way made him feel like a super human. He stated "I don't see myself as anybody better than another person. Be humble; it is God that gives. If you feel you are intelligent, what did you do to get it? It is God that gave you the high intelligence quotient. The best people are those who will keep quiet. Everything is the blessing of God. It is God and His mercies. Everything is by His grace, if you have anything, it is from God". Faruk Yahaya noted that "the Academy laid the foundation for everything and I have maintained what was inculcated. He humourously quipped "I became a course senior for life. I was just doing my thing in NDA without 'patching' for anything. I did not know, when I was made a Cadet Senior Under Officer. A critical takeaway from his submission is for one to be him or herself and know thyself as cautioned by Socrates, an Athenian moral philosopher, who said, "man, know thyself. Lt Gen Faruk Yahaya could be said to have self- identity towards himself and others, which he exemplifies through his empathy, patience, tolerance and simplicity. After being commissioned as an Officer, Gen Faruk Yahaya has also attended several courses as his career has demanded.

Other Military Training and Civil Accomplishments

In the course of Lt Gen Faruk Yahaya's illustrious career in the Nigerian Army, he was privileged to have attended all courses commensurate with his ranks. These are the Young Officers' Course (Infantry), Machine Gun Platoon Commanders' Course, Air Defence Platoon Commanders' Course, Junior Course and Company Commanders' Course. Others include Basic Range Management Course, Senior Course, Commanding Officers' Course, and Civil-Military Coordination Course. He is a fellow of the National Defence College, Chile.

It is important to note that in all the courses listed above, Gen Faruk Yahaya excelled greatly, with a good grade being the least he obtained. This attests to his brilliance and intellectual superiority, which he has exhibited right from his primary and secondary school education, where he topped all his classes. In the short stint he had at the University of Sokoto, Faruk emerged overall best in the 100-level class. During his trainings at C Company, 3rd Battalion, 3rd Special Forces Group (Airborne), Fort Bragg, USA, the Commanding Officer, Maj David A. Duffy wrote the following in respect of Maj F Yahaya in 2001:

> The United States Training Team recognises Maj Yahaya as being the best officer during the course of the training. As the Commander of C Coy, Maj Yahaya never failed to attend training, routinely inspiring his men by participating in all the training, regardless of the rigors involved. His company was split up among three US Training Teams by platoon, yet he was easily the most visible of the commanders of the 20th Mechanised Battalion. It is further hoped that this memorandum will in some way aid him in garnering further promotions and keeping him in leadership positions within the Nigerian Army.

The foregoing report from the US Army aptly underscores General Faruk Yahaya's commitment to duty, visibility, and proactive leadership competencies. During General Yahaya's senior course, it was reported that he had the ability to absorb knowledge quickly. In his Commanding Officer Course Report, he was said to have exercised effective command and control, won the Commandant's prize for the best service paper, and came first in order of merit. Lt Gen Faruk holds a Bachelor of Arts (BA) Degree in History from the Nigerian Defence Academy in 1990 and a Master in International Affairs and Diplomacy from the Ahmadu Bello University (ABU), Zaria in 2008. He equally holds a Certificate of Fellowship of the Nigerian Army Resource Centre Abuja in 2020. Gen Faruk Yahaya is a life member of the Historical Society of Nigeria and a Fellow of the Institute of Disaster Management and Safety Science. Gen Yahaya's military training at the NDA and other reputable institutions around the world thoroughly prepared him for effective military leadership and service to the nation and humanity.

A Life of Service to Nation and Humanity

Do your job to the best of your ability. If nobody sees, God sees. Be humble because it is God that gives. Having done everything correctly, luck is more than 50 per cent
Lt Gen Faruk Yahaya

This chapter explores the career experiences of Lt Gen Faruk Yahaya. It explores his military career from a Second Lieutenant to his position as the 22nd Chief of Army Staff. The chapter highlights the high and low points of his military career. It signposts the hallmark of each rank and what was his driving force as a young officer. The chapter identifies his career mentors and role models as well as the downside of his military career. It narrates his military career obstacles and how he triumphed. The chapter closes with a brief account of Lt Gen Faruk Yahaya's contributions to humanitarian causes through the Fatima Yahaya Foundation, a not-for-profit charity organisation he established to render educational and health services support to humanity, especially in Sifawa, Bodinga Local Government Area of Sokoto State and Nigeria in general. Faruk Yahaya in 2019 envisioned immortalising his beloved parents by establishing a foundation to touch and change the lives of people from all walks of life.

The foundation was named after his mother, Hajia Fatima Yahaya who was so dear to him and to whom he was a close confidant. It is underlined that the Hajia Fatima Yahaya Foundation is just one channel through which Lt Gen Faruk Yahaya exhibits his devotion towards promoting the welfare of humanity. He can be rightly described as an adherent of humanitarianism, which entails an active belief in the value of human life and the provision of assistance to other humans to reduce their suffering and improve their conditions of existence. A humanitarian act is based on moral, altruistic and emotional reasons. It is usually done without ulterior motives.

Humanitarians such as Lt Gen Faruk Yahaya believe that human beings deserve respect and dignity and should be treated as such. They abhor all forms of discrimination and violation of basic and human rights on the basis of gender, religion and ethnicity among others. Lt Gen Yahaya throughout his life and military career has proven to be a philanthropist par excellence.

The Young Officer and a Gentleman

Second Lieutenant Faruk Yahaya was granted Regular Combatant Commission as a member of 37 Regular Course on 22 September 1990 with seniority in the same rank effective 27 September 1985. His first posting after passing out of the NDA was to 181 Battalion Bida. Ever since he left the NDA, he has served at all levels all over the country and beyond, rendering quality military service to the nation. Faruk Yahaya sees his work and profession as a call to render service to the nation, humanity and God Almighty. There is no doubt that Faruk Yahaya's call into the military profession is divine and he reflects the joy of service rendered from his heart.

Faruk Yahaya has held several command, instructional and staff appointments which include Platoon Commander 181 Mechanised Battalion and 82 Motorised Battalion. He was also a Company Second in Command at 81 Guards Battalion and 20 Amphibious Battalion. He was also appointed Aid de Camp (ADC) to Col Dominic Oneya, Military Administrator of Kano State and later Benue State. He was Company Second in Command, 20 Amphibious Battalion and Officer Commanding 7 Battalion. Furthermore, Faruk Yahaya was General Staff Officer Grade 2 (Field Exercises), Army Headquarters Department of Army Operations, Staff Officer Grade 2 (Admin), Headquarters Guards Brigade, Staff Officer Grade 1 (Admin and Quartering), Headquarters Guard Brigade and Garrison Commander, Headquarters Guards Brigade and Directing Staff, Armed Forces Command and Staff College, Jaji. Faruk Yahaya also served as Deputy Director Military Secretary 3, Deputy Director Military Secretary 2, Deputy Director Research and Development and Chief of Staff Headquarters, Joint Task Force (Operation PULO SHIELD). He also served as Deputy Director Military Secretary 1, Principal General Staff Officer- Honorable Minister of Defence, Commander HQ 4 Brigade, Commander HQ 29 Task Force Brigade and Director Manpower, Army Headquarters, and Department of Army Administration. Faruk Yahaya also had the privilege to serve as Military Secretary (Army), General Officer Commanding, Headquarters 1 Division and Theatre Commander, Headquarters Threatre Command Op HADIN KAI before his appointment as the current Chief of Army Staff, Nigerian Army.

Instructional Experience

In instructional appointment and experience, Faruk Yayaha was a Directing Staff (DS) at the Armed Forces Command and Staff College, Jaji, from 12 September 2006, to 11 September 2008. He was noted to have contributed immensely to the success of junior courses during his tenure, and he also sponsored several exercises. Due to his sound knowledge of tactics, he was made head of the Tactics Team and as usual, he gave it his best shot. While in the AFCSC as a DS, Faruk Yahaya planned and conducted two Ex UBIAK ISIN (final exercises for the Junior Course). The conduct of the exercises was highly commended as the best in the recent history of the college. Faruk Yahaya taught and instructed his students from a strong foundation of knowledge and intellect. His depth, knowledge and commitment to duty made him the golden fish who had no hiding place during his tour of duty in the AFCSC, Jaji. This was exemplified through his appointment as the chairman assessment team on Peace Support Operations (PSO) Case Study. Faruk Yahaya's diligence and high sense of equity, fairness, and justice commended him for being appointed in the Promotion Board of Soldiers. A task he carried out with empathy, humility and wisdom. Lt Col Faruk Yahaya was also awarded Passed Staff College Daggar (psc(+)) with effect from 11 September 2008 in recognition of his service as a member of the Directing Staff in the AFCSC. A letter of congratulations written by Brig Gen AB Maitama reads thus: "Your professional conduct as a member of the DS in the AFCSC has done me proud and indeed all infantry officers and soldiers".

Command Appointments

In his Command experience, Faruk Yahaya served as an Officer in Charge (OC) in 20 Battalion and took part with his company during Op FOCUS RELIEF Phase III Training and Exercises. Owing to his professionalism, dedication to duty, and superlative performance, he was awarded a Letter of Achievement and memorial matchete as the best officer during the training by the US Department of the Army, 3rd Special Forces Group (Airborne), Fort Bragg. In his role as the Commander Guards' Brigade Garrison, he organized regular training programmes and consequently scaled up the level of professionalism of his unit.

As the Commander, 4 Brigade, Faruk Yahaya effectively coordinated the training and preparation of the 3 Battalion for a hitch-free mobilization and induction into Op LAFIYA DOLE. With commendable professionalism, he ensured that the mandate to curb crude oil theft, illegal oil bunkering and related crimes was carried out to the letter. He also provided security to oil and gas facilities, which immensely contributed to revenue generation for the Federal Government of Nigeria. Commendably, Faruk Yahaya's Brigade destroyed more than 45 illegal bunkering spots, 58 boats, 1,438 surface tanks, 9 vehicles, and 37 pumping machines. These efforts significantly downgraded and reduced criminal enterprises in his Areas of Responsibility (AOR). As Brigade Commander, Faruk Yahaya launched Op CLEAN UP to curb the proliferation of small arms and light weapons in his AOR. The operation led to the recovery of 21 x AK 47 rifles, 3 x FN rifles, one MMG, Improvised Explosive Devices (IEDs) and ammunitions of varying calibre among other dangerous weapons and devices. Additionally, his Brigade launched Op MOP UP to check the nefarious activities of the Niger Delta Avengers. These gallant efforts were carried out altruistically and patriotically by Faruk Yahaya and his men as a sacred mandate/service to Nigeria.

In the cause of engaging criminal elements operating in the Niger Delta, Faruk Yahaya placed his life and those of his troops on the line for the sake of the fatherland. Combating the flourishing and debilitating criminal enterprise in the Niger Delta could be a very dangerous engagement as these criminals who are feeding fat by illegally extracting and stealing the commonwealth have developed a network that is difficult to unbundle and dismantle. The wanton theft of Nigeria's crude oil in the Niger Delta over the years has continued to deal a catastrophic blow to the Nigerian economy since oil and gas account for the bulk of government revenue. The experience gleaned from combating these criminal organisations in the Niger Delta speaks to the need to integrate both the kinetic and non-kinetic approaches in dealing with insecurity and other criminalities in the society. This is akin to the experience gathered from counter-terrorism and counterinsurgency operations in the North Eastern part of Nigeria, where the military has engaged the Boko Haram sect and ISWAP in a protracted battle for over a decade. It has been argued that the military alone cannot completely destroy and obliterate crude oil theft and even piracy in the Niger Delta, just like insurgency, as long as some of the undesirable socio-economic conditions such as poverty, unemployment, and environmental degradation still persist.

The experiences gained combating criminalities in the Niger Delta through a military or kinetic approach speak to the need for an integrated and whole-of-society approach to dealing with this problem. This is why the steps taken by the FGN in addressing these precipitating conditions that are fueling criminal enterprise in the Niger Delta, such as the Ogoni Clean Up Initiative, the passage of the Petroleum Industry Act (PIA), and the award of pipeline surveillance contracts to some persons in the Niger Delta region, among others, are commendable. It is hoped that these measures will usher in a more peaceful and prosperous Niger Delta region.

As the Commander of the 29 Task Force Brigade, Faruk Yahaya, through his creativity and foresight, improved the troop's mobility and firepower through the repairs of several unserviceable Armoured Personnel Carriers (APCs) and B vehicles. This effort immensely aided his forward units in repelling several Boko Haram terrorist attacks in the North East. Using his initiatives, Faruk Yahaya procured additional ICOM ground-to-air radio for effective interface with the Nigerian Air Force (NAF) and BAOFENG UV-5R for the Brigade. He maintained an effective and efficient liaison with the NAF, which enabled the seamless supply of food and logistics to locations that were inaccessible after heavy rainfall. This intervention boosted the morale of troops and enhanced service delivery in pursuit of national security.

Staff Appointments/Experience

Faruk Yahaya served as the Acting Second in Command 7 Battalion and he creditably and commendably discharged his duties. As Staff Officer Grade 2 (SO2) Administration and later GSO1 Training/Operations at Headquarters, Guards Brigade, Faruk assisted the Brigade to successfully execute its 2005 training activities and mounted several internal security operations. As an officer with empathy and human milk of kindness he kept a close tab on the Senior Non-Commissioned Officers (SNCO) and promotion examination cadres which resulted in the improved standard of soldiers in their duties and the success of the officers in promotion examinations. Faruk was also the ACOS G1 at Headquarters 1 Division, Kaduna where he was the coordinator of the Second Commanding Officers' Workshop which took place at the Division's HQ. He was a member of the HQ 1 Division Complex Renovation Committee and he clearly demonstrated an uncompromising desire for a quality job to be done through constant and effective supervision. In 2009, Faruk Yahaya was appointed an umpire during Exercise OLOGUN META and he made profound and significant contributions to the exercise as well as developed team momentum. The exercise was adjudged to be very successful and insightful.

Faruk Yahaya in the course of his illustrious career and service to the nation was Deputy Director, Military Secretary 3 (DDMS3) and later Deputy Director Military Secretary 2 (DDMS2). Due to his penchant for quality service and his unalloyed dedication, he "handled all his responsibilities with determination, seriousness, professionalism, confidentiality and a high level of integrity". A case in point was during a Short Service Combatant (SSC) Selection Board where his efforts led to the detection of an attempt by 2 ex-cadets of SSC 39/2010 who were withdrawn from NDA for fraudulent conduct to rejoin the service as well as another individual who attempted to undertake the 3.2 kilometers run on behalf of a candidate. In addition, Faruk Yahaya was saddled with the responsibility of administering the department and he worked tirelessly to successfully accomplish all assigned tasks as scheduled.

Furthermore, Faruk Yahaya served as the Deputy Director, Research and Development (DDR&D) at Army Headquarters, DAPP. He was also appointed the Secretary of the Nigerian Army Systems Development Central Management Board Meeting, and he played a pivotal role in identifying, initiating, monitoring, and prioritizing the Nigerian Army's research needs, as well as in sourcing alternative options for research in the Nigerian Army. As a dedicated and untiring officer, Faruk Yahaya compiled a compendium of all Nigerian Army research projects, which now serves as a data base for details on all Nigerian Army research activities. He was duly commended for these initiatives. He equally represented the department and prepared accurate briefs in meetings, including the Nigerian Army R&D Conference and National Emergency Management Agency (NEMA) meetings on floods and other disasters, among other tasks and responsibilities he carried out.

Faruk Yahaya also served as Chief of Staff (COS) Headquarters Joint Task Force (JTF) Operation PULO SHIELD. He was reported to have performed excellently, above and beyond the call of duty. He prepared and coordinated effectively the JTF Commander's briefs to the Chief of Defence Staff, Chief of Naval Staff, and Chief of Training and Operations Defence HQ. As an officer who is dependable and reliable, he was saddled with coordinating Operation CLEAN SLATE in 2013 to flush out militants responsible for the death of 11 policemen. True to his character, Faruk Yahaya delivered on the mandate.

It is often said that the reward for hard work is more work and this expression has been proven time and time again in the course of the military career of Faruk Yahaya. He was briefly Director of Logistics at the National Defence College in April 2014, before he was appointed the Principal General Staff Officer (PGSO) to the Honourable Minister of Defence (HMOD), Lt Gen Aliyu Gusau. Consistent with his professionalism and dedication, he advised the HMOD on military matters and attended Services Council/Board meetings. He effectively and efficiently handled all correspondences to the Ministry of Defence and prepared real-time and relevant briefs, drafts, and executive summaries as appropriate for the HMOD. He also brilliantly drafted speeches, lectures, and remarks for the HMOD, among other assignments. He served as PGSO-HMOD from April 2014 - August 2015.

Peace Support Operations Appointment

Faruk Yahaya has contributed to global peace support operations and stability operations within and outside Nigeria. He served in NIBATT 16 Op LIBERTY, from 1993-1996 in diverse capacities during the first Liberian civil war (1989- 1996). It was reported that the first Liberian civil war was one of Africa's bloodiest civil conflicts in the post-independence era. The war claimed more than two hundred thousand lives and displaced more than one million Liberians. Faruk Yahaya was inducted into this war in 1993 and as a child of destiny, he survived the war and contributed his quota to peace and security in Liberia.

Faruk's attitude and aptitude positioned him to be appointed as Security Officer to the Interim President of Liberia, Dr. Amos Claudius Sawyer. Dr. Sawyer emerged as Interim President after Charles Taylor's insurgency led to a full-scale breakdown of law and order that resulted in the death of Samuel Doe, who served as Liberia's Interim President from 22 November 1990, to 7 March 1994. Dr.

Sawyer was described by Lindsay Barret as Liberia's peace-seeking leader and one of West Africa's most profound advocates of post-colonial representative government. He was always in search of peace, whether in or out of office. Dr Amos Sawyer died on 17 February 2022 at the age of 76. Faruk Yahaya, as Adjutant participated actively in all exercises and training for peace enforcement and peacekeeping in the mission. As the Intelligence Officer, Faruk Yahaya used his tact and friendly approach to collect vital information from various warring factions in his unit's AOR, including the National Patriotic Front of Liberia (NPFL), led by Charles Taylor, the United Liberian Movement of Liberia for Democracy (ULIMO), and the Independent National Patriotic Front of Liberia (INPFL), led by Prince Johnson, among others. In August 1996, Nigerian officials forced major warring factions to sign the Abuja Accord, requiring that they all agree to disarm and demobilize by 1997 and abide by UN-monitored elections. The election gave victory to Charles Taylor.

Strategic Appointment

Lt Gen Faruk Yahaya was also at the Army Headquarters Department of Army Administration as Director of Manpower Planning. He was also the Military Secretary (Army) before his appointment as the General Officer Commanding 1 Division Kaduna. Until his appointment as the 22nd Chief of Army Staff on 27 May 2021, he was the Theatre Commander Joint Task Force North West, Op HADIN KAI. Apart from Lt Gen Faruk Yahaya's military service to Nigeria and the world, he is such an officer and gentleman with uncommon humanitarian and philanthropic missions. Daily, he seeks to promote the welfare of others in the Nigerian Army, his community, Sokoto State, and Nigeria as a whole.

Honours and Awards

Lt Gen Faruk Yahaya has proven himself to be a generous and benevolent General of our time. In the course of General Yahaya's close to four decades of meritorious service to his fatherland and humanity, he has received several accolades and commendations from diverse quarters. These include the Nigerian Army Medal (NAM) for exemplary leadership and the provision of administrative and operational guidance and motivation as the Chief of Army Staff, Nigerian Army Field Command Medal of Honour (FCMH), Nigerian Army Distinguished Service Star (DSS) and the Nigerian Army General Operations Medal (GOM), among others. In October 2022, he was awarded the national honour of Commander of the Order of the Federal Republic (CFR), which is the third highest national honour in Nigeria after the Grand Commander of the Order of the Federal Republic (GCFR) that is exclusive to President and the Grand Commander of the Order of the Niger (GCON), which is the second highest national honour in Nigeria. The GCON is conferred on Vice Presidents, Chief Justices and Senate Presidents. However, in 2011, business mogul Alhaji Aliko Dangote, Chairman of Dangote Group was awarded the GCON honour due for innovative business leadership in Nigeria.

Reacting to the national honours bestowed on one of his illustrious sons, the District Head of Sifawa, Alhaji Muhammadu Buhari Tambari MON, described the award as a testimony to the fact that Lt Gen Faruk Yahaya is doing a great job in securing the country from the problem of insecurity. In recognition of Lt Gen Faruk Yahaya's outstanding leadership of the Nigerian Army, the Historical Society of Nigeria (HSON) on Tuesday 28 September 2021 conferred the Honorary Award of Associate Fellowship of the Historical Society of Nigeria (AFHSN). According to Professor Okpeh Okpeh, the Acting President of HSON, the award is well deserved, considering the visionary and astute leadership provided by Lt Gen Faruk Yahaya since his assumption of command. He further pointed out that the COAS leadership has culminated in the successes being recorded in ongoing Nigerian Army campaigns and operations across the country.

The Guardian Newspaper of 1 July 2022, described Lt Gen Faruk Yahaya as "Yahaya: The Working, Not Talking COAS". It goes on to state "Lt Gen Faruk Yahaya has surpassed the mark of a mere hero and has launched himself into the nobility of greatness to be reckoned with worldwide". Furthermore, Moses Oche, a public affairs analyst, penned passionately the following eulogies on Lt Gen Faruk Yahaya thus: "over time, Lt Gen Faruk Yahaya, has proven himself qualified with unique skills such as his vast wealth of experience as a war veteran, a peacekeeper, and an administrator with efficiency in maintaining order and stability in conflict- ridden areas around the country. The General respects every religion by showing no discrepancy in his judgements and decision-making. Apart from his gift of looking beyond religious fanaticism, he is loved by all due to his large heart of giving and donations to soldiers and citizens around without showing any tolerance for worldliness in his dealings" (Oche, The Guardian, 1 July 22). In the course of Lt Gen Faruk Yahaya's illustrious military career, he has experienced some highs and lows. According to him, "I cried as a Captain, wishing to dash from my duty post. There were indeed tough times. I was the ADC to the Military Administrator of Kano and Benue States but things were still difficult". Despite some of the career challenges he encountered, he remained resilient and determined to finish strong. Gen Faruk Yahaya's promotion history reveals that he has earned his promotions as follows:

a. Lieutenant   27 September 1990
b. Captain   27 September 1994
c. Major   27 September 1998
d. Lieutenant Colonel   27 September 2003
e. Colonel   27 September 2008
f. Brigadier General   27 September 2013
g. Major General   27 September 2017
h. Lieutenant General   7 July 2021

The history of Lt Gen Faruk Yahaya's career promotion underlines the important and significant date of 27 September in which he earned all his promotions up to the rank of major general. One could be tempted to state that 27 September is a lucky and watershed date for the General. "If I didn't join the military, perhaps I would be a teacher. I like books and reading. I have plenty of books and I still buy books. I like memoirs. I like to go to bookshops to buy books by different authors especially *Maliki*, which is one of the schools of thought in Islam. Mostly, people from Sokoto State align with this school of thought, he said".

Lt Gen Faruk Yahaya noted with a high sense of humility and gratitude to God that "by divine providence, I have been in all the places. I have had staff, instructional, operational and command appointments in the Nigerian

Army". Having operated at the tactical, operational and strategic levels, Faruk Yahaya has been thoroughly groomed and equipped for the command of the Nigerian Army. His professional pathway, which has seen both high and low levels of tipping points, has molded and inculcated in him a robust and deep commitment to humanity and humanitarian causes. Moses Oche aptly captured the natural and undiluted philanthropic blood that flows through the veins of Gen Faruk Yahaya when he observed, "those who have known Lt Gen Faruk Yahaya from his teenage years loudly attest to his open-minded and compassionate nature. They know the Army Chief as humane and passionate about the afflictions and plight of the less privileged. Anyone can easily touch his soft spot irreversibly when he extends assistance to the needy or comes to the rescue of anyone in a consuming dilemma. He is kind to a fault, humble, and amiable". Oche submits that Lt Gen Faruk Yahaya has grown up with these attributes in his chosen profession, the Army, and exhibits them everywhere he has served his country.

The foregoing graphically exhibits the milk of kindness that flows in the spirit, soul, and body of Gen Faruk Yahaya, which led him to establish a humanitarian foundation to immortalize his beloved parents' years before he became the Chief of Army Staff. The moral lesson of the pioneering efforts of Faruk Yahaya in promoting human empowerment and development is that one does not have to wait until he or she occupies a high position in society to become impactful. We all can start small in our little corners to alleviate poverty, abolish illiteracy, and contribute to the development of human capital for national development and security. Lt Gen Faruk Yahaya has taught us that it is little drops that make an ocean.

Humanitarian Services

Lt Gen Faruk Yahaya has been a compassionate and benevolent person since childhood. This was attested to by the District Head (Sarki) of Sifawa, Alhaji Muhammed Buhari Tambari MON, who stated that in Sifawa, nobody will ever point a finger at Faruk for having ever fought anybody. In the words of the Chief Imam of Sifawa, who was a primary school mate of Faruk Yahaya, "he is religious, generous to a fault, and humanely conscious". Lt Gen Faruk Yahaya, as captured by one of his NDA course mates, Maj Gen IM Yusuf, has empathy as a major attribute. "He is gifted with empathy and the human angle is uppermost in his mind".

It is worthy of note that in all his close to four decades of meritorious service to the nation, Lt Gen Faruk Yahaya has no disciplinary record of any kind. This is an uncommon feat and speaks eloquently to the General's impeccable character, integrity, loyalty, and total dedication to the service of the nation and humanity.

In Sifawa community in particular, the projects built in the community were achieved largely through the efforts of Lt Gen Faruk Yahaya. He instituted a foundation in honour of his parents named Fatima Yahaya Foundation. The foundation has built primary and secondary schools and a school of nursing and midwifery. In the primary and secondary schools, there are about 500 students from different parts of the country studying and enjoying a highly subsidised tuition fee. The Fatima Yahaya School of Nursing and Midwifery has students from different parts of the country and is serviced by a hospital established by the Foundation. These humanitarian efforts have provided quality education to hundreds of students and also created employment for many people in Sifawa and Bodinga Local Government.

Hajiya Fatima Yahaya Foundation

The Hajiya Fatima Yahaya Foundation being promoted by one of her beloved sons, Faruk Yahaya, has a vision to empower and uplift the weak and the less privileged in society. The vision, mission, and objectives of the foundation are outlined below.

Vision

To achieve a happy, healthy, disciplined, and self-reliant society in which the weak and less privileged members are not excluded, but supported and encouraged to have access to basic education, health care and means for livelihood, leading to higher intellectual, social, and economic status.

Mission

To raise and invest funds, support educational and health institutions, acquire and manage assets, organize programmes and activities, and collaborate with private and public organizations towards sustainable human resource development, empowerment of women, youths and less privileged individuals, as well as general social services to humanity.

Objectives

- To foster unity, harmony, and love among the members of society through various humanitarian services, including economic, social, religious, and educational support and services.

- To succor, empower, and cater for the welfare of the needy, widows, orphans, oppressed, and other less privileged members of the society.

- To facilitate human resource development, build the minds of the youths, motivate them to maximize their talents, sensitize and enlighten them on their civic duties, and opportunities.

- To promote the welfare of women and girl-child education, advocate equal access for the vulnerable population to education and health care services, and inculcate in them discipline and good values of living.

- To initiate empowerment programmes or activities and collaborate with community development associations as well as government agencies to make a positive impact on humanity.

- To support the establishment of educational and health institutions, including the College of Nursing and Midwifery, for the training of qualified nurses, midwives, and other health care personnel.

Units and Services

The Hajiya Fatima Yahaya Foundation has several units. These include the education and human resources development unit responsible for education and health issues, public enlightenment, scholarship and students support, research, and publication. The social and humanitarian service unit is responsible for food assistance, medical assistance, school materials assistance, shelter construction and rehabilitation, clothing materials, sanitary facilities, and community projects. The economic empowerment unit oversees training on entrepreneurial skills, youth empowerment activities, women empowerment activities and loans. The last unit is the fund-raising and investment unit. The unit is in charge of investment, asset management and maintenance, public collection and donation, revolving fund management, bank and non-bank facility operations, and zakah and endowment management.

The target beneficiaries are orphans and widows, the aged and incapacitated- victims of disaster, students and youths, women and vulnerable children, internally displaced people, and the general public. The Foundation facilities are all located in Sifawa. These include the foundation secretariat, office accommodations, skills acquisition centres, classrooms and event halls, computer laboratories and CBT centres, store rooms and a mosque.

The achievements recorded by the Foundation are underpinned by the guiding principles. Some of them include the registration of beneficiaries and documentation, adherence to specific criteria in selecting beneficiaries, consideration of frequency and priority, collaboration with micro finance banks, and collaboration with individuals and corporate bodies.

Hajiya Fatima Yahaya Foundation has, since inception in 2019, made some remarkable achievements in education, capacity building, the provision of health care services, scholarships and other welfare programmes. The foundation runs the Fatima Yahaya International School, an ICT Centre, a Skills Acquisition Centre, the Fatima College of Nursing Sciences, as well as the Fatima Yahaya Hospital in Sifawa. The impact of its services to the people is typified by the International School and the College of Nursing Sciences. The primary school has 422 pupils receiving first-class education in the conventional section and 312 pupils in the Islamiyya section, while the college has 337 students comprising 199 student nurses and 138 student midwives from Sokoto State and beyond. After nursing/midwifery training and certification, their lives would never be the same again.

Fig 20: Hajiya Fatima Yahaya Foundation

Fig 21: Fatima Yahaya International School   **Fig 22**: Fatima College of Nursing

The foundation would surely impact more people with the support of well-to-do Nigerians and other philanthropists, even beyond the shores of Nigeria. The Foundation has touched the lives of many Nigerians across ethno-religious divides and could do more with greater support from both the government and other individuals, including the private sector. Lt Gen Faruk Yahaya's vision and benevolence are worthy of emulation by other military and non- military persons in order to assist the Nigerian government in addressing poverty and unemployment. The Foundation could serve as a model to be replicated in other parts of the country.

Lt Gen Faruk Yahaya's life of exemplary service to nation and humanity built in him some time-tested leadership competencies that culminated in his well-deserved appointment as the Chief of Army Staff. The trajectory of his military career, right from the NDA, points to the conclusion that Faruk Yahaya was destined by God to lead. This was succinctly captured again by Maj Gen IM Yusuf, when he stated that "I saw in him great leadership potential from cadet till now, and this was instrumental to his selection as the Course Senior in the NDA. It's just about destiny". Destiny has called Faruk Yahaya to be a strategic leader, with uncommon and unobtrusive leadership traits.

Narrating his passion and drive towards humanitarianism, Lt Gen Faruk Yahaya stated that "I am from a humble beginning. We lived in a one-room house. My background contributed to the foundation, and it is also a gift from God". He noted further, "I can feel people's pain because I was there. The women feel poverty more. In a typical community, there are things she cannot do. We all need help, but women need it more". The COAS stated that his effort is to support women. The women are my concern because they are more compassionate and also provide more help than men. Women are very industrious and have a natural tendency to help". In addition, he posited that "one of the things I like doing most, is supporting those who have nobody but God. I am not expecting anything from them. Every time you see me, I have something to give to people around".

The future of the Fatima Yahaya Foundation is very bright, given the growing demand for its offerings both in education and other empowerment and human capital development programmes. The School of Nursing and Medical Sciences is expected to award degrees in the near future. The foundation will grow someday and transmute into a major academic hub in Northern Nigeria in particular and the country in general. The Fatima Yahaya Foundation looks forward to deeper collaboration with partners within and outside the shores of Nigeria. It is salutary to note that the Foundation has a database of all orphans in Sifawa and Bodinga Local Government Area, and there is enough room to expand the scope of documenting orphans not just in Sokoto State but in Nigeria. What the Hajiya Fatima Foundation has done could be a pathfinder for states and the FGN to begin to document and generate a database of orphans in the country.

Another area in which the Hajiya Fatima Yahaya Foundation is looking forward to intervening is that of taking care of senior citizens. Currently, the foundation is taking a census and studying, and researching to see what areas of intervention are needed for older people. This is another uncharted course in Nigeria where senior citizens are left without much support from society or the government. The support system for senior citizens, both in terms of pension and for those who are not pensionable, leaves much to be desired. The Hajiya Fatima Yahaya Foundation has discovered this area of need and is working towards ameliorating the poor living conditions of aged people. The future is also bright for the foundation to actively engage in policy advocacy and programmatic initiatives that will impact the living conditions of the less privileged in society.

Lt Gen Faruk Yahaya is committed to giving to humanity. Indeed, he is a gift from God to humanity, as God Almighty continues to empower him to ameliorate and pull many out of the firm grip of poverty. He strongly believes that it is God that gives and when He gives, you don't close and clinch your palm. Be a channel of blessing to others, even when they cannot do anything for you. The Hajiya Fatima Yahaya Foundation is a role model for any person who is called to humanitarianism and who has empathy for fellow human beings especially the less privileged in society. The Foundation is a clarion call to action for all well- meaning individuals, military and civilians to take up a humanitarian cause in their domain, which would be tantamount to changing one life at a time. That is how change happens. One gesture, one person, one moment at a time, one life changed can change the world. According to Mahatma Gandhi "Be the change you wish to see in the world". Let us mirror the world, the country, and the community we want to see, and don't just sit and wait for others to lead.

Leadership Grooming and Selection

Great leadership results from the collision of the intangible and the malleable, from that which is given and that which is exerted. Scope remains for individual effort – to deepen historical understanding, hone strategy, and improve character.
Henry Kissinger

Concept of Leadership

Every nation, society, organization, military, army, formation, unit, and subunit craves leadership. Leadership is the process of directing the affairs of a group of people (followers) towards arriving at a destination or attaining their aims and aspirations. It includes the ability of an individual or group to influence and guide another group of individuals or organization in a particular direction, primarily towards the achievement of goals or otherwise. Leadership involves the application of some skills, both hard and soft, to attain the set goals and objectives. Some of these skills are acquired over a period of deliberate regime of training or imbibed unconsciously through association with people in leadership positions. Some other skills are inherent. Both ideas agree with General S Patton's view that 'leadership is a complex phenomenon; leaders are both born and made, but mostly made'. Be that as it may, leadership skills are developed over time. Some schools of thought argue that leadership is a natural phenomenon, while others see leadership as an acquired. Whichever way it is viewed, both ideas could apply to leadership within the military.

Military Leadership

Military leadership is about how leadership is viewed and practised within the military as an organization. The military structure is hierarchical. The structure is built around the commander, his troops, and other material resources. Though the concept of command is not exactly the same as the concept of leadership, the commander needs to exhibit good leadership to succeed in his assigned tasks in order to become an accomplished commander.

Leadership is an element of combat power. Military leadership is thus about leading men and controlling resources. Military leadership, in several situations, entails making critical decisions under high pressure with attendant risks. Leadership in the military is purpose driven. It involves a lot of motivation, compulsion, influence, direction, and bold actions towards a successful mission accomplishment.

Importantly, leadership in the Nigerian Army is exercised through command, which is the authority conferred on the leader to lawfully control his subordinates by virtue of his rank and assignment or position. The leader exercises authority through the chain of command to accomplish assigned missions while caring for personnel and other resources placed in his care. Effective leadership in the Nigerian Army would clearly demand leaders that can provide purpose, direction and motivation to accomplish missions. Alternatively, it requires leaders that understand their subordinates and take a keen interest in their welfare. Nigerian Army officers therefore ought to lead by example, supervise and train their soldiers as a team, make sound and timely decisions and instill a sense of responsibility in subordinates. Furthermore, they will be required to employ the unit in accordance with its capabilities and also take responsibility for their actions. The troops must have confidence in their leader before they can follow him or her in such a manner as to get the job done. A good military leader is one who is able to get the job done irrespective of the risks involved with minimum casualties. Lt Gen Faruk Yahaya is the epitome of good leadership in the Nigerian Army. He has been able to get most of his jobs done while ascending the military hierarchy over the years with minimum casualties, even in very turbulent situations and a somewhat chaotic environment. Lt Gen Yahaya was able to achieve this feat due to some qualities he developed, values he held so dear and principles he adhered to while making his way up the mantle of leadership in the Nigerian Army in particular and the Armed Forces of Nigeria in general.

Attributes Values and Principles of Leadership in the Armed Forces of Nigeria

The attributes, values, and principles of leadership constitute a crucial component of the officer cadets' training curriculum right from the commencement of military training, especially at the NDA. Regular combatant officers of the Armed Forces of Nigeria are usually moulded at the NDA from raw civilians, young men and women, from different parts of the country. The ex-boys, junior ratings, junior air men/women or those from the military schools, command, navy, or air force secondary schools, also constitute a significant percentage of the young entrants into the Academy. Officer cadets are taken through modules on leadership and management as well as exercises in the field to train them on leadership and management in the field. The cadet battalions lines under the Cadets' Brigade are also managed and led by senior cadets who hold different cadets appointments at different terms/levels.

They start with syndicate or group leaderships to course senior-ship, cadet lance corporal through cadet corporal, cadet sergeant, and cadet company sergeant major, cadet regimental quartermaster sergeant to cadet regimental sergeant major. Other cadets' appointments are cadet company senior under officer, cadet battalion senior under officer, academy cadet adjutant, and academy senior under officer. All of these appointments imbue in the cadets a sense of responsibility over their subordinates in terms of control, training, and welfare. The ability to also take care of military properties and accommodation infrastructure; through interior economy, is also developed at this early stage of the officer cadets' upbringing. Faruk Yahaya, who came straight from Sifawa, Bodinga Local Government Area of Sokoto State, without any prior military training, began his leadership grooming right from Mogadishu Battalion of the Cadets' Brigade, NDA, and was only a course senior until he became a Cadet Company Senior Under Officer in his final year before his commission into the Nigerian Army in the rank of second lieutenant in 1990.

According to Maj Gen IM Yusuf, "I recall how in the NDA Class of 1985, we unanimously elected Cadet Faruk Yahaya as our course senior. You know it is rotated, but each year, we said he should continue. When we got to the final year (Army Class), that was how we also said you are our Course Senior, and he continued as Course Senior throughout the time". He was never a cadet lance corporal, cadet corporal or cadet sergeant in his second, third, and fourth years, respectively, until he became a company senior under officer in the Mogadishu Battalion in his fifth year. This is quite unusual for a final year cadet appointment, but it goes to show the peculiarities of Cadet Faruk Yahaya as a special one whose leadership traits must have been keenly observed by the instructors in his battalion and the

Academy. His course mates still kept him as their Course Senior even with his appointment as a Company Senior Under Officer of a battalion. It is important to note that while appointing him as their course senior, there was neither rancour nor contest, it was a unanimous decision, which made him somewhat acceptable to all of them. Yusuf (2023) attested that the qualities of empathy, patience, and humility stood him out among others.

The motto of the NDA is loyalty and valour. An officer cadet of the NDA is thus taught that a leader must have some basic qualities to be successful. Such qualities include morals, courage, integrity, intelligence, self-discipline, manners, and humility. Others are knowledge, proficiency, and instructional ability; mastery over language; loyalty; willpower; keenness; judgement; flexibility; good character; personal example; and self-sacrifice. It is expected that if the cadet is able to grasp all of these basic qualities and operate with them as an officer in the field, he would likely turn out good results whenever tasked with or assigned any mission. Reports from course mates, superiors, and subordinates confirm that Lt Gen Faruk Yahaya imbibed these qualities right from the training days in the Academy and lived through them as an officer in his service with the Armed Forces of Nigeria. According to Lt Gen Yahaya, "The training in the NDA has prepared every officer for the task ahead up to the highest level. The Army has procedures for doing things; cadets train cadets on the way things are done. If you build on them and adapt yourself, you will improve. Our training curriculum is good, but we can improve." This is in consonance with the views of many other officers of the Armed Forces of Nigeria that the NDA is second to none in the country, as well as across the African Region, in terms of the quality of training bequeathed to its graduates. The values of the Academy are proudly held and guarded jealously by its products.

Growing through the Ranks from Tactical to Operational Level of Leadership

The stratification of warfare into tactical, operational and strategic levels laid the foundation for building command and leadership in the military on the hierarchy of tactical, operational, and strategic levels. A commissioned combatant officer in the army begins his career as a platoon commander and rises through the ladder of command and leadership (company, battalion, brigade, division, corps) until getting to the peak of commanding an army as the Chief of Army Staff, as is the case with the Nigerian Army, or Commander Land Forces in other climes where the military command structure has been fully integrated into a Joint Force Doctrine. As a platoon commander, Faruk Yahaya was already observed to possess some of those basic character traits that ultimately define good leadership. He was found to be promising right from the outset as a young lieutenant in 181 Battalion of the Nigerian Army. According to his Commanding Officer, Colonel JL Kum, who wrote his first Performance Evaluation Report signed on 25 January 1992, Lt Faruk Yahaya ..., I observed him to be a very hardworking, loyal, disciplined and efficient [officer]. Lt Yahaya is a very young officer, healthy and energetic, who has great determination to do very well in his chosen career. So far, he has been on the right footing and should endeavour to maintain the pace. Although he was young and recently posted to the unit, he took an active part in the unit's command and administration at the platoon level. He acted competently as the unit adjutant, whenever required to do so.

Faruk Yahaya thus set the right foundation for himself and his career from the word 'go' and he never looked back as he built on it till the end. He also served in 82 Battalion (NIBATT 16) Op LIBERTY ECOMOG Operations in Liberia from 1993 – 1996 as a platoon commander, where he was found capable of being selected and appointed as the Battalion Adjutant and also Intelligence Officer. Such appointments are not usually made for all officers in a battalion at the junior command and leadership level. Subject to availability, only young officers with the right potentials and dispositions are selected to serve as unit adjutants or intelligence officers. At that level, being a Battalion Adjutant and Intelligence Officer exposes an officer to some special tasks and responsibilities that eventually develop those qualities of good accountability, administration, confidence, confidentiality, probity, prudence, quick thinking, robustness and reliability that enhance an officer's competences. He was found so competent that he was appointed as a Security Officer to the Interim President of Liberia, Dr Amos Sawyer during which he was noted to be a very humble and intelligent officer who could be relied upon. He carried out his duties creditably.

Before becoming a Company Commander in 7 Battalion, Serti, Taraba State, Faruk Yahaya served in 81 Guards Battalion Keffi and 20 Amphibious Battalion Warri as Company Second-in-Command. He was also an Aid-de-Camp to Colonel Dominic Oneya as the Military Administrator of Kano and later Benue State. His principal noted that Yahaya had carried out his duties satisfactorily. Some striking qualities that the principal commended him for were his bearing, conduct both on and off duty, punctuality, commitment to duty, efficiency, dedication, and concerns for the welfare of his colleagues and subordinates. Colonel Dominic Oneya defined Capt Faruk Yahaya as 'a confident and trusted officer' whom he enjoyed working with. He was also noted to be quite humorous, cheerful and open-minded. Most of these qualities appeared consistently in Faruk Yahaya's evaluation reports throughout his career in the Nigeria Army.

As a company commander in Serti, he was noted for having used his comportment, wealth of experience, and vastness knowledge of service to produce quality results on any task assigned to him. His relationship with both superiors and subordinates was noted as outstanding. This quality had remained constant all through his career. It was not a surprise then that the troops were very excited, such that they were singing and dancing on the announcement of his appointment as the Twenty-Second Chief of Army Staff, Nigerian Army, on 27 May 2021. He also served as a Recruitment Officer for the Nigerian Army during a recruitment exercise in Jalingo, Taraba State, in 2002, while he was still a major. His Commanding Officer in Serti noted that he had high potential and the capacity to develop in the future for the benefit of the Nigerian Army.

Faruk Yahaya kept developing himself continuously in his acquisition of professional knowledge, skills, and expertise. He also developed his character as an officer in particular, and most importantly, as an individual. This is something that is not common, yet very important for leadership development both in the military and even in society at large. Good leadership has a lot to do with the possession of good character traits. Faruk Yahaya attained such a level of proficiency that he was qualified to be used as a utility officer for all jobs when his unit eventually redeployed from Serti in Taraba State to Warri in Delta State, Nigeria. During his service in 7 Battalion, Warri Delta State, some qualities that came out clearly were his discipline, dedication and integrity. Lt Col GAR Dogo, his commanding officer, remarked that:

> Major Yahaya is a disciplined, dedicated, and honest officer. He is an officer

full of integrity and knowledge in both military and world affairs. Major Faruk can be relied upon to achieve results in any given task assigned to him and does not need to be prompted to carry out his duties.

Faruk Yahaya is thus highly knowledgeable, possesses a high level of integrity, and has good crisis management skills. It was remarked that he commanded different sectors in the heat of communal clashes in the Niger Delta and successfully brought situations well under control in all the sectors he commanded. He repelled several militant attacks on oil facilities and even Koko town. At the height of the Ijaw/ Itsekiri crisis, he restored confidence to the Koko people and represented his battalion in several meetings. He also conducted the 53 Regular Intake Recruitment Exercise in Delta State objectively and came up with results that were not disputed anywhere. On the whole, he was seen as a valuable asset to the Nigerian Army, and his service knowledge as well as his personal interest in the job were observed to be influential on his subordinate. Faruk Yahaya was thus an embodiment of leadership by example, which should be the standard for leadership development in the Armed Forces of Nigeria in particular and contemporary Nigerian society in general.

As a unit commander, that is the Guards Brigade Garrison Commander from 7 April 2006 to 7 September 2006, he took the training of his men seriously. He was noted to have organized regular training programmes for them, thereby improving the level of professionalism in the unit, which ultimately resulted in high levels of performance by his troops during competitions that were held in the brigade within the period of his command. Before his assumption of command of the garrison, he had served at the Brigade Headquarters as a Staff Officer Grade 2 in charge of administration. Subsequently, he served as Staff Officer Grade 1, in charge of training and operations. All of these eventually prepared him for his future leadership role as the Commander of the Brigade Garrison. He had acquired some experiential knowledge and skills in the course of his duties as a staff officer before assuming a position that demanded a higher level of responsibilities as the commander. Such is the kind of practical grooming for leadership that is available within the military organization rather than leadership by inheritance or by circumstance. Nevertheless, some circumstantial or situational leaders may emerge in the military due to certain unforeseen circumstances. Such circumstances may include the unexpected demise of a commander or the task behaviour demanded by the higher authority, which is akin to Hersey and Blanchard's situational leadership model. Whoever emerges in such a circumstance must have undergone the requisite training and acquired adequate knowledge and experiences to shoulder the responsibilities expected of the new status.

Faruk Yahaya was a Directing Staff at the Armed Forces Command and Staff College, Jaji, Nigeria as a lieutenant colonel before he was promoted to the rank of colonel in the Nigerian Army. The Armed Forces Command and Staff College focuses on tactical and operational level training of middle level career officers of the Armed Forces of Nigeria. The command and leadership packages constitute a significant percentage of the training curriculum, and they are very important to the development of military leaders in Nigeria. Graduates of the college are expected to take up unit command in the field and also operate as Grade 2 or Grade 1 staff officers at the formations and services headquarters. It was noted that he "imparted positively on his students' performance". His attributes of honesty and prudence as with many others were also noticed and adequately acknowledged in the college by his Chief Instructor, Col EG Ode. According to Col Ode:

> Owing to his diligence, sense of justice and fair play, he was appointed Chairman of the Assessment Team on Peace Support Operations Case Study Presentation Junior Course 66/2008, and Armed Forces Command and Staff College Promotion Board Soldiers in 2008. Faruk proved that he was an honest officer and a very good resource manager when, as a Term Coordinator A Division, he adequately utilized over Two Million Naira for Junior Course 65/2008, including Exercise UBIAK ISIN. He never waited to be prompted before acting. These virtues were also displayed when, Exercise UBIAK ISIN for Junior Course 66, which he organized, was adjudged to be the best organized in recent years. Faruk has proven to be professionally competent and dedicated to duty.

He was promoted to the rank of colonel at the end of 2008 and was posted to the Army Headquarters Department of Military Secretary and appointed the Deputy Director Military Secretary 3 (10 August 2009 - 3 June 2010). He served in this capacity to oversee the career progression of Nigerian Army commissioned officers of the rank of captain and below. After about 10 months on this appointment, he was redeployed within the Department as Deputy Director Military Secretary 2 (3 June 2010), who takes care of the career progression of officers of the rank of major and lieutenant colonel. He returned to the Department later as Deputy Military Secretary 1 (23 January - 10 March 2014), in charge of the career of officers of the rank of colonel and above, before growing to become the Military Secretary (Army) (31 October 2017 - 8 February 2019), who is in charge of career management of all commissioned officers of the Nigerian Army. He handled the commissioning, posting, promotion, and retirement of all categories of officers in the Nigerian Army during his different tours of duty in the Military Secretary. Having been well-groomed and developed as a professional military officer, he was also directly involved in the selection, training, development, posting, promotion, and career reviews of other officers.

Faruk Yahaya served on a couple of staff appointments before becoming a formation commander in the field. He was Deputy Director Research and Development at the Army Headquarters Department of Policy and Plans and was briefly Director of Logistics at the National Defence College. He was also Chief of Staff Operation PULO SHIELD in the South-South geo-political zone of Nigeria, during which he supported his Theatre Commander with necessary staff inputs to aid command decisions. Faruk Yahaya communicates effectively. He was remarked to be "articulate, orally and in writing. He was very clear, confident, and deliberate in his briefs and presentations." All of these are products of good knowledge and professional competence. Similarly, they are good followership skills that a future leader should possess and exhibit on his way up, so as to know the extent of what to demand and expect from his subordinates when he is eventually saddled with the mantle of leadership.

He was a Commander in the 4 Brigade Nigerian Army located in Benin, Edo State, from 5 August 2015 to 30 June 2016. He was also Commander of the 29 Task Force Brigade in the North East Op LAFIYA DOLE. As Commander 4 Brigade, he was under Headquarters 2 Division of the Nigerian Army but had his units and troops deployed to cover both Edo and Delta States. He also had one of his units operating in the southern part of Ondo State. His units were at Auchi, Benin City and Ekenwa in Edo State; Koko, Ughelli, Warri, and Asaba in Delta State, and Okitipupa in Ondo State. He trained his units so well that they emerged as the best formation during inter-brigade competitions within the Division. He was also highly committed to their welfare, accommodation, and other administrative needs.

He participated in Operation PULO SHIELD and other internal security operations as part of military aids to civil authority. Commanding operational formations and units in these parts of Nigeria usually comes with its own challenges and peculiarities that put to task the tact, patience, and decisiveness of a field commander. He exhibited total commitment in the pursuit of Operation PULO SHIELD mandate to check illegal oil bunkering and related crimes. He remained upright and maintained zero tolerance for compromise and indiscipline. He was thus tested and exhibited full competence at the tactical/operational level of command. General Yahaya was therefore found to have had practical knowledge and understanding of the security dynamics in the South-West and South-South geopolitical zones of Nigeria, thus preparing him for some of his future roles at the higher strategic management level of the Nigerian Army operations.

While commanding 29 Task Force Brigade, he reported directly to Headquarters Sector 2 Damaturu as his one up and his units were located at Borgozo, Benisheilk, Mauli, and Allagarno. In 2016/2017, as a commander in the field, according to Col AN Ezeh, one of his subordinate unit commanders in 29 Task Force Brigade Borgozo, "one thing that went well for General Faruk Yahaya was that he enjoyed the good will of his subordinates and people around him. He motivated well, and his troops as well as Civilian JTF were always ready to go for any operation he ordered." Borgozo village is located in an area referred to as Allagarno Forest within the general operations area. It is in Kaga Local Government Area of Borno State. It is within the Maiduguri – Biu - Damaturu triangle along the Buni Yadi Maiduguri rail line, as shown in the map of the area overleaf. Borgozo is about 20 km to the east of Benisheikh in Borno State and 37 km north of Goniri in Yobe State, 60 km north west of Damboa, and also about 60 km south of Maiduguri, as the crow flies.

Gen Faruk Yahaya was noted to have re-engineered 29 Task Force Brigade into a more effective fighting force. He improved the troops mobility and firepower through the repairs of many unserviceable armoured personnel carriers, 'B' vehicles, and recovery vehicles. He also improved their communication assets and interfaced very well with the Nigerian Air Force component for logistics supply and resupply to his forward troops in locations that were not accessible during the rainy season. The brigade's area of operations poses many challenges during the rainy season, like many other locations in the North East, due to waterlogged terrain. He was able to bring his leadership to bear to overcome most of these challenges. He also liaised effectively with flanking formations such as the 25 Task Force Brigade, Damboa, and 27 Task Force Brigades, Buniyadi, for operations. Terrorist activities in such notorious Boko Haram infested areas as Bulabulin, Gongon, Goniri, Ajigin, Talala, Buk, Kafa, Afa, Abalam and Dogoma were brought under control during his tenure as the Brigade Commander.

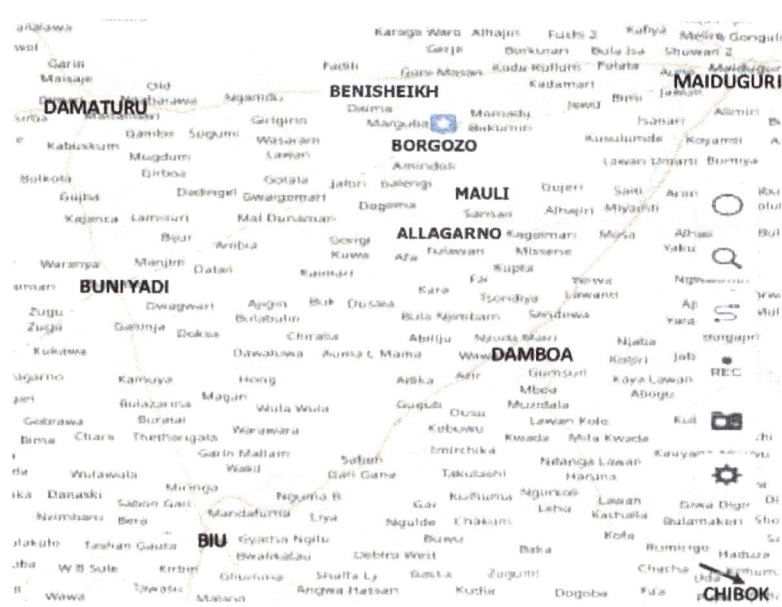

Fig 23: Map highlighting locations of 29 Task Force Brigade Units Source: Adapted from Guru Maps Pro Apps.

As a major general, he was appointed the General Officer Commanding (GOC) 1 Division Nigerian Army, which was deeply involved in anti-banditry operations in some North-Central and North-West States like Niger, Jigawa, Kaduna, Kano and Kebbi States. He also provided troops for the

CTCOIN operations in the North East. His holding areas were usual transit points for movement of troops and equipment to the North East Theatre. He served as GOC 1 Division from 11 February 2019 to 10 April 2020. He gave a good account of himself in the 1 Division area of operations as GOC, such that his troops were hoping he could remain with them but for the call of duty to serve at a higher level of responsibility as Theatre Commander North East Operations. Command and leadership in the Nigerian Army from the platoon level up to the division level could be grouped under the tactical level. However, the Theatre Command level could be classified as operational command and leadership. Faruk Yahaya was adequately exposed to a varying degree of tactical operations during which his tactical command and leadership competencies were tested and he was found highly capable of serving in the North East Operation LAFIYA DOLE as the Theatre Commander.

Military Strategic Leadership

The military is a key instrument of national power through which nations pursue their national interests and achieve their national security objectives. Its leadership structure at various levels thus plays a key role in providing direction, guidance, and policies in the drive to accomplish its roles. The Armed Forces of Nigeria comprising the Nigerian Army, Nigerian Navy, and Nigerian Air Force, have developed a management structure as well as professional cultures that establish what leaders must be, know, and do. The Nigerian Army specifically manages its affairs through three key levels of leadership: tactical, operational and strategic. These could be interrogated by the Three Levels of Leadership Model developed by James Scouller in 2011. Scouller's three levels are personal, private, and public levels which he further grouped into inner and outer levels. The personal leadership level is seen as the 'inner behavioural level' in which a leader's self-awareness, self-mastery, technical proficiency, and sense of connection to those around them come into play. The inner level thus concerns the leader's emotion, presence, skills, beliefs, and unconscious habits. "Personal leadership is the inner source of a leader's outer leadership effectiveness" (Scouller, 2011). This kind of leadership is inculcated in the individual cadet or officer being groomed at the different training schools of the Armed Forces of Nigeria. The public and private levels are seen as the 'outer behavioural level' which has to do with influencing others. This is also thought about and practised in all the military training schools in Nigeria. The three military levels thus resonate with Scouller's 'outer behavioural level', in which the leader or commander organizes and directs the affairs of the led or troops. This exists right from the frontline tactical echelons within battalions through the brigade and divisions. These two could also be seen at the operational level, as they were in the North East Theatre Command, which Lt Gen Faruk Yahaya commanded.

The strategic level exists at higher levels, such as the Service Headquarters and the level of national defence activities. Military strategic leaders are therefore responsible for establishing the force structure, allocating resources, and articulating the military strategic vision. The strategic leadership of the Nigerian Army thus involves running the army, which encompasses developing strategic plans, policies, guidelines, and laws. It also entails determining force structure based on likely future mission requirements and capabilities, as well as prioritizing over-arching army programmes against competing interests. Additionally, it involves articulating army programmes and policies to the highest level of government. A military strategic leader should understand the political dynamics of national security, strategy, and decision making. According to Admiral Bill Crowe, 'a military strategic leader must be an expert in war fighting and also be able to assist national decision-makers in matters of strategy, policy, resource allocation, and operations. Efficient and effective military strategic leaders keep themselves abreast of developments both within and outside the Armed Forces. They make judicious use of their influence and inculcate their ideas in others for the benefit of national security. They must understand the views of their subordinates, have self-control, create and express a vision, and persistently drive it to accomplishment.

Some of the key components of military strategic leadership include strategic direction, objective appointment of commanders, training and welfare, effective customs, ethical practices, as well as strategic controls. Strategic direction refers to the actions that should be taken, usually in the form of plans and directives to operational-level commanders, to achieve military's strategic objectives. It is a product of the military strategic planning process. Another important component of military strategic leadership is the ability to select the right commander for the right job.

Knowledgeable and resourceful commanders are critical to the attainment of military objectives. Training and welfare are also important components. Military strategic leadership must devise means to train and retrain personnel in their core competencies as a prerequisite for success. Additionally, welfare issues that have a direct bearing on morale must be accorded the utmost attention. Similarly, the maintenance of effective customs and ethical practices is imperative. This will assist in inculcating established patterns of action and sustaining cohesion amongst military personnel. Thus, devising a means of monitoring these standards is imperative. Another important component is strategic control. Military strategic leadership must design feedback and control mechanisms for the operational and tactical levels of command. This will ensure that information to improve the cyclic planning process is readily available, credible, and reliable.

Military effectiveness is the process by which Armed Forces convert resources into fighting power. A fully effective military is one that derives maximum combat power from the resources physically and politically available. Accordingly, the decisions and actions of military strategic leadership seek to achieve maximum efficiency in the use of their allocated resources while performing their task. Clearly, the 3 Services of the Armed Forces of Nigeria are responsible for waging and winning the nation's wars. Consequently, it is important that they are able to identify, develop, and implement the best military strategy to achieve national security objectives within the limits of available resources. It is also important to highlight that military strategic leadership can bolster national power and influence outcomes without committing troops to actual combat. This is often achieved by suggesting pre-emptive actions or non-kinetic measures to the political masters that could negate the adversary's war-fighting potential. For instance, the imposition of diplomatic and economic sanctions could deter aggressive action by an adversary and ultimately preserve the peace. According to Sun Tzu, "to win one hundred victories in one hundred battles is not the acme of skill. To subdue the enemy without fighting is the acme of skill". Similarly, deterring the adversary by displaying the right force posture is an art that could be directed by military strategic leaders. To properly put the concept of military strategic leadership in context, the views and experiences of General Martin Luther Agwai, Lieutenant General Tukur

Yusuf Buratai, and Lieutenant General Faruk Yahaya would be discussed.

General Martin Luther Agwai's Perspective

General Martin Luther Agwai's leadership philosophy was transformational. As the Chief of Army Staff, General Agwai envisioned a Nigerian Army that is mobile, compact, and professional, respected by its allies, feared by its adversaries, and a source of pride to Nigerians. He opined that this could be achieved within a decade. Akin to the principle of collective responsibility of the United Nations, where he served prior to his appointment as Chief of Army Staff, General ML Agwai believes in collective leadership, constructive engagement, and shared responsibility. He therefore constituted a committee on the transformation of the Nigerian Army and pursued attitudinal change across the Army. He devoted a lot of resources and energy to presenting and discussing the concept of the "army of the next decade", looking at the likely threat perception of the next decade and the appropriate responses that such threats demand. He believed in his vision and pursued it with all he had. Unfortunately, many of the personnel were not in tune with the ideals of a compact army. Many saw the idea as inimical to their career progression in the Army, and they passed negative comments at the slightest opportunity. Fortunately, the chairman of the transformation committee was General OA Azazi, who succeeded Agwai as the Chief of Army Staff in 2006. However, he came with his own vision as Chief of Army Staff but his stay was short-lived. General Azazi could no longer drive the project any further as he spent less than a year as the Chief of Army Staff. Nevertheless, Agwai's spirit of transformation, albeit with modifications, permeated the Nigerian Army and was escalated to the entire Armed Forces of Nigeria on his appointment as the Chief of Defence Staff in 2006.

From what started as an idea at the beginning of the Agwai era in 2003, the Nigerian Army now has a full-fledged Department of Army Transformation and Innovation. A lot of work has thus gone into transforming everything about the Nigerian Army, and, indeed, the Armed Forces of Nigeria. The Nigerian Army has expanded in size, scope, and resources to tackle the contemporary security challenges of terrorism, armed banditry, the farmers-herders crisis, separatists' agitation, cybercrime, and other adversarial activities of non-state actors. From a 5-division force in 2003, the Army now has 8 divisions and a Special Force Command. There are several other specialized forces, such as the Cyber Warfare Command, that also take care of different threats within the framework of national defence and security. There are still several avenues for further expansion. Similarly, the Defence Headquarters now have a Department of Transformation and Innovation, while the Nigerian Navy has a Transformation Branch. In the Nigerian Air Force, the Directorate of Transformation is under the Department of Policy and Plans. All of these evolved from an idea that was initiated during the Agwai era. Additionally, the Armed Forces of Nigeria can now boast of the Defence Space Administration and Defence Research and Development Bureau. All facets of Nigeria are now coming to terms with the need for change in the way things are done in the country. People now preach for a change in attitude across all strata of society. Generally, there are cries for value reorientation in the country.

Martin Luther Agwai also believes in participatory leadership, presence and accountability. He was always inspecting units and formations, sometimes unannounced. He went round all units of the Nigerian Army, responding promptly and effectively to all their challenges. He rewarded good performances and resented incompetence. He ensured that merit and competence were duly considered during appointments to leadership positions and the nomination of officers for overseas training. He clearly and unapologetically stood against lobbying in any form, shade, or shape, while he was in service. He popularly recommended the 'football strategy of the first eleven' when selecting personnel for leadership positions. Even in his retirement, he still propagates the idea of putting your best foot forward, especially when selecting officers to take up appointments at the military strategic leadership level. He views considerations for merit, competence and capacity ahead of political correctness or federal character in the appointment of military strategic leaders.

Agwai stressed the importance of observing rules and regulations as well as sticking to correct values in leadership in as much as leaders try to empathise. Empathy should not be at the expense of military values and the observance of rules and regulations. He views loyalty as a comprehensive concept that a leader is obliged to express to his subordinates, peers, superiors, the military as a system, the Nigerian people, and the constitution. Thus, loyalty should not be seen in the military as the sole preserve of the immediate superiors. As a peacemaker of international repute, Gen Agwai sees Nigeria's active participation in peacekeeping as a strategic platform to drive Nigeria's interest in the global arena. He was of the view that, irrespective of the domestic commitments of Nigerian troops, the Armed Forces of Nigeria should scale up their participation in peace support operations across the globe so that the country will not miss out on the benefits accruable to countries participating in global peacekeeping.

As a military strategic leader, Gen Agwai projected the importance of logistics to military operations. He remarked that "logistics limitations determine operational deployment rather than operational planning". He believes in high quality and opines that a leader must make a difference that impacts the people positively. He also propagated mentoring while he was in service. He groomed and adequately prepared his successors for the tasks ahead, a practice that he recommends to strategic leaders since leadership is a continuum. It is a process that should engender continuity and change, for the security and development of society. He believes that a pool of middle cadre career officers should be identified based on merit, competence and capacity, and should be properly groomed through exposures, postings, and appointments so that they would be adequately prepared to take up strategic leadership positions in the future. At the end of his tenure as the Chief of Defence Staff, General Agwai was appointed Force Commander of the UN-AU Hybrid Mission in Darfur in 2007, a position he held until his disengagement from service in December 2009. During his pulling-out parade, he acknowledged the wonderful and overwhelming support he received from his superiors, mates, and subordinates. According to Gen Agwai "it is impossible for me to claim any unique achievement without acknowledging the support of all those around me". He emphasized the need for authorities to always enter into dialogue with stakeholders for collective decisions on tasks. "A leader should not be afraid to dialogue, and they should not dialogue out of fear"(Agwai 2009). The Honourable Minister of Defence, Maj Gen Godwin Abbe (rtd), remarked that "the magnificent parade accorded Agwai is an indication that the nation is happy… the country is proud to produce a fine officer and a gentleman who gave a good account of himself. I am expressing the Commander-in-Chief's pleasure, President Umaru Yar'Adua, for the service he rendered to his country and beyond and that is what an officer should be" (Abbe, 2009).

Since his disengagement from the service of the Armed Forces of Nigeria,

General Agwai has been re-engaged on other national assignments, counting on his past experiences and dedication to duty especially at the strategic level. He was appointed Chairman of the Subsidy Reinvestment and Empowerment Programme (SURE-P) of the Federal Government of Nigeria by President Goodluck Jonathan from September 2013 – March 2015. He was also Chairman of Leadway Assurance Company Limited. Currently, he is the Pro-Chancellor of the University of Calabar. Gen Agwai believes that everything needs change, right leadership is important, and integrity matters (Agwai, 2023).

Lieutenant General Tukur Yusuf Buratai's Perspective

Lt Gen Tukur Yusuf Buratai was the Chief of Army Staff from 13 July 2015 to 26 January 2021. Shortly before then, he was Force Commander of the Multinational Joint Task Force with its headquarters located in Ndjamena. The Joint Task Force is a combined force constituted by Nigeria, Cameroun, Chad, Niger, and the Benin Republic to fight terrorism and insurgency launched by the Boko Haram group against Nigeria and, subsequently, other nations within the Lake Chad Basin region. The joint task force was also designed to curb other forms of transnational crimes within the region. TY Buratai was a visionary leader whose perspective on strategic leadership was leading from the field, as he was constantly in the North East Theatre during his tenure as the Chief of Army Staff. His vision was "to have a professionally responsive Nigerian Army in the discharge of its constitutional roles". According to Lt Gen TY Buratai, "professionalism is about doing things the way they should be done … Responsiveness is the ability to respond adequately to situations by being proactive." He believes that the military leadership needed the political strategic leadership to function properly. He thus courted the political leadership and cultivated the media well during his tenure as the Chief of Army Staff. Under his watch, public confidence was restored in the Nigerian Army, and by extension the Armed Forces of Nigeria's capability to secure the country and protect the population. He expanded the Nigerian Army across all facets; size or strength, force structure and capability.

As an infantry general, TY Buratai believes in the strategy of employing special forces to penetrate the adversary's fortresses and the tactics of long range patrol or living off the land. He believes in leadership through motivation. He motivated the troops and boosted morale on the frontlines through different welfare packages and special promotions. Many see him as a bridge builder. According to Abraham Ogbodo, Buratai came to re-invent the Nigerian Army.

I wouldn't know what others think but for me, you have come to reinvent the army ... Within a very short time, you have stamped on the army some measure of dignity and confidence through a leadership style that bridges much of the gap between the strategic and tactical levels of army operations.

General Buratai introduced the army's Super Camp strategy in 2019 and re- emphasised the mobile strike team concept during Op LAFIYA DOLE in the North East. The idea of the army Super Camp was essentially to have operational and logistics bases that are held in strength to deal decisively with the adversary when attacked and from where forces could be projected to dominate the area of operation while denying the adversary freedom of action. Similarly, the idea of the mobile strike team was to have a strong mobile force that could fight out any adversary encountered while on patrol. They are meant to be on the move continuously to dominate and secure the Main Supply Route (MSR), and to ensure that they are free from Boko Haram terrorists' ambushes and Improvised Explosive Devices (IEDs). During the Op LAFIYA DOLE, the army's super camps became the main operational bases.

The super camps were commanded by officers of the rank of colonel but had the same command and administrative status as a brigade. They were meant to have forces of battalion plus an armour company and other combat support as well as logistics support elements. However, this strategy was widely criticised by politicians. This was because the strategy led to a reorganization of troops deployment such that some locations that were thinly held by troops were redesignated as response areas that were to be dominated by patrols and other routine activities. While the troops were pulled together to concentrate at the super camps, many villages that were hitherto occupied by a small number of troops were exposed. The strategy enhanced force protection, but it was noted that many civilian populations in the local communities were vulnerable to Boko Haram attacks.

One of the famous critics then was His Excellency, Prof Babagana Zulum, Executive Governor of Borno State, who opined that "the super camp strategy was 'unwise and not working' and lamented that the withdrawal of troops from many towns to be concentrated in a particular area was the reason for the increasing attacks on Borno communities by insurgents". While Boko Haram avoided the troop's concentration areas, they directed their attacks on soft targets in the communities, killing and maiming civilian populations. The super camps as well as the mobile strike teams also had the challenge of inadequate platforms on the frontlines. The assumption of leadership of the Nigerian Army by Lt Gen I Attahiru on his appointment as the 21st Chief of Army Staff on 26 January 2021, saw the reorganisation of the 'super camps', converting them to Forward Operational Bases (FOBs).

Lt Gen TY Buratai was the longest-serving Chief of Army Staff in the history of Nigeria having served for 5 years and 6 months on the appointment. He was assigned as the Federal Republic of Nigeria Ambassador to Benin Republic upon his disengagement from the Service in 2021. He resigned his appointment as an ambassador in May 2022 to be fully engaged in partisan politics under the platform of the All Progressive Congress, just like his colleague, Air Marshal Sadique Abubakar, Chief of Air Staff, July 2015 – January 2021. Air Marshal Abubakar resigned from being the Nigerian Ambassador to Niger Republic to contest the gubernatorial election in Bauchi State under the platform of the All Progressive Congress. Lt Gen TY Buratai has been a great mentor to Lt Gen Faruk Yahaya while he was in active Service with the Nigerian Army. He remained a rallying figure around Lt Gen Faruk Yahaya, the current Chief of Army Staff, since his appointment.

Lieutenant General Faruk Yahaya's Perspective

Lt Gen Faruk Yahaya's perspective is that for the Nigerian Army to perform well on its assigned roles, it requires strategic leadership that operates based on a sound professional philosophy. To that extent, he couched his command philosophy on 4 strategic pillars: professionalism, readiness, administration, and cooperation.

He is of the view that these are the key requirements needed to reposition the Nigerian Army to deal with all existing threats to national security. He opines that professionalism entails the execution of all Nigerian Army operations and activities in line with established military, national, and international best practices. It involves the display of excellent military skills and competencies, high ethical standards, and reasonable work motivation. Professionalism requires realistic training to meet the changes in the contemporary security environment. Thus, he postulated that:

> ...to have a professional Nigerian Army, we must return to the tenets of basic soldiering, adhere strictly to the traditions, customs, and ethics of our Army, uphold regimentation, and emplace an effective sanctions and rewards system. I shall rely on the astounding discipline of all Nigerian Army personnel as it is key to my success. Good leadership at all levels will also be required. Leaders at all levels must show a good personal example to troops under their command while curtailing their excesses.

General Yahaya has exhibited exemplary leadership from the beginning of his career to the peak. Therefore, he is of the view that exemplary leadership at all levels of command is no doubt a prerequisite for the success of the Nigerian Army in all assigned tasks. He sees readiness as the ability to properly man and operate available equipment by his troops, which can only be achieved by well-trained and well-administered troops who are in a high state of morale to perform. The combat readiness of Nigerian Army troops is thus vital to the success of all operations. He opines that the Nigerian Army's roadmap to readiness would entail improved training, optimal resourcing, innovation, firm leadership, and pro-activeness. He promised to ensure that adequate platforms and equipment are procured both locally and abroad to engender effective performance of our roles, while the Nigerian Army as a whole will improve its maintenance system to ensure operational efficiency and effectiveness. He also views it as important to propagate research and development at all levels throughout the Nigerian Army.

To General Faruk Yahaya, sound administration is essential to operational effectiveness and high morale. It consists of all tangible and intangible efforts aimed at putting the Nigerian Army troops in the best state of mind to discharge their duties effectively. It engenders the right attitude and frame of mind that are prerequisites for mission accomplishment as well as organisational success. Therefore, he promised to ensure that good administration of troops is emplaced at all levels of command so as to improve morale. He prioritized welfare of personnel, promoted merit, celebrated gallantry, honoured heroes, and supported troops families. Gen Yahaya viewed sanctions and rewards seriously to ensure that those well deserving of accolades were recognized while those that erred were corrected or sanctioned appropriately in line with the provisions of the law.

His perspective on cooperation covers interoperability, integration and synergy with the other Services, security stakeholders, and Ministries, Departments and Agencies. It requires adaptable Tactics, Techniques and Procedures, flexible mind sets, and the acquisition of military hardware and software to operate in a joint environment for the defence of Nigeria. Cooperation while working with all stakeholders is an essential factor for success in Nigerian Army operations. He emphasized synergy at all levels and a cordial working relationship with all stakeholders in the security sector to fulfill the common goal of defending Nigeria. He undertook to bridge all existing gaps in the Nigerian Army's relationship with the Services and agencies through a robust joint, inter-agency and inter-governmental framework configured to confront current security challenges. As such, General Yahaya's military leadership philosophy emphasizes jointness in all national security endeavours. He set out to strengthen the quality of the Nigerian Army by modifying and expanding the force structure, maintaining effective war fighting doctrine and building technological capacity. He also worked hard to sustain civil-military relations and explored means of generating revenue internally while advocating for more funds for the Army. On the whole, Lieutenant General Faruk Yahaya promoted purposeful and responsible leadership in the Nigerian Army.

General Faruk Yahaya believes that strategic leaders must be adequately trained and equipped with the requisite capacity to carry out their tasks. After observing some gaps in the leadership capacity of Direct Regular Commissioned or Direct Short Service Commissioned officers and the opportunities available for them in the existing training institutions in the Nigerian Army, General Faruk Yahaya introduced compulsory capacity development training for this category of commissioned officers. The young officers among them are made to go through the Young Officers Course Infantry in the Nigerian Army School of Infantry. The middle career group now undergoes mid-career courses designated as the Junior Leadership and Staff Course as well as the Senior Leadership and Staff Course at the Nigerian Army College of Logistics in Lagos. Due to this development, the institution has been renamed Nigerian Army College of Logistics and Management. Similarly, the senior officers attain strategic leadership training at the NigerianArmy Resource Centre, Abuja.

They go through the Strategic Management and Policy Studies Course at the Resource Centre. Leadership grooming in the Nigerian Army is thus a continuous process. Before officers are selected to hold certain leadership positions, they must have met some criteria; passed through certain levels of training, held some preparatory positions, possessed required character traits, and demonstrated competence in previously assigned roles.

It is generally believed that most officers in the military just command without actually leading. However, Lieutenant General Faruk Yahaya is a commander with a difference. He does not just command; he also leads. This is an aspect of his command and leadership style that inspires his officers and soldiers to be willing to go to any length to carry out their assigned tasks in the service of their country, Nigeria. He is loved by his troops.

Section Two

Nigeria's National Security Problematic

Lt Gen F Yahaya
Chief of Army Staff

Precedence, Origin, and Dynamics of Insecurity in Nigeria: Theoretical and Empirical Notes

Background

Security is a critical component of the international system, bearing in mind that the survival of the global system is tied to human security. The Hobbesian analysis of the state of nature and the eventual social contract reflects the importance of security as a fundamental need. Throughout the pre-Cold War era, the concept of security has been traditionally perceived or associated with the whole gamut of processes defined in terms of the capacity of the coercive apparatus of the state to uphold sovereignty, defend territorial integrity, ensure stability and peace, as well as pursue armed conflict. Nevertheless, the end of the Cold War in the1990s marked a paradigm shift and a fundamental departure from the state-centered approach to security. Thus, human security involves protecting the citizens from poverty, hunger, diseases, unemployment and national disaster (Orhero, 2020: 470). Security is an important requirement for the sustenance of every modern state in the international political system. This is based on the need for states recognised as independent to maintain their territorial integrity without the control of their territories by other states. The maintenance of internal security has remained a primary duty of the state, and this endeavour in the history of Nigeria dates back to the colonial period when the colonial masters mobilised all the machinery of cohesion (police and army) in their bid to suppress the indigenous people into total submission to the colonial administration (Okolie-Osemene, 2019).

Nigeria as a major player in global affairs and a leading nation in Africa has had its fair share of insecurity emanating from or arising from diverse sources such as civil war, insurgency, recurring violent religious crises, the nature of Nigerian politics, ethnic and poverty-induced militancy, as well as crises occasioned by clamour for self-determination. It is therefore evident from the history of Nigeria since independence, that the issue of security remains on the front burner of national discourse (Adediran, 2016). Since the 1970s, when the aftermath of a thirty- month civil war induced criminal activities and various acts of voilence, senseless killings have been part of our society's social burden. Nigeria has had its share of robbery kingpins and minions. Bandits such as Oyenusi, Anini, Shina Rambo, and others had their time unleashing violence and mayhem on the psyche of Nigerians. Yet, never has the nation witnessed violent crimes with such pervasiveness, brazenness, and sophistication as in the present times, when a combination of socio– political and economic factors conspire to encase us in a cocoon (Eme & Anyadike, 2013). The capacity of a state to guarantee national defence and security is germane to its survival. The Nigerian state has been grappling with a series of security threats that undermine the sovereignty and coercive prerogatives of the state. Terrorism, banditry, militancy, insurgency, trans-border crimes, farmers-pastoralist conflicts, ethno-religious conflicts and other forms of violent communal conflicts are other major manifestations of insecurities threatening the peace and stability of Nigeria (Adejoh and Ukhami, 2021).

Conceptual and Theoretical Parameters

Understanding the precedents and consequences of insecurity in Nigeria will require some conceptual and theoretical parameters. Concepts and theories are important components of social science research.

The Concept of Security

The concept of security is omnibus and plethora in nature, and as such several scholarly attempts and efforts have been put in place to conceptualise security. The concept has also been evolving as scholars now view security from both the traditional state centric approach and a modern understanding of security. Whether national or regional, security transcends the definitive rubric of military alertness or valour. It extends to the interlocking realms of economic self-reliance, human security considerations, cohesion, and political stability (Adamu, 1990).
McNamara (1968:149) wrote that:

> In a modernizing society, security means development. Security is not military force though it may involve it, security is not military hardware, though it may include it. Security is development, and without

development, there can be no security... the security of any nation lies not solely or even primarily in its military capacity; but equally in developing relatively stable patterns of economic and political growth.

It is the existence of conditions within which people in a society can go about their normal daily activities without any threats to their lives or properties. It embraces all measures designed to protect and safeguard the citizenry and the resources of individuals, groups, businesses, and the nation against sabotage or violent occurrences (Ogunleye, et al', 2011). To understand security, one must be able to evaluate the prevailing threat situation, which depends on the values and interests of the nation as they relate to threat perceptions. Threatening situations are also dynamic and, in many cases, highly politically determined (Ochoche, 1997:11). Security has to do with freedom from danger or from threats to a nation's ability to protect and develop itself; and promote its cherished values and legitimate interests (Imobighe 1990: 224). The promotion of human security has become the central focus of the new development paradigm because the building of arms and ammunition does not bring peace, security, or political stability. Eradicating hunger, diseases, poverty, and unemployment through sustainable development programmes holds the key to enduring national security (Orhero, 2020).

It was Freedman (1998:53) who once asserted that:

> Once anything that generates anxiety or threatens the quality of life in some way becomes labeled as a "security problem" the field risks losing all focus. Such an agenda is potentially rich, and is certainly inclusive, but it can also be off-puttingly vague. ... Insecurity is "the state of fear or anxiety stemming from a concrete or alleged lack of protection." It refers to a lack of or inadequate freedom from danger, and inappropriate conclusions are likely to be reached when issues that are quite different in kind are squeezed into an unsuitable conceptual framework geared to military threats. The notion of economic security thus encourages a confrontational approach to tracing policy, while that of "environmental security" has often served more to confuse than to clarify by encouraging a search for adversaries.

Just as there are several perspectives on security, there are similarly several theoretical parameters for explaining and understanding the drivers of insecurity. Theories are scientific tools that enable one to understand, explain, and predict social phenomena. It is like a lens that gives clearer vision and like a sign post that gives direction. Scholars in political science, security studies, international relations, sociology, and criminology among others have evolved several theories of security. The Marxist conflict theory, the Human needs theory, the Frustration aggression theory, the State failure/failed state theory, the Theory of anomie, the Securitization theory, Structural functionalism, System theory, Quid ladder theory, and Resource conflict theory, among others are theoretical frameworks designed by scholars to further understand the nature and drivers of insecurity.

Human Needs Theory

The human needs theory stresses the fact that every human has basic needs that allow for survival. When such needs are not met, the tendency for conflict and insecurity is high. "Human needs theorists' offer a new dimension to conflict theory... approach provides an important conceptual tool that not only connects but also addresses human needs on all levels. Furthermore, it recognizes the existence of negotiable and non-negotiable issues. Needs theorists understand those needs. Interests, on the other hand, cannot be traded, suppressed or bargained." (Marker, 2003). Maslow categorises needs at physiological (food, water, warmth, shelter and sleep), security or safety (free from danger and the fear of job loss, property, food or sleep), affiliation or acceptance (social needs—belong and be accepted), esteem (power, prestige, status and self-confidence) and self-actualization (what one is capable of becoming—maximization of potential) needs (Maslow, 1970). Therefore, the Human Needs Theory serves well in the enhancement of human security for it does not only emphasize the physical security of the individual but also fulfills the aspect of freedom from want.

The various manifestations of insecurity can be understood within the context of the state's inability to enhance the promotion of the needs of its citizens. Hence, citizens now use other means, such as violence and crimes, to achieve their needs.

Frustration Aggression Theory

The Frustration Aggression Theory is a very unique and profound theory that is multidimensional in its explanation of human behaviours. This theory is key to understanding the trajectory of insecurity in Nigeria. It is more commonly known as the frustration–aggression hypothesis, and it ranks among the most seminal and prolific theories in research on aggression. From its beginnings in the late 1930s until date, it has been applied and studied in a variety of areas, including clinical and social psychology, ethnology, sociology, criminology, and medical research (Berkowitz, 1983; Scott, 1948).

The original formulation of the frustration–aggression hypothesis by Dollard, Doob, Miller, Mowrer, and Sears (1939) stated that "the occurrence of aggressive behaviour always presupposes the existence of frustration and, contrariwise, that

> ...the existence of frustration always leads to some form of aggression". Unlike the use of the word in everyday language, frustration here is not understood as an emotional experience but as "an interference with the occurrence of an instigated goal-response" (Dollard et al., 1939, p. 7). The presumption that occurrence of aggressive behaviour always presupposes the existence of frustration" suggests that aggression does not occur without any form of prior frustration, and the assertion that frustration "always leads to some form of aggression" implies that aggression is a certain outcome of any frustration. These deterministic assumptions were somewhat qualified in a 1941 publication by the same authors, in which they stated that "frustration produces instigation to aggression, but this is not the only type of instigation that it may produce" (Miller, Sears, Mowrer, Doob, & Dollard, 1941, p. 339).

Fig 24: Frustration - Aggression Theory

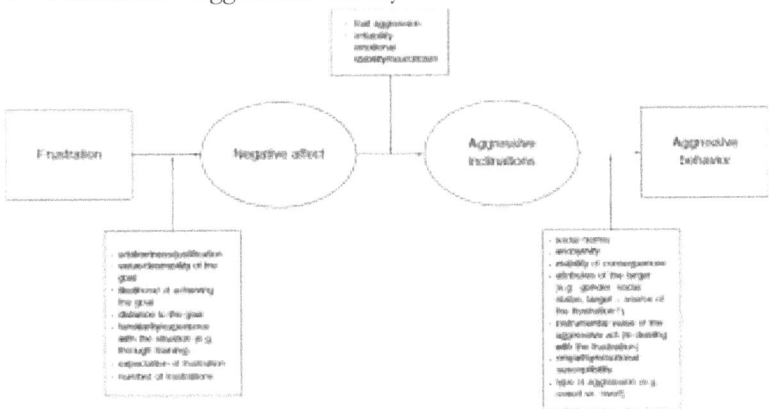

Source: Breuer, J., & Elson, M. (2016). The frustration–aggression hypothesis according to Berkowitz (1989). Figshare.

The analysis of this theory clearly indicates the nexus between frustration and aggression in several contexts. The rate of insecurity in Nigeria has been linked to a large extent to the level of frustration amongst Nigerians and groups within the country. Several scholars have argued, for instance, that terrorism, militancy in the Niger Delta, and secessionist agitations in the South East are all products of frustration since the state has failed to holistically aggregate the collective interests of the diversities that make up Nigeria.

State Failure/Failed State Theory

In recent years, a growing number of states have experienced severe crises. In some cases, the erosion of the state has gone so far as to lead to widespread political violence. Against the background of these developments, it is not surprising that 'state failure' and 'state collapse' have become catchwords in recent discourse about political development in 'the third world'(Mark and Crawford, 2002). Nation-states fail because they are convulsed by internal violence and can no longer deliver positive political goods to their inhabitants. Their governments lose legitimacy, and the very nature of the particular nation-state itself becomes illegitimate in the eyes and in the hearts of a growing plurality of its citizens (Robert, 2016).

According to William Zartman (2005), a state has collapsed 'when the basic functions of the state are no longer performed'. Strong states unquestionably control their territories and deliver a full range and a high quality of political goods to their citizens. They perform well according to indicators like GDP per capita, the UNDP Human Development Index (HDI), Transparency International's Corruption Perception Index (CPI), and Freedom House's Freedom of the World Report. Strong states offer high levels of security from political and criminal violence, ensure political freedom and civil liberties, and create environments conducive to the growth of economic opportunities (Robert, 2003).

Weak states include a broad continuum of states that are: inherently weak because of geographical, physical, or fundamental economic constraints; basically strong, but temporarily or situationally weak because of internal antagonisms, management flaws, greed, despotism, or external attacks; or a mixture of the two. Weak states typically harbor ethnic, religious, linguistic, or other inter-communal tensions that have not yet, or not yet thoroughly, become overtly violent (Robert, 2003). Even though the Nigerian state cannot be characterised as a failed state, it is pertinent to note that the increasing emergence and activities of violent non-state actors threaten the integrity and sovereignty of Nigeria. It questions the capacity of the state to protect its citizens and territories, and if the needful is not done, Nigeria may be fast sliding into a failed state.

System Theory and Structural functionalism

The system theory and structural functionalism theory have certain kinds of similarities in their explanation of the nature of the political system, especially when it comes to the issue of functions and survival of the system. Originating in biology, systems theory was developed in the 1950s against the backdrop of a need to have a set of systematic theoretical constructs to discuss the empirical world (Boulding, 1956; von Bertalanffy, 1951). Systems theory aims to explicate dynamic relationships and interdependence between components of the system and the organization– environment relationships. A system is established based on the structure and patterns of the relationships emerging from interactions among components (Lai and Huili, 2017). System theory presents an analysis of the political system as being made of several sub-systems, each responsible for the survival of the system, as the political system cannot survive if one sub-system fails to function. In a similar vein, the structural functionalism theory presents the political system as having different structures, each saddled with functions.

Resource conflict theory

Homer-Dixon's theory of environmental scarcity provides an analytical relationship between environmental factors and conflict in human society. Scarcity of renewable resources, - or what I call environmental scarcity, - can contribute to civil violence, including insurgencies and ethnic clashes" (Homer-Dixon, 1999). Homer-Dixon predicted that "in coming the decades, the incidence of such violence will probably increase as scarcities of cropland, fresh water, and forests worsen in many parts of the developing world."

Issues of drought, water/rain, inadequate pastures, population expansion, migration, deforestation, and the land tenure system are all environmental factors. The scarcity of these environmental variables and the increasing demand for them by both farmers and pastoralists constitute the triggers for pastoralist-farmer conflict. The insecurity in the Niger Delta region of Nigeria, orchestrated by the militants, is also precipitated by the impact of the activities of oil multinationals in that region, which have a negative impact on the environment. The government's perceived neglect of the economic development of the area is also another contributory factor. However, without the natural resources in the Niger Delta, the Transnational Corporations would not have been there in the first instance (Adejoh, and Anya, 2021).

In the following section, we deploy the historical and socio-economic perspectives to empirically explore the crisis of security in Nigeria.

Political History and Socio-Economic Environment of Insecurity in Nigeria

Understanding the antecedence of insecurity in Nigeria necessitate a political- economic and historical retrospection of Nigeria, as it provides a clearer perspective on Nigeria's configuration in relation to the internal contradictions that now constitute the major drivers of insecurity. There have been pockets of crime and insecurity in Nigeria from the pre-colonial,

colonial, and post-colonial eras manifested in the forms of ethnic, tribal, regional, and political conflicts. Nigeria's political nature since independence has been one of a long-drawn-out decay or decline, whose empirical elements are first political instability occasioned by high turn-over of governments - regime structures, institutions, and personal - leading to military coups; inconclusive and contested electoral outcomes; frequent changes in policy; political violence; and a crisis of legitimacy. Second is a low level of national cohesion, which defies every element of healthy ethnic competition, and third is an economic crisis, all of which reinforce one another (Osaghae, 2011).

The series of military coups and counter coups was a dangerous trend that took advantage of the fault lines of conflict in Nigeria. One major event that set the pace for insecurity in Nigeria was the Nigerian civil war which also led to the loss of lives and properties. The consequences and legacies of the war seem unending.

Ike-Muonso (2021:1) asserted thus:

> The 1966 coup is unarguably the ugly cornerstone for the insecurity experienced today in Nigeria. The coup was staged and led by Igbo Christian officers, while Northern soldiers, primarily Muslims, led the counter-coup. With the excuse of curbing corruption, the highest-ranking military officers from the northern parts of Nigeria, including the then Prime Minister, Tafawa Balewa, and the Premier of the Northern Region, Ahmadu Bello from the Muslim North, lost their lives in the coup. The counter-coup staged by northern military officers resulted in the killing of Major-General Aguiyi Ironsi, who seized power after the coup in what was considered the Igbo's conspiratorial plot to control the country. The immediate consequence was mutual distrust between Igbo ethnic groups and the Hausa/Fulani ethnic groups. That distrust provides strong subterranean currents that drive insecurity today.

The Movement for the Actualization of the Sovereign State of Biafra (MASSOB), formed in 1999, led the pack in these agitations. The successful operations of the Niger Delta militants were a strong inspiration and seemed to boost the possibility of successful military engagement. MASSOB quickly became a dreaded militant group. Street cult groups such as the Aba Boys also assembled to resist the government headed by Northerners believed to be behind the Southward migration. The split in MASSOB eventually resulted in the emergence of the Indigenous Peoples of Biafra (IPOB) in 2012, currently proscribed by the federal government as a terrorist organization (Ike-Muonso, 2021:1).

Remote and Immediate Precipitators of Insecurity in Nigeria

Security is the most critical and fundamental responsibility of the state. However, the level of insecurity across the globe has raised a lot of concerns as to whether or not states and the international community are living up to the basic responsibility of securing the lives and properties of citizens. This section attempts to identify and interrogate the remote and immediate drivers of insecurity in Nigeria with a view to offering actionable recommendations and measures to address them. As Andrew and Kennedy (2003) pointed out, it is necessary to distinguish between different causes as each may require a different remedy.

State Failure and Prevalence of Ungoverned Spaces

State failure and the challenges associated with massive un-policed landmass and ungoverned spaces are major remote and immediate triggers of insecurity in Nigeria. Evidently, as Igbuzor (2011) observed, the state of insecurity in Nigeria is greatly a function of government failure or can be linked to government failure. This is manifested by the incapacity of government to deliver public good and services and to provide for the basic needs of the masses. The limited availability of basic necessities for the people in Nigeria created people who were easily incited to violence. The Armed Forces of Nigeria are the country's major element of national power, and Nigeria's involvement in several regional and United Nations peacekeeping operations relative to the performance of the military has earned Nigeria a lot of respect in the community of nations. However, the increasing security challenges in Nigeria and the inability of the defence and security agencies to nip them in the bud have raised a lot of questions regarding the capability of the Nigerian state (Adejoh and Ukhami, 2021).

One major index of a weak state is the increasing rate of internal conflicts, which could be politically motivated or precipitated by socio-economic issues, especially since these states reflect some degree of plurality. Failed states reflect the total collapse of state institutions and an increase in non-state actors who challenge the monopoly of state coercion.

Such states are unable to exert authority and ensure their territorial integrity. Failed states are characterized by economic underdevelopment, a gross deficiency in basic amenities, and an increasing rate of unemployment, and in most cases, the state is unable to provide for the basic human needs of its citizens (Tar and Adejoh, 2021). For Baldwin, seven questions are sacrosanct to the issues of national security and they are: (1) Security for whom? (2) Security for which values? (3) How much security? (4) From what threats? (5) By what means? (6) At what cost? (7) In what time period? These questions justify, to a large extent, not just the economics of defence but also the political economy of defence and security. The determination of who gets what, when, and how, and the authoritative allocation of values for defence and security in Nigeria do not seem to tally with Baldwin's analysis of security. Just as there are basic economic problems, there are also basic defence and security problems that must be identified to ensure efficient and effective utilization of scarce resources.

Forests in Africa have emerged as marginal spaces that are susceptible to capture by criminal and clandestine elements who seek shelter and a safe haven to carry out nefarious activities. Insurgents, armed bandits, and kidnappers who would normally be rejected by society find sanctuaries in forests and use them as staging posts to conduct their terror activities. Unless the state takes adequate control of these forests, they are bound to become a permanent safe haven for criminals and terrorist organizations (Tar and Safana, 2021). The measures could include government effort to introduce subsidiary laws in the form of policies and programmes aimed at achieving sustainable utilization of forest products, and the outcome should also be economically viable, ecologically sound, and socially just. The difficult nature of the Niger Delta forests and creeks in South-South Nigeria conferred some degree of strategic advantage on the militants over government troops, who were not sufficiently conversant with the terrain (Okoli 2016). This geographical feature boosted the operations and sustainability of the Niger Delta militant movement in the focal area. Such a feature was leveraged by the Boko Haram insurgents to sustain a stranglehold on the Sambisa Forest to enhance their operations through the laying of mines, bomb blasts, cattle rustling, hostage taking, and arms smuggling (Okoli and Atelhe 2014).

Climate Change, Environmental and Resource-Induced Insecurity

The ecosystems reflect a complex interdependent web of living organisms and natural resources and, play a critical role in supporting human wellbeing and driving economic growth through the valuable services they provide such as food, water for drinking and irrigation, pollination, and climate regulation. Yet human society has systematically undermined these natural allies, treating forests, arable land, and rivers as though they are inexhaustible (UNEP, 2013). The concept of environmental security falls within the purview of the modern understanding of security. It is an attempt to explain the nexus between environment, ecological variables, and national security (Adejoh and Anya, 2021).

Environmental security has been described as a bundle of issues that involve the role that the environment and natural resources play in peace and security, including environmental causes and drivers of conflict, environmental impacts of conflict, environmental recovery, and post-conflict peacebuilding. The major remote and immediate precipitators of the conflict between pastoralists and farmers across West Africa and the Sahel hinge basically on the environment. Issues of drought, water/rain, inadequate pastures, population expansion, migration, deforestation, and the land tenure system are all environmental factors. The scarcity of these environmental variables vis-à-vis the increasing demand for them by both farmers and pastoralists constitutes the trigger for pastoralist-farmer' conflict (Adejoh and Anya, 2021).

The crisis in the Niger Delta region of Nigeria is a typology of resource-based violence with the impact of human activities on the environment. The major activities of the oil industry that negatively impact the Niger Delta area are gas flaring and oil spillages. These unchecked environmentally unfriendly activities of the oil industry make the utilization of the environment for the livelihood of the local people unsustainable (Obi 1997). The insecurity in the Niger Delta Region of Nigeria is also precipitated by the unwholesome activities of oil multinationals in that region which have a negative impact on the environment. Oil spillage, environmental degradation, gas flaring, and water pollution have adverse effects on human, aquatic, and other agricultural activities within the Niger Delta. Contestations of over ownership of resources have accounted for series of conflicts (Adejoh and Anya, 2021).

Nigeria has also witnessed how climate migration dynamics contribute to increasing violence and conflicts. The shrinking of Lake Chad has become a threat to over 15 million Nigerians living in the area and about 10 million others living outside Nigeria's shores (Akubor, 2017). Abbass (2012) argues that the exacerbation of vulnerability and conflict in Northern Nigeria is both a product of the impact of climate change and drought leading to competition between farmers and pastoralists. Okoli and Atelhe (2014) argues that the historical trajectories of Fulani herdsmen militancy show that the phenomenon has progressively transmitted from rudimentary communal skirmishes to organised armed confrontation while its contemporary manifestations has further transformed itself into a genre of guerrilla warfare characterized by immense brutal sophistication and efficiency.

Proliferation of Small Arms and Light Weapons

The proliferation of Small Arms and Light Weapons (SALWs) has transformed Africa's political, economic, demographic, and socio-cultural landscapes in spectacular, but gory ways. Light weapons include heavy machine guns, hand-held under-barrel and mounted grenade launchers, portable anti-aircraft guns, portable anti-tank guns, recoilless rifles, portable launchers of anti-tank missile and rocket systems, portable launchers of anti-aircraft missile systems, and mortars of a calibre of less than 100 mm (Saferworld, 2012). SALWs constitute one of the key factors in the escalation of conflict and instability in Africa's *zones of violence*.

The proliferation of SALWs in Africa is both a cause and manifestation of diverse conflicts that are internal and/or external to the continent, and are driven by the forces of demand and supply, predicated on weak structures that sabotage preemptive conflict management mechanisms. In particular, arms control enables governments and institutions to mobilize and enhance their capacities for addressing the free flow of arms among unauthorized persons (Tar, 2021).

It is obvious that the failure of states to provide necessary political goods can snowball into the proliferation of SALWs, which could aggravate series of political crises. The use of force is traditionally the exclusive preserve of states. However, the emergence of militias, insurgents, terrorists, and bandits' militants in several African countries clearly suggests symptoms of state failure (Tar and Adejoh, 2020).

Political instability, poor border management, illicit arms transfers, state failure and the fflorescence of ungoverned spaces, stockpiling and diversions of arms and ammunition as well as the illicit arms market, constitute the major drivers of the proliferation of SALWs in Nigeria. Below is a theoretical matrix and diagrammatic attempt by Tar and Adejoh (2020) to explain the proliferation of SALWs.

Fig 25: Theoretical matrix and diagrammatic explaining the proliferation of SALWs.

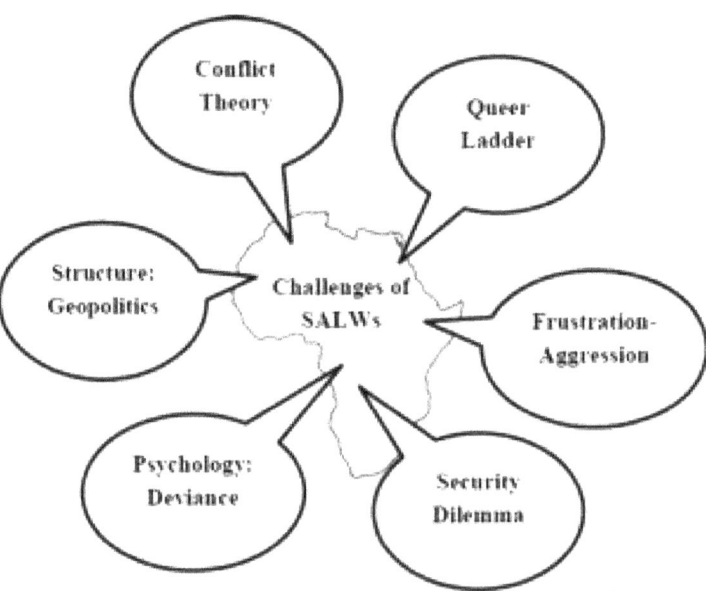

Source: Tar and Adejoh (2021:46). Theoretical matrix on small arms and light weapons proliferation in Africa in Tar, A.U., and Onwurah, C.P. (eds), Palgrave Handbook of Small Arms and Conflicts in Africa. Switzerland: Palgrave Macmillan

Porous Borders and Poor Border Management

Criminals in the country also have easy access to both heavy and light arms as a result of these porous borders (Hazen and Horner, 2007). The porous nature of Nigeria's borders has enabled non-documented migrants from countries like Niger, Chad, Benin, Mali, and Niamey to infiltrate Nigeria with their criminal activities (Adeola and Oluyemi, 2012). The security challenges facing a nation could be internal or external. The internal ones in Nigeria include armed robbery, sea piracy, kidnapping, and hostage-taking. Others are ethnic, religious, and electoral violence, as well as the Niger Delta crisis. On the other hand, external security challenges emanate from outside the nation. Apart from the boundary disputes between Nigeria and Cameroon along the shared land and sea borders from the Atlantic coast in the south to the Lake Chad basin in the north, the country had no external threats from its neighbours. The problems of arms and human trafficking often reported by the media all result from the country's inability to effectively police its borders (Albert, 2018).

Violent Non-State Actors (VNSAs) and armed militias are able to cross borders easily in conflict zones, and cross-border shipments of arms and ammunition are generally on the increase. Smugglers also exploit irregular sea and land routes in an effort to bypass the law in the transportation of weapons, making it difficult for security forces to detect the movements of illegal arms and other contraband commodities. Terrorist and violent extremist groups, such as Boko Haram and al-Shabaab, also operate across borders using irregular routes and taking advantage of poorly secured border points to smuggle weapons (Onuoha, 2013).

Poverty, Unemployment and Pervasive Material Inequalities

There is no doubt that poverty and inequality can trigger insecurity for several reasons. Drawing from McNamara's explanation of the nexus between underdevelopment and insecurity, one will clearly see how poverty is a causative factor for insecurity. According to Awaka (2012), as cited by Akwara (2013), more than 80 per cent of conflict-related deaths occurred in economically disadvantaged states. Conflict, violence, and insurgency are caused by poverty and other factors that are inimical to the development of any society (Gurr 1970; Burton 1997). Ikejiaku (2009) argues that poverty is a multidimensional problem that goes beyond economics to include, among other things, social, political, and cultural issues, social strife and revolutions are not brought about by the conspiratorial or malignant nature of man; rather, revolutions are derived from poverty and distributive injustice. Therefore, when the poor are in the majority and have no prospect of improvement in their condition, they are bound to be restless and could seek restitution through violence. Poverty is a principal cause of political, social, and economic conflict in the country. Poverty is anti-thetical to the principles and core values of democracy. Poverty in the midst of plenty creates disaffection among the populace and leads them towards violent behaviour (Ighodalo, 2012:171).

The failure of successive administrations in Nigeria to address the challenges of poverty, unemployment and inequitable distribution of wealth among ethnic nationalities is one of the major causes of insecurity in the country. In spite of the myriad policies and programmes initiated by successive Nigerian governments such as the Better Life Programme (BLP), National Directorate of Employment (NDE), Family Support Programme (FSP), Family Economic Advancement Programme (FEAP), Poverty Alleviation Programme (PAP), National Poverty Eradication Programme (NAPEP), Agricultural Development Projects (ADPs), National Economic Empowerment and Development Strategy (NEEDS), SURE-P, N- Power, Trader Money, and so on, their inability to affect the real target (the youths and the vulnerable); reflects the lacuna between policy formulation and implementation in Nigeria (Nwagbosa, 2013).

Ethnic and Religious Dichotomy

Nigeria is a pluralistic state with over 350 ethnic nationalities and over 500 languages. As a pluralistic society, it is diverse in culture, language, and ethnic background (Adamolekun, 1991:68). Christianity, Islam, and traditional religion are the three major belief systems in the country. Over the years, the dichotomy, especially in religion and ethnicity has become a major security threat to the Nigerian state. This is why Nigeria is often described as a conglomeration of nation-states. The political history of Nigeria has also clearly shown that these factors constitute the major security environment in Nigeria. Notwithstanding the quest for national unity and integration, violent conflicts have thrived on the shoulders of these primordial sentiments in Nigeria. By virtue of its complexity in identities and history of seemingly intractable conflicts as well as instability, Nigeria can be rightly described as one of the most deeply divided states in Africa (Osaghae and Suberu, 2005:23).

The political geography called Nigeria is dynamic for several reasons. The plurality of Nigeria in terms of the different ethnic groups, cultures, and religion attests to the dynamic character of the Nigerian state. These pluralities notwithstanding, the Nigerian state has undergone a series of ideological and political clashes precipitated by the desire of each side of the divide to promote their own agenda through the instrumentality of the state and its apparatus. Of all these variables, religion has been the most entrenched in the social fabrics and political schemes of Nigeria. Since the attainment of independence in 1960, religion has been the major determinant of both domestic and foreign policies in Nigeria. These attest to the fact that most crises in Nigeria have religious underpinnings. The Maitatsine crisis, the Bulunkuttu crisis, the 2015 post-elections crisis, the Miss World crisis, the Boko Haram crisis, etc. are pointers to the above arguments (Adejoh and Onuh, 2017).

While religion can be a unifying factor, it can also be a divisive platform and a driver of violence. No wonder, Basedau and de Juan (2008) claimed that religion is both the "maker and/or breaker" of the African continent. This clearly shows the synthetic and antithetical relationships between Christians and Muslims in Nigeria. The idea of a federal character, quota system, and secularity of the Nigerian state, as enshrined in Section 10 of the 1999 Constitution of the Federation of Nigeria, among others, was precipitated by the agitations and perceived insecurity of people of different ethnic and religious background in the country. Nigeria's multi-ethnicity makes it susceptible to conflict and insecurity, especially when a group claims marginalization or when ethnic or religious minorities are systematically excluded from governance or political representation; they may resort to open revolt against the system (Oshita, 2011).

There is no doubt about the need to understand the full ramifications of the connections between religion, secularism and politics in Nigeria, or the strategic urgency of secularism in that country. The problem lies in how religion is instrumentalised in politics, how secularism is rhetoricised and how politics is erratically constructed to serve the egoistical interests of the country's ruling and governing elites. Further, the contested nature of the state says a lot about the difficulties of institutionalising a secular state: capitalist structures (a key to secularism) remain blocked and distorted. It goes without saying that Nigeria is an ambiguous example of a capitalist formation, even by the standards of developing states. There is an emerging consensus that "the national bourgeoisie is relatively weak and divided by sectarian differences" (Tar, 2009:65).

The presence of different religions with their diverse interpretations is a potential source of inter- and intra-religious rivalry in Nigeria. The way some Muslims and Christians preach, teach, and practice their religions betrays the intolerance of the various religious adherents. Their inability to accommodate other religious views, their false devotion to religious founders and their seemingly zealous but fanatically uncompromising practices are contrary to the fundamental claims of their religion and religious founders (Mala, 1984). Religion is a key factor as far as the political scheme of things in Nigeria is concerned. Nigeria's political architecture clearly manifests the politicization of religion and the religionization of politics, which generated a lot of internal contradictions and a clash of civilizations between Christians and Muslims (Adejoh and Onuh, 2017). In addition, the political elites have always sought to manipulate the multifaceted identities (ethnic, regional, minority-majority, and religious divisions), especially during political competition, and this has given rise to conflicts and instability in Nigeria (Nnoli 1978; Dudley 1973).

Repercussions and Cost of Insecurity in Nigeria

The Nigerian state has been grappling with a series of security threats that undermine the sovereignty and coercive prerogatives of the state. Terrorism, banditry, trans- border crimes, farmer-pastoralist conflicts, ethno-religious conflicts, militancy, and insurgency, among others, are major manifestations of insecurities threatening the peace and stability of Nigeria. Regardless of the resources allocated to addressing these challenges, the country seems to be sinking deeper into insecurity (Adejoh and Ukhami, 2021). The consequences of insecurity in Nigeria are multifaceted and multidimensional. Thus far, it has been empirically proven that security comes with a lot of implications. Beyond the political and economic impacts of security, it has socio-cultural consequences as well. Nigeria has recorded huge losses of lives and properties due to insecurity, which has also affected the Nigeria's international image. Terrorism, banditry, militancy, pastoralists-farmers conflict, secessionist agitations, kidnappings, and several other security challenges have also come with one form of implication or the other. Just as development thrives most in a secure environment, underdevelopment thrives in an insecure environment.

Underdevelopment is a sure bait of insecurity, as development is never realized in an atmosphere of instability, fear, threats, and hopelessness. For people to invest in developmental projects, they must be certain of at least relative stability and a guarantee of safety. In the absence of these, the stark reality of underdevelopment takes center stage (Ozoigbo, 2019). The Global Terrorism Index (2020) indicates that Nigeria is among the countries with the most fatal terrorists attack in 2019.

Fig 26: Figure indicating the twenty most fatal terrorist attacks in 2019

#						Description
1	COUNTRY	SRI LANKA	CITY	MUTLIPLE LOCATIONS	DEATHS 268	Eight coordinated attacks took place in Sri Lanka on Easter Sunday targeting churches, hotels and a housing complex.
	DATE	21/4/19	GROUP	ISLAMIC STATE OF IRAQ AND THE LEVANT (ISIL)		
2	COUNTRY	MALI	CITY	OGOSSOGOU AND WELINGARA	DEATHS 157	Assailants opened fire on the villages of Ogossogou and Welingara in Mopti, Mali.
	DATE	23/3/19	GROUP	DAN NA AMBASSAGOU		
3	COUNTRY	AFGHANISTAN	CITY	MAYDAN SHAHR DISTRICT	DEATHS 126	A suicide bomber detonated an explosives-laden vehicle and assailants opened fire on a National Directorate for Security (NDS) base in Maydan Shahr district, Wardak, Afghanistan.
	DATE	21/1/19	GROUP	TALIBAN		
4	COUNTRY	CAMEROON	CITY	DARAK	DEATHS 101	Several hundred assailants armed with rocket launchers attacked military positions in Darak, Extreme-North, Cameroon.
	DATE	9/6/19	GROUP	BOKO HARAM		
5	COUNTRY	AFGHANISTAN	CITY	KABUL	DEATHS 93	A suicide bomber detonated an explosives-laden vest at the Dubai City wedding hall in Kabul, Afghanistan. At least 93 civilians were killed and 142 others were injured in the blast. The Khorasan Chapter of the Islamic State claimed responsibility for the incident.
	DATE	17/8/19	GROUP	KHORASAN CHAPTER OF THE ISLAMIC STATE		
6	COUNTRY	SOMALIA	CITY	MOGADISHU	DEATHS 84	A suicide bomber detonated an explosives-laden truck at a police checkpoint in Darkheynley, Mogadishu, Somalia.
	DATE	28/12/19	GROUP	AL-SHABAAB		
7	COUNTRY	AFGHANISTAN	CITY	JAWDARA	DEATHS 74	A suicide bomber detonated targeting a mosque in Jawdara, Nangarhar, Afghanistan.
	DATE	18/10/19	GROUP	KHORASAN CHAPTER OF THE ISLAMIC STATE		
8	COUNTRY	NIGERIA	CITY	BADU	DEATHS 70	Assailants attacked a funeral in Badu, Nganzai, Borno, Nigeria.
	DATE	27/7/19	GROUP	BOKO HARAM		
9	COUNTRY	AFGHANISTAN	CITY	SHAKAR SHILI AND MAJID CHAWK	DEATHS 65	Assailants attacked an unknown number of security outposts in Shakar Shili and Majid Chawk in Sangin district, Helmand, Afghanistan. At least 65 people were killed and 38 people were injured across both attacks. The victims included soldiers, police officers, intelligence officers, and civilians.
	DATE	23/3/19	GROUP	TALIBAN		

Source: Global Terrorism Index, 2020

Citizens' lives are the casualties of the insurgency in the country. According to the Nigerian security tracker, there have been 17,285 civilian deaths due to insecurity between May 2015 and March 2022. Within this period, Boko Haram was responsible for 8,230 deaths, sectarian actors were responsible for 7,280 deaths, and state actors accounted for 10,315 deaths. Other armed actors were responsible for 10,419 deaths.

Figur 27: shows Months with Highest Civilian Deaths Caused by Boko Haram

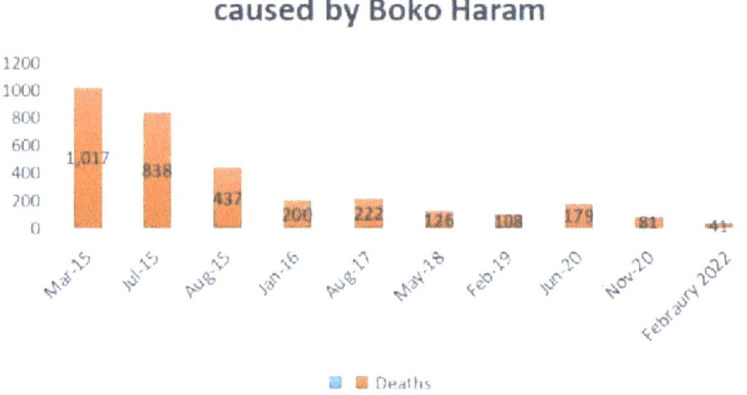

Source:https://www.dataphyte.com/latest-reports/analysis-what-are-the-implications-of-nigerias- growing-insecurity/

The implication is that Nigeria symbolizes an unsafe place of abode and has also been included among one of the terrorist countries of the world. Therefore, investors, foreigners, expatriates, and even citizens of Nigeria are scared of investing and committing their hard-earned resources in businesses in Nigeria. The economic cost of insecurity is enormous. People who joined the fighting forces can no longer work productively; schools, power stations, and roads that are destroyed reduce the productive capacity of the economy. Further, displacement of people reduces the production of goods for exports, thereby reducing foreign exchange earnings, import potentials, and consequently further constraining output, leading to a decline in employment and earnings (Stewart, 2004). Achumba and Ighomereho (2013) noted that insecurity discourages investment as it makes investment unattractive to business people. This is because it increases the cost of doing business, either through direct loss of goods and properties or the cost of taking precautions against business risks and uncertainty. Insecurity in Nigeria has led to the destruction of lives, properties and equipment; relocation and closing down of businesses (Adeleke, 2013). In the absence of security, economic growth and development cannot be sustained as they destroy economic, human, and social capital. Under conditions of peace and security, people and governments can direct their efforts and resources towardsi mproving human life. Insecurity is a threat to sustainable development globally. It is a bane to economic growth and development and can simultaneously frustrate and undermine the dreams and aspirations of citizens owing to its obvious negative consequences.

The emergence of the Boko Haram terrorist organization and its activities has precipitated a range of security challenges for the Nigerian state. Thousands of Nigerians have been killed, properties worth millions have been destroyed, there has been increase in IDPs and IDP camps, and other forms of humanitarian crisis and post-conflict reconstruction challenges. Boko Haram has employed sexual violence such as rape, sexual slavery, forced prostitution, forced pregnancy, forced abortion, enforced sterilization, forced marriage, and other forms of sexual violence of comparable gravity perpetrated against women and girls directly or indirectly as part of its strategy towards achieving its goals and objectives (Adejoh, 2019). According to the UNOCHA, nearly 300,000 people in Adamawa, Borno, and Yobe states – 70 percent of them women and children have fled their homes since early 2013. The Office of the United Nations High Commissioner for Refugees (UNHCR) puts the figure of IDPs in Nigeria at more than 650,000, with a majority of them staying with families in other parts of Nigeria. The UNHCR estimates that over 60,000 Nigerians have sought refuge in neighbouring countries since May 2013. For instance, there are about 40,000 Nigerian refugees in Niger Republic and about 28,000 in Cameroon, with the majority coming from border communities (Human Rights Watch, 14 March, 2014).

Response of Government in Combating Insecurity

In combating the challenges posed by insecurity and crime in Nigeria, the state and non-state actors have come up with different measures to tackle insecurity. The Nigerian government, for instance, has applied both kinetic and non-kinetic strategies in countering terrorism and insurgency, banditry, andeven militancy in the Niger Delta. Since the advent of Boko Haram, a series of efforts have been made both at the national and regional levels. There have been series of military operations in the Northeast, including military alliances like the Multinational Joint Task Force between Nigeria and some other Lake Chad Basin Commission (LCBC) countries, especially Cameroon, Chad, Niger and the Republic of Benin. Military alliances are an important strategy for curbing threats, and the MNJTF as a military alliance has contributed in no small way to combating Boko Haram activities within the Sub-Region (Tar and Adejoh, 2017). As a way of combating the challenges of terrorism, the government has also put in place several policies such as the Counter-Terrorism Strategy, the National Cyber Security Policy, and other forms of anti-terrorism laws. Funding for defence and security has also consistently been on the increase so as to ensure the procurement of military softwares and hardwares. Evidence also abounds of technical collaborations and assistance from some western countries.

It is also important to note that the increase in insecurity has, like never before in Nigeria's history, increased the agitation for the establishment of state police. Even though there are a series of arguments for and against state police, several regions in Nigeria have established regional security outfits as a mechanism to address security challenges within their regions. Notable examples are the South-West security network known as Amotekun and Ebube-Agu in the South-East zone. Community policing and civil military relations, especially in terms of intelligence gathering, are another major response of the state towards addressing the challenges of insecurity.

Conclusion and Prognosis

There is no doubt that Nigeria is grappling with several security challenges that constitute major threats to the lives of citizens and the image of Nigeria in the comity of nations. The activities of terrorists and insurgents, the escalated dimensions of banditry, the increasing rate of kidnapping for ransom and the separatist agitations of the IPOB are major security threats to Nigeria. A more dynamic threat is the issue of resource conflict and climate change, which in turn are also threat multipliers. These insecurities are connected to the internal contradictions within the Nigerian state, and they come with immense consequences.

The level of instability being experienced in Nigeria has had political economic and socio-cultural implications. Resources that would have been channeled to developmental endeavours are used for procuring arms and weapons to combat insecurity in Nigeria. Since 2009, there has been a visible increase in the budgets of defence and security agencies with a view to restoring peace and stability in the country. Worthy of note is the fact that the Nigerian state has adopted both kinetic and non-kinetic approaches in the fight against insecurity. The government has also evolved several strategic security policies to serve as a road map in the fight against insecurity.

However, despite the government's efforts at reversing the recurrent insecurities, the threats have persisted, thereby requiring intensified responses. Therefore, there is an urgent need for the Nigerian state to address the remote causes of insecurity, especially the issues of poverty and unemployment, as the lack of an equitable distribution of wealth constitutes a springboard for crime and insecurity in most societies. Also, there is a disconnect between the National Security Strategy and the National Counter Terrorism Strategy and what is going on at the theatre of operations. Hence, the government needs to identify the lacuna with a view to ensuring harmony and the implementation of strategies.

The government also needs to device modern techniques of border management, which require the use of technology, as this will help control the illicit flow of SALWs into the country. The use of satellites imagery, surveillance, and remote sensing mechanisms are contemporary security strategies, especially in countries like Nigeria with a very large land mass. It therefore means that the National Space Research and Development Agency (NASRDA) and the Defence Space Administration (DSA) need to be strengthened and better coordinated so as to supply relevant intelligence in the fight against insecurity. The level of synergy and collaboration between strategic security agencies and parastatals is still very weak. Inter-agency collaboration needs to be strengthened.

Factors and Actors of Insecurity in Nigeria: Manifestations and Impacts

Introduction

The unprecedented outbreak of multiple and often overlapping security challenges has become a troubling feature of Africa's most populous country, Nigeria, in the last two decades. The result of an October 2022 online poll conducted by *Premium Times*, indicates that the majority of Nigerians (42.2 per cent) want the next president to prioritise the tackling of insecurity across the country before other national challenges (Iroanusi, 2022). The economy (30.1 per cent), was a distant second, followed by electricity (14.2 per cent), and lastly by corruption (13.5 per cent). Behind the wave of insecurity is the astonishing growth in scale, spread, and sophistication of criminally-oriented Non-State Armed Groups (NSAGs) such as terrorists, insurgents, bandits, kidnappers, ritual killers, militants, separatists, armed pastoralists, pirates, and cultists among others. The motivation, size, structure, and capabilities of these criminally oriented NSAGs vary differently.

While there are some NSAGs with some form of centralized command structures, such as terrorists and bandits, there are many other small groups, such as kidnappers and armed pastoralists, that are decentralized in structure and operate fluidly across the country. Notwithstanding these characteristic variations, the use of violence is a trademark common to all. Death and destruction associated with the activities of these NSAGs are daily occurrences in Nigeria. For instance, between January and July 2022, an estimated 7,222 Nigerians were killed while 3,823 were abducted as the country experienced 2,840 incidents of violent criminal attacks (Odeniyi, 2022).

Given the frequency and intensity of violent activities by these criminal groups, a large percentage of Nigeria's military personnel are currently deployed in Internal Security Operations (ISOs) across the 36 states of the federation in response to the state of insecurity (Isamotu, 2022). Inevitably, billions of naira are expended on defence and security. For instance, a total of ₦11.18tn was spent on security, from 2015 to 2022. Despite extensive military deployment and a huge expenditure on security, the security challenges remain, causing concerns both within and outside the country.

This chapter, critically examines the contributions of violent groups to widespread insecurity in Nigeria. The objective is to discuss the nature of these violent groups while highlighting the factors underpinning their emergence and persistence. The chapter consists of five sections. The first section is the mapping of violent groups in Nigeria, including the nature and state responses. In the second section, factors contributing to the rise of violent groups and insecurity in Nigeria were highlighted. The third section discusses the impact of insecurity in Nigeria, while the fourth section proffers some recommendations towards addressing the problem of violent actors that underpin insecurity in Nigeria. The last section concludes the discourse.

Mapping Violent Groups in Nigeria: Nature and Some State Responses

Although Nigeria's internal security landscape is blighted with several potent threats, analytical commentaries tend to isolate and underscore the possible concentration of some violent groups as per geopolitical zones (Duerksen 2021). A careful survey of Nigeria's internal security landscape reveals that Nigeria is not short of violent groups whose existence and activities significantly undermine internal security. The drivers of violence for these myriad of NSAGs include political, religious, economic, financial and other interests (International Committee of the Red Cross, 2020). This mapping will highlight the profile, threats posed and the geopolitical zones where they are dominant. These groups include Boko Haram, rural bandits, armed herdsmen, separatist groups, unknown gun men, and Niger Delta militants. Others are cult gangs, maritime pirates, kidnap gangs, and ritual killers.

Boko Haram Terrorists

Since 2009, Nigeria has been embroiled in conflict in the Northeast region with Boko Haram Terrorists (BHT), a terrorist group that originally preferred to be addressed as the *Jama'atu Ahlus Sunna Lidda'wati Wal Jihad*

(JAS). The rise of the BHT group has witnessed substantial fragmentation over the years, given rise to factions such as the *Ansaru al-Musulmina fi Bilad al-Sudan* (Ansaru) in 2012 and the Islamic State West African Province (ISWAP), which emerged between March 2015 and 2016. Attacks by BHT continue to be one of Nigeria's most serious security threats (Duerksen, 2021).

Attacks by the BHT have claimed at least 37,000 lives, displaced more than 2.6 million people, and caused about $9 billion worth of damage in Nigeria since 2009 (World Bank Group, 2015; Onuoha and Oyewole, 2018). Rivalry among the jihadist factions – Ansaru, JAS, and ISWAP – has been a feature of the insurgency in Nigeria's northeast. Differences in ideology, the quest for territorial control or expansion, and the desire for dominance in membership recruitment underpin the rivalry. Despite internal schism, the BHT has continued to launch deadly attacks on military, civilian, and humanitarian targets, as the data/graph in Figure 28 shows.

Fig 28: *Boko Haram Incidents and Fatalities in Nigeria, 2014 - 2021*

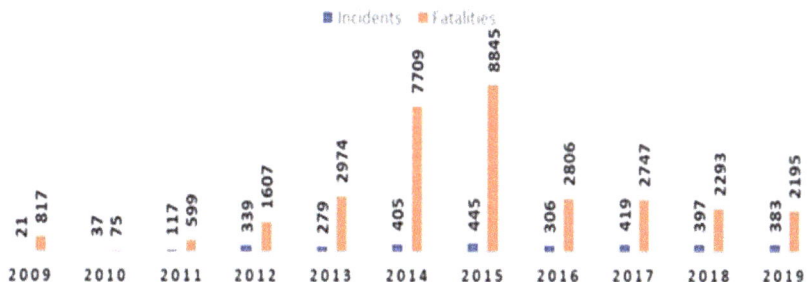

Source: Authors' compilation from the Armed Conflict Location & Event Data (ACLED).

Attacks by the group peaked in 2015, but an obvious trend is the remarkable decline in reported fatalities associated with the group activities since then. The fluctuation is attributed to several factors, including but not limited to offensive operations by the Nigerian military in collaboration with the MNJTF, which has seriously degraded the combat capability of the group.

Armed Herdsmen

The activities of armed herdsmen add a complex dimension to the insecurity landscape in Nigeria. Primarily affecting the Middle Belt and northwest states, clashes between armed herdsmen and farmers have expanded to other parts of the country. Historically, the northwest and northcentral states have been the fertile plains and grazing lands of Nigeria, where nomadic pastoralist and sedentary agriculturalist groups coexisted, traded, and turned to local conflict resolution mechanisms when disputes arose (Duerksen 2021). However, population explosion and urbanisation have pushed herders off their historical grazing routes and forced them to move further South.

In addition, climate change, depleting natural resources, cattle rustling, and the weak capacity of state institutions to manage the grievances of herdsmen have made the attacks more frequent and explosive. From 2001 to 2018, for example, about 60,000 deaths were recorded in multiple clashes, while more than 300,000 were displaced across four states; 176,000 in Benue, about 100,000 in Plateau, another 100,000 in Nasarawa and about 19,000 in Taraba (Ogune, 2021).

Pervasive clashes between herdsmen and farmers have deepened the level of ethnic disharmony and distrust in the affected communities. This is often the case given that the herdsmen are predominantly Fulani and the host communities are mainly of a different ethnic group such as Agatus, Anagos, Baribas, Beroms, Hausa Sabes, Ohoris, Igbos, Tivs, and Yorubas, among others. In the face of growing classes between herdsmen and farmers, the country witnessed an increase in the formation of ethnic militias and vigilantes in local communities.

Rural Bandits

Criminal gangs, referred to locally as 'bandits', are present across northern Nigeria, particularly in the North-West. Banditry, which has long afflicted northern Nigeria, has assumed a dangerous dimension, mostly in Zamfara but also in Kaduna, Katsina, Kebbi, Niger, and, more recently, Sokoto and Taraba states (Nextier SPD, 2018). The violence began as a farmer-herder conflict in 2011 and intensified between 2017 and 2018 to include cattle rustling, kidnapping for ransom, sexual violence and killings (Muvunyi, 2021).

Although particularly active in the northwest geopolitical zone, they have gradually spread to other states outside the region like Adamawa, Benue, Nasarawa, and Plateau to some degree.

The scale, frequency, and intensity of rural banditry are a source of serious security concerns in Nigeria. For instance, while about 1,100 people were murdered in 2018 in the six states of northwest Nigeria, over 2,200 were killed in 2019 (Ademola, 2021). The situation is worst in Zamfara State considering the frequency of kidnapping and ransom payment (Altine, 2021).

Colonies of bandits operate from several forests, namely Maradi, Kuyambana Dansado, Rugu, Guljba, Balmo, Dajin Rugu, Kamara, Kunduma, and Sububu forests located within or traversing the affected states in the region. About 100 different bandit camps exist in Zamfara, Sokoto, Kebbi, Kaduna, Niger, and Katsina, with no fewer than 300 bandits in each of these camps having sophisticated weapons with them (Sabiu, 2021). The commanders of these criminal groups cut across different ethnic nationalities (Babarbare, Fulani, and Hausa, etc). Some of the notorious bandit leaders included, Abdulhadi Dan Nashe (late), Bala Na Dama, Buharin Daj (late), Dogo Gide Illiya, Dogo Idi, Farun Bod'ore, and Kare Moba. Other notorious bandit leaders known by a single name include Dangote (Bazamfare), Baleru, Dankarami, Gajere, and Garso (Anka, 2021). With the emergence of these high-profile leaders, banditry in northern Nigeria has transitioned from the use of crude weapons to sophisticated weapons like the AK47, General Purpose Machine Gun (GPMG), and other assault rifles. Armed with these weapons, they engaged alternately or simultaneously in cattle rustling, community raiding, extortion, high-way robbery, kidnapping for ransom and racketeering in natural resources. The federal government has responded to the threat through the deployment of the military and the police, leading to the killing of some bandits and the destruction of their safe havens and logistics. The Federal Government also declared bandits as terrorists on the strength of a Federal High Court judgement in Abuja on 25 November 2021, which granted an ex parte application by the Federal Government for Yan Bindiga (a Hausa word for gunmen or - bandits) and *Yan Ta'adda* (a Hausa word for terrorists) to be declared as terrorists (Oyero, 2022). Similarly, the State Governments in some of the affected states have experimented with peace deals or amnesty for bandits. These approaches have largely failed, prompting vulnerable communities in some states to resort to self-defence by establishing groups such as vigilantes, which complicates the insecurity climate. The activities of these groups have further heightened the proliferation of SALWs, cases of reprisal attacks, and instances of extra-judicial killings. These developments in turn feed into the cycle and culture of violence, further exacerbating insecurity in the region. The operations launched by the Nigerian Army with the support of the Nigerian Air Force, particularly, Op FOREST SANITY have been crucial in tackling the bandits' threats and creating an enabling condition for other governmental activities aimed at addressing the root causes.

Violent Separatists

Activities of separatist groups in the South-East zone have led to a significant deterioration of security in an area that used to be one of Nigeria's safest. These separatists consist of groups like the Movement for the Actualization of the Sovereign State of Biafra (MASSOB), Biafra Zionist Movement (BZM), MASSOB International, Biafran Zionist Front (BZF), Biafra Independent Movement (BIM), the Biafra Youth Congress (BYC), the Biafran Liberation Council (BLC), and the Indigenous People of Biafra (IPOB) (now proscribed by the Federal Government), among others. They have leveraged the opportunities provided by the return to civil rule in 1999 to openly express their hitherto suppressed grievances against the Nigerian state, agitating for a separate state of Biafra in Nigeria's South-East and part of the South-South zones (Nwangwu, et al. 2020).

The agitation has, however, intensified since President Buhari came into office in 2015 (Hassan, 2018). The most radical group amongst them is the IPOB, led by Mazi Nnamdi Kanu, which has consistently called on its supporters to boycott and disrupt elections unless the government calls for a referendum on independence. The IPOB leader exploited the situation to establish a regional security system widely yearned for in the region and quickly created its own outfit known as the Eastern Security Network (ESN) (Onuoha and Akogwu, 2022a). Their tactics included using hate speech, rumours, threat messages, and the imposition of sit-at-home orders. At the onset, the group declared sit-at-home to celebrate Biafra Day. However, it has continued to impose sit-at-home more frequently in recent times, every Monday, following the repatriation or rendition of Mr Kanu to Nigeria in June 2021.

Members of the ESN have reportedly clashed with state security forces in parts of Southeast and Southsouth zones. Data from Nextier SPD (2021) shows that from October 2020 to September 2021, Nigeria recorded 74 alleged secession-related violent incidents in the Southeast and South-south regions of Nigeria, resulting in 352 casualties (comprising 98 civilians and 78 security agents) with 17 persons injured, and two persons kidnapped. Nigerian security forces have firmly responded to separatist agitation and violence, thus containing the threats. In this regard, the Nigerian Army launched Op UDOKA in January 2023, which helped to improve the security situation and enabled the safe conduct of the 2023 general elections.

Unknown Gunmen

Amidst the evolving tense security situation in the South-East, security personnel and formations began to experience attacks by a seemingly faceless group described as 'unknown gunmen' (UGM). These armed non-state actors also target strategic government facilities, and citizens, especially business people, traditional rulers, and other innocent citizens. They are alleged to be behind the surge in attacks in the southeast in particular and some parts of the south-south zone (Njoku and Ogugbuaja, 2021). Some schools of thought believe that UGM is a creation of IPOB with elements of ESN. Of note is that the Southeast zone has recorded an increase in cases of arson, attacks, and killings blamed on these faceless, roving armed hoodlums.

More than 25 police stations were attacked in parts of the south-east and south-south in the first five months of 2021, resulting in the killing of over 127 policemen and other security personnel (Adepegba, 2021). Data in Figure 2 reveal killings in the Southeast from 1 January 2020, to 12 December 2021. The compilation revealed that the southeast recorded 97 deaths in reported violent attacks between 1 January 2020, and 12 December 2020, while 636 deaths were recorded inreported violent attacks between 13 December 2020, and 12 December 2021. Imo State has been the scene of some of the most audacious attacks with state security facilities and personnel bearing the brunt of this vicious attacks.

Fig 29: Killings in the South-East, 2020 – 2021

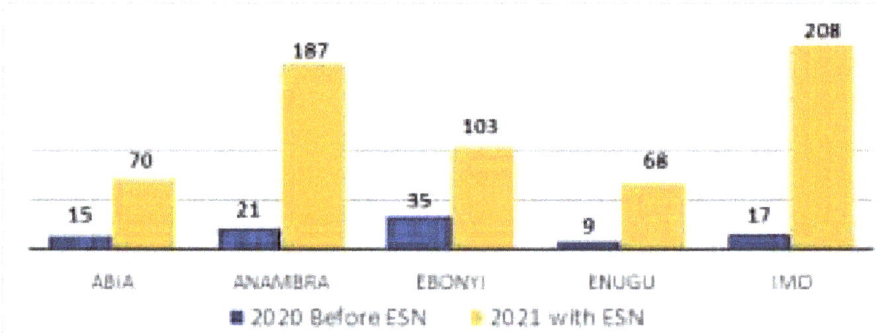

Region	2020 Before ESN	2021 with ESN
ABIA	15	70
ANAMBRA	21	187
EBONYI	35	103
ENUGU	9	68
IMO	17	208

Source: Adapted from Chime (2022).

The compilation further corroborates the arguments of Ojewale and Onuoha (2022, para.4) that "the dramatic surge in the activities of the criminals described as 'unknown gunmen' has not occurred in a vacuum. It is a result of separatist agitation by IPOB and the activities of ESN. Both have contributed to insecurity in the South-East. It is pertinent to note that the killing of security forces by violent groups is not limited to the southeast. For instance, armed groups killed at least 81 soldiers, 65 police officers, two correctional service officials, two anti-drug law officers, five officers of the Civil Defence Corps and two road safety officials; between January and June 2022 (Ayitogo, 2022). The killings spread across the country but were mostly carried out in the northwest, northcentral and southeast. The response of the government, particularly the use of the military, has helped to contain the threats. The Nigerian Army has been exemplary in the use of patrols, checkpoints, and intelligence operations to dominate flash points. Non-kinetic efforts through CIMIC Operations by the Nigerian Army are also worthy of note. Notable among these efforts are the renovation of schools, and hospitals, as well as the provision of boreholes, among other things, in some villages in the South-East.

Niger Delta Militants

The activities of violent criminal gangs particularly militants, cultist groups and pirates constitute a significant source of insecurity in the South-South zone. For years, armed militant groups straddled the landscape of Nigeria's oil-rich Niger Delta region. Local grievances over destructive environmental practices by multinational oil companies and the lop-sided distribution of oil wealth by the Nigerian state sparked a popular backlash against the oil industry in the region. Foremost groups like the Movement for the Survival of the Ogoni People (MOSOP) and later the Niger Delta Peoples Volunteer Forces (NDPVF) mounted protest movements and violent resistance in the Niger Delta against the perceived marginalisation of the region. The mobilisation by MOSOP and other organised groups and subsequent violent resistance by the NDPVF eventually culminated in a decade of instability and targeted attacks on oil infrastructure. This was led by the Movement for the Emancipation of the Niger Delta (MEND), which was active from 2006 to 2009, and the smaller but equally dangerous Niger Delta Avengers (NDA), which took up arms between 2016 and 2020.

The economic consequences for Nigeria were drastic, as the activities of MEND reduced Nigerian oil outputs by about 25 per cent, while attacks by the NDA reduced oil production by an estimated 40 per cent in 2016, driving outputs to a 20-year low. Kidnappings and illegal oil bunkering or oil theft also gave these militant groups new sources of funding, as well as political notoriety. It is estimated that criminal groups were stealing between 100,000 barrels per day (bpd) and 400,000 bpd from oil wells and pipelines in the Niger Delta, resulting in the loss of about $42 billion between 2009 and 2018. An estimated 12,000 barrels of crude oil are stolen daily in Nigeria (George, 2019).

Over time, the Nigerian government adopted several initiatives and measures to combat militancy and oil theft, including the launching of military operations such as Operation DELTA SAFE, conduct of waterways patrols, the award of pipeline surveillance contracts, and the deployment of maritime domain awareness (MDA) infrastructure to monitor the movement of vessels (Onuoha, Iroezumuo, and Onuoha, 2022). However, the realisation that strictly military operations cannot end attacks on critical oil infrastructure in the region led to the adoption of soft measures such as the presidential amnesty programme, which drastically reduced attacks on oil installations and

---

Note: The data for 2020 covered January 1 to December 12, 2020. ESN was launched on December 13, 2020. The Data for 2021 covered December 13, 2020 to December 13, 2021

allowing oil production to restart in earnest. While the amnesty programme contributed to the improved security situation and oil production, it was undermined by several challenges, including the documentation and administration of ex-militants. Despite the gains of these official responses, the quest for sustainable peace and security in the Niger Delta has remained difficult to achieve. Oil production dropped to a record low of 1.015 million bpd in September 2022. However, the efforts of the security forces yielded positive outcome such that as at February 2023, oil production in Nigeria increased to 1.3 million mpd (Addeh, 2023).

Cult Gangs

The threat posed by violent cult groups remains pervasive, if not growing, in different parts of Nigeria. The cult groups are of various names, sizes, and operational reach. In terms of membership, they could be either gender-inclusive or restrictive. Some of the prominent cult groups include Buccaneers, Pyrates, Black Axe, Eiye, Vikings, Greenlanders, Icelanders, Deewell, and Deebam, among others. Notable female cult groups include Daughters of Jezebel, Black Brazier, White Angels, Viqueens, Damsels, Sisters of Darkness, and Pink Ladies, among others. Cult- related activities such as inter- and intra-cult clashes have been prevalent in mostly owns hosting tertiary institutions in Nigeria. However, these cult activities are not restricted to schools or towns, as the menace has penetrated rural communities as well. The prevalence and escalation of violent cultism are partly connected to the dynamics of politics in Nigeria and dates back to the formation of the Pyrates Confraternity in the 1960s. Since 1999, political actors have either employed cult groups as informal security or used them to intimidate or kill their opponents, especially during elections. As politicians increasingly leverage cult groups in pursuit of their political interests, cultists are, in turn, demanding all kinds of favours from politicians, including access, resources, contracts and political or security service positions (Stakeholder Democracy Network, 2020). However, the threat is particularly acute in the Niger Delta region. Data in Figure 30 show that fatalities from cultism have expanded over the past few years in the Niger Delta, especially in Rivers, Delta, and Edo states. Rivers State recorded the highest rate of cult-related incidents. Cult-related incidents and deaths are now recorded every year in each of the nine Niger Delta states.

Fig 30: Cult-related incidents in the Niger Delta Q1 2016 – Q2 2020

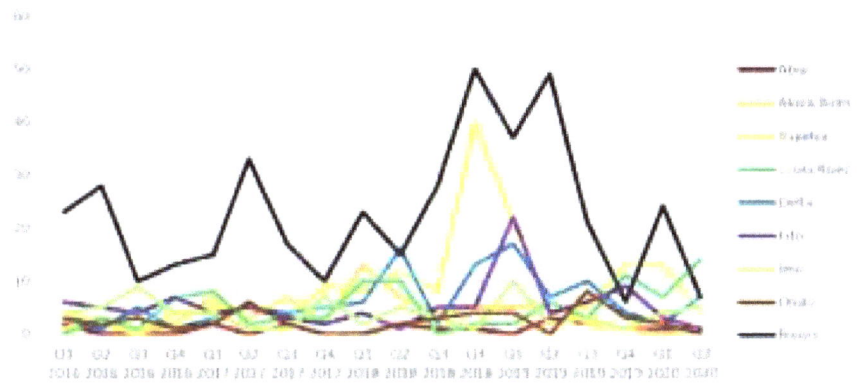

Source: Stakeholder Democracy Network (2020).

The clashes which are violent in nature are carried out by youths who belong to one cult group or the other (Nwaogu, Weli and Mbee, 2019). In some instances, many lives are lost in the most vicious and gruesome manner such as the decapitation and dismemberment of victims. In July 2021, for instance, Mr. Alex Umezuruike, the leader of a vigilante group in Emorhua Local Government Area of Rivers State, the Omudioga Security Planning and Advisory Committee (OSPAC), was beheaded and his body dismembered by suspected cultists (Godwin, 2021).

To curb the menace, the government and other stakeholders have initiated and encouraged campaigns against cultism in schools and institutions of higher learning. School authorities have also tried to deal with the problem by rusticating some students or sanctioning staff found to be cult members or connected to their activities. In addition, the police maintain Special Anti-Cult Squads (SPACS) in most of the states afflicted by cultism. Despite these and other measures, authorities across the various levels of government in Nigeria have failed to end the menace of cultism in the country. The reason is that the financiers, supporters and godfathers of the majority of the violent cults are some of the most influential members of society (Canada: Immigration and Refugee Board of Canada, 1999).

Maritime Pirates

Criminal elements such as militants, cultists, armed robbers and kidnappers have pivoted to sea robbery and piracy in Nigeria's waters, with significant implications for safety and security in the internal waterways and the Gulf of Guinea coast. It is estimated that between 65 per cent and 75 per cent of maritime crimes, particularly piracy, in the Gulf of Guinea emanate from Nigeria's territory. Figure 31 reveals that Nigeria recorded a total of 312 cases of pirate attacks between 2010 and 2021, with the highest number of incidents occuring in 2018 with 48 cases.

Figure 31: Incidents of Piracy in Nigeria Waters, 2010-2021

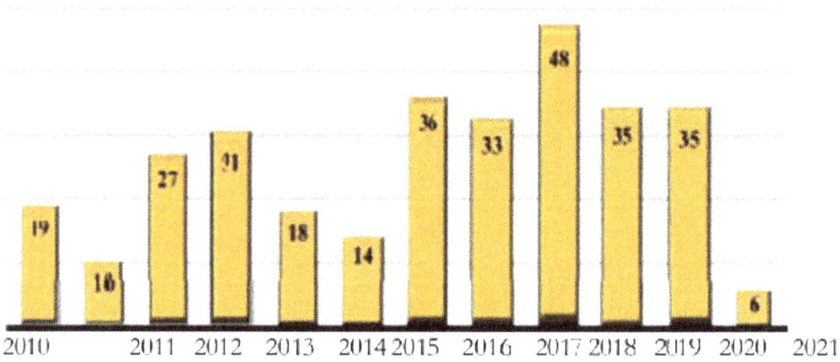

Year	2010	2011	2012	2013	2014	2015	2016	2017	2018	2019	2020	2021
Incidents	19	10	27	41	18	14	36	33	48	35	35	6

Source: Complied from IMB Annual Reports

This worrying trend compelled the Nigerian government to undertake bold measures, such as the enactment of the Suppression of Piracy and Other Maritime Offences Act (the SPOMO Act 2019) and operationalisation of the Deep Blue Project to tackle maritime insecurity and illegal activities on inland waterways (Onuoha, 2021). These initiatives, coupled with collaboration with regional and foreign navies, have led to a significant drop in the number of incidents of piracy in Nigerian waters. For instance, Nigeria reported only 6 incidents in 2021, in comparison to 35 in 2020. Evidently, of the 58 incidents of piracy reported globally in the first six months of 2022, none occurred in Nigeria (Sanni, 2022).

Kidnap Gangs

Acts of kidnap are perpetrated by different criminal elements, such as militias, gangs, ritualists and terrorists, among others, for a variety of reasons. An SBM Intelligence (2022) report documents that at least 500 incidents of kidnap were recorded and 3,420 people were abducted across Nigeria, with 564 others killed in violence associated with abduction between July 2021 and June 2022. However, the increased frequency, geographical spread, and operational sophistication of kidnapping for ransom (K4R) is a major source of concern. A report revealed that between June 2011 and March 2020, at least $18.34 million (N7 billion) was paid to kidnappers as ransom in Nigeria, and the larger proportion of that figure (about $11 million) was paid out between January 2016 and March 2020 (SBM Intelligence, 2020). While the accuracy of these figures was contested, it still highlighted the nature of the threats. Apart from the deployment of the military to address the problem, the 2022 Naira redesign policy of the Central Bank of Nigeria was also meant to tackle the amount of illegal cash in the possession of kidnappers and other organised criminal groups.

Obviously, kidnapping has become a lucrative crime in Nigeria. No part of the country is immune from the threat of kidnapping or abduction. The targets of abduction are as diverse and include expatriates, business people, school-children, women, politicians, government officials, diplomats, and traditional rulers, among others. While there are instances where abductees whose family members could not raise ransom were gruesomely killed, there are also situations where some abductees were killed even after the ransom was paid (Onuoha and Okolie-Osemene, 2019).

In response, the Nigerian Police and other security agencies have deployed anti- kidnap units and tracking devices, but the forested areas where gangs hide, coupled with their ability to relocate victims has sometimes frustrated security efforts. The Nigerian government has also tried alternative methods to curb kidnapping, such as registering the Subscriber Identification Module (SIM) cards of mobile phone users to better track their owners. Some state governments have enacted laws either prescribing life imprisonment or the death penalty for any person convicted of kidnapping. In April 2022, the payment of kidnap ransom was criminalised by the Senate as they passed the Terrorism (Prevention) Act 2013 (Amendment) Bill, 2022. Despite these interventions, kidnapping has persisted because some of the underlying drivers of criminality such as poverty, unemployment, and inequality, remain unresolved.

Ritual Killers

Although not new in Nigeria, ritual killing is a major criminal activity that has significantly contributed to the current wave of insecurity pervading the country. Stories of ritual killings are reported daily in traditional and social media. The collapse of moral values, the get-rich-quick syndrome, and other constraints inherent in the criminal justice system have allowed ritual killings to fester in Nigeria. Often time, victims are decapitated and some body parts are harvested for ritual practices such as producing charms, concoctions, and portions. Those who engage in ritual killings are mainly motivated by the desire for self-protection, the pursuit of political ambitions, and success in business ventures, especially the quick money syndrome.

It is instructive that an alleged commander of IPOB's ESN, identified as Emeoyiri Benjamin, confessed to how he and his gang members fortified themselves with charms prepared with the heads of ten young girls abducted in Imo State (Hanafi, 2021). Also, some politicians are known to engage in ritual killings for self-protection and electoral victory as evidenced by confessions of some suspects and witch doctors, who mentioned politicians, government officials, and wealthy businessmen as their sponsors (Peterside, 2021). In addition, it is believed that young Nigerian scammers known as 'Yahoo Boys' are increasingly resorting to ritual killings to charm potential victims into doing their bidding. The practice is referred to as "Yahoo Plus" or "Yahoo Plus-Plus", depending on the nature and degree of charm and ritual undertaking involved.

Factors Contributing to the Rise of Violent Groups and Insecurity in Nigeria

The preceding section demonstrated that the activities of violent groups constitute the major sources of insecurity in Nigeria. Several factors are responsible for this state of affairs, but at the root of the problem is governance failure. The failure of political leadership at all levels of government (federal, state, and local) to judiciously utilise state resources to provide basic social services has created conducive and permissive conditions for the outbreak and persistence of violence, conflicts, and criminality.

In Nigeria, corruption among public office holders has long meant that privation, poverty, inequality, and unemployment blight the majority of the citizens despite the enormous national wealth. In 2019, it was revealed that an estimated $582 billion has been stolen from Nigeria since its independence in 1960 (Asadu, 2019). About 70 to 75 per cent of the national budget is lost to corrupt practices at all levels of government in the country (Daily Trust, 2022). This explains why 63% of the people living within Nigeria (133 million people) are multidimensionally poor (National Bureau of Statistics, 2022, p.22), despite the country having earned $741.48 billion from oil and gas in 21 years (Ekekwe, 2022). The diversion or outright embezzlement of public funds, undermines the ability of the state to provide social services or create jobs for its teeming population.

Consequently, unemployment and poverty, especially among the youth have become major factors implicated in rising criminality in the country. The unemployment rate in Nigeria has more than quadrupled since 2016 when the economy slipped into a recession. As of April 2022, an estimated 83 million people, or 39% of the total population, live in extreme poverty earning less than $2 per day. This is a significant 18 per cent increase from the 70 million people recorded in 2016 (Agusto & Co., 2022). High unemployment and poverty rates readily predispose the youth to several criminal behaviours including being recruited into violent extremist organisations. The limited capability of state institutions to effectively discharge their duties complicates the tenuous security situation. Factors such as politicization, nepotism, and a culture of corruption have also undermined the effectiveness of state institutions.

In addition, the ability of the criminals to coordinate their illicit activities via mobile phones without being apprehended further suggests some compromises in the functioning of the country's security architecture which needs to be effectively tackled. In May 2011, the Nigerian government mandated that all telecom operators in Nigeria register the SIM cards of all existing mobile phone subscribers before the January 2012 deadline. The registration of mobile phone users was primarily to mitigate the incidences of crime and criminalities perpetrated through the use of phones. In December 2020, Nigeria started to enforce the SIM-National Identification Numbers (NIN) linkage. Despite these laudable initiatives, criminals have continued to make use of mobile phones to plan and coordinate their nefarious activities. Corruption, incompetence and pecuniary interests have frustrated attempts to have such a vital system operating in Nigeria. The setback from the poor SIM registration regime is further compounded by the lack of a reliable electronic national identity management system in Nigeria. This situation has created a terrible security gap in the absence of a national database for reliable identification of people, thereby severely constraining the evolution of robust security and crime management system in the country.

Furthermore, insecurity and the prevalence of violent groups are exacerbated by the country's porous borders. Most of the border areas are in mountainous areas, desert plains, thick jungles, or along sea edges. Almost all are not clearly demarcated and are easily penetrable without detection. As of 2013, it was revealed that Nigeria had over 1,499 illegal and 84 legal entry routes into or out of the country (Ojeme and Odiniya, 2013). The porosity of borders facilitates easy cross-border movement of criminals, smuggling of SALWs, and the transfer of stolen items.

The heightened circulation of illicit SALWs has become both a cause and a consequence of insecurity in Nigeria. Weapons such as 9mm semi-automatic pistols, assault rifles, shotguns and sub-machine guns, among others, are readily available in the underground (black) market in Nigeria. These weapons come largely from local fabrication, cross-border smuggling by criminal elements, and thefts from government armouries. Gun runners smuggle SALWs from war-torn zones like Libya, the Central African Republic, and Mali into Nigeria through the nation's porous borders (Onuoha, Okafor and Femi-Adedayo, 2021). The easy availability and accessibility of SALWs have enabled and emboldened violent groups to launch attacks against diverse targets depending on their motivations.

Another factor contributing to the rise of violent groups and the persistence of insecurity is the dearth of elite consensus on how to manage dissent and grievances in a heterogenous society. Some of the existing violent groups in Nigeria take on ethnic or religious colouration and this complicates attempts at defeating them. For instance, the IPOB is believed to be of Igbo extraction; the Niger Delta militants, especially MEND, are seen as representing Ijaw interests; and armed herdsmen are perceived as Fulani people. The bulk of Boko Haram is of Kanuri extraction. The ethnic character of these groups undermines the quest for elite consensus in tackling and defeating them. The focus of the government on the engagement of elites, civil society groups, and traditional and religious institutions is meant to address the problem.

There is also the problem of misguided policy responses to insecurity. Relevant here is the nature of amnesty and peace deals with criminal groups such as terrorists, bandits, and militants by the Nigerian government. The peace deal or amnesty approach is often fraught with several challenges, such as the absence of clear policy and legal frameworks to anchor the initiative and the lack of an institutional platform to facilitate sustainability, inclusivity, and transparency in the process. How government authorities were able to correctly identify who was a "repentant" criminal is equally a nagging concern. The continued activities of these violent groups have exposed the fragility and weakness of this approach. Moreover, "in the absence of robust accountability mechanisms, the risk of politicisation and incentivisation of criminal violence through amnesty becomes high" (Onuoha and Akogwu, 2022b, p.42).

Impact of Insecurity in Nigeria

Insecurity has continued to have grave consequences for Nigeria. Firstly, the activities of violent groups have resulted in huge loss of lives. Between May 2015 and May 2022, over 55,430 Nigerians were killed by terrorist groups and criminal gangs operating across the country (Bukarti, 2022). The killing of any family member leads to a deep fracturing of kinship structures. Some children have been orphaned, while spouse have sometimes become widowed or widowers because of the deaths caused by these criminal armed groups. In 2015, it was estimated that there were about 17.5 million orphans and vulnerable children live in a nation of about 200 million people representing nine per cent of the population (Dada, 2021). The number has increased over the years due to violent conflicts and insecurity in Nigeria.

This reality has placed Nigeria among the countries with children worst affected by conflict. For instance, an estimated 57,000 children at IDP camps in Borno state lost their parents to the Boko Haram insurgency (Haruna, 2022). The number will be far higher if we tally deaths from banditry, farmer-herdsmen clashes, and kidnapping. Needless to say, the failure to address the plights of orphaned children will lay the foundation for 'security anarchy' in years to come.

Insecurity in Nigeria is also contributing to forced population displacement and the rising trend of emigration. As of 2020, Nigeria has the third-highest number of IDPs in Africa after the Democratic Republic of Congo and Somalia. In 2021, the number of registered IDPs in Nigeria was 2.18 million (Uduu, 2022). Conflicts associated with the Boko Haram insurgency, farmer-herdsmen clashes, mass kidnappings by bandits, and other criminality accounted for 94 per cent of IDPs. In places where camps have been provided, most of the IDPs have limited access to basic amenities such as health facilities and portable water (Ahmed & Sulaiman, 2022, para 6). Forced displacement is also leading to a massive influx of people to relatively safer parts of the country, exacerbating the strain on public resources. Besides, Nigeria is also a refugee receiving-country, as several thousand Cameroonians fleeing the conflict in the Anglophone region have fled to Nigeria for refuge, thereby sparking new security challenges of refugees by day and separatist fighters by night between Nigeria and Cameroon (C. N. Okereke, personal communication, January 7, 2023).

Nigerians are equally leaving the country for relatively more prosperous countries due to insecurity and economic challenges. According to data from the United Nations World Population Prospects, Nigeria had a net migration rate (per 1,000 population) of -0.3 between 2015 and 2020. This translates to three of every 10,000 Nigerians emigrating annually within the period (Agusto & Co., 2022). The desperation of many Nigerians to leave the country is now referred to as the "Japa" syndrome. "Japa" is a Yoruba word for "to run, flee, or escape." The word takes firm root in the aspiration that young Nigerians have to leave the country for good (Dayo, n.d.). Security challenges have force people, mostly local farmers and fishermen, to abandon their sources of livelihood. As a result, most farmers are no longer able to produce in sufficient quantities to meet the demand of the masses in the country. This trend is particularly worrisome because it is aggravating food scarcity, hunger, and malnutrition in the country (WFP, 2022).

Insecurity is equally harming economic activities, as many businesses are closing down or relocating to safer environments (Adegbami, 2013, p. 9). The production units of most manufacturing businesses depends largely on the availability and regular supply of raw materials for production. Insecurity in most parts of the country, particularly the threat of kidnap, is contributing to inability to access such raw materials; hence, jeopardizing production activities. It also scares foreign investors and discourages domestic investors from re-investing their returns. According to the National Bureau of Statistics (NBS), Nigeria's Foreign Direct Investment (FDI) fell from $1.028 billion in 2020 to $698 million by 2021, indicating a drop of about $322 million. This is the lowest Nigeria has recorded in 10 years. (Ahmed & Sulaiman, 2022, para 6). There is also an increase in security spending as most business organisations operating in Nigeria spend a lot on hiring private security outfits. This adds to the cost of doing business in Nigeria, further stifling economic growth and development.

Another major consequence of insecurity has been in the tourism sector, which is in near comatose, particularly in Northern Nigeria. Some of Nigeria's most attractive tourist sites are located in Plateau, Bauchi, Adamawa, Taraba and Kaduna States where insecurity is now rife. The ripple effect on the local economies has been devastating, especially on jobs and consumer demand. This, in itself, is likely to further fuel insecurity (Agusto & Co., 2022).

Security challenges are also undermining education in Nigeria and children are among the worst hit. About 1,436 schoolchildren and 17 teachers were abducted from their schools by bandits and 16 school children lost their lives, across Kaduna, Katsina, Niger, and Zamfara states. A total of 11,536 schools in Nigeria have been closed since December 2020 due to abductions and security issues (Adedigba, 2022). The attacks and resultant closure impacted the education of approximately 1.3 million children in the 2020/21 academic year. Moreover, some schools in remote areas of Northwest states were closed indefinitely due to the precarious situation of the areas in which they were located (Ahmed & Sulaiman, 2022, para 7). This contributes to forcing children out of school. In 2018, there were an estimated 10.2 million out-of-school children in Nigeria. The number has increased to about 18 million as of 2021 (Adedigba, 2022).

Another notable consequence of insecurity is rising expenditure on defence and security. The Nigerian government has reportedly spent over N8 trillion in the last seven years on defence, including the purchase of military hardware. Indeed, the defence sector has consistently received the highest budgetary allocation, in addition to other extra-budgetary allocations, like the $1billion withdrawal from the Excess Crude Account for the procurement of

12 Super Tucano aircrafts for the military (Ajaja, 2022). While these have helped to contain the activities of violent groups, insecurity has persisted in the country.

Towards a Sustainable Solution to Escalating Insecurity in Nigeria

Nigeria has been facing security challenges since the return to democratic rule in May 1999. The ugly situation is partly a product of the activities of violent groups or non-state actors. These security challenges result in records of daily deaths, displacement, destruction, and economic devastation. The Nigerian government has reacted in diverse ways, with the reliance on kinetic measures standing out as the most prominent conflict and security management tool. Non-kinetic measures have also been applied in several cases with positive results. Beyond coercive and reactive engagement with violent groups, the Nigerian government should prioritise efforts at understanding the current dynamics of insecurity, with particular attention on addressing the drivers of violence in Nigeria, structural vulnerabilities underpinning state fragility and social issues that fuel the emergence of violent groups.

Therefore, there is a need to aggressively explore alternative approaches to conflict and security management in Nigeria. To be effective, the approach must naturally proceed from addressing the root causes of violence and conflicts to the immediate causes. Economic marginalisation and social injustice are at the root of the explosion of violent groups in Nigeria. Situational factors such as porous borders, weak state institutions, and the proliferation of SALWs, among others, tend to exacerbate the scourge. Studies have shown that poverty and idleness are among the major drivers of people getting recruited by violent groups. The Nigerian government needs to ramp up measures aimed at stemming the level of poverty, hunger and unemployment in the country. This could be achieved through huge investments in public infrastructure, the revival of strategic industries, and aggressive anti-corruption campaigns to save the funds needed to accelerate development initiatives and targeted youth empowerment interventions.

In addition, measures should be taken to strengthen the capacity of state institutions to address marginalisation and injustice that drive groups into taking up arms. The Nigerian state should promote equity and merit in the allocation of national resources to curb the menace of ethnic agitations which eventually culminate in the formation of violent groups. Recent experiences and emerging lessons have shown that excessive use of force also seems to be fueling continued agitations. Thus, there should be proactive measures in early warning mechanisms, which are essential to identifying and addressing grievances and marginalisation before they fester and feed into violent conflicts. Furthermore, the government needs to collaborate with civil society organisations to strengthen community-based dispute resolution mechanisms as well as bolster community-driven disarmament initiatives. There is also a need to enhance community policing to better leverage the vantage position of rural communities in gathering intelligence and effectively responding to low-level threats.

In addition, strengthening robust collaboration among the nation's security agencies, and between them and their counterparts in neighbouring countries, is equally vital in stemming the inflow of SALWs that encourages the culture and cycle of violence in Nigeria. The Office of the National Security Adviser should initiate a robust framework of multi-agency and multi-lateral collaboration to curtail cross-border smuggling of SALWs in the region.

Conclusion

It is obvious that insecurity has undermined peace, progress and social cohesion in the country. The violent actors (groups) behind the escalating insecurity in Nigeria are as diverse as the factors fuelling and sustaining their existence. The outbreak and persistence of insecurity have resulted in huge losses of lives, widespread destruction of properties, and humongous displacements of people as IDPs and refugees. The Nigerian government has adopted several measures to tackle insecurity, with a growing reliance on the military as a prominent tool for managing violent conflict and criminality. The approach has proven largely effective in addressing the problem, but more effort is required.

Addressing the drivers and enablers of violence and crime is therefore key to reversing the wave of insecurity in Nigeria. At the root of Nigeria's lingering security challenges are poor socio-economic performance and misgovernance. To be more effective, Nigeria's response to insecurity should adopt multidimensional and multifaceted approaches to addressing the actors and factors destabilising the peace of the country. Good governance, commitment to social justice, and judicious utilisation of resources are critical for a more effective and sustainable solution to insecurity.

Terrorism and Insurgency in Nigeria

Introduction

Since her attainment of political independence in 1960, Nigeria has continued to experience varying incidences of extreme violence perpetrated by various Non- State Armed Groups (NSAGs) that neither the Nigerian government nor the international community has designated as terrorist organization. This is essentially because those behind such acts did not indiscriminately targeted unarmed civilians, let alone justify their operations on ideological grounds. However, by the second decade of the twenty-first century, the country gradually became one of the top ten countries most affected by *terrorism* on account of a brutal insurgency waged by the *Jama'atu Ahlus-Sunnah Lidda'Awati Wal Jihad (JAS)*, known the world over as Boko Haram. The pseudo-Islamist militant group has since 2009 sought to overthrow the Nigerian government and replace it with a regime based on Islamic laws (Onuoha, 2010).

Although the group evolved from Nigeria's North-East under different names, its violent campaigns transformed into an insurgency in the aftermath of the short-lived July 2009 revolt in its area of dominance. The July uprising was quelled by the joint operations of the military and other security agencies, including the police and Department of State Services (DSS), among others, leaving more than 800 dead, most of whom were sect members (Onuoha, 2010; Adibe, 2019). The group's leader, Mohammed Yusuf, was also captured and subsequently extra- judicially killed while in police custody (Onuoha, 2010). Since then, the threat posed by Boko Haram has continued to challenge the capacity of the Nigerian state to govern. The splintering of the Boko Haram terrorists (BHT) into two factions in 2012, namely the original Boko Haram (JAS) and the *Ansaru al- Musulmina fi Bilad al-Sudan* (Ansaru), further compounded the complexity of the terrorist threat in Nigeria (Office of the National Security Adviser - ONSA, 2019).

As attacks on civilian and military targets grow in frequency and intensity, the Nigerian government, on 4 June 2013, proscribed Boko Haram and *Ansaru* as terrorist organisations. The order, gazetted as the

Terrorism (Prevention) (Proscription Order) Notice 2013, was approved by President Goodluck Jonathan pursuant to Section 2 of the Terrorism Prevention Act, 2011 (as amended). The group was subsequently designated as a terrorist organization by foreign powers such as the United Kingdom (July 2013), the United States (November 2013), and Canada (December 2013), as well as the United Nations (UN) (May 2014). In 2014 Boko Haram transformed into a major regional security threat following the intensification of cross-border attacks in Cameroon, Chad, and Niger and the seizure of several territories in Nigeria's northeast (Mahmood, 2016). On account of the death and brutality unleashed by its fighters, Boko Haram was designated as the world's deadliest terrorist organisation in 2014 (Institute for Economics and Peace, 2015).

At the height of the insurgency, the group controlled about 12,427 square kilometres of territory in Nigeria (Blair, 2015). After a peak in terror-related violence in 2015, the number of casualties attributed to the group declined significantly, as did operating space. This is partly due to sustained military-led CTCOIN operations by the Nigerian government. Renewed CTCOIN operations – with assistance from Benin, Cameroon, Chad, and Niger under MNJTF, helped push Boko Haram out of several territories it previously held. In 2015, Shekau pledged allegiance (bay'a) to ISIS's now-deceased caliph, Abu Bakr al-Baghdadi. However, internal rivalry again caused a major split within the Boko Haram leadership in August 2016, leading to the emergence of another faction: the Islamic State West African Province (ISWAP). Notwithstanding, the splintering into three factions - Ansaru, ISWAP, and JAS - the terrorists have continued to plan and launch deadly attacks on military, humanitarian, and civilian targets. Despite a general decrease in terror- related deaths, and the degradation of BHT combat capability, Nigeria recorded the ninth-highest number of terrorism related deaths worldwide in 2021 (Sasu, 2022).

Against this backdrop, this chapter examines the challenge posed by Boko Haram Terrorist (BHT) in Nigeria. The BHT was selected because it was the first such group in Nigeria to be gazetted as a terrorist organisation by the Nigerian government, some major foreign powers, and the UN. In addition, it is the only group that sought to combine terrorist and insurgent tactics by seizing territories at the height of the insurgency in 2015. Though this situation has been reversed by the Armed Forces of Nigeria, the reference to

BHT in this chapter encapsulates militants belonging to the three main factions of the group. The chapter has two major objectives. The first is to examine the dynamics of BHT in Nigeria focusing on the evolution, operations, splintering, and trajectory of the group. The second objective is to provide a brief evaluation of the diverse CTCOIN measures adopted by the Nigerian government to tackle the BHT, highlighting key successes and setbacks and offering actionable recommendations.

The remainder of this chapter is organized as follows. First, we present a clarification of key terms used in the analysis. Next, we briefly highlight Boko Haram's evolution and ideology. In the section that follows, we discuss the trajectory of BHT manifestation in terms of the emergence and operations of the three factions. We then highlighted the impact of the insurgency. This is followed by a reflection on the diverse measures adopted by the Nigerian government to combat terrorism and insurgency, highlighting some successes and setbacks characteristic of these initiatives. Finally, we present our conclusions and recommendations.

Clarification of Key Concepts

Before undertaking the substantive analytical component of this chapter, it is necessary to provide clarification of some key concepts. These concepts are terrorism, insurgency, counterterrorism, and counterinsurgency.

Terrorism

The concept of terrorism continues to be widely used in academic, media and official circles. Yet there is no single definition that is generally agreed upon. Simon (1994, p.29), for instance, identified no fewer than 212 different definitions of terrorism in use, with 90 of them used by governments and other institutions. The multitude of definitions derives from the fact that terrorism is 'intended to be a matter of perception and is thus seen differently by different observers' (Cronin 2004, p.40).

In this regard, Section 2(c) of the Terrorism Prevention Act of Nigeria defines terrorism as an act which is deliberately done with malice aforethought and which has the capacity to seriously harm a country or an international organization, and which is intended to unduly compel a government or international organization to do or abstain from doing any act; intimidate a population; destabilize the fundamental, political, constitutional, economic, or social structures of a country or an international organization; and otherwise influence such government or organization by intimidation or coercion.

Notwithstanding the absence of a universal definition, scholars contend that there is almost general agreement that terrorism encompasses the premeditated use or threat of use of violence by an ideologically motivated individual or group to cause fear, injury, death, or destruction, intended to compel those in political authority to accede to the demands of those behind such acts (Sampson and Onuoha 2011). Terrorism is defined here as the use or threat of use of violence by an ideologically motivated individual or a group, whether acting for or in opposition to established authority, when such action is designed to create extreme anxiety and, or fear, including effects in a target group larger than the immediate victims, to coerce that group into acceding to the political demands of the perpetrators (Wardlaw, 1982). Thus, "at the minimum, an act becomes labelled as terrorism when it has been defined as such in the ATL of a specific state or in international instruments or legal texts it subscribes to" (Sampson and Onuoha, 2011, p.35).

Insurgency

As with terrorism, the concept of insurgency does not lend itself to a universally accepted definition. Some writers have used the concepts of terrorism and insurgency interchangeably. Although they are closely related in terms of their application of violence, they are different in some respects. The United States Department of Defence defines insurgency as 'an organized resistance movement that uses subversion, sabotage, and armed conflict to achieve its aims (Department of Defense, 2001). O'Neill offers a different definition that views it as a "struggle between a non-ruling group and the ruling authorities in which the non-ruling group consciously uses political resources (organisational expertise, propaganda, and demonstrations) and violence to destroy, reformulate, or sustain the basis of legitimacy of one or more aspects of politics" (O'Neill, 1990). According to Hammes, insurgency has been the most prevalent form of armed conflict since at least 1949 (Hammes, 2005). The ultimate goal of an insurgency is to challenge the existing government for control of all or a portion of its territory or to force political concessions in sharing political power. Insurgencies, therefore, require the active or tacit support of some portion of the population involved. External support, recognition, or approval from other countries or political entities can be useful to insurgents but is not required (Reider, 2014). However, it is more often than not a decisive factor in the success of an insurgency (Reider, 2014).

In contrast, terrorism does not require and rarely has the active support or even the sympathy of a large percentage of the population. While insurgents will frequently describe themselves as "insurgents" or "guerrillas", terrorists will not refer to themselves as "terrorists" but describe themselves using military or political terminology like "freedom fighters" or "activists". Terrorism relies on public impact and is therefore conscious of the advantage of avoiding the negative connotations of the term "terrorists" in identifying themselves (US Joint Publications, 2014). Insurgencies combine violence with political process in pursuit of revolutionary purposes in a way that terrorism cannot duplicate. Terrorists may pursue political, even revolutionary, goals, but their violence replaces rather than complements a political process.

Counter Terrorism

The concept of CT, has gained significant currency among government officials, media practitioners, scholars, and security officials, especially since the terrorist attacks of 11 September 2001. However, the formulation of a single definition of CT that will enjoy global acceptance has proved to be a difficult task given the very controversial and contested nature of the term terrorism. The US Joint Publications define CT as activities and operations taken to neutralize terrorists, their organizations, and networks to render them incapable of using violence to instill fear and coerce governments or societies to achieve their goals (Pratt, 2010). In this chapter, CT is defined as "actions or strategies aimed at preventing terrorism from escalating, controlling the damage from terrorist attacks that do occur, and ultimately seeking to eradicate terrorism in a given context" (Harris-Hogan et al, 2016). Overall, CT measures involved military action, increasing policing powers, and expanding intelligence services to combat or prevent terrorism

(Olawoyin, 2021). In fact, CT "operations require a timely and accurate response from the state armed forces to carry out assigned missions and forestall terrorist actions that threaten the territorial integrity, independence, and sovereignty of the state" (DoD Dictionary version, 2008). The ability of a state to deploy the right mix of policies, practices, personnel and resources holds the greatest prospect of reducing the spread and scale of terrorism within its territory.

Counter Insurgency

There is no universally accepted definition of COIN due to the amorphous nature of insurgencies and the fact that each insurgency has its own unique driving force. The United States Department of Defence (2001) defines COIN as all political, economic, military, paramilitary, psychological, and civic actions that can be taken by a government to defeat an insurgency. Though this definition identified the ingredient of COIN, it remains less than satisfactory in its failure to address the root causes of the insurgency (Moore, 2007). Also, its emphasis on defeating an enemy portrays a military bias. As a working definition, COIN is defined as "an integrated set of political, economic, social, and security measures intended to end and prevent the recurrence of armed violence, create and maintain stable political, economic, and social structures, and resolve the underlying causes of an insurgency in order to establish and sustain the conditions necessary for lasting stability" (Akanji, 2009). This definition implies that COIN is hugely political; it seeks not just to eliminate the insurgents but also to resolve the underlying causes of an insurgency.

Evolution of Boko Haram Terrorism in Nigeria: A Synoptic View

The actual date of the emergence of Boko Haram is a source of debate in literature. The origin of Boko Haram dates back to the early 1990s, but its influence began to grow steadily in 2002, when Mohammed Yusuf, a charismatic preacher, became its leader. Its "ultimate goal was to overthrow the existing political order [in Nigeria] and establish and replace it with a strict Islamic system" (ONSA, 2014, p.11). Boko Haram, which literally translates to 'western education is forbidden', opposes Nigeria's secular government and western-style institutions such as schools, universities, and the civil service.

Boko Haram members are motivated by the conviction that the Nigerian state is a cesspool of social vices; thus, "the best thing for a devout Muslim to do was to 'migrate' from the morally bankrupt society to a secluded place and establish an ideal Islamic society devoid of political corruption and moral deprivation" (Onuoha, 2010). Non-members were therefore considered *kuffar* (disbelievers; those who deny the truth) or *fasiqun* (wrong-doers). Although some Chadians, Cameroonians, and Nigerians were among the group's early members, an estimated 80 per cent of its members are believed to be of the Kanuri ethnic group.

In the aftermath of the July 2009 revolt, the group went underground and later adopted Yusuf's hard-line deputy, Abubakar Shekau, as its new spiritual leader. Thereafter, the militants referred to themselves as the JAS. The evolutionary trajectory of BHT since then has been characterised by internal revolt, factionalisation and splintering amidst continuity in the perpetration of extreme violence in Nigeria and the Lake Chad region.

Trends and Trajectory of Boko Haram Terrorism in Nigeria

Boko Haram remains a somewhat impenetrable creation, splintering into multiple factions after Yusuf's death. To date, three main factions have their roots in the original Boko Haram was led by Yusuf. Their evolution, core ideology, operations, and dynamics are discussed subsequently.

Jama'atu Ahlissunnah Lidda'awati wal Jihad (JAS)

Following Yusuf's death during the July 2009 revolt, Shekau moved quickly to consolidate the *Salafi Jihadi* ideology of the group while propagating *Takfirism*,- which classifies all non-practicing Muslims as *kafirs* (infidels) and even justifies their killing. The ideology of *Salafism* seeks to purge Islam of outside influences and strives for a return to the Islam practiced by the "pious ancestors", that is Muhammad and the early Islamic community (European Commission's Expert Group on Violent Radicalisation 2008). *Salafist Jihadism* is the specific interpretation of *Salafism* that extols the use of violence to bring about such radical change (Mneimneh, 2009). It stresses adherence to a rigorist interpretation of the

Quran and the Hadith and aims at reforming the personal behaviour of every Muslim. It also involves the duty to advise other believers to change their way of life in the same sense. Only "one specific interpretation of Salafism focuses on the use of violence to bring about such radical change and is commonly known as Salafist Jihadism" (European Commission's Expert Group on Violent Radicalisation 2008: 6). In other words:

> Salafi jihadi groups are motivated by a mix of religious and political objectives: they embrace a strict, literal interpretation of Islam, and combine it with an emphasis on jihad, understood here as holy war. They view jihad as the primary instrument through which their Salafi desire to 'return' to the original message of Islam will become reality. Unlike radical Islamists, they approach jihad as a global struggle that knows no borders.... They form an amorphous, transnational movement, and disseminate an ideology that is fundamentally hostile to modernity, the secular, democratic nation- state, to the logic of globalization, and the peaceful coexistence of different cultures and religions. (Denoeux and Carter 2009, p.86)

In this light, Boko Haram's Salafi Jihadist inclination became evident in the aftermath of the July 2009 revolt. In March 2010, for instance, Boko Haram declared that it was "joining Al-Qaeda to avenge the murder of some of its members and leaders in a series of explosions across Nigeria" (The Jihadi Websites Monitoring Group 2010, p.14).

Under Shekau's brutal leadership, Boko Haram became more violent, adopting the strategy of terrorism and insurgency in 2010. The group mounted deadly suicide bombing attacks targeting Police Headquarters in June 2011 and the United Nations House in August 2011, both in Abuja. These incidents, among other violent operations brought Shekau to the global limelight. The group draws its fighters mainly from the Kanuri ethnic group, with CIA officials estimating that it boasted around 9,000 fighters in 2015 (Institute for Economics and Peace, 2010). They established safe havens in the Lake Chad basin area which hosts a complex terrain of deep forest, lakes, islands, and caves. The JAS has sustained a deadly insurgency that has overwhelmingly targeted civilians in Adamawa, Borno, and Yobe States in Nigeria's Northeast region, although the group has equally mounted attacks in other states. Shekau's approval of the indiscriminate killing of civilians led some disgruntled members to splinter from the group to form the Ansaru in 2012.

In April 2014, Boko Haram drew international condemnation after it kidnapped 276 girls from the Government Girls Secondary School in the town of Chibok, Borno State. It subsequently started seizing towns and villages in Borno, Adamawa, and Yobe States and proclaimed the establishment of an Islamic caliphate with Gwoza town as its capital in August 2014. On account of its brutal attacks, Boko Haram emerged as the world's deadliest terrorist organisation in 2014 (ADF Staff, 2018). By early January 2015, the insurgents had emerged as a serious regional security threat to the Lake Chad region, following the staging of cross-border attacks on Cameroon, Chad, and Niger. A renewed military operation by Nigerian-led regional forces known as the Multinational Joint Taskforce (MNJTF) helped to turn the tide against the group. Boko Haram became badly degraded and mostly resorted to asymmetric tactics such as suicide bombings. Between April 2011 and June 2017, the group was responsible for a total of 238 suicide bombings in the 4 riparian countries of the Lake Chad namely: Nigeria (208); Cameroon (22); Chad (5); and Niger (3) (Warner and Matfess, 2017).

In March 2015, when Shekau pledged allegiance to Abu Bakr al-Baghdadi, then ISIS's leader, the group was rebranded as the ISWAP. In 2016, the group experienced a major fracture, with Abu Musab al-Barnawi, the son of the group's original leader, Yusuf, leading a majority of the militants under ISWAP, while Shekau remained the head of the JAS faction or Boko Haram. His faction became very dominant in the Southern Borno and Mandara mountain areas, covering parts of Nigeria and Cameroon, with a branch outpost in the Lake Chad area between Tumur in the Niger Republic and Kangar in Northern Borno. Hoever, on May 19, 2021, Abubakar Shekau, was killed during a clash with the ISWAP fighters after he allegedly detonated his suicide vest. Before Shekau's killing by rival militants, the Nigerian military had on several occasions (at least four times between 2009 and 2017) claimed that it had killed Shekau. The Boko Haram leader will always debunk such claims via video or audio messages (Owete, 2017). The fact that Shekau was eventually killed by ISWAP fighters denied the Nigerian military that strategic and symbolic victory.

In the aftermath of Shekau's death, both factions reportedly resolved to work together after pledging allegiance to one Aba Ibrahim Al-Hashimiyil Al Khuraishi, designated as Khalifa Muslimai, or 'the Leader of all Muslims' (AFP, 2021). However, some JAS fighters led by Bakoura Buduma, a former Shekau lieutenant, refused to surrender to the ISWAP leadership. In September 2021, for instance, JAS fighters invaded and dislodged ISWAP militants based at Kirta Wulgo island. Subsequently, the ISWAP has been fighting JAS remnants who have refused to be absorbed into its fold to consolidate its grip in the northeast (Onuoha, 2013; Makama, 2022).

Ansaru al-Musulmina fi Bilad al-Sudan (Ansaru)

The Ansaru, which roughly translates as "Vanguards for the Protection of Muslims in Black Africa", was founded shortly after the 20 January 2012 Boko Haram attack in Kano that killed at least 180 people, mostly Muslims. On 2 June 2012, its self-identified leader, Abu Usmatul al-Ansari, released a video proclaiming the creation of the group and outlining its doctrines. Abu Usamatul Ansari' was a pseudonym for a former Boko Haram commander, Khalid al-Barnawi, who received jihadi training from Al-Qaeda in the Land of the Islamic Maghreb (AQIM) in Algeria in the mid-2000s (Lobe, 2012). Khalid al-Barnawi was among the three leaders of Boko Haram designated as 'global terrorists' by the US State Department on 21 June 2012. The other two leaders were Abubakar Shekau and Abubakar Adam Kambar (Mamu, 2012). Very little is known about Ansaru's command structure, funding streams, recruitment tactics, or the number of fighters at its disposal. It boasts a smaller fighting force, hovering around 300 to 500 members.

Unlike the JAS which is composed largely of Kanuris, the Ansaru drew from diverse ethnic groups, but most of its core members were Hausas and Fulanis. It operates mainly in the northwest zone of Nigeria with light footprints in Niger Republic. Although it shares *Salafist ideology*, the Ansaru:

> Considers anybody who accepted the *khalimatush shahada* (believing in one God and Prophet Muhammad as the messenger of Allah) as a Muslim who must not be killed unless, he/she has committed an act that is punishable by death as stated in the holy Qur'ran. Islam forbids the killing of innocent people including non-Muslims. This is our belief and we stand for it (Shuaib, 2012).

Thus, Ansaru's understanding of Jihad in Islam is different from that of JAS, which claims to be engaged in Jihad for the sake of Allah (Ajani & Edeh, 2013). While Shekau's JAS faction considers every non-Muslim, including Christians, an enemy that should be killed, the Ansaru abhors the killing of innocent non-Muslims except in self-defence or if they attack Muslims. Hence, Nigerian security forces and foreigners (Westerners) constitute Ansaru's main targets. Its first major attack on 26 November 2012 involved a raid on the Special Anti-Robbery Squad detention centre in Abuja, to free its members and other detainees.

Ansaru's second attack was the kidnapping of Francis Colump, a French citizen working for the French company - Vergnet, in Katsina State in December 2012. However, the kidnapping of seven foreigners – a Briton, an Italian, a Greek, and four Lebanese – on 17 February 2013, by Ansaru, was the biggest of its kind since the outbreak of terrorist violence in northern Nigeria. The group justified the abduction thusly:

Based on the transgressions and atrocities done to the religion of Allah SWT by the European countries in many places such as Afghanistan and Mali, by Allah's grace, *Jama'atu Ansarul Musilimina Fi Biladissudan* have the custody of seven persons.... It is stressed that any attempt or act contrary to our condition by the European nations or by the Nigerian government will lead to the happenings as it was in the previous attempt (Abdulkadir, 2012).

The phrase "previous attempt" apparently was a reference to the killing of Franco Lamolinara (Italian) and Christopher McManus (Briton) in Sokoto State, in March 2012, during a botched attempt by the Nigerian Forces and British Special Boat Squad to rescue them. Both hostages, who were working for an Italian construction firm, B Stabilini, in Birnin Kebbi, Kebbi State, were taken hostage in March 2011. The Ansaru was later placed on the UK Proscribed Terror List on 23 November 2012, for the kidnapping and killing of these Europeans while operating under the name *al-Qa`ida in the Lands Beyond the Sahel* (Zenn, 2019a).

The trend of Ansaru-claimed attacks from 2011 to 2013 further confirms it initially operated within Nigeria's northwest zone, such as in the states of Katsina, Kebbi, Sokoto and Kano but also extended its attacks to Abuja and Kogi in the northcentral before becoming prominent in Bauchi and even Sambisa in Borno (Nwabufo, 2016). The Ansaru has remained largely dormant from 2013 to late 2019 when it re-emerged. Violent rivalry from JAS and successful CT raids against its top leaders by Nigerian security forces greatly emasculated the group. For instance, state security service (SSS) operatives arrested its leader, Khalid al-Barnawi, in Lokoja, Kogi state, on 1 April 2016. His capture was described as "a major milestone in the counterterrorism fight." His presumed second-in-command, Bello Danhajiya, was also arrested on 13 April (Odita, 2020). Khalid al-Barnawi was among the high-profile terrorists that escaped during the ISWAP-led July 5 attack on the Kuje medium security prison.

Although the group largely restricted its presence to periodic online statements to reassure of its existence, it has increased its online and offline footprints in the terrorism landscape since 2019. For instance, Ansaru released its first message in Fulfulde, a language widely spoken across northern Nigeria and the Sahel in May 2019. Later in October 2019, the group announced its return through the Al Qaeda propaganda channel, the Global Islamic Media Front, which released a photo of Ansaru fighters and unveiled a new media outlet for the group, the Al Yaqut Media Center. The group was blamed for the December 2019 kidnapping of two expatriates, Zaid Alas from Jordan and Isah Jabour a Syrian, both working with Traicta Ltd., in Shiroro, Niger State. They were released after the payment of ₦120 million in ransom (Nasi, 2020). The terrorists were also responsible for the kidnapping of some employees of Mothercat Construction Company, as well as Magajin Garin Daura in Katsina State. An event of notable significance in the group's resurgence was the 17 January 2020 attack on a military contingent escorting the convoy of the Emir of Potiskum along Kaduna-Zaira Road (Sadiq & Yaba, 2022). The incident, which resulted in the death of at least six people, was the group's first attack since 2013. On April 5, 2021, suspected members of the Ansaru attacked a military formation along the Kaduna-Birnin Gwari highway, killing 11 soldiers and four villagers and injuring many others (Sadiq, 2021). These attacks represent Ansaru's attempt to revive its operational strength The group is currently exploiting vulnerable rural communities and the existing climate of insecurity in the Northwest zone to deepen its recruitment, radicalisation, and fund-raising drives. In October 2021, a violent clash between members of the Ansaru group and bandits claimed the lives of at least 30 bandits around the Damari axis in Birnin Gwari, Kaduna State (Sadiql & Yaba, 2022). They also engage in recruitment and indoctrination activities in communities such as Damari, Farin Ruwa, Gobirawa, Kakini, Kazage, Kwasa Kwasa, Kutemeshi, Kuyello, Tabanni, and Unguwar Gajere. Such activities included the distribution of Sallah gifts in the form of biscuits, the performance of motorcycle stunts to the delight of villagers, and the sharing of pamphlets, flash disks, and other accessories in the activities of the group (Gaffey, 2016). It has equally kidnapped youths as part of its recruitment strategy.Analysts believe thatAnsaru militants maintain links withAl-Qaeda affiliated jihadist groups in the Sahel, such as the *Jama'at Nusrat al Islam wa al Muslimeen* (JNIM).

The Islamic State in West Africa Province

The ISWAP faction emerged in June 2016, when it was reported that Boko Haram has fractured internally, with a large group splitting away from Shekau over his failure to adhere to guidance from ISIS (Idris, 2016). On 2 August 2016, ISIS named Abu Musab al-Barnawi as the new leader of ISWAP. He was previously the spokesman for Boko Haram under Shekau. Shortly after his nomination, al-Barnawi made a caustic rejection of Shekau's leadership, lambasting him for targeting ordinary Muslims and promising to concentrate attacks largely on Christians.

The designation infuriated Shekau who denounced al-Barnawi in an audio message as an infidel (Idris, 2016). Shekau's outburst triggered a propaganda tirade between the two jihadi leaders. On 6 August 2016, al-Barnawi's faction with the support of Mamman Nur, released an audio message denouncing Shekau as a hypocrite and coward. They claimed that Shekau was ousted because of various offences, including the killing of fellow Muslims, living in luxury while his fighters starved, and committing sacrileges that affected the sanctity of their jihadist campaign. As with past infighting, the schism was primarily driven by ideological and tactical differences between Shekau and those who oppose his *takfirist* approach to Islamic jihadism.

Like the Ansaru, the ISWAP also disagreed with Shekau's takfirist stance (Samuel, 2019). Hence, ISWAP has sought to distance itself strategically and operationally from the Shekau-led JAS. The ISWAP operates largely in the northern parts of Borno and the islands in the Lake Chad area covering Nigeria, Cameroon, and Chad, providing some services in the communities it occupies (Campbell, 2021). This has enabled it to generate huge amounts of funding from the areas it controls by collecting taxes from farmers and fishermen and imposing passage and protection fees on business people. In February 2019, it was estimated that ISWAP boasts around two to three times more fighters (3,500-5,000) than Shekau's faction (1,500- 2,000) (Zenn, 2019a). It is reported to have an unspecified number of foreign terrorist fighters, possibly of Chadian, Libyan or other North-African origin, including Caucasian foreign fighter commanders (GlobalSecurity.org, n.d.; Zenn, 2019b; Salkida, 2021).

The ISWAP focuses mainly on attacking military and government targets. The group has attempted to avoid targeting Muslims although it has carried out attacks on civilians, including executing captured humanitarian actors and Christians. In July 2020, for instance, ISWAP fighters reportedly executed Mr. Ishaku Yakubu, Action Against Hunger (ACF) staff member, and four other aid workers, whom they abducted on 8 June 2020 (France24, 2020). Its attacks in Nigeria include a few notable ones. In February 2018, the group abducted 110 schoolgirls in Dapchi and in March, it kidnapped three aid workers during an attack that killed dozens of other people. On 18 November 2018, the group attacked an army base in the village of Metele, in northeastern Borno State, Nigeria and killed some Nigerian soldiers. In June 2019, the group attacked two military bases in the towns of Marte and Kirenowa, near the Borno state capital Maiduguri, Nigeria.

As it has grown in influence in the intervening years, its leadership has changed due to internal rivalries as well as successful airstrikes by the Nigerian Air Force and ground offensives by the Nigerian Army. In 2018, Abu Musab al-Barnawi's long- time ally, Mamman Nur, who had ties historically to AQIM and Al-Shabab was purged from ISWAP and eventually killed on orders from ISIS (Ibraheem, 2020). In March 2019, Abu Musab al-Barnawi himself was purged from ISWAP in favour of the more hard-line Abu Abdullah Ibn Umar al-Barnawi, *alias* Ba Idrissa. Meanwhile, Ba'a Idrissa was reportedly overthrown in February 2020 and was replaced by Abba Gana aka Ba-Lawan (Oyema-Aziken, 2022). In May 2021, Abu Musab al-Barnawi was reinstated as the "caretaker" leader of ISWAP. He was later killed in August 2021, paving the way for Malam Bako to assume leadership of the ISWAP. Mallam Bako was killed by Nigerian security forces in October 2021, forcing the group to name Sani Shuwaram as its leader in November 2021. Following the killing of Sani

Shuwaram in February 2022 in an airstrike by the Nigerian Air Force, Bako Gorgore became ISWAP's leader in March 2022 (Olaniyi, 2022).

Impacts of Terrorism and Insurgency in Nigeria

The ongoing terror attacks by BHT have had devastating effects on Nigeria economically, politically, socially, and environmentally among others. Since 2009, Boko Haram has killed 350,000 people in northeast Nigeria and displaced three million people in the Lake Chad Basin region. The insurgency reportedly destroyed infrastructure worth $9bn in Nigeria (Punch 2019; Onuoha and Oyewole 2018). Low levels of education and literacy in northeast Nigeria have been exacerbated by the Boko Haram insurgency. Activities of BHT in the North-East have undermined education in the zone, with more than 910 schools destroyed between 2009 and 2015, and 1,500 forced to close (Udegbunam, 2022).

Beyond the destruction of lives and properties, the insurgency has negatively impacted socio-economic activities, as attacks, abductions and the imposition of levies on farmers, fishermen, and business people have contributed to a collapse of productivity or livelihoods as well as growing food insecurity in Nigeria. On 28 November 2020, for instance, BHT massacred more than 100 rice farmers in Zabarmari, Jere Local Government Area of Borno State. This has implications for human wellbeing, particularly with regard to food insecurity (Agbelusi, 2022). Nigeria has an estimated 91 million people living in extreme poverty, which is projected to reach 106.6 million by 2030.

Security-wise, BHT has heightened other challenges in Nigeria such as the proliferation of small arms and light weapons and the rise in kidnapping for ransom due to close networking with other criminal groups such as bandits operating in the Northwest. The result is that Nigeria has become less peaceful and largely insecure. The Global Peace Index for 2021 ranked Nigeria 146th out of 163 countries with a score of 2.712, while among Sub-Saharan African countries, the country was ranked 39th out of 44 countries examined in the region (Agbelusi, 2022).

The insecurity associated with the insurgency affects economic growth by drying- out investments, increasing unemployment, and bloating the government's expenditure on security, among others. The impact is reflected in the performance of macroeconomic indicators, investment inflow, and economic performance. As of 2020, over $40.6 billion worth of foreign investments were diverted from the Nigerian economy as a result of insecurity (Okafor, 2021). The insecurity challenge also affected other sectors in terms of government revenue allocation as the security budget continues to increase year after year. Data from BudgitIT shows that in 2020 the Federal Government allotted ₦1.78 trillion for security expenses, which is approximately an 83.7 percent increase from the ₦969 allocated for the same in 2015 (UNODC, 2020).

Furthermore, Nigeria's inability to defeat the insurgency more than ten years after it started, greatly undermines its image in the comity of nations. It has led several foreign countries to issue repeated disparaging reports against Nigeria, including advising their citizens on the dangers of visiting the country. This, in turn, adds to the loss of foreign earnings that accrue from foreign direct investments and tourism. In addition, the BHT has forced Nigeria to contribute less of its military to peace support operations, an engagement in which Nigeria once prided itself as the leading actor in Africa in that global responsibility. Another obvious impact of BHT is the false sense of confidence their daring attacks bestow on their fighters. By boldly attacking military formations, the terrorists have tended to demonstrate their audacity despite the degradation of their combat capability.

Notable Counterterrorism and Counterinsurgency Measures to Defeat the Boko Haram Terrorists

The activities of the BHT constitutes existential threat to the Nigerian state. Diverse CTCOIN initiatives have been adopted by the Nigerian government to defeat the group. These include legislative, prosecutorial, law enforcement, military, and socio- economic measures. A few notable ones are worth highlighting.

Legislative Initiative

The Nigerian government enacted some legal or statutory instruments to facilitate national efforts at combating the threat of terrorism and insurgency. These include the Terrorism Prevention Act 2011 (as amended in 2013 and 2022); Money Laundering (Prohibition) Act, 2011, and the Nigerian Financial Intelligence Unit Act 2018, among others. These instruments provide comprehensive legal, regulatory and institutional frameworks for the detection, prevention, prohibition, and prosecution of terrorism and insurgency. They equally enable multi-agency cooperation and strategic partnerships for CTCOIN in Nigeria. To strengthen the operationalisation of these laws, the Nigerian government has partnered with the European Union and the United Nations Office on Drugs and Crime (UNODC) to deliver over 82 capacity-building activities, including providing extensive training to select groups of investigators, legal advisors, defence attorneys, prosecutors, and judges on a range of practically-focused terrorism-related criminal justice issues in Nigeria (UNODC, n.d). However, it takes more than ambitious legislation to effectively tackle terrorism.

Strategic Guidance Initiative

The federal government has also evolved strategic frameworks to underpin a holistic response to the wave of insecurity associated with violent extremism and terrorism. Such guidance frameworks include the National Counter Terrorism Strategy (2014), the National Security Strategy (2019), and the Policy Framework and National Action Plan for Preventing and Countering Violent Extremism (2017), among others. The Policy Framework highlights access to justice, human rights, the rule of law, and community engagement to prevent and counter Boko Haram extremism. Overall, these strategic policy documents provide the overarching blueprint for a whole-of-society 'soft'approach to dealing with the threat of terrorism, insurgency, and violent extremism (Nseyen, 2020). Notwithstanding their adoption, terrorism thrives partly due to the failure of the government to address the objective conditions that enable it to fester such as pervasive poverty, widespread unemployment, a sense of injustice, and impunity by security forces, among others.

Policing Initiative

Law enforcement measures in the form of routine and special operations are being executed by the police as well as intelligence, customs, immigration, and drug officials to detect, disrupt and defeat criminal elements involved in terrorism. These interventions have led to the arrest and prosecution of BHT. Recently in February 2020, the Police's Special Forces raided the Kuduru

Forest, in Birnin Gwari, Kaduna State, which hosts members of the Ansaru terrorist group, bandits, and kidnappers (Odita, 2020). The police claimed they killed over 250 terrorists and bandits in the operations. In May 2020, nine members of the group who had received training in Libya were also arrested by the police in their hideouts in Kaduna, Kano, and Katsina States (Elumoye, 2022). Notwithstanding the modest successes recorded, weak inter-agency collaboration, a faltering intelligence structure, and a deficiency in forensic skills have limited the impact of law enforcement operations.

Prosecutorial Initiative

Leveraging extisting legal instruments, the Nigerian government has successfully prosecuted some BHT and their corroborators. In August 2022, for instance, the Attorney-General of the Federation, Abubakar Malami, revealed that the Federal Ministry of Justice has secured no fewer than 1,000 convictions on terrorism within 18 months (Ngari & Olojo, 2020). However, the prosecution of suspected Boko Haram members has been characterized by several shortcomings: - weak investigation capacity; arbitrary arrests; unlawful detention; alleged exclusion of victims from observing or testifying in the legal proceedings; lack of official interpreters/use of untrained unofficial interpreters; absence of legal aid; and a dearth of prosecutable evidence (Onyedinefu, 2022). The government's prosecutorial approach has thus failed to inspire public confidence in its anti-terrorism campaign. In February 2022, for instance, the Federal Government claimed that it had uncovered 96 terrorist financiers, 424 associates of the financiers, 123 companies and 33 bureau de change linked to terrorism (Onuoha et al, 2020). Several months later, these accused persons were yet to be duly prosecuted.

Military Operations

The deployment of troops in CTCOIN operations remains the most visible kinetic response to BHT. This takes place at the national and regional (Lake Chad Basic Commission) levels. At the national level, successive military operations against the group include *Op FLUSH* (2009) *Op RESTORE ORDER* (2011), *Op BOYONA* (2013), *Op ZAMAN LAFIYA* (2013), and *Op LAFIYA DOLE* (2015), and *Op HADIN KAI* (2021). These operations were geared toward degrading, deterring, and defeating the insurgents (ReliefWeb, 2022). Military operations against the BHT have recorded modest successes, such as the arrest and killing of commanders, the interdiction of their logistics, the destruction of safe havens, and the disruption of networks, among others. CTCOIN operations have significantly decreased Boko Haram's fatalities, although attacks have persisted, as evident in Figure 32.

Figure 32: Incidents and Fatalities from the Boko Haram Insurgency, 2009–2021

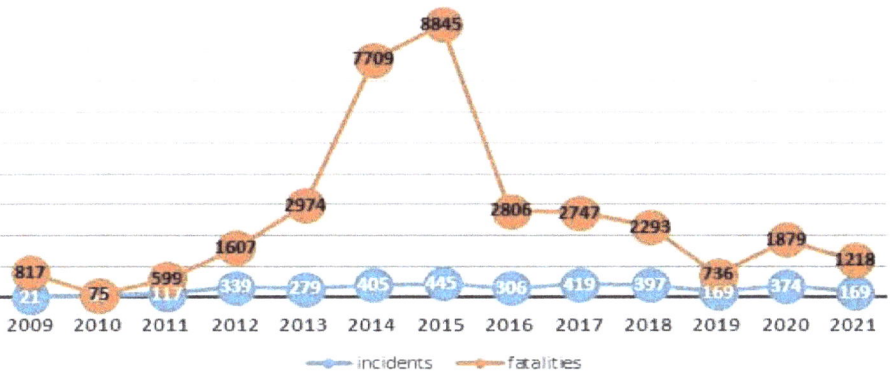

Source: Authors' compilation from the Armed Conflict Location & Event Data (ACLED).

Deaths dropped by 92% from 2,131 in 2015 to 178 in 2021. The decline in BHT casualties contributed to Nigeria recording the second-largest reduction in deaths from terrorism in 2021, with the number falling by 47% to 448 (ReliefWeb, 2022). At the national level, the low manpower strength of the military presents a challenge to the prosecution of its operations. The challenge of holding on to manpower to effectively cover the North-East theatre and other parts of the country is being addressed by the Nigerian Army through increased recruitment of soldiers. The Depot Nigerian Army in Zaria currently trains two strings of soldiers yearly towards boosting the personnel strength of the Nigerian Army. The positive effect is visible in the increased footprints of the Nigerian Army in trouble areas nationwide.

In addition, the Nigeria Police and the Nigeria Security and Civil Defence Corps have proven incapable of holding territories cleared by the military, thereby stalling the ability of the troops to advance into the Tunbuns (island) of Lake Chad as well as the Sambisa Forest, where remnants of the terrorist operate from (I.N Abbas, personal communication, August 24, 2022).

At the regional level, Nigerian troops are deployed with the MNJTF to combat Boko Haram in the Lake Chad region. As of August 2022, the MNJTF had over 13,000 troops drawn from Cameroon, Chad, Niger, Nigeria, and Benin (A.K. Ibrahim, personal communication, August 22, 2022). The intervention of the MNJTF has contributed to reducing the threat of the BHT and pushing them back into their sanctuaries in the Tunbuns of Lake Chad and caves in Sambisa Forest. The operations of the regional force have largely failed to achieve their objectives due to the pursuit of vested interests by states, frequent change of the leadership of the military component of the MNJTF, inadequate military assets, and resource constraints. There is also the challenge of the absence of an integrated, region- wide deradicalisation programme. While Nigeria and Niger have deradicalisation programmes, Cameroon and Chad do not. The MNJTF is thus left with no option but to hand over terrorists who surrender to their country of origin for processing.

Reconstruction and Resettlement Initiatives

The Nigerian government has also undertaken some initiatives aimed at addressing poverty, unemployment, and destitution, which contribute to the security threats. Interventions such as the N-Power Programme, for instance, seek to deliver large- scale skill development for Nigerian youth to remove the conditions that terrorist ideologues have exploited in recruiting youths.Additionally, the Presidential Initiative for the North-East (PINE) is a large-scale intervention being implemented to jumpstart the economy of the North-East while repositioning the region for long- term prosperity (State House, 2016). The paucity of funds, patronage politics, and corruption have meant that these interventions hardly benefit the intended targets – vulnerable individuals and impacted communities (Kazeem, 2016).

Reformation and Rehabilitation Initiatives

A notable non-kinetic initiative to deal with the threat of terrorism and insecurity is a defection programme known as 'Operation Safe Corridor' (OPSC) (Onuoha, 2020). Conceived in September 2015, it is a multi-sectoral programme involving 17 government agencies administering specific projects but coordinated by the military. The programme exposes the beneficiaries to psycho-social therapy, training on citizenship, and the acquisition of vocational skills, such as carpentry, tailoring, vulcanising, welding, and barbeing, among others. Upon completion, they are assisted with grants to set up businesses in their various communities. In February 2020, a government official revealed that about 1,400 repentant Boko Haram suspects had been released in three tranches and re-integrated into society since the OPSC started in 2016 (Olugbode, 2020).

The conception and delivery of the OPSC program, however, are fraught with challenges such as a lack of discernible legal framework, weak coordination among relevant agencies, the absence of gender mainstreaming, overt militarisation, and limited consultation with prospective communities that will receive rehabilitated Boko Haram members (Ugwueze et al, 2021). As at 8 April 2023, 93,900 former Boko Haram fighters and their families have surrendered to the military. It is unlikely that Operation Safe Corridor has adequate capacity to effectively process, deradicalize, and rehabilitate the large number of fighters surrendering.

Conclusion

Boko Haram has demonstrated resilience and remains a formidable threat to the Nigerian state despite sustained national and regional CTCOIN operations against it. Nigeria's CTCOIN measures have yielded some successes amidst several setbacks. In spite of the various measures adopted by the Nigerian government, Boko Haram continues to demonstrate resilience and adaptability enabled by the transnational flow of ideological influence from global Salafi Jihadist Islamism.

To defeat the insurgency, there is a need for a major review and reinforcement of the nation's strategy. The Nigerian government's overall strategy and trial procedures need to conform to constitutional safeguards and international standards. In addition, authorities should prioritize the prosecution of those most responsible for providing financial and material support to the group's atrocities, leveraging opportunities offered by global collaborative initiatives such as the Global Programme on Detecting, Preventing, and Countering the Financing of Terrorism (CFT Programme) and relevant universal legal instruments that prohibit money laundering, terrorist financing, and transnational organised crime. Such collaborations at the bilateral, regional and multilateral levels promote intelligence sharing, lessons adaptation, and the acquisition of high-end technology that is critical to defeating ideologically driven and formidable terrorist organisations.

There is equally a need to re-assess and strengthen frameworks for civil-military- humanitarian cooperation and cross-border collaboration to stem the flow of terrorists, the influx of weapons and the prevalence of organised crime. The breadth of past and ongoing CTCOIN operations calls for the Presidency to establish a specialised body (the Strategic Review Team - SRT) to provide an independent and objective evaluation of military operations to ascertain what has been achieved and identify lessons to improve current and future operations. Nigeria's political leadership needs to prioritise and galvanise investment in the local defence manufacturing sector, to minimise the country's strategic vulnerability to the external defence sector and shore up military combat efficiency through defence self-sufficiency.

The military should take reports and petitions of human rights abuses seriously. A robust feedback and dissemination strategy is required to ensure that reports of human rights abuses are thoroughly investigated and the findings are publicly disseminated. A robust feedback mechanism will help to rebuild and sustain public trust and confidence between the population, government, and military. Concerted measures should be taken by the government and civil society to work collaboratively in addressing the root causes or drivers of conflict and violence in Nigeria through a comprehensive peace-development nexus approach. The ONSA should properly resource its strategic communication programme to more effectively counter the violent incentives and narratives of Salafi jihadi ideology.

Section Three

CTCOIN: Leading From The Front

Yahaya, Chief of Army Staff as Theatre Commander, Operation LAFIYA DOLE

Lt Gen F Yahaya, Chief of Army Staff as Theatre Commander, Operation LAFIYA DOLE

Evolution of CTCOIN Operations in North East Nigeria

Is killing a known terrorist wrong? I ask this, did the terrorist allow any of his victims quarter? No, then allow him no quarter, and hoist the black flag.
TR Wallace

We can't accommodate terrorism. When someone uses the slaughter of innocent people to advance a so-called political cause, at that point the political cause becomes immoral and unjust and they should be eliminated from any serious discussion, any serious debate.
Rudolph Giuliani

Globally military operations are organised to resolve certain security challenges that threaten the peace and security of states or actors. Military operations could be carried out in peace time, during a crisis, or during war. It could be combat operations or non-combat operations, depending on what the situation demands. Military operations could be typified on the basis of scale and scope. Military operations could be orchestrated through a coalition of global military efforts against a common adversary. When it is beyond the scope of a nation's effort, military operations, could be on a sub-regional basis as we had in ECOMOG or by a group of contiguous countries such as the Multinational Joint Task Force in the Lake Chad Basin region, which was organised by Nigeria, Niger, Cameroun, Chad, and Benin Republic. It could also be an aggregation of regional forces, such as the African Union Mission in Sudan, or transregional forces, as exemplified by the North Atlantic Treaty Organization forces in different theatres of operation in Kosovo, Iraq, and Afghanistan. Additionally, military operations could be organised under the auspices of the United Nations and replicated all over the world. By scope, it is possible to have a theatre-level operation, a military campaign, a battle, an engagement, strikes, and other offensive or defensive military engagements.

The Nigerian military has been involved in one form of operation or another since Nigeria's independence from Great Britain in 1960. The Armed

Forces of Nigeria had participated in several operations within and outside the country prior to the commencement of the Boko Haram crisis. Lt Gen Faruk Yahaya participated in these operations in different capacities. In Nigeria, Boko Haram terrorism and insurgency began in 2009 following the killing of their leader, Mohammed Yusuf. The group of terrorists and insurgents attacked military locations, police stations, and other security agencies. Boko Haram also attacked government installations, critical national infrastructure, schools, villages and other soft targets. Accordingly, the Federal Government of Nigeria ordered the military and other security forces to curb the activities of this terrorist and insurgent group. This sets the stage for the series of operations that were conducted to counter terrorism and the insurgency that ensued within the Nigeria security space for over a decade. The counter terrorism effort of the Nigerian Army began in the form of minor internal security operations, keeping the peace in the usually quiet commercial city of Maiduguri amidst its traditional social and political environment which influences entire Borno State and extends up to Yobe State. The internal security operations were initially conducted by 21 Brigade of the Nigerian Army, under whose area of operation the entire Borno and major parts of Yobe were. Situation soon went out of control, and that more deliberate effort had to be put in place. The countering efforts started under the 21 Brigade but in a more organized operational space with different nicknames before developing into what they are today. The operations began with Op FLUSH OUT I & II then Op RESTORE ORDER I, II & III before transiting into Op BOYONA, then Op ZAMAN LAFIYA, Op LAFIYA DOLE before the ongoing Op HADIN KAI.

Operation FLUSH OUT

Op FLUSH OUT I was set up in 1998 by the Borno State Government as an internal security operation against bandits that usually attack traders, commuters and businessmen and businesswomen in the state. Their bandits' activities were prevalent at the fringes of the Lake Chad Basin. They usually attack from their hide outs in the forests and rural communities or waylaid commuters on the roads, especially in the deserted or unfrequented stretches. Prior to 2009, the activities of these bandits were on the increase, and the security forces involved in the operations were really hard on them. Subsequently, the unrelenting banditry metamorphosed into radical, violent extremist activities, including those of the Boko Haram Islamists movement. Though Boko Haram Islamists were aggressive in their religious disposition, they avoided violence in pursuit of their beliefs. They carried out public debates and embarked on public awareness campaigns in order to propagate their ideology. As they continued with their doctrine, they attracted huge followership amongst the unemployed youths and soon spread across the northern region of Nigeria. They soon became violent in their approach following the enlightened public's resentments of their ideals and ways. Though they were predominantly in Borno State, they had followers in Adamawa, Bauchi, Kano, Plateau and Yobe States. Op FLUSH OUT was therefore aimed at curbing armed banditry and restraining the activities of the Boko Haram Islamists in Borno State and environs.

The Nigeria Police Force was the lead agency for the operations, which were internal security operation, as enshrined in the 1999 Constitution of the Federal Republic of Nigeria and re-echoed in the National Security Strategy. However, Op FLUSH OUT I had other agencies such as the DSS, NIS and NCS. The Police Mobile Force was initially in charge, but as the situation deteriorated, 21 Brigade, Nigerian Army was invited to support the police. The brigade was deployed to some key points and vulnerable points, such as motor parks, markets, and other public places. Though the activities of these bandits were somewhat under control with the reinforcement of Op FLUSH OUT I by the Nigerian Army troops of the 21 Brigade, especially in Maiduguri City, they continued to deteriorate as Boko Haram Islamists ideology spread, uptil to sometime in 2009. Highways were becoming more unsafe, residents were living in fear, and the ideology of Boko Haram extended to other North Eastern States of Nigeria. Many of the attacks on people within Maiduguri City and on highways were then traced to Boko Haram Islamists. There were also attacks on security forces, especially Nigerian Police Force personnel. The Borno State Government then initiated Op FLUSH OUT II to give more bite to the Internal Security architecture. The military component of the operation was expanded and the entire Op FLUSH OUT II was placed under a military commander, Col BI Ahanotu (NA Publication, 2022).

Troops for the operation were generated within 3 Division Nigerian Army. All units and formations within the division contributed troops. The Multi-National Joint Task Force in Baga as well as the 79 Composite Group of the

Nigerian Air Force in Maiduguri also contributed some troops to this operation. All the military troops were playing basic infantry roles. However, the paramilitary and other security agencies personnel were not fully under the command of the military commander. They report to and through their statutory command and control channels. The operation also involved the employment of sub-conventional security forces such as local vigilantes and hunters, leveraging their local knowledge for intelligence purposes. At that time, the Nigerian Army in particular and the entire Armed Forces of Nigeria were new to counter terrorism and counter insurgency operations. At best, the Armed Forces of Nigeria had been involved in Internal Security Operations across the country, but not on the scale of terrorism and insurgency being displayed by Boko Haram Islamists. The AFN had to learn how to adapt conventional military training to non-conventional employment in the form of counter-terrorism and counter-insurgency. During Op FLUSH OUT II, many special operations were conducted to rid Maiduguri and its environs of armed bandits and Boko Haram Islamists who had become terrorists and insurgents. Mohammed Yusuf, the leader of the Boko Haram Islamists had undertaken to avenge the alleged highhandedness of the security forces on his followers. Accordingly, there were many attacks on security forces, especially the Nigeria Police Force personnel, equipment, and stations. Troops embarked on different types of patrols to dominate flash points and vulnerable areas, including cordon and search operations, raids, established control points, road blocks, and check points as well as VIP escorts and protection duties. Soon the Boko Haram terrorists and insurgents violent attacks spread across many northern states especially Borno, Yobe, Bauchi, and Kano.

In response, the security forces, including the Armed Forces of Nigeria, had to go after Mohammed Yusuf and his followers to check their violent attacks against citizens and security forces, which resulted in inflicting casualties on some of them. On 27 July 2009, Op FLUSH OUT II troops arrested Mohammed Yusuf and neutralised some of his men. Mohammed Yusuf was subsequently handed over to the police for prosecution. Unfortunately, he was declared dead by the police after a few days in custody. His death sparked a more violent round of attacks against ordinary citizens, and security forces, including the military, across Maiduguri, Galadima, Kasuwan Shanu, and Low Cost areas. There were hues and cries across the country for a state of emergency to be declared, especially in those affected local government areas. However, the government exercised some restraints. The Nigerian Army troops were therefore reinforced with men and equipment to restore law and order in the affected areas.

Troops cracked down heavily on the terrorists and insurgents from 2009 to 2010. Subsequently, many of the terrorists went into hiding in different places; a new leader, Abubakar Shekau, emerged, and Boko Haram re-strategized. Some of their fighting forces were sent for training in different parts of the world such as Somalia, Libya, and Afghanistan, as would be revealed by some of the terrorists that were later arrested at different locations or captured in battle. Apparently, Abubakar Shekau was more violent than his erstwhile leader, Mohammed Yusuf. By late 2010, Boko Haram violent attacks returned and became more sophisticated. They used guerrilla tactics and assault rifles to attacks security forces, including the Nigerian Army troops. In 2011, the government reassessed the security situation, disbanded Op FLUSH OUT II and launched Op RESTORE ORDER. Some issues were observed during Op FLUSH OUT II, which include the force generation process, the state of readiness of troops, kitting and equipment, and the information and intelligence sharing mechanism. Leadership and command issues in the field, media operations issues, support from the local population, as well as weather and terrain issues, were also noted. Nonetheless, the operation recorded some successes in the capture of Mohammed Yusuf, enhancing cooperation amongst security agencies, reducing banditry and promoting of joint intelligence sharing. It also espoused the need for the development of indigenous capacity in counterterrorism and counter insurgency tactics and strategies in the Armed Forces of Nigeria. At the twilight of Op FLUSH OUT, Col Faruk Yahaya was serving in the Army Headquarters Department of Military Secretary, generating the officers to be posted to the field as part of the manpower requirements for the operation. A role he also played during Op RESTORE ORDER.

Operation RESTORE ORDER

Op RESTORE ORDER (ORO) effectively commenced on 15 June 2011 (NA Publication, 2022). Its main objective was to defeat Boko Haram terrorists and insurgents in all their strongholds, restore peace, and facilitate law and order in Borno and Yobe States. At this time, the notorious activities of the Boko Haram group had surrounded the entire

Borno State and extended to Yobe State as well as the northern fringes of Adamawa State. ORO employed both land and air power to orchestrate its forces and it leveraged the efforts of other security agencies within the joint operation area. It also relied on intelligence from the local populace. The Borno State capital, Maiduguri, was mapped into 11 sectors and sub-sectors under different commanders who reported to the Joint Task Force (JTF) Commander. Forward Operation Bases were also established in some important towns like Azare (in Bauchi State), Biu, Daban Masara, Damasak, Damboa, Dikwa, Gamboru, Krenoa, all in Borno State, and Mubi (in Adamawa State).

ORO had a strength of over 3800 troops from the NA, NN, NAF, NPF, DSS, NCS, NIS, and DIA. Most of the NA troops were from within 3 Division, with some special forces elements from 72 SF Bn. The specific tasks of the JTF ORO were to defeat insurgency, restore law and order to the North East especially Borno State, regain control of areas under Boko Haram occupation, support local security agencies in restoring peace in areas affected by the insurgents, protect the civilian population, reduce collateral damage, defeat the radical ideology, and mitigate its impact in Borno, Yobe, and Adamawa States. The complexity of the crisis in Borno State soon increased to the point that ORO had to be enhanced so that it could be more effective and have wider coverage up to Yobe State. Thus ORO I was scaled up to ORO II to cover both Borno and Yobe States.

However, tt was observed that the situation in both states soon went out of the control of ORO II. Accordingly, ORO III was established by merging both ORO I and ORO II as a more potent response to Boko Haram terrorism. ORO III embarked on serious intelligence-led operations. There were significant civil-military relations activities in ORO III, thus engaging both kinetic and non-kinetic strategies to execute operations. One very interesting aspect of ORO III was the positive engagement of the civil population network and local hunters for community policing, information/intelligence gathering, and embedding some of them during operations to identify Boko Haram terrorists or collaborators. Some willingly repented Boko Haram members were also engaged on the side of government forces to provide intelligence. ORO III was a joint operation between the Nigerian Army, Nigerian Navy, and Nigerian Air Force. The troops welfare and other incentives were better handled, and quick intervention forces were introduced at some vulnerable locations.

Personnel from the Nigeria Police Force, the State Security Service and other security agencies were also involved. ORO III and the MNJTF in the Lack Chad Region worked in close collaboration. The joint intelligence cell of ORO was very effective and assisted in the successes recorded within the joint operation area. The operation was better resourced than the previous ones and it made some remarkable impacts. ORO banned the use of motorcycles in Maiduguri and environs to reduce IED attacks in the towns and conducted several cordon and search operations, long-range patrols, and CIMIC activities to win the hearts and mind of the locals. The operation was able to significantly isolate the insurgents from Maiduguri and its environs. The insurgents then sought refuge in the Sambisa Forest, and other adjoining forests from where they coordinated their guerilla attacks.

Despite the successes achieved, ORO recorded a major setback with the attack on Bama on 7 May 2013. The terrorists attacked key points in the town, including the police barracks, and the 202 Tank Battalion in Kur Mohammed Cantonment, Bama. It was apparent that the local population cooperated with the terrorists by keeping information about the attack away from security forces, which brought to the fore the significance of the people in any irregular warfare. It was thus clear that the nature and enormity of the threat were strategically misunderstood. The porosity of the nation's border within the North East region was a challenge to the quick resolution of the problems. Similarly, the nature of the North-East terrain constitutes a major logistical burden for troops. There were instances when troops' equipment and vehicles bogged down, thus rendering them vulnerable to terrorists who had better knowledge of the ground. The capacity of the Nigerian military for counter insurgency or other non-conventional operations was also a problem. These issues kept growing, and Boko Haram ideology, terrorism, and insurgency spread in the North. The operation was reviewed, and Op BOYONA was established.

Operation BOYONA

From 2012 to 2013, Boko Haram's insurgency evolved into a serious national security concern. The Nigerian Army was at the forefront of CTCOIN operations as the government responded to this challenge. The previous JTF made attempts at restoring normalcy and building confidence in the populace through checking, monitoring, and controlling the influx of illegal immigrants into the country, especially in the adjoining areas of the affected states. It should be noted that the initial response to the Boko Haram insurgency was not holistic. According to the Nigerian Army Pamphlet on Op BOYONA 2022, "This largely explains the gradual but steady metamorphosis of the terror group. Initially, the group was viewed as mere irritants and religious fanatics that would fizzle out over time. Secondly, the politicization of the responses to the threat was another undoing that facilitated the transformation of the terror group. When it became clear that the attacks and terror of the group continued unabated, accentuated by incessant killing, destruction of properties, and the setbacks suffered in the CTCOIN operations, there was a need to rejig the security architecture by establishing a new outfit to contain the escalating menace of Boko Haram terrorists. By this time, the casualty level in the North-East from Boko Haram attacks kept increasing and became unacceptable". That was the situation before Op BOYONA was launched.

Consequent upon the deteriorating security situation in the North-East, the president and Commander-in-Chief of the Armed Forces of Nigeria, Goodluck Jonathan, declared a state of emergency in Borno, Yobe, and Adamawa States on 14 May 2013 (Nigerian Army, 2022). The then Chief of Defence Staff, Admiral Ola Sa'ad Ibrahim, was subsequently directed to restore law and order in the affected states.

In line with the directives, troops made up of men of the Armed Forces of Nigeria, Nigeria Police Force and other para-military and security organisations were deployed under Op BOYONA to secure the affected states and restore peace and order. The acronym BOYONA stood for Borno, Yobe, Nasarawa, and Adamawa. The addition of Nasarawa was attributed to the menace of Ombatse cult activities experienced in the state between late 2012 and 2013. The untoward activities of the Ombatse Militia Group, under the spiritual leadership of Baba Alakyo in Nasarawa Eggon, resulted in the killing of over 70 policemen and 10 DSS officials. However, the cult was subdued before Op BOYONA was launched. The inclusion of Adamawa to the Area of Operation was because it was contiguous to Borno State, where Boko Haram was gradually establishing itself among the locals, especially in the northern part. The Boko Haram sect also had sleeper cells in

Yola, the state capital. This led to the coinage of Op BOYONA meaning Op Borno, Yobe, Nasarawa, and Adamawa. For continuity, the commander of the subsumed Op ORO Maj Gen JAH Ewansiha, was assigned the command of Op BOYONA based on experience. The headquarters of Op BOYONA was at Maiduguri, under the operational control of the DHQ (Nigerian Army, 2022).

The main target of Op BOYONA was to contain the nefarious activities of Boko Haram terrorists and insurgents and to restore of law and order in Borno, Yobe, and Adamawa states, with some specific objectives including the destruction of terrorist camps/bases in Borno, Yobe and Adamawa states, identify and arrest the perpetrators of terrorism in the states of Borno, Yobe and Adamawa, and bring perpetrators of terror in Borno, Yobe and Adamawa states to justice. Op BOYONA leveraged the existing organisation of ORO with a little modification in the grouping of forces. More troops, weapons, and equipment were inducted to clear the terrorists and insurgents from Northern Borno, Sambisa Forest, Gwoza Hills, and Maiduguri metropolis. On 16 May 2013, Combat Team A in the Northern Sector of 21 Bde advanced from Monguno and dislodged the BHI from old Marte, Krenoa, and Hausari on 17 May 2013. Concurrently, on 16 May 2013, combat Team B commenced its offensive from Gamboru Ngala through Bagara Waji and secured Wulge, Wulgo, and Chikun Gudu. Team B thereafter pushed further to Kala Balge LGA before returning to Gamboru Ngala. Combat Team C dislodged terrorists and insurgents from New Marte, Sand Ridge Pump Station, Logomani, and adjoining villages.

In the Southern Sector of 21 Brigade, the Sambisa Forest, covering 1,024 square kilometres and identified as the major stronghold of the insurgents, was the main focus. The offensive operation was led by Lt Cols M Danmadami and AG Laka along with Capt Nandang of the Engrs in support. The troops were sourced from the 202 Bn Bama, 82 Bn, and HQ JTF ORO in Maiduguri. Combat Team D, comprising 202 and 82 Bns supported by artillery, was used to find, fix strike, and prevent further infiltration of Boko Haram insurgents from the forest. However, due to adverse weather conditions, the NAF was unable to provide the planned Close Air Support to the advancing troops. The 2 teams subsequently advanced in order to achieve surprise, but failed to secure central Sambisa on 20 May 2013. The team had an encounter with the insurgents, killing scores of them, while Abubakar Shekau was wounded in the operation.

On 13 June 2013, based on the intelligence that Ibrahim Gontalek was holding out on Gwoza hills in the Mandara Mountains, the Rapid Deployment Force (RDF) was tasked to dislodge the miscreants from Gwoza hills and to hold the area. In this operation, Maj AT Fanbiya, who displayed exceptional gallantry during the operation, contributed largely to the success recorded by troops in Gwoza. However, the valiant officer was KIA during the hard-won battle. Usually, when an operation requires massive manpower, reinforcement is provided from adjoining sectors. There were also surveillance aircraft such as the Beechcraft ATR that were called upon for recce support; however, the Alpha Jets and the Mi35 Helicopters were not equipped with night navigation and fighting capabilities, thereby limiting operations to daylight and good weather conditions only. Additional fire support from the artillery regiment attached to Op BOYONA played an enabling role in the operation. The artillery regiments from Kachia and Bauchi, which had earlier arrived in Maiduguri on 20 May 2013 with six 105mm Pack Howitzer guns, were used to dislodge Boko Haram insurgents from Harasa Hills in Gwoza.

The JTF troops within Maiduguri metropolis continued to conduct cordon and search raids and road blocks to apprehend escaping Boko Haram insurgents and those trying to infiltrate the town from the northern and southern sectors. The cordon and search operations were conducted based on intelligence and led to the arrest of several Boko Haram insurgents and criminals. This was the highest number of arrests since the commencement of CTCOIN operations in the North-East. Also deployed to Maiduguri metropolis was the AHQ MP K-9 unit with its military trained dogs. The dogs were used for searches after Boko Haram fighters and their Amir Abu Kaka were dislodged from Bulabulin Nganaram while this was complemented by intermittent searches at the Maiduguri Airport. Furthermore, the Bulabulin area of Maiduguri, comprising Aljajeri, Umarari, and some parts of Baga road were the main Boko Haram insurgents enclave in Maiduguri metropolis. The houses in the area were linked by mouse holes and a network of tunnels made by insurgents, which aided their operations and facilitated easy escape when pursued. Some of the houses also had bunkers that could shelter over 100 people, and some corpses were found in soak-away pits as well as some graves in houses. The areas were cordoned off and secured by troops on 3 July 2013.

During Op BOYONA, some weapons were recovered, including RPGs, different rifle variants, including AK-47 rifles, locally made guns, grenades, and single and double-barreled guns, machine guns, a large stock of IED, and various calibers of ammunition. Other items recovered include vehicles, military and police uniforms, knives, machetes, bows and arrows, charms, walkie-talkies, gun trucks, vehicle plate numbers, bomb detonators, tricycles, and telephone handsets. These recoveries were made in major towns and villages such as Chikun Gudu, Krenoa, Monguno, Bama, Banki, Gwoza, Kala/Balge, Gubio, Biu, Damboa, Konduga, Magumeri, Marte, and Kukawa. The conduct of the operation led to several deliberate engagements leading to the liberation of territories and the neutralization of the adversaries in the Sambisa Forest, which was a major den of the terrorists. The advance into Sambisa Forest heavily degraded the adversaries and led to their relocation to other areas they thought could afford them safe havens. Most of the 27 LGAs of Borno State were traversed to liberate them from Boko Haram insurgents. Troops of the Nigerian Army had serious and frontal encounters and confrontations with Boko Haram, particularly in Monguno, Boma, Gwoza, Gubio, Dam insurgentsboa, Konduga and Marte. The intensity of Op BOYONA and the casualties suffered by Boko Haram insurgents led to their maneuvering through the borders into neighboring Niger Republic, Chad, and Republic of Cameroon. Initially, the neighboring countries saw the problem as Nigeria's and did not understand the dynamics of the problem. Thus, the countries were reluctant to provide assistance despite insurgents crossing into their territories with arms, ammunition, and gun trucks.

The use of CJTF was a novel and welcome development during Op BOYONA. These were youths who volunteered to support the mission being executed by the JTF Op BOYONA. The youths were absorbed, trained, and deployed into various sectors of the operation. They were indigenes who were familiar with the terrain and contributed immensely to the success of the operation through their clandestine employment known as "Black Maria" to identify Boko Haram members. The operation gave them maximum protection throughout the period, but their identities were kept under wrap. In specific terms, the youths provided information to HQ JTF which subsequently informed HQ 23 Bde and this led to the arrest of 38 Boko Haram members, mostly at a shopping complex in Yola from 20-23 July 2013. The CJTF members also provided information and travelled at the expense of the JTF to Lagos and Ogun States to effect the arrest of 82 Boko Haram members in conjunction with 81 Div between 12-16 July 2013. They also provided information on other BH members who had fled to Port Harcourt, Kano, Damaturu, Kaduna, Abuja, Sokoto, Keffi, and Asaba. Lt Col MA Suleiman formed and coordinated the activities of the JTF. A significant number of other officers and men participated actively during Op BOYONA, prominent among whom were the JTF Commander Maj Gen JAH Ewansiha, his Chief of Staff was Col Abdulmalik who later handed over to Col KO Ogundele. The Operation Officer was Col V Ebhaleme, who also handed over to Col M Danmadami, while the Deputy Chief of Staff personnel was Col J Ekparere.

During Op BOYONA, the Nigerian Army, as part of its non-kinetic operations and CIMIC responsibilities, engaged in various activities aimed at reducing the impact of the insurgency and winning the hearts and minds of the populace during Op BOYONA. Citizens of the 3 affected states were the most impacted by the terrorists' activities. They suffered killings, invasions, and displacement from their homes; disruption in socio-economic activities, kidnappings; and rape. To forestall this carnage, the state took actions through the deployment of troops to mitigate the Boko Haram activities and protect the people. In order to gain the support of the citizens, a robust enlightenment campaign was deployed to propagate the position of the government during the troops' deployment to the effected states. The troops also provided logistics needs, particularly in IDP camps, as well as repairs and rehabilitation of damaged infrastructure at schools, places of worship, and medical outreaches amongst other things. Degrading the terrorists also contributed towards building the confidence of the citizens in the Armed Forces of Nigeria for their protection and preservation.

One of the strategies employed by the terrorists was the recruitment of minors, vulnerable women, and girls as shields and foot soldiers. They were used for surveillance against troops of the military and members of other deployed security agencies. Boko Haram also employed them as Persons Borne IED (PBIED), bomb riggers, informants, suicide bombers, and human shield to prevent them from attack and capture by troops. Also, the cultural norms that prioritises the male child over the female predispose the female child towards being deployed as PBIED. The

Boko Haram insurgents also capitalized on the impoverished socio-economic situation of the locals and induce them with financial gains as low as ₦5,000. Furthermore, Boko Haram engaged in the use of social media for their recruitment purposes, the propagation of fake news, and the dissemination of inciting videos. The Insurgency negatively impacted the people, the social life, and the environment of the 3 states. Families were separated, socio-economic activities were disrupted, and social infrastructure was damaged. The people were under perpetual fear of attack and thus psychologically derailed. Poverty increased, and many were internally displaced. Some Nigerians also became refugees across the border in Cameroon, Chad, and the Niger Republic. A review of Op BOYONA after three months saw the need to change the modus operandi. This brought about the establishment of Op ZAMAN LAFIYA.

Operation ZAMAN LAFIYA

Op BOYONA was disbanded following the formation of 7 Division Nigerian Army in Maiduguri and the directive for the Army to take over operations in the North- East from the DHQ. On 19 August 2013, under the leadership of the COAS, Lt Gen AO Ihejirika, Op ZAMAN LAFIYA was launched, and the handing over of the operation was done in Abuja on 25 August 2013 to the COAS by the Commander JTF Maj Gen JAH Ewansiha. Maj Gen OT Ethan now became the pioneer GOC of the Division and thus the commander of the operation. The frequent changes in the nomenclature of operations against Boko Haram insurgents meant that the concept of operations was significantly different, and not just for change's sake or due to the perceived failure of the preceding operation. This was necessitated essentially by the emergence of a new operational command structure for CTCOIN in the region, as well as the revamped, strategised, and reenergised CTCOIN operation. It is also necessary to state that following an assessment of the Boko Haram insurgents capabilities, intentions and desire to harm the Nigerian state, the FGN, under the leadership of President Goodluck Jonathan proscribed the Boko Haram Sect, amongst others, as a terrorist group and gazetted it through Notice 2013 on 24 May 2013. Hence, they were now designated Boko Haram Terrorists (BHTs) and no longer insurgents. Furthermore, on 14 November 2013, the BHT group was designated as a "Terrorists Group" by the US State Department, which described them as a deadly group linked to international terrorist organizations such as the Al Qaeda terrorist group.

From the codename Op ZAMAN LAFIYA, one could easily decipher that it was an operation that was designed to involve both kinetic and non-kinetic means.

ZAMAN LAFIYA in Hausa Language simply means live in a peace or peaceful coexistence and Hausa is the widely spoken language in the operational area. The name reflected the projected state that the Nigerian Army authorities, at the time of its anticipation, wanted this particular operation to achieve. In other words, the cardinal objective of Op ZAMAN LAFIYA was the philosophy and desire for peaceful coexistence among the people living in Borno, Yobe, and Adamawa States. Therefore, it conveyed an appeal to the terrorist group and thinking in line with the belief that counter insurgency operations should typically involve 80 per cent non-kinetic operations, while the military (kinetic) component of them should make up 20 per cent of the entire operational construct.

Op ZAMAN LAFIYA was fundamentally executed as a robust operation with the primary objective to destroy the insurgents' camps, incapacitate their chain of command, regrouping, and reinforcement capabilities, arrest terrorists, and bring them to justice. The whole idea was to consolidate and improve on the gains of the preceding Op BOYONA, as well as rectify the notable setbacks. The operation combined both military and civil measures to defeat the insurgency and leverage hard and soft power approaches in achieving its mission. It therefore envisaged the use of coercive means as well as the capacity to realize preferred outcomes through greater civil engagements and interactions. In other words, it was referred to as the carrot and stick approach. The goal of Op ZAMAN LAFIYA was to defeat Boko Haram. The specific objectives were to liberate the 3 affected states from Boko Haram Terrorist and insurgent incursions, facilitate peaceful coexistence amongst the people, and ensure that no territory in North-East Nigeria was occupied by the insurgents. The fulcrum of the operation rested on the newly established 7 Division of the Nigerian Army. Other troops from the 3 Division were also involved. The Army Headquarters also set up AHQ Teams A and B as a task group of battalions plus strength made up of highly mobile force to be able to respond to changing situation at different locations rapidly within a short time. The NAF troops, the Naval Special

Boat Service, the Nigeria Police Force, and other security agencies also participated actively.

Op ZAMAN LAFIYA was anchored on asymmetric warfare because the adversaries were non-state actors, comprising disgruntled elements, terrorists, and insurgent groups operating guerrilla tactics. The major tactical approach adopted by Op ZAMAN LAFIYA was the conduct of long and short-range patrols into the positions of the terrorists and their adversaries. Initially, the BHT disappeared underground throughout the course of Op BOYONA in order to regroup and refit, and thereafter launched several attacks, starting from the attack on 202 Bn Kur Mohammed Barracks, Bama. On 4 August 2013, the Kaka Alai's group moved in from the Niger Republic and attacked the 174 Bn's location in Malam Fatori. There were heavy casualties among their own troops, with survivors crossing into the Niger Republic. This was the second attack on the base; the first was in June 2013, which was decisively repelled. The second attack dislodged the units with a lot of material and equipment lost to the terrorists while a large portion of the barracks was burnt down. However, the BHTs attack on Bama town which was aimed at capturing the weapons in NPF Barracks arms store was successfully repelled. During the attack, the soldiers fought bravely despite the BHTs overwhelming strength. In the fierce battle, the soldiers neutralised Momodu Bama nicknamed Abu Saad who was shekau's second-in command. He was also personally responsible for slaughtering of captured victims, including policemen.

The third attack on Kur Mohammed Barracks was on 20 December 2013. The 7 Division had been in place 15 August 2013. The terrorists burned many structures in the barracks including the MRS and MT Yard. They also burnt the unserviceable AFVs in the unit and kidnapped some family members of soldiers. Capt Usman (rtd) and his son Zachariah, along with 17 other soldiers, were slaughtered; and unspecified number of teachers, women, and children were also killed; 5 soldiers were wounded, including Lt Mustapha, the unit's adjutant. The attack completely dislodged the unit. A new Chief of Army Staff, Lt Gen KTJ Minimah, was appointed on 16 January 2014. His focus was to quickly tackle the Boko Haram issues. However, this did not intimidate the terrorists and insurgents. The fourth attack by BHT was on 19 February 2014, but the soldiers rapidly mobilized to engage the BHTs before arriving at the Barracks. The Shilka gun was effectively used even after being hit by a VBIED. The Bama Terrorists retreated and burned the place of the Emir of Bama on their way to Sambisa Forest. The fifth attack was on 1 September 2014. The attack completely dislodged the 21 Bde Tac HQ, while the officers and surviving soldiers withdrew to Konduga. The BHT's successes were attributed to low morale and fighting spirit among the soldiers for various reasons, including poor training, non-functional or inadequate equipment. It seemed the soldiers had lost the will to fight as most of them fled on sighting the adversary even before the battle was joined, thus abandoning the officers, who had no choice but to withdraw as there were no soldiers to fight with.

Most of the structures in Bama were destroyed, and Shekau proclaimed one of his lieutenants as Emir of Bama. It is pertinent to state that most of the youths in Bama, Kawuri, and Konduga formed the bulk of BHT fighters. They had knowledge of the terrain and the support of the people who saw the activities as "Aikin Allah" meaning "God's Work". The locals who bought into the BHT ideology were solidly behind the terrorists, despite the military's friendly disposition; hence, their reluctance to change their attitude. Not until BHT turned their guns on the locals and imposed a draconian rule that the towns were recaptured in early 2015. The BHTs attacked the NAF Base, Maiduguri destroying the two MI-35 helicopters, thus temporarily limiting their own air support. They also staged mass attacks on troops between Benishek and Maiduguri, in which the Comd 21 Bde and CO 202 Bn's vehicles were destroyed. Within the same period, the terrorists attacked Kauri, Konduga, and other settlements along the Bama-Maiduguri axis. They also dislodged troops at Monguno, Kukawa, Cross Kawa, and MNJTF troops at Baga, thus gaining control of the whole of Northern Borno. The BHT also audaciously attacked a battery of 333 AR locations at Jimtilo in Maiduguri. This led to the formation of 271 TF Tk Bn, equipped with 10 x T-72 tanks, and commanded by Lt Col AM Usman. Some tanks were quickly mobilized to Yola as the city was threatened by the terrorists. The game changer was the introduction of the 10 x T – 72 tanks, Multi Barrel Rocket Launchers, and the inclusion of foreign technical partners. The Op ZAMAN LAFIYA was conducted using a 2-pronged offensive approach.

The advance from the Adamawa axis was led by Brig Gen VO Ezugwu, who was the then Commander 28 TF Bde. The Bde had a 143 Rangers Bn commander, Lt Col C Ogbuagbo, 114 Bn commanded by Lt Col MK Gara, and 117 and 115 Bns, which were deployed for support roles and were commanded by Lt Col MA Sadiq and Lt Col DJ Abdullahi, respectively. The advance commenced on 2 fronts using 114 TF Bn to dislodge BHT in Maraban, Mubi, Uba and Kuzum. While 143 Rangers Bn was to clear Mubi, Vintim, Kwa and Kuzum, it was also tasked with linking up with 26 TF Bde at Gwoza. The advance on both axes crisscrossed at Baza, which was the major stronghold of the terrorists. The advance recorded huge successes, which resulted in the elimination of key BH leaders and the recapture of lost territories and Boko Haram's acclaimed caliphate. The advance from the Yobe axis was led by Brig Gen AA Adefarati. The Yobe axis has 27 and 29 TF Bde as its fighting formations. The advance from the Yobe axis recorded minor attacks on the fringes of the state.

Op ZAMAN LAFIYA recorded some remarkable successes with brave and courageous commanders, officers, and troops at different levels of their engagement with BHTs. The successes came with significant losses of men and equipment.

Most of the successes recorded were particularly in terms of arrests and neutralization of BHTs, the seizure and recovery of weapons, as well as the destruction of BHT operational bases. The other remarkable successes recorded during Op ZAMAN LAFIYA included the liberation of territories, the execution of raid/cordon and search operations, and the rescue of kidnapped Chibok girls. The liberation of occupied territories was one of the successes recorded by Op ZAMAN LAFIYA. For instance, on 19 November 2014, the Nigerian Army, alongside the other collaborating security agencies and partners, recaptured the Gombi, Maraban Pella, and Hong communities in Adamawa State. Several BHTs were captured, while many others were KIA. Weapons and equipment, which had been taken by the sect, were equally recovered. The Nigerian Army lost Capt Adeba while Acting Comd 23 Bde Col AB Popoola was WIA in Hong by BHT. Similarly, the Nigerian Army recaptured several other towns, including Mubi North, Mubi South, Michika, Shuwa, Wuro Gyambi, Gombi, Vintim, Uba, and Bazza in Adamawa State. Counter offensives by the terrorists to reclaim those liberated territories were decisively repelled by our own troops.

There were several successful raid operations conducted during Op ZAMAN LAFIYA. The objectives of the operations were to degrade and neutralize the adversaries as well as deny them freedom of action. A good example was the raid operation conducted following some debilitating ambush attacks by the terrorist elements. A company under the command of Maj I Saleh laid ambush on 26 November 2015, at Limankara, which is a known crossing point of BHTs. The operation resulted in the killing of unspecified numbers of BH commanders and the recovery of many weapons and vehicles that had hitherto been carted away by the terrorists from our own troops. Several other successful raid operations were conducted in other areas of operation in the theatre, which also led to the degrading, neutralization, and capture of equipment by own troops. The Chibok story was one of the significant experiences during the lifespan of Op ZAMAN LAFIYA. The kidnapping scenario and narratives went global and became a source of security concern for the Nigerian Army and the country. Consequently, concerted efforts were made at rescuing and reuniting the kidnapped girls with their families. In this regard, precisely in April 2014, troops of 7 Division conducted a search and rescue operation for the 276 kidnapped Chibok school-girls at the 3 remote camps at Madayi, Dogon Chuku, and Meri, where the girls were suspected to be held as hostages. These camps were located in the North of Kukawa, along the western corridors of Lake Chad. The troops eventually had a breakthrough and rescued about 21 of the kidnapped girls.

Due to the strategic importance of the Sambisa Forest to the BHTs, its penetration and conquest by the Nigerian Army troops was fundamental and desirous. This was in response to political and public pressure to find and return the Chibok girls. The Nigerian Army troops began an offensive in Sambisa Forest; the troops went as far as Injimiya amid heavy fighting between them and the BHT fighters. Prior to this, the BHTs had anticipated an offensive against its positions thus; it prepared for it by planting belts of IEDs at the various entries into the forest. This was observed by the troops, who made efforts to deactivate them, unfortunately, two soldiers fell victim to the IEDs. The belt of mines strategy, as well as the use of combat security outposts by the insurgents, made it difficult for the Nigerian Army troops to enter the Sambisa Forest. Consequently, the strategic desire to capture Sambisa Forest was not achieved. There were enormous challenges that confronted the troops. The challenges encountered during Op

ZAMAN LAFIYA included poor knowledge of the terrain. The North-East terrain is sandy, with isolated quicksand areas and forests as well as extreme weather conditions. This situation was made worse by the fact that BHT fighters were conversant with the terrain and took advantage of it in their fight against Nigerian Army troops. They were mostly indigenes of the area and had good knowledge of how to navigate their ways through. They had a clear advantage in this regard, unlike Nigerian Army troops fighting against them.

Poor force generation and logistics planning were significant challenges to Op ZAMAN LAFIYA. Prior to operation, no detailed attention was paid to personnel employment, logistics requirements, and force protection. Thus, plans for Op ZAMAN LAFIYA were made hurriedly without due consideration for these factors. The forces were haphazardly generated from different units, while the formations were largely deployed with deficient equipment holding. Some of the troops were batmen, orderlies, and office clerks who had lost touch with regimental duties. This created a huge capacity gap and a lack of cohesion and bonding among troops that fighting force requires for optimal performance. Furthermore, available equipment could not be effectively deployed because the troops were largely unfamiliar with it. For instance, troops of the 157 TF Bn took a defensive position and deployed ahead of Gudumbali village on 10 November 2015. Unfortunately, the unit was dislodged 7 days later with considerable casualties in men and material. This was substantially due to a lack of cohesion, knowledge and mastery of the equipment at their disposal and a lack of adherence to Tactics Techniques and Procedures (TTPs). Thus, it had a negative impact on the unit's output.

The sympathetic disposition and attitude of the locals towards the BHT in the theatre was a challenge to the troops at the time of Op ZAMAN LAFIYA. Most of the locals were sympathetic to bandits and later, BH insurgents. For instance, suspects being pursued by security forces sometimes escaped into houses, due to restrictions of entry as most of the houses had *Ba'ashiga* (No entry) boldly written at the entrances, thus restricting further action by soldiers in pursuit. Some locals were informants and couriers for BHT logistics with some even donating their daughters for suicide bombings. There were problems of media interference in the operation, such as sensational news, fake news, and misrepresentation of facts thereby sending out the wrong narratives to the general public and the international community on the operation. For instance, it was reported by the media that a filling station was set ablaze by the Nigerian Army, which was completely false. These misleading media representations led to the accusation of human rights violations against the Nigerian Army by local and International Civil Society Group (CGS) and engendered further sympathy from the local populace towards the BHTs. Also, Nigerian Army troops were inexperience in asymmetric warfare operations at the onset of Op ZAMAN LAFIYA. This impacted negatively on the troops. Many pieces of equipment were destroyed and others captured thereby affecting troops' morals. To curtail this, attention was drawn to the need to commence robust in-theatre trainings on asymmetric warfare, even whilst the terrorists were being contained. This aided troops' knowledge and developed their skills in this warfare.

The failure to identify the root causes of the insurgency hampered the successful conduct of Op ZAMAN LAFIYA. The cause which was attributed to socio- economic issues, poverty, illiteracy and fanaticism among others were however, identified but the right solutions were not applied by the government as total reliance was on kinetic efforts. The activities of NGOs operating in the region constituted yet another challenge. There was evidence that the NGOs operating in the troubled areas were surreptitious in reporting the Nigerian Army activities. They accused the Nigerian Army of violating the human rights of civilians in the conflict area even without concrete evidence to prove their allegations. This notion made the international community reluctant in assisting the Nigerian Army in the procurement of hardware and platforms, technical aid as well as critical intelligence assets to be employed against the BHTs. It also affected own troops' morale and decisiveness in their engagements with BHT. Other challenges include inadequate knowledge of the adversary and their capability, inadequate intelligence gathering for the operation, limited night fighting capability and a long line of communication which created an avenue for the adversaries to lay IEDs on supply routes. Some of the GOCs/Commanders of Op ZAMAN LAFIYA were Maj Gen A Mohammed, Maj Gen MY Ibrahim – 7 Division, Maj Gen ZS Zaruwa - 3 Division , Maj Gen FO Ali – 3 Division and Maj Gen LO Adeosun – 7 Division Maj Gen LO Adeosun tenure was particularly eventful as most territories lost to the insurgents were recovered during his tenure.

During Op ZAMAN LAFIYA, Brig Gen Faruk Yahaya served as Deputy Military Secretary 1 during a period in which he identified officers that could hold higher command and staff responsibilities at the operations theatre as part of the Military Secretary's input into the Chief of Army Staff's manpower generation for the operation. During the time, he also served as the Principal General Staff Officer to the Honourable Minister of Defence at the strategic level. He provided the Honourable Minister with necessary staff advice regarding the operations in the North East, especially amidst several challenges. He was a source of hope to officers whose careers were on the line for several reasons, either rightly or wrongly. His presence on the ministerial staff team was reassuring to the personnel in the field that, at least, the correct information and right advice would be provided for the Honourable Minister to take his decisions regarding the conduct of Op ZAMAN LAFIYA, which eventually transmuted into Op LAFIYA DOLE.

Operation LAFIYA DOLE

The appointment of Lt Gen TY Buratai as COAS in 2015 and the establishment of HQ Theatre Command witnessed the redesignation of the operation as Op LAFIYA DOLE and the appointment of the late Maj Gen YM Abubakar as the first Theatre Commander. He served as Theatre Commander from August 2015 to 4 January 2016 before he was appointed Chief of Training and Operations (Army). Gen YM Abubakar eventually died in an auto crash in the North East Theatre along Maiduguri – Damaturu road on 8 March 2016. Thereafter, Op LAFIYA DOLE had Maj Gen Hassan Umoru as Theatre Commander (4 January – 17 March 2016), Maj Gen LEO Irabor (17 March 2016 – 30 May 2017), Maj Gen IT Attahiru (30 May 2017 – 11 December 2017), Maj Gen IR Nicholas (11 December 2017 – 31 July 2018), Maj Gen AM Dikko (31 July 2018 – 27 November 2018), Maj Gen BO Akinroluyo (27 November 2018 – 17 August 2019), Maj Gen OG Adeniyi (17 August 2019 – 3 April 2020) before Maj Gen F Yahaya was appointed as Theatre Commander. He served from 3 April 2020 until he was appointed Chief of Army Staff on 27 May 2021. Faruk Yahaya, then a Brigadier General, has earlier served in Op LAFIYA DOLE as Commander 29 Task Force Brigade in Borgozo. During Maj Gen Nicholas' tenure, the Theatre had Op LAST HOLD commanded by

Maj Gen AM Dikko before he eventually assumed command of Op LAFIYA DOLE and subsequently wound up Op LAST HOLD. Op LAST HOLD was seen as an operation within another operation which was widely criticised. Op LAFIYA DOLE particularly lasted very long for about 5 years and 6 months due to the long tenure of the initiator, Lt Gen TY Buratai.

Battles are generally preceded by careful preparation and a detailed operational plan taking cognizance of the threat, adversary capabilities, equipment and other factors. This is done with resources available to a commander both human and material, higher commander's intent and other tactical factors. Plans are therefore translated into directives and orders issued to subordinate commanders for implementation. The mission of formations in Op LAFIYA DOLE was derived from COAS and Theatre Commander's intent which was to retake all lost territories and clear Boko Haram fighters from the North East to restore the territorial integrity of the Nigeria State. The security situation at the time was relatively tensed in some locations as Boko Haram terrorists still controlled Sambisa Forest and large portions of the LGAs within Borno State. They also had sizable pockets of foot soldiers in some enclaves within the Southern and Central Senatorial districts of Borno state. Thus, series of oral and written directives and orders which provide the needed guidelines and operational guidance to clear Boko Haram Terrorists from Borno State were issued. Furthermore, these instructions were well executed by subordinate commanders leading to the operational successes achieved. However, it was observed that some units did not obey key timings and instructions issued in operations orders/directives thereby taking unilateral decisions like withdrawal from defended areas without the Appropriate Superior Authority's approval. On the whole, the implementation of directives and orders in Op LAFIYA DOLE was very satisfactory as evidenced by the numerous successes recorded against BHT in Op LAFIYA DOLE. Also, military deployments for special operations were based on the assessment of the scale of the threat and the operational end state.

The manpower generated for Op LAFIYA DOLE was raised from other divisions of the Nigerian Army. While some units were inducted immediately on return from Peace Support Operations, others were hurriedly assembled from various formations and units without formal Pre-

Deployment Training (PDT) or unit integration. The entire 7 Division as of then was made up of an amalgamation of different troops which adversely affected command and control, administration, regimentation and success in battle. This lack of cohesion and unity of purposeexplained why several units were easily overrun by BHT at the beginning of the operation in the North-East. it has therefore become imperative that a new concept of force generation be put in place to achieve spirit-de-corps and synergy of troops inducted in the theatre. However, the establishment of the Nigerian Army Special Forces School (NASFS) at Buni Yadi greatly addressed the issue of training and integration of troops. The PDT given to troops before being inducted in the theatre provides an avenue for appropriate marrying up of units and integrating them into an efficient and effective fighting force. Specifically, the PDT conducted for 22 Bde and affiliated units before induction in February 2016 accounted for the recapture of Rann and Kala-Balge LGAs in the space of 3 weeks. It was therefore suggested that the School be expanded to cover jungle, mountain and desert warfare training as well as other terrain-oriented training for the Nigerian Army.

    The AHQ took several initiatives to further contain the activities of the Boko Haram Terrorists in the North East. Such initiatives included 3 reviews of the Nigerian Army Order of Battle and the introduction of some policies, all of which further resulted in induction of more troops into the North East. A few of these were the creation of the 7 Division in August 2013 and also in December 2015, the Tactical HQ of the 3 Division was relocated to Damaturu while the 8 Division was established with its temporary HQ in Monguno. The introduction of these 3 formations with a coordinating theatre command and the establishment of new brigades and battalions under them altered Nigerian Army force structure in the North-East region. The new structure ensured wider deployments and engendered a major force buildup in conformity with the new threat by Boko Haram terrorist. To this end, the strength of the Nigerian Army personnel in the North-East increased from about 10,000 troops under ORO I in 2011 to about 38,000 in 2018. This was, in a bid to meet the large manpower requirements of the new formations and units. Deployment of a large force to a vast theatre of operation as covered by Op LAFIYA DOLE requires good coordination organization of Op LAFIYA DOLE however was devoid of good coordination, record management and plan for rotation of troops. The lack of coordination in deployment of Op LAFIYA DOLE had overtime contributed to the prolong deployment of troops, at both AHQ and Corps level and has not been efficiently managed. At some point, the posting of officers to the North East was done at Army Headquarters, Department of Army Training and Operations, which made records of such service unavailable at the Department of Military Secretary (Army). The haphazard force generation for several Task Force units in the theatre further complicated forecasting for possible rotation.

The PDT for Op LAFIYA DOLE took place in Jaji. However, specialist Corps such as the Nigerian Army Armoured Corps and Nigerian Army Corps of Artillery conducted PDT at their various schools in Bauchi and Kachia respectively. The training was mission-specific and concentrated mainly on CTCOIN tactics as well as the employment of fire support assets in a CTCOIN environment. The Op LAFIYA DOLE comprised components of the Nigerian Army, Nigerian Navy and Nigerian Air Force troops under a joint command. Asides from the core military force, a police component was also inducted into the operations on 4 January 2019 at 333 Artillery Regiment, Njimtilo. These specially trained police officers and men were inducted after 4 weeks of training at the NASFS Buni Yadi, Yobe State. Incidentally, some of the police officers left after the training following information that they would be posted to the crisis region to complement the military efforts. This speaks to the apprehensions that greeted postings to the North East, especially amongst paramilitary agencies.

The Op LAFIYA DOLE engagements in the theatre of operation were facilitated and coordinated by the Theatre Command in Maiduguri. The engagements were expected to dominate the entire Area of Operations and to facilitate the effective flow of logistics support to formations/units. For instance, the 3 divisions of the Nigerian Army involved in Op LAFIYA DOLE were deployed to cover the states affected by the Boko Haram terrorists' insurrection. These Divisions were organized based on their tasks to effectively discharge their assigned responsibilities. The 3 Division, Nigerian Army, with tactical HQ at Damatutu had 4 brigades under the command and covered Adamawa, Bauchi, Gombe and Yobe States. The brigades in the Division were 23 Brigade, 33 Artillery Brigade, 27 Task Force Brigade and 29

Task Force Brigade with their headquarters at Yola, Bauchi Buni Yadi and Borgozo respectively. The core engagement of this Division was ensuring safe corridors within the areas of operations.

The 7 Division Headquarters was in Maimalari Cantonment Maiduguri and had 5 brigades under command. These included 21 Brigade, 22 Brigade as well as 25 Task Force Brigade, 26 Task Force Brigade and 28 Task Force Brigade with Headquarters at Bama, Dikwa, Damboa, Gwoza and Chibok respectively. In the past, the 28 Task Force Brigade was under the command of the 3 Division in Mubi and later relocated to Chibok to come under the command of the 7 Division. The operations of the 7 Division covered the entire Southern part of Borno State. The Headquarters of the 8 Division was in Monguno. It has 2 brigades designated as 5 Brigade and 7 Brigade with their headquarters at Gubio and Baga respectively.

The 8 Division's Area of Operations covered the Northern area of Borno State. These military formations conducted several offensive operations within their areas of responsibility. For example, 21 Brigade liberated Konduga, Kawuri and Mairari up to Bama while 26 Task Force Brigade conducted offensive operations to link up with the 21 Brigade in Bama, thereafter, proceeded to liberate Pulka, up to Gwoza and its surroundings. The core tasks were that of the liberation of territories dominated by BHT and blockage of their logistics supply routes around the North East.

The Nigerian Navy operations in the theatre of operation involved the deployments of Special Boat Services personnel as well as naval personnel in the Armed Forces Special Forces Battalion. The Nigerian Navy also deployed about 300 personnel with gunboats at the Naval Out Post in Lake Chad. The logistics support for the naval component was coordinated by the Naval Headquarters Logistics Branch. The naval component provided maritime support which was crucial in achieving victory through the neutralization of the insurgents along the fringes of the Lake Chad area. The establishment of the Theater Command brought the Nigerian Navy under command thereby enhancing synergy among the military forces. The naval component also participated in subsidiary operations especially the Special Boat Services, which operated alongside the Nigerian Army troops.

The Nigerian Air Force provided air power which was essential in aerial bombardment, reconnaissance, resupply and casualty evacuation among other tasks. The Nigerian Air Force was pivotal to most of the operational successes in Op LAFIYADOLE with the limited manned and unmanned platforms. They helped with interdiction fires and close air support. The role of the Nigeria Air Force was very significant and their active involvement in the operation helped to dislocate and inflict heavy casualties on the insurgents. The Nigerian Air Force operated under the command of the Theatre Commander. However, the deployment of air assets was under the control of the Headquarters Nigerian Air Force. This sometimes made timely deployment of air assets challenging arising from the bureaucratic processes that had to be followed. Climatic conditions also constituted a challenge as unfavourable weather conditions impeded air operations. Aside from air engagements some of the personnel were deployed to safeguard air force installations and other Key Points and Vulnerable Areas within the Maiduguri metropolis.

The role of the Civilian Joint Task Force (CJTF) in the theatre of operation was strategically impactful particularly when viewed from the social dynamics perspective.

The social dynamics of asymmetric warfare encourage the use of human intelligence gathering and the participation of indigenous people. It was in this light that the CJTF featured prominently. For instance, the CJTF was made up of mainly personnel from the Kanuri ethnic extraction in Borno and Yobe States. They understood the local terrain especially the hunters among them and they could traverse the Sambisa Forest with less difficulty than the soldiers. More importantly, they knew their kinsmen who belonged to the terrorist group. The knowledge of the environment assisted the CTCOIN efforts immensely. The CJTF fought alongside the military in dislodging insurgents from several locations. However, the major role of the CJTF was in providing intelligence and serving as guides to locations. It is important to reiterate that engagement in the theatre of operation was essentially by the conduct of special operations like raids as well as cordon and search operations with limited manpower. This presupposes that the deployment of troops on the ground to cover the entire geographical area of North East, inch for inch, was impracticable. The implication is that the insurgents often leveraged this limitation to reoccupy cleared areas during operations after the government troops must have pulled out. This explains the fluctuations experienced, which prolonged the operations in North East Nigeria.

Given the fragility of the security situation in the North East, there was the need for subsidiary operations to address specific security threats as they develop. Thus subsidiary operations were conducted intermittently. Such operations include - Op ASIYO TAMUNOMA which was charged to bombard all targets along Alagarno general area. In 2016 Op CRACK DOWN was conducted in 4 phases to capture the Sambisa forest to completely flush out Boko Haram terrorists from the forest. Phase I was the logistics buildup; Phase II was the actual conduct of the operation; Phase III was the consolidation phase and Phase IV was the force recovery phase. Advance into Sambisa Forest commenced on 30 April 2016 and was concluded on 17 May 2016. The operation succeeded in dislodging terrorists from Alafa I, Alafa II, Alafa Yaga, Kulburi, Dar-El-Salam as well as Bula Bello villages and Njimia. In 2017, Op RESCUE FINALE was charged with the responsibility of bombarding Bulabulin from Jakana; blocking Matari, Kasamti, Gramari and Madamtari. The operation led to the capture of Gorgori, Djuballa and Doksa I, II and II Joko and Mangrove camps which were neutralized during the operation. In 2017-2018, Op DEEP PUNCH I and II were charged with the responsibility of eliminating security threats which led to the capture of Camp Zairo and the displacement of Mohammed Shekau from his operational base. It also paved way for the successful conduct of the 2019 general elections.

Op FIRE BALL was introduced in 2020 to continue with the degradation of Boko Haram terrorists as well as ISWAP elements and the destruction of their logistics installations. In the same Year 2020, Op TURA TAKAIBONGO was meant to dislodge Boko Haram terrorists/ISWAP elements from the Timbuktu triangle, Alagarno and Sambisa forests. This led to the neutralization of scores of Boko Haram terrorists/ISWAP in the general area. It is important to note that this operation was critical but challenging because the terrain was difficult and the general area was booby trapped and heavily laid with IEDs. This constituted a huge challenge for troops to conduct patrols, ambushes, as well as routines in defense, and conduct fire missions on registered targets, carry-out surveillance, deploy observation posts, conduct CIMIC activities such as visitations to local officials and other local leaders. The subsidiary operations were short-spanned as they depended on the security objectives that had to be met. The other subsidiary operations conducted under Op LAFIYA DOLE include; Op TAKUN GIWA, Op AIKI TAFKI and Op RUFE KOFA. Others were

Op QUICK BLOW, Op KATANA JIMLA and Op LAST HOLD. Within the framework of military success, Op LAFIYA DOLE recorded considerable successes in the theatre of operation. Several pointers support this position. The operation decimated hundreds of terrorists through airstrikes and artillery bombardments around Sambisa Forest, the fringes of Lake Chad and strongholds in the North East. The capacity of the group to hold swathes of land which was the pre-2015 situation was significantly diminished. The LGAs hitherto under the control of the group were liberated and some semblance of normalcy was restored. Following large-scale raids on terrorist camps, a great number of arms and ammunition were captured by troops thereby incapacitating the insurgents and degrading their capacity to take on "hard targets".

Statistics exist to further support the successes recorded. For instance, from January 2015 – May 2018 alone, about 4,609 active Boko Harram fighters fell causalities in action. These include; 1,087 in 2015, 1696 in 2016, 1,210 in 2017 and 606 between January and May 2018. The Nigerian Army also arrested about 4,876 Boko Haram terrorists since 2015. Arms recovered in the same period stood at 2,045 weapons. Within the same period of 2015 – May 2018, the total quantity of ammunition of various calibers recovered from the Boko Haram terrorists is put at 116,714. It was this momentum of success that made some commentators and well-meaning Nigerians like the Minister of Information and Culture, Alhaji Lai Mohammed, announce to the nation that Boko Haram had been "technically defeated". The extent to which the "technically defeated" phrase is understood may differ and the description of the situation in the North East is contestable. This notwithstanding, significant successes were recorded during Op LAFIYA DOLE.

Further examples suffice as success indicators. In December 2016, troops of Op LAFIYA DOLE captured Boko Haram terrorist's operational and "spiritual headquarters" "Camp Zairo" in Sambisa Forest. Furthermore, the Nigerian Army Small Arms Competition 2017 was conducted from 26-31 March 2017 within the Sambisa Forest. This measure enabled the Nigerian Army to dominate the general area of the forest that was close to Banki Junction and Bama. In 2020, it was reported that Op LAFIYA DOLE troops conducted several operations; aggressive patrols, ISR missions and air offensive operations against Boko Haram terrorists/

ISWAP. This led to the destruction of Boko Haram terrorist camps as well as the neutralization of their Amirs and other fighters. Similarly, on 15 July 2020, the Air Task Force of Op LAFIYA DOLE coordinated air offensives on terrorists camp at Ngwuri Gana Village, along the Gulumba Gana-Kumshe axis in the northern part of Borno State. The massive air strikes led to the destruction of the terrorists camp while several terrorists were neutralized.

In April 2021, the Nigerian Army reported that the troops of Op LAFIYA DOLE eliminated 21 Boko Haram terrorists/ISWAP terrorists in the border town of Geidam in Yobe state. Gallant troops successfully recovered a Gun Truck with an Anti- Aircraft gun mounted on it, 8 AK-47 rifles with 10 magazines as well as 2 RPG bombs and 5 chargers. Other recoveries were 1000 rounds of different calibers of ammunition, one Commando Mortar tube, 3 IED blasting devices, toolboxes, communication radios and phones amongst others. These kinds of successes are inexhaustive, but they serve as few examples to indicate combat operations that have largely degraded BHT's capacity. In fact, the conduct of the 2019 general elections in the North East was largely possible because of the successes recorded by Op LAFIYA DOLE.

The CTCOIN operations are replete with low points occasioned by commissions or omissions by commanders at all levels. During Op LAFIYA DOLE, there were some challenges in tactics, logistics and administration which negatively affected the tempo of operations. In asymmetric warfare, one of the success criteria is the ability to achieve surprise against an adversary. During most operations in Op LAFIYA DOLE, own forces were reacting to the BHT battle plan. The failure to adopt a more proactive posture by some units and formations resulted in casualties of men and equipment. During the rainy season, the defensive operations plan led to the insurgents seizing the initiative to attack and ambush own forces along own MSR. The ambush on the convoy of Brig Gen Victor Ezugwu on 19 April 2016 and that of the UNICEF convoy along road Bama-Maiduguri on 28 July 2016 were instructive. This has made the need for an all-season proactive posture to deny the insurgents freedom of action inevitable. Another area of concern was over-dependence on Armoured Fighting Vehicles (AFVs) for mobile operations. Mobile patrols with AFVs, which are often road bound was generally associated with noise which in most cases give away the element of surprise. This most probably accounted for the futility of many mobile patrols conducted by troops as the Boko Haram terrorists abandoned targeted locations at the approach of own troops. As much as AFVs afford troops protection, their negative impact in achieving surprise in CTCOIN operations must be considered as mobile patrols, which are mainly road bound also made troops' movement predictable and susceptible to IED attacks leading to disruption of operation plan and also resulting in human and equipment casualties. A well-planned and coordinated foot patrol would attain surprise and achieve better results in degrading the adversary.

The conduct of CTCOIN operations globally is intelligence driven. Accurate and actionable intelligence is therefore a critical factor, which shapes military operations. During Op LAFIYA DOLE, A great percentage of the quantum of intelligence on Boko Haram terrorists was often speculative, unverified and misleading. For the Nigerian Army CTCOIN efforts to be steps ahead of its adversary, there is the need for coordinated and timely dissemination of Human Intelligence (HUMINT), Signal Intelligence (SIGINT), Electronic Intelligence (ELINT) and air intelligence. There is also the need for appropriate vetting and protection of intelligence sources.

The standard of discipline among troops in the theatre of Operation was also an issue. The general conduct of troops in their area of operations and within Maiduguri Metropolis called to question the standard of discipline within Op LAFIYA DOLE troops. Crimes ranging from illegal trafficking in ammunition, drug abuse, rape, AWOL, and desertion among officers and soldiers were recorded. As of 7 September 2016, a total of 15 officers and 304 soldiers were on AWOL within 7 Division while the number of deserters stood at 11 soldiers. Similarly, a total of 4 officers and 16 soldiers stood trial at 7 Division General Court Martial as of 7 September 2016. The level of indiscipline by troops affected the operation's efficiency and fighting spirit. To address this challenge, the commanders constantly sensitised and sanctioned erring personnel, measures which assisted in stemming the level of indiscipline. Another area of concern was the poor handling of WIA/KIA personnel in the theatre. Many of the evacuated WIA soldiers did not receive timely medical attention due to the limited number of ambulance and medical personnel. Some WIA had to wait for over a year to be evacuated for level 4 medical treatments within and outside the country. In particular, the COAS later authorised expeditious MEDEVAC of some critically WIA officers and soldiers outside the country. Due to the resultant negative effect on troops morale, it is expedient that proper attention be given to WIA personnel during operations.

Logistics was also an issue during Op LAFIYA DOLE. The scale of the operation, the terrain and the lethal capacity of the terrorists among other factors combined to stretch the armed forces and military resources profoundly. The most prominent challenge revolved around deficits in logistics. The logistics challenges range from inadequate lift capability, inadequate fuel supply facilities and a dearth of skilled manpower in the maintenance of equipment. Others were a lack of efficient CASEVAC system dependence on overseas sources of military hardware, inadequate and substandard storage facilities and insufficient spare parts among others. The logistics challenge was compounded by the ineffective management of funds. Several military commanders and officers in the theatre of operation indicated that the logistics available for combat operations were grossly inadequate, nonfunctional and often broke down during operations. Lt Gen LO Adeosun (rtd) (2022) however explained that the Nigerian Army was not oriented to fight asymmetric warfare and the equipment available was meant for conventional engagements. It was therefore not unexpected that there were challenges with equipment. However, as the operations progressed, better weapons and platforms commensurate with the threats were inducted.

The troops' generation mechanism and deployment during Op LAFIYA DOLE were problematic for a few reasons. The logistics for the operation were coordinated by the Combat Services Support Corps involving units of the Nigerian Army Corps of Supply and Transport, Nigerian Army Medical Corps, Nigerian Army Ordinance Corps and Nigerian Army Electrical and Mechanical Engineers. These Combat Services Support corps provides essential CSS to troops. Some of these troops were deployed not on corps specific roles but on general duty tasks or pure infantry roles. Aside from the Nigerian Army, the Nigerian Air Force provides air power to support the operation. This was crucial in the success of combat operations. A former Air Component Commander of Op LAFIYA DOLE, Air Commodore E Anebi explained that apart from the air operations conducted, the Air Force also supported the ground forces with ground troops. About 390 Nigerian Air Force personnel were deployed for the operation. The personnel were extracted from units under the 5 tactical commands of the Nigerian Air Force. The Nigerian Navy was also a functional component of ground operations.

Limited manpower available for deployment and troops mobilization for the operation which was done without strict adherence to the specialities of personnel were some recorded challenges. Secondly, the mobilization of troops from various brigades and battalions did not allow for cohesion and team spirit which is an important factor for military success. Thirdly, the shortage of manpower also accounted for the thin deployment of troops at locations which rendered them susceptible to dislodgements by Boko Haram terrorists. This problem resonated across the area of deployment. Fourthly, the deployments were also fraught by the lack of skilled manpower for effective equipment support. The Nigerian Army Electrical and Mechanical Engineers technicians responsible for the repair and maintenance of equipment were not given sufficient training. Commanders had to rely on residual technical knowledge. For example, no Nigerian Army Electrical and Mechanical Engineers technician was trained in the maintenance of 155mm Self Propelled Gun (BEGUWA) and Multi Barrel Rocket Launchers. This made maintenance of the equipment problematic.

The lethal impact of IEDs on troops and equipment was one of Boko Haram terrorists' greatest strengths in terms of weaponry the IEDs were rampantly used on both military and civilian targets. Most of them were in form of VBIED, PBIED, ABIED and MBIEDs. For instance, between January and June 2016 out of the 51 recorded KIA troops of 7 Division Maiduguri died as a result of the impact of IEDs. Several commanders and officers confirmed that this was a general problem across the theatre. Sadly, efforts by it engineer troops at C-IED operations were also recording some causalities among the EOD personnel.

Given the imperative of logistics to military success and the challenges that ensured it; several perspectives have been put forward to explain the depth, nature and dynamics of the problem. Some of these challenges included failing platforms procured long ago such as the Russian T-55 MBTs first produced in 1955 and uses during the Soviet era. A fundamental problem with this platform was the closure of the production line by the Original Equipment Manufacturers leading to lack of spare parts. Attempts to remediate this challenge led to the procurement of the T-72 tanks which became a game changer in the theatre, although it also had issues with the availability of spares. Another instance was a situation where some shilka guns had to be 'cannibalized' to fix another until they broke down completely and had to be withdrawn from the operation. Even the Vickers MBTs were older than the T-72; however, these narratives do not explain the unwillingness of troops to fight arising from poor training, poor handling of equipment, battle fatigue and poor strategy. More so, Nigerian never had a history of asymmetric warfare until the outbreak of the insurgency in the North East. Thus there were obvious gaps in equipment but as the insurrection progressed, better equipment was introduced.

There was a perspective that debunks the insinuation that setbacks in Op LAFIYA DOLE were due largely to inadequate and ageing equipment. These sources disagree that the Boko Haram terrorists had better weapons than the military and blamed the setbacks in the theatre of operation on cowardice by some ill-trained soldiers, the haphazard manner in which troops were generated and poor knowledge of newly inducted weapons. Also, poor tactics techniques and procedures, the nature of the relations between commanders and troops as well as a poor maneuver of the terrain in the North East were among others issues that created problems for the Armed Forces of Nigeria. This perspective is reinforced by an Infantry Corps Commander, who debunked the simplistic excuse that troops had inadequate and non-functional equipment. Rather, the failures stemmed more from the lack of commitment by commanders and troops' will to fight, deliberate sabotage of operational strategies/equipment and poor leadership (especially Junior leadership) in the theatre of operation. He argued that some commanders exhibited less interest in defeating the enemy and as a result excuses were magnified to explain constraints. However, an instructive context is often missed in criticisms of combat equipment deployed to the North-East at the beginning of operations. The Table of Equipment of the military before the start of the Boko Haram insurgency was meant for conventional warfare and not asymmetric warfare. But as the conflict progressed, it became clear that Boko Haram had evolved asymmetric tactics. This development led to a restructuring of the Table of Equipment to accommodate asymmetric equipment. However, some commanders, despite the induction of asymmetric equipment, still showed some form of lack of will to fight.

Setbacks during Op LAFIYA DOLE were not necessarily the lack of weapons but also attitudinal. Some sources affirmed that once a commander on a battlefield expresses fear, it automatically affects the fighting spirit of his soldiers. It suffices to add that Boko Haram terrorists were successful in carrying out lethal attacks not necessarily because of the sophistry of their weaponry but because they were daring, energized with illicit drugs, warped in a brain-washed ideology and with no thought for the future, thus, dying in the war was less considered. The Super Camp concept was adopted in early 2020 when soldiers were under regular attacks and dislodged from the thinly held location due to over dispersal of troops. They were therefore created as a strong defense structure of protection and necessitated the concentration of troops from the thinly held location into the Super Camps. Concentrated forces within the Super Camp were expected to project power and dominate the area of operational responsibilities using Mobile Strike Teams. However, the employment of this strategy created vast swathes of rural communities which were left unprotected. As a result of this, Boko Haram terrorists exploited these gaps and had more freedom of action thus deepening their roots and reinforcing their supply chains. It is important to also indicate that the Super Camps were in garrison towns where the military in recent years settled thousands of civilians. The garrison towns were ringed by ranches to slow Boko Haram terrorist's invasions. The distance between one Super Camp and the other did not also allow for mutual support as well as an effective and efficient response to attacks. The Boko Haram terrorists took advantage of the new concept by attacking civilians' soft targets and isolated communities. They also resorted to laying ambushes and IEDs against own troops. Several Theatre Commanders confirmed that the concept failed because of poor implementation. The Super Camp concept was an excellent idea and a global best practice in warfare but its execution in the North-East was not up to par.

Non-adherence to Mission Command Philosophy was also an identified challenge in Op LAFIYA DOLE. The philosophy postulates that junior commanders be given freedom of action in the conduct of their assigned missions without interference. However, this was not the case in Op LAFIYA DOLE as the operation was micro managed by Appropriate Superior Authority. This development created a frosty relationship among commanding officers. The micro-management of operations outside the theatre was a challenge because the field realities and intelligence available to commanders on the geography, threat and equipment state did not often align with directives from above. It is a considered view that commanders in the theatre of operation were better placed to evolve effective strategies for executing battle missions. Thus there is a need to allow commanders some functional flexibility in conducting operations in consonance with the Mission Command philosophy.

Inter-service rivalry amongst the military components of Op LAFIYA DOLE also profoundly constrained the operation. This challenge was prominent especially when the central control of operations shifted from Joint Task Force to the Nigerian Army. Several covert grumblings were expressed in ways that did not facilitate inter-Service cohesion and cooperation. Several instances of frosty inter-personal relationship among some commanders within and across services greatly affected the sharing of actionable intelligence and joint timely confrontation of security threats in the theatre of operation. The bottlenecks that ensued adversely affected efficient operations, oftentimes resulting in the loss of men and equipment. Even among the paramilitary, the police, for instance, were unwilling to hold on to liberated territories to enforce civil order and in the same light, a few policemen reportedly fled from the theatre of operation. Also, some Nigeria Immigration Service and Nigeria Customs Service personnel abandoned the border posts and moved their statutory responsibilities hinterland thereby jeopardizing Op LAFIYA DOLE and risking national security. In all of these, Lt Gen Faruk Yahaya's tenure as Theatre Commander brought some stability to the operations theatre. He was the last Theatre Commander during Op LAFIYA DOLE before the operation was redesignated Op HADIN KAI.

Operation HADIN KAI

Op HADIN KAI was launched on 30 April 2021 by the Late Lt Gen I Attahiru on his appointment as COAS. He redesignated the operation as Op HADIN KAI still under command of Lt Gen Faruk Yahaya as Theatre Commander. The Theatre Command has retained its modus operandi as a JTF but is led by the Nigerian Army. According Brigadier General Mohammed Yerima, Army Spokesperson then, the redesignation was premised on the fact that the Nigerian Army has made a lot of progress in the operations over the years and needed a re-alignment for better efficiency. The Army Super Camps were also redesignated as Forward Operational Basis. All these were done in line with Gen Attahiru's vision to have "A Nigerian Army that is repositioned to professionally defeat all adversaries in a joint environment". He believes that Boko Haram can only be completely defeated with the participation of the whole elements of power of the nation. He promised to pursue the line of jointness to carry out his mission. Op HADIN KAI was commanded by Gen Faruk Yahaya until he was appointed as the 22nd Chief of Army Staff, Nigerian Army.

A total of 5 major operations and not less than 18 subsidiary operations were identified to have been conducted under the North-East military campaign against insurgency. Some of the subsidiary operations of Op HADIN KAI which are still ongoing are: Op DESERT SANITY and Op LAKE SANITY. The continuous presence of BHT and ISWAP insurgents within Alargano, Sambisa Forest, Mandara Mountains and other areas of the North-East necessitated another major offensive within the Joint Operations Area. Hence, HQ JTF (NE) Op HADIN KAI directed the operation be conducted in 3 phases; shaping, decisive and consolidation phases.

The formations were to conduct operations to destroy ISWAP/BHT in their enclaves in Alagarno Forest, Sambisa Forest, Mandara Mountains, Tumbuns of Lake Chad area and other areas across the theatre to facilitate the return of normalcy to the NE region.

Operation DESERT SANITY

Op DESERT SANITY was conducted simultaneously across Sector 1 by the 5 CTs. Having completed Phase 1 of Op DESERT SANITY within Sector 1, CT 1, CT 3 and 402 SF Bde commenced the Decisive Phase 2 of the operation on 21 March 22. The operation was conducted using 2 fronts simultaneously. CTs 1 and 3 advanced through the Abu Ali range axis, while 402 SF Bde advanced from Aulari axis towards the Ukuba. On 21 March 2022 (Day 1), troops commenced advance along the Abu Ali range axis. The CTs advanced and cleared Galdekore, Izza, Maiyankare, and Garin Ba'abba but there was no contact despite signs of habitation. On the other hand, 402 SF Bde commenced advance from assembly area Aulari at about 1200hrs to clear and destroy ISWAP/BHT camps within Sambisa Forest with Ukuba as their first objective. On 22 March 2022 (Day 2), at about 0610 hrs CTs 1 and 3 repelled the insurgents attack on the harbour position. Thereafter, the troops continued their advance and at about 0935hrs a VBIED rammed into CT 1's leading APC. Next day, at about 1411hrs, CT 1 and 3 made contact with ISWAP/BHT in Njimia destroying the 2 VBIED that attacked them. On 24 March 2022 (Day 4), CT 1 and 3 cleared a network of insurgent hideouts including Kuruba, Alafa, and Yaga 2 and encountered a pocket of terrorists on foot neutralizing 3.

In line with the operation plan, the CTs linked up with 402 SF Bde at Ukuba and Camp Zairo. 402 SF Bde conducted a clearance operation to Ukuba and Camp Zairo with no resistance from terrorists as they fled before the arrival of the troops. The camp was searched and one 122mm gun, 2 x 105mm guns, one MRAP, one gun trucks and one MOWAG APC were recovered. On 25 March 2022 (Day 5), a stretch of enclaves including Parisu-1, Parisu-2, and Sabil Huda was searched making some seizures. Further exploitation between Ukuba and Camp Zairo by 402 SF Bde recovered one Eagle MBT and one 155mm Bofors gun. On 26 March 2022, CT 1 patrol team found the wreckage of the Nigerian Air Force aircraft that crashed in March 2021. A pilot helmet, flying suit and human bones were recovered. By Day 7, CT 1, CT 3 and 402 SF Bde withdrew to Bama, Gwoza and Maiduguri respectively. On 4 April 2022, CT 1 married up with CT 3 at Pulka and proceeded to the concentration area in Ngoshe. The next day, a fire mission was conducted from a gun position at Ngoshe and engaged targets at Agapalwa, Kwadale, Gava and Ashigashiya before advance commenced. On 6 April 2022, at about 0853hrs, CTs encountered heavy fighting with insurgents at Gava and Chinene fighting from the mountains. A Cameroonian ISR was on hand to provide situation awareness while an Alfa Jet conducted airstrikes. Troops later returned to Ngoshe.

On 7 April 2022, at about 1130hrs, a fire mission was conducted from a gun position at Gwoza and engaged Guduf, Kwatara, and Razah respectively. On 8 April 2022, CTs advanced from Gwoza to clear terrorist camps at Kwatara. Troops made contact with insurgents who retreated to the Mandara Mountains, thereby forcing own troops to withdraw to Gwoza due to a lack of access road to Razah. On 23 April 2022 (Day 1), all CTs commenced advance as CT1 pushed on to Kashimeri - Gargash axis from Kur Mohammed Barracks. The same day, at about 0900hrs, troops of CT2 commenced advance to Boboshe and adjoining villages. CT 2 cleared Boboshe general area but 3 gun trucks and one MRAP developed a fault and were evacuated to Mafa for repairs. On 25 April 2022, at about 0820hrs, troops of CT 2 made contact with the insurgents in Merkas 1 and Merkas 2 and engaged in a pursuit up to Yale neutralising 16 insurgents.

On 25 April 2022, at about 1000hrs, troops of 402 SF continued to advance from the harbour area clearing Gremari, Goniri, Mgobdori, Kagimari, Kajimari, Kolori, Karimi 2, Jaltawa, Bulagalda and Yale. No contact was made and all villages were observed to be deserted with a few newly built makeshift accommodations. On 26 April 2022, troops of CT 1 conducted a patrol to evacuate 278 persons rescued on days 2 and 3 to Bama. The same day, 195 Bn (M) cleared Ladin Mbuta, Kasha Kasha and Maasharafti. Contact was made with the insurgents at Kasha Kasha during which 6 insurgents were neutralised. Items recovered include 2 x AK 47 rifles, one G3 rifle, 2 motorcycles and one Techno phone. The same day, troops of 402 SF Bde conducted a patrol from Yale firm base and cleared Khachazara, Agulari, Shigabaja, Bone, Chingori and Amchille. The settlement was deserted but spotted at Amchile were 2 new camps which were set ablaze.

On 27 April 2022 (Day 5), at about 1210hrs, troops of CT 1 arrived in Maiyanti and dropped 156 persons rescued from Chongolo - Jeree general area. On 28 April 2022, at about 0733hrs, CT 3 was attacked at Manjo Ali and 4 insurgents were neutralised (Including one Mallam Shehu the Amir and spiritual head of Galta general area). Some items recovered include 2 x LMGS, one AK 56 rifle, 3 x AK 47 rifles, 156 x 7.62mm rounds and a gun-turret. Additionally, troops rescued terrorist family members comprising an adult male, 13 women and 15 children.

The troops also discovered a mass grave and a recently burnt gun truck in Dissa. Fanning out from the assembly area Gajigana, 212 Bn advanced to clear its area of operation to ensure freedom of movement on Road Maiduguri – Monguno. After 5 days, 212 Bn completed all assigned tasks and withdrew to Maiduguri. A total of 29 settlements were cleared but no contact was made. A major challenge of the force was the incessant breakdown of vehicles due to the thorny and soft ground that becomes marshy during the rainy season. 212 Bn opined that the insurgents that often block MSR Maiduguri – Monguno come from the Gubio axis and not Gajigana.

Operation LAKE SANITY

Op LAKE SANITY commenced with the marrying-up of TF Marte (CT 2) and TF Wulgo (CDF) at Wulgo on 27 March 2022. On 28 March 2022 (Day 1), combined troops of TF Marte and TF Wulgo commenced advance from Wulgo to Bagadaza and Zanari. Bagadaza was deserted but contact was made with a pocket of ISWAP/BHT at Zanari village killing 2 terrorists. Items recovered included 22 bicycles and 18 motorcycles. A total of 21 women, 11 male children and 9 female children were also set free from captivity. At about 1945hrs troops repelled ISWAP/ BHT attack with VBIED and gun trucks in the harbour area at Zanari village. The next day an ambush was repelled killing 2 terrorists and recovering 2 gun trucks, 2 RPG tubes, 3 RPG bombs, one NSVT gun, 2 GPMGs, 3 GPMG belts, 4 belts of PKT rounds, 600 rounds of 7.62mm NATO and one FN magazine. The combined troops advanced and cleared the Fulatari village en-route to Chikin Gudu. There was no contact at Fulatari but later encountered slight resistance at Chukun Gudu and recovered a terrorists' drone. Sadly, at the same location, combine troops encountered an IED killing a CJTF personnel and a soldier of the CDF.

On 30 March 2022 (Day 3), combined troops cleared Afunori village along their axis of advance to Arina Waje. Although the settlement was deserted, fresh trenches were seen. At about 1742hrs, while preparing to harbour, ISWAP/BHT attacked the troops using a VBIED and gun trucks. The attack was repelled with the support of Air Component. Regrettably, one soldier was killed, 7 soldiers were wounded and own 2 gun trucks were destroyed. On the other hand, 8 terrorists were neutralised. Items recovered included one RPG, 2 RPG bombs, one AA gun, 2 GPMG with 7.62mm NATO rounds, and one G3 rifle while 2 gun trucks were destroyed. On 31 March 2022 (Day 4), the troops cleared a deserted settlement along the axis of advance to Arina Waje. Terrorists' vehicle workshop and IED equipment seen at the settlement were destroyed. However, combined troops could not access Arina Chiki and Kolaram because the 2 routes to the locations were muddy and sandy. Eventually, the combined troops withdrew to Wulgo to refit and evacuate their casualties. On getting to Wulgo, combined troops encountered IED behind Government Girls Secondary School Wulgo which damaged a CDF MRAP tyre. At about 1340hrs the same day, the Multinational Joint Task Force helicopter evacuated the corpse of its soldier and the 7 wounded to 7 DMSH. On 7 April 2022 (Day 11), the troops advanced from New Marte and cleared Old Marte but encountered 2 IEDs planted along Road Dikwa - Kukawa. Subsequently, detonation was carried out by the EOD Team. The troops returned to their harbour location at New Marte at about 1645hrs. On 11 April 2022 (Day 15), having obtained intelligence on the presence of insurgents at Arina Waje, the combined troops set out and discover a VBIED fabricating workshop. A 105 mm artillery gun, 2 toolboxes, a sewing machine and a dane gun were recovered while 11 vehicle scraps, a stolen Nigerian Police vehicle scrap, a CJTF vehicle scrap, 3 unserviceable heavy duty power generating sets as well as many bunkers were destroyed.

Several challenges highlighted for Op LAFIYADOLE persist with the ongoing Op HADIN KAI. However, the obvious issues in the conduct of Op HADIN KAI were; The inability of the 7 Division to hold Sambisa Forest, the inability to conduct full-scale night operations, the high rate of tyre damage due to rough terrain and thorny scrubs and incessant bugging down of vehicles which delayed movement thereby breaking the momentum. Despite these challenges, however, a lot of successes were achieved during Op HADIN KAI. They include the continuous domination of Sambisa Forest, Mandara Mountains and other key locations within the Joint Operations Area. Re-opening Road Maiduguri – Damboa for commuters and dominating the road to deny the terrorists freedom of action, clearing of bushes on each side of Road Maiduguri - Damboa and the excavation of anti-vehicular ditch on the right side of the road as well as the patching of the road to curtail the terrorists' ability to plant IED are also signs of good successes. The neutralisation of several terrorists, recovery and destruction of several arms, artillery guns, ammunition, fighting vehicles and equipment, recovery of the wreckage of the NAF aircraft that crashed in March 2021, freeing of 213 terrorists' captives mostly women and children and shoring up troops' confidence and placing them on a better stead for success in subsequent operations. Most importantly, the massive surrender of 93, 900 terrorist fighters, wives, and children to the government between 7 July 2021 and 8 April 2023, has been unprecedented in the history of counter insurgency all over the world. Op HADIN KAI, thus put forward some lessons for the whole world to study.

Commanding the North East Theatre

Guns and tanks and planes are nothing unless there is a solid spirit, a solid heart, and great productiveness behind it.
Eisenhower, 1946

Prevailing Situation before Gen Faruk Yahaya Assumed Command

The situation in the North-East theatre of operations in the First Quarter of 2020 was very fluid. Operations were at high tempo across the Theatre. At the beginning of 2020, there were renewed offensive operations by Boko Haram insurgents. There was a failed Boko Haram attack at Headquarters 29 Task Force Brigade location on 4 January 2020, there were attacks on Main Supply Routes across the theatre. This necessitated Nigerian Army troops to embark on offensive operations into identified strong holds of Boko Haram insurgents to rid those areas of Boko Haram. One of such operations was Op AYISO TAMONUMA which was an advance into the Timbuktu Triangle on 22 March 2020. The operation however was unsuccessful. There were huge losses on own troops, 3 officers and 30 soldiers were killed in action, 7 officers and 32 soldiers were wounded and much equipment was destroyed in the Boko Haram ambush combined with IEDs attack on troop's convoy. Morale in the theatre went down which began to affect operational fortunes. The Nigerian Army troops suffered some major setbacks within the Quarter, especially within the Sector 2 Area of Operations.

There were several attacks on troops' deployments despite efforts to maintain an aggressive posture while IED attacks constituted the most prevalent threat in the Theatre. A major straw drawn was Op AYISO TAMONUMA and its failed assault conducted by troops of Op LAFIYA DOLE on the popular 'Timbuktu Triangle' through the Gorgi-Goniri corridor. The failure brought to the fore obvious shortfalls of the campaign in the North East at the time. The logistics and equipment support situation were not in a good state. Commanders were not fully and promptly supported in repairing equipment requiring funds beyond their resources, as such many unserviceable pieces of equipment were not adequately funded for repair. They were thus accumulated in the main repair group. Similarly, fast-moving spares such as tyres, recovery vehicles, and vulcanising equipment were not adequately provided for. Many equipment casualties were therefore abandoned and unrepaired.

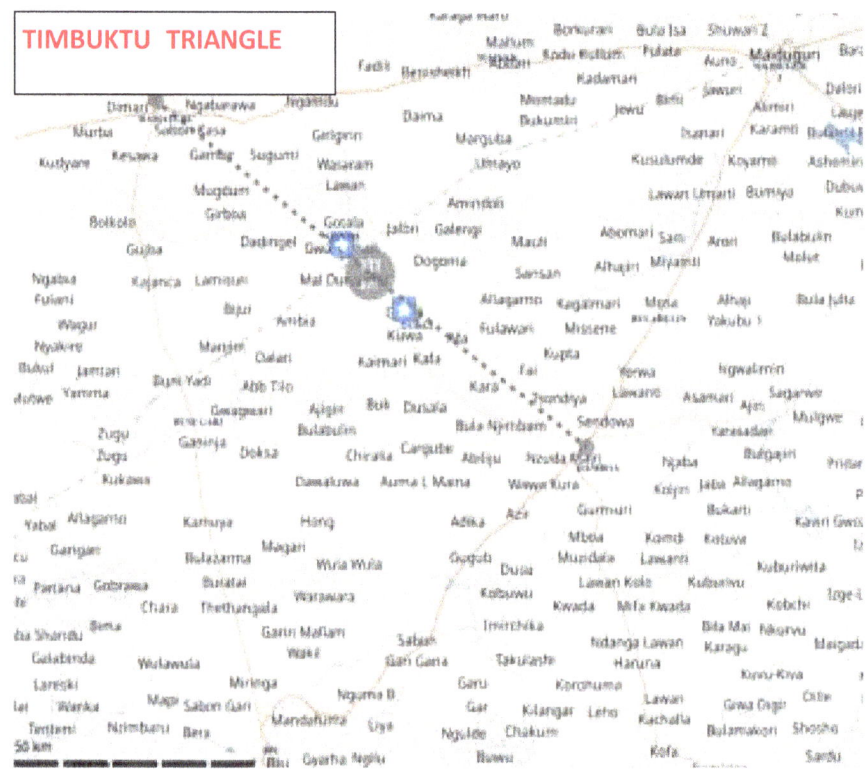

Fig 33: Map of Timbuktu Triangle (Triangle enclosed by Roads Maiduguri-Damaturu, Damaturu- Biu and Maiduguri-Damboa-Biu)
Source: Adapted from Guru Maps Pro Apps.

After considerable assessment of the situation, it was evident that the Nigerian Army needed a reorganization in the North East Theatre towards refocusing its efforts for enhanced performance. Thus, it was no surprise that then Major General Faruk Yahaya – General Officer Commanding 1 Division, Nigerian Army (now Lieutenant General and the Chief of Army Staff) was appointed Theatre Commander, Op LAFIYA DOLE, on 30 March 2020 with effect from 1 April 2020, which was indeed considered a timely decision.

On the adversary side, their numerical strength and equipment capability were usually uncertain and mostly underestimated right from the inception of the military campaign against terrorism and insurgency in North East Nigeria. What was certain was that there had been a steady build-up of resistance by Boko Haram, culminating in what could be termed 'the 22 March 2020 debacle of the Timbuktu Triangle'. The terrorists were emboldened, more daring and were ready to give in whatever it could take to stop the Nigerian Army from penetrating the Timbuktu Triangle which provides access to their 'Allagarno Spiritual Headquarters'. The Islamic State in West African Province (ISWAP) under the leadership of Al-Banawi were the main force in this general area. They were ready to hold the fort there to prevent them from going into Sambisa at that time to avert confrontation with the Abubakar Shekau faction of BHT.

Apparently, the JAS faction of Boko Haram under the leadership of Shekau and the Al-Banawi's ISWAP faction were not on the same page. They, ISWAP, did all they could to make the Triangle impenetrable to the Armed Forces of Nigeria. The terrorists indeed had a field day, in a generally believed below par offensive into the 'Triangle', a fortress of some sort, impermeable until Maj Gen Faruk Yahaya arrived on the scene. He was thus seen as The 'Slim' of the era. The state of jointness within the Theatre was not delivering optimal value towards overall mission accomplishment. Similarly, the local authorities were beginning to have issues with the operation especially with the implementation of the Nigerian Army Super Camp concept, removing permanent deployment of troops away from many villages thereby giving the people a false sense of insecurity. The civil society groups were beginning to question the objective and sincerity of the military towards a quick resolution of the crisis. The arrival of General Faruk Yahaya brought about stability in the area and restored confidence in the people and troops in the North East.

Assumption of Command

Armed with the mandate to reverse the trend of operation, against the terrorists/ insurgents, in favour of own troops and motivate the troops, he wasted no time in reporting to the operations theatre. He arrived in Maiduguri on Friday 3 April 2020 and assumed command as the Theatre Commander, Op LAFIYA DOLE the same day. He took over command from Maj Gen Olusegun Adeniyi, who was redeployed to the Nigerian Army Resource Centre as a Senior Research Fellow. At the Theatre Headquarters and Maiduguri circles, the general tone was 'here in comes Slim'. General Yahaya! the 'Field Marshal William Slim' of some sort! Field Marshall William Slim, a Brit, is best known for commanding the Fourteenth Army in Burma (Myanmar) during World War II. He had inherited a disastrous situation. However, with pragmatic skill and quiet charisma, he turned the situation into an ultimate victory for the Allies. What was most compelling, was General Yahaya's striking resemblance to Slim from a close view. He was pragmatic, visionary, possesses a calm mien, quietly charismatic, but with a keen sense of humour. It is therefore not surprising that he could turn the tide within a short time, albeit with some usual periodic operational challenges akin to the 'Clausewitzian Friction or Fog of War'.

More so, there had been an upsurge in the terrorists' activities across the Theatre, which indicated that the criminals have begun to enjoy the freedom of movement across sectors. For example, there was an attack on civilian commuters in Auno on 12 April 2020, along the Maiduguri-Damaturu Road as well as Buni Gari on 18 April 2020, along the Damaturu – Biu Road amongst others. The renewed adversary engagements, particularly along Main Supply Routes necessitated the restriction of movement through the imposition of a curfew from 1600 hours daily. Unfazed by the daunting task ahead, Gen Yahaya immediately set out his Vision to restore the fighting spirit of the Theatre troops, through in-Theatre training, adequate logistics, sound administration, and bold handling of troops. These were immediately translated into relevant directives upon assumption of duty, with particular reference to the Theatre Commander's maiden directive on 'Additional Security Measures to restrict Boko Haram's Freedom of Movement Across the Theatre.'The Maiden Directive was premised on the need to sustain efforts to deny the Boko Haram Terrorists their operational objectives across Op LAFIYA DOLE Theatre, which need not be over-emphasized at that time.

There was also the need to enhance civil-military relations and support civil authority, which formed his key operational ethos to further guarantee public support. Hence, the restriction of movement and imposition of curfew enhanced the Borno and Yobe State Governments' efforts to restrict movements in line with the outbreak of the COVID-19 Pandemic, prevalent at that time. It could be recalled that Borno State, for instance, had at that time recently recorded a death in Pulka in Sector 1 Area of Operations due to the dreaded COVID-19. This measure also enabled commuters to vacate these major routes, thereby providing an opportunity for complete domination by own troops, in line with the Boko Haram Terrorists'pattern of staging most attacks at that period.

On assumption of command, he sought the support of all the components in the North East theatre which include the Land, Maritime, Air, Logistics, Police and all the paramilitary as well as other security agencies to enable his success in the operations.

> I solicit the support of all components in the theatre; I am talking about Maritime, Air Force and other security agencies to enable us to achieve total peace and sanity in the North East.
> Yahaya, 2020

He addressed troops at the Headquarters Theatre Command, tried to boost their morale, and shifted their focus from groaning over their recent losses to looking forward to surmounting the tasks ahead which were to ultimately lead to the defeat of the terrorists. His assumption of command brought a reinvigorated zeal amongst troops of Op LAFIYA DOLE, particularly due to his antecedents as an astute professional, fantastic administrator and leader of men. Memories of the multitudes recently departed, and in particular the indefatigable SO2 G3 Headquarters Theatre Command, Major Daniel Udoh who fell to the adversary's bullet in the Timbuktu Triangle still filled the air, then came in the Theatre Commander. His presence, the charm, and his firm but fair disposition, all gave hope. Real hope as he was armed with the mandate to reinvigorate Theatre Operations and galvanize troops. He quickly got down to the task ahead. Daunting as it may seem, he made it look easy. So much at ease, calmness personified. Indeed the turn of a new era is a new vista for the Theatre! His assumption of duty also marked a re-organization of processes at the Theatre Headquarters and the entire operation. He brought back the conduct of daily operational briefs and, the production of a weekly summary of incidents across the Theatre. The summary of incidents helped to keep up with the overall operational tempo while acting as a repository to enhance the War Diary.

Firm in disposition, yet fair, Maj Gen Faruk Yahaya on the assumption of duty, tackled head-long the challenge of leadership, perceived sabotage and weak behaviour hitherto condoned by commanders. It could be recalled that there was a hitherto worrisome spate of mission failures and incessant reports of equipment breakdown, which had characterised Op AYISO TAMONUMA. There were also traces of poor junior leadership observed during subsequent operations. On 17 April 2020, there was a failed advance into the Timbuktu Triangle, there were also 3 failed patrols, coupled with frequent reports of 'A' vehicle clutch plate damage, vehicle over-heating and other sundry complaints, which suggested that commanders were not in the firm grip of their subordinates and were possibly tolerating sabotage. A case in point was Sector 2/Combat Team 1 Patrol Team, which was tasked on 2 occasions to patrol to Doksa but failed to get to the objective. Reasons adduced among others included, faulty gun control panel. This led to the AHQ directive to relocate the Sector 2 Headquarters to Doksa from Buni Yadi.

The Theatre Commander tackled this directly with commanders at all levels. Accordingly, defaulters were immediately sanctioned and this was the first sign of paradigm change and a glimpse into what was to follow. According to General Faruk Yahaya "failure is failure, no matter the excuses". He was not ready to accept any form of failure under his watch. He believes that "when you take over any command or office, whatever you fail to change in the first few days or weeks of your assumption of command, you may not be able to change them even throughout your tour of duty". The Theatre began to witness a steady resurgence of able leadership, particularly at the junior command cadre, a few weeks into his tenure. This effect of renewed able junior leadership was manifested in the gallant repelling of Boko Haram attacks at Buni Gari on 19 April 2020 and Geidam on 20 April 2020, with resultant operational gains. This is a lesson for future commanders at all levels. Once you take over your command or a new appointment, let the transformation begin as soon as possible.

While the Boko Haram Terrorists strove to intensify their offensives across the Theatre, Op LAFIYA DOLE under General Yahaya's watch adopted a more offensive posture with tremendous positive outcomes.

This necessitated the immediate commencement of offensive operations across the Theatre such as Op KANTANA JIMLAN, Op TIGER HUNT, and Op FIRE BALL, which metamorphosed into Op TURA TAKAI TABONGO amongst others. There were likewise, various subsidiary operations across the Theatre in a bid to off-set the adversary's hitherto enhanced tempo.

Operation KANTANA JIMLAN

Op KANTANA JIMLAN was intended to dislodge Boko Haram Terrorists from the entire Theatre in stages, beginning with the Timbuktu Triangle and subsequent sweeps to the Sambisa Forest and the Lake Chad area, which were hitherto strongholds of the adversary. The first stage was intended to dislodge and destroy the terrorists in the Timbuktu Triangle, recover lost equipment and further frustrate the terrorists' operational objectives, which were intended to completely turn the tide on Boko Haram Terrorists in the Theatre. The first stage of the operation was conducted from April-June 2020 followed by an operational pause. The Theatre Command's Tactical Headquarters was initially established at Ngamdu before the further directive was given to relocate to Buni Yadi. Subsequently, Op KANTANA JIMLAN fully commenced on 17 April 2020 with an advance into the Timbuktu Triangle along the Buni-Yadi-Lariski-Gwagwari-Malumti-Ajigin-Talala-Buk-Dusula axis, while the Main Effort rested with Sector 2. This was complemented by Artillery fire missions, Air Interdiction and blocking operations at Jemyeri, Mal Dunamari and Kassachia. Troops were tasked to destroy Boko Haram Terrorists in camps, logistics bases, and crossing points in the Timbuktu Triangle to set conditions for the final defeat of the Boko Haram Terrorists elements. Characteristic of General Faruk Yahaya, The Theatre Commander, his disposition was indeed the needed boost to reinvigorate an offensive spirit, which was observed in the troops for this phase.

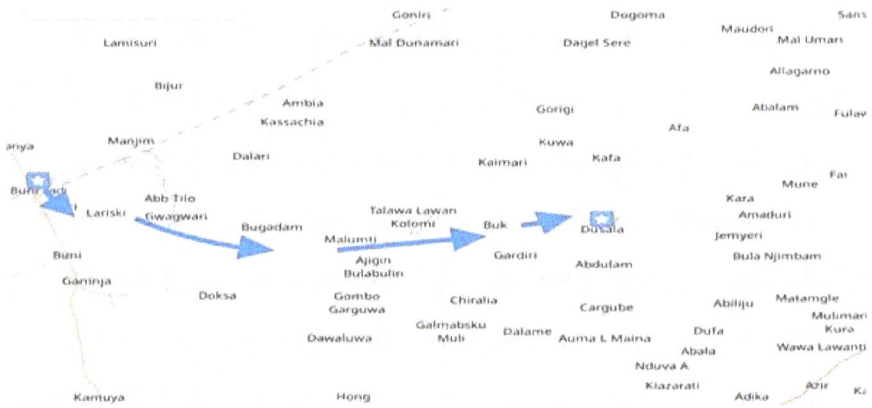

Fig 34: Axis of Advance for Operation KANTANA JIMLAN Source: Adapted from Guru Maps Pro Apps.

The operation also incorporated aggressive deep fighting patrols across varying fronts in conjunction with Artillery fire missions and air interdictions as the immediate precursor operations. There were indeed quick gains at the commencement of this stage. It could be recalled that on 18 April 2020, an unconfirmed number of Boko Haram Terrorists attacked Buni Gari village. Gallant troops of Op KANTANA JIMLAN swiftly mobilized to engage the criminals with a high volume of fire forcing the assailants to withdraw in disarray. The Air Task Force also provided Air Interdiction. As a result, several terrorists were killed while troops recovered Anti- Aircraft guns, GPMGs, PKT Machine Guns, AK47 rifles, RPG bombs, and a host of other equipment. There was an operational pause in June 2020. Cognizant of the need to interface with troops to uplift troops' morale and improve confidence, the Theatre Commander immediately set out on operational visits to sectors, taking advantage of the operational pause declared in June 2020, during the conduct of Op KANTANA JIMLAN. Operational visits and durbars were held in Sectors 1, 3 and 2 in that order in June – July 2020. The visits enabled first-hand insights into common operational challenges bedevilling the forces, and this helped craft initial response measures.

The Second Phase of the operation commenced with the Precursor Phase on 24 August 2020, with emphasis on Human Intelligence, continuous Intelligence Surveillance and Reconnaissance (ISR), Air Interdiction (AI) and artillery engagements. During this phase, Sector 2 established blocking positions at key Boko Haram Terrorists crossing points and approach routes around the Timbuktu Triangle, while other sectors conducted subsidiary operations in support of the Sector around the Triangle. ISR, artillery and air bombardment were also conducted on some identified Boko Haram terrorists enclaves and hideouts such as Buk, Doksa, Gwagwari, Abbtilo, Wass, Lariski, Digamari, Manjim, Degel Sere and Alagarno. Phase 2 of the Second Stage, took place from 2-15 September 2020 and entailed a limited incursion into the Timbuktu Triangle. Sector 2 had been directed by the Theatre Commander to project limited incursions into the Triangle to choke the adversary, while sustaining the Artillery bombardments. Sectors 1 and 3 continued to conduct subsidiary operations in support of Sector 2 around the Timbuktu triangle while maintaining blocking positions to destroy fleeing Boko Haram Terrorists from the Triangle.

Phase 3 of Op KANTANA JIMLAN, which was the final assault into the Boko Haram Terrorists identified enclaves commenced on 21 September 2020 with Sector 2 as the lead while Sectors 1 and 3 were tasked to conduct subsidiary operations in support of Sector 2. Key objectives included clearance of Mauli, Sansan, Quari, Mamanti, Dakwari, Marguba, Borgozo, Masamari and Gelnori, all in the 'Timbuktu Triangle'. Troops also undertook several forays into the Wajiroko - Sabon Gari corridor, although encountered a setback with the unfortunate demise of the Commander 25 Task Force Brigade, Col Bako in an ambush cum IED attack. This indeed had a negative effect on troops' morale, although did not in any way slow down the operational tempo. Op KANTANA JIMLAN was subsequently paused at the end of September 2020, with another offensive planned into the Triangle using an entirely different axis, due to terrain and weather effects.

Operation FIRE BALL

Limited success was achieved during Op KANTANA JIMLAN, which was largely attributed to the weather and difficulty in navigating the Timbuktu Triangle terrain. Furthermore, recent intelligence had revealed that the Boko Haram criminal elements had continued to converge in Gwagwari and its environs from where they intended to project their nefarious activities. Thus, Op FIRE BALL was activated on 6 October 2020 with the intent to destroy, clear and dominate the general areas of the Timbuktu Triangle. The objective was to effectively dominate these areas with clearance operations, patrols, ambushes and blocking positions as well as long- range patrols and raids. To strengthen these efforts in Phase 1, the Special

Firepower Concentration on the Timbuktu Triangle, involving the coordinated use of direct and in-direct weapon systems along with the Air Task Force and other fire support units including the establishment of Artillery Manoeuvre Areas to support manoeuvre formations/units was successfully conducted.

The first phase, which was the precursor phase, focused on the Timbuktu Triangle. Phase 2 was the limited incursion phase while Phase 3 was the assault into Boko Haram terrorists' enclaves and Phase 4 was the recovery phase. Furthermore, the persistent weather effects led to the short-lived Op FIRE BALL as offensive troops were subsequently withdrawn from their already established Artillery Manoeuvre Areas to the concentration areas of Ngamdu, and Buni Gari in order to re-strategise. This necessitated the review of the concept of operations and the insertion of the 4 Special Forces Command to bolster troops' efforts in the subsequent Op TURA TAKAIBANGO. Op FIRE BALL ended on 30 December 2020 to pave way for Op TURA TAKAIBANGO.

Operation TURA TAKAIBANGO

Op FIRE BALL also achieved limited success just like Op KANTANA JIMLAN. This was largely attributed to the difficulty in navigating the Timbuktu Triangle terrain. Thus, Op TURA TAKAIBANGO was launched on 31 December 2020 with the intent to destroy, clear, and dominate the general areas of the Timbuktu Triangle, Lake Chad Basin/Northern Borno and Sambisa Forest in Phases 1, 2 and 3 respectively. The objective was to effectively dominate these areas with offensive operations to clear villages and settlements, fighting patrols, ambushes and blocking positions as well as long-range patrols and raids. To strengthen these efforts in Phase 1, the Special Firepower Concentration on the Timbuktu Triangle, involving the coordinated use of direct and in-direct weapon systems along with the Air Task Force and other fire support units including the establishment of Artillery Manoeuvre Areas to support manoeuvre formations/units was successfully conducted.

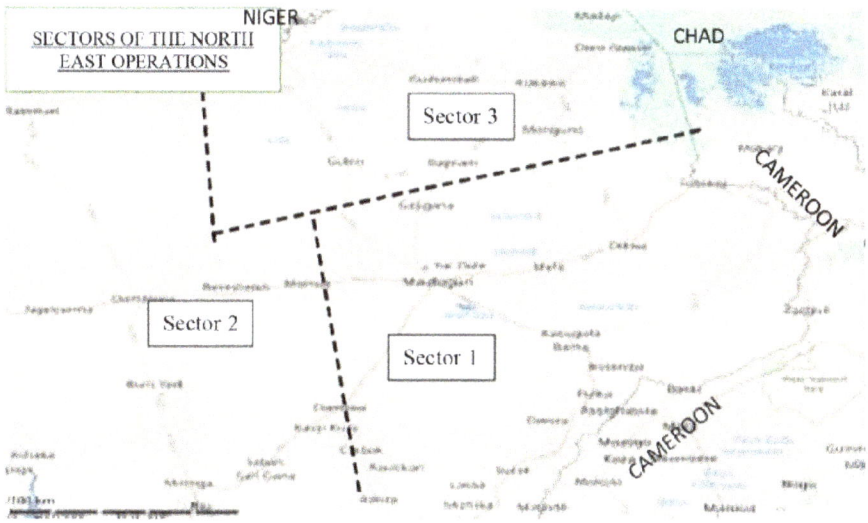

Fig 35: Deployment of Troops for Operation TURA TAKAIBANGO Source: Adapted from Guru Maps Pro Apps.

Phase 1 of Op TURA TAKAIBANGO was concluded on 3 February 2021 with the capture of Gwagwari, which was preceded by the capture of major enclaves including Talala, Ajigin, Buk, Doksa, Gorgi, Kafa, Muchima A and Muchima B. It is pertinent to state that Op TURA TAKAIBANGO was largely successful owing to the dogged and visionary leadership of the Theatre Commander. Furthermore, given the significant in-roads that the troops made within the Triangle, there is no gainsaying the fact that this feat into the Triangle had never before been achieved and in this magnitude of significant defeat of the terrorists. The TC thereafter set out plans to consolidate on these gains before his departure from the Theatre. Careful planning, forecasting, efficient battle preparations, robust logistics build-up, as directed by the TC, were largely responsible for this feat. The appointment of Lieutenant General Ibrahim Attahiru as the Twentieth Chief of Army Staff Nigerian Army on 26 January 2021 brought about a total review of the Operations in the North East. The fact that Major General Faruk Yahaya was retained as Theatre Commander even with all the changes made, including the redesignation of the North East Operations as Op HADIN KAI speaks volumes of his competence and personality.

Subsidiary Operational Efforts

Many subsidiary operations were conducted under Maj Gen Faruk Yahaya's watch as the Theatre Commander Op LAFIYA DOLE. It is also noteworthy to mention the successful deployment of 403 Amphibious Brigade to Baga on 23 August 2020 during his tour of duty as the Theatre Commander. Upon assumption of duty, General Yahaya had remained consistent in his resolve to stabilize Baga and its environs, and the relocation of the brigade, which was considered key to the security and stability of the area, was at the top of his list of priorities. The Theatre also made several efforts to dominate the Baga general area through constant patrols and ambushes, while seeking out the terrorists' hideouts. The Brigade troops also provided security for the rehabilitation of the Internally Displaced Persons (IDPs) returning to Baga town and its environs.

Long-range patrols were activated to seize the initiative and deny the criminals freedom of movement in troubled routes and enclaves. This necessitated the TC's directive to all sectors to scale-up long range patrols to counter the effect of the terrain during the rainy seasons. The effort largely yielded results, as witnessed on 7 September 2020, when own Patrol Team of the 402 Special Forces Brigade dealt decisively with the terrorists along Gubio-Maigumeri Road, killing several of the terrorists and recovering key equipment and vehicles.

In recognition of the need to support other collaborative actors within the operational space, the Theatre under General Faruk Yahaya's command provided security and escorted United Nations agencies, International Non-Governmental Organizations, Non-Governmental Organizations, and other humanitarian agencies in the discharge of their humanitarian duties. This included logistics movements, food and medical aid distribution, fertilizer movement as well as distribution. The Theatre also assisted the Borno State Government with escorts and security to ensure that necessary amenities were provided in several communities even in the face of terrorists' acts.

The Theatre facilitated the efforts of some Federal Ministries, Departments and Agencies in the implementation of the Federal Government's housing, education, agricultural, and IDPs' initiatives. Furthermore, troops conducted joint operations with federal law enforcement agencies like the National Drug Law Enforcement Agency, National Immigration Service, and the National Correctional Service, among others, towards implementing government policies and directives. Indeed, the Theatre Commander was so passionate about these requests for support for other actors that from their inception he directed a review of the request process to make it more efficient. These efforts were sustained under his watch, as such collaborations helped enhance the much-needed cross-governmental synergy in line with the Comprehensive Approach to warfare.

Protection of IDP camps was given top priority under his watch. The most vulnerable targets are usually the IDP camps, which currently house large populations. There were 59 major IDP camps with over 1,000 IDPs in the Theatre including men, women, and children. The terrorists sometimes attack the camps to raid for logistics supplies and eliminate persons suspected to be informants supporting own operations. However, Theatre troops under his command rose to the occasion to ensure lives and properties at the camps were adequately protected as attempts to infiltrate or attack IDP camps were mostly repelled.

Similarly, the improved operational posture under General Yahaya continued to translate to gains in stability and normalcy. This led to a gradual return to normalcy in the Theatre, with civilians steadily returning to their ancestral homes. The Theatre under his command also facilitated the Borno State Government's successful relocation of IDPs to their ancestral homes. It could be recalled that on 10 September 2020, a total of 750 households in the Kawuri community displaced by the terrorists in 2013 returned to Kawuri for the Phase 1 occupation of the community, an exercise supervised by the officials of the Borno State Government.

Most notable was that Baga, the erstwhile economic and commercial centre in Northern Borno, was re-opened to receive its inhabitants on 26 September 2020, with the return of over 1,500 of its original occupants on the same day and about 9015 inhabitants relocated under a month. Baga has since stabilized and normal socio-economic activities have resumed. Other notable towns that the IDPs were relocated to included Gwoza, Pulka, Izge, Bama, Banki, Ajiri, and Ngoshe amongst others. The relocation of civilians indeed was a key indicator of progress made in Gen Yahaya's efforts to ensure stability under his command. His efforts indeed provided the enabling environment for this feat, which has been sustained in the Theatre. Similarly, in 2020, residents of Chibok witnessed the peaceful conduct of the West African Examination Council School leaving examination. It is pertinent to note that this examination had not taken place in Chibok since 2013.

Reconstruction and rehabilitation of Main Supply Routes, which was a key responsibility of the state governments, were undertaken during his command upon his recommendation to Army Headquarters. Suffice to state that the Theatre Command had also commenced palliative repairs of the Maiduguri-Damboa road to enhance its own operations. Consequently, Army Headquarters directed the Theatre to commence reconstruction of the Buni Gari-Kamuya-Buratai road, the Ngamdu-Goniri road, the Ganija-Doksa-Ajigin road, and the Goniri-Kafa-Jimyeri- Damboa road.

Some Personal Close Encounters with the Insurgents

General Faruk Yahaya always had the knack for maintaining a forward presence in various locations, as he made several tours and visits to forward troops during his tenure. Considering the low state of morale preceding his assumption of duty, these visitations greatly enhanced troops' spirits across the Theatre. He was keen on seeing to the well-being of his troops and 'problem solving' during such visits was his passion. He also undertook several on-the-spot assessments of equipment, vehicles, and troops' living conditions and would always direct immediate provision of financial and logistics support as appropriate, regardless of the level of command at hand. However, he would demand prudent and efficient utilization of such resources and was very keen in that aspect of administration. It is worthy of note that on two occasions during such tours, the entourage/convoy of the Theatre Commander, Major General Faruk Yahaya, had its own fair share of the adversary's attack 'first-hand', with his tactical prodigy coming to the fore. 'calmness and boldness were exemplified' during these encounters.

It could be recalled that Boko Haram insurgents sprang a well-coordinated attack on Monguno in Sector 3 on 13 June 2020. Credible intelligence had indicated that the attack was planned for 12 June 2020. However, due to the Theatre Commander's operational visit to Monguno on the same date, the attack was delayed till his departure on 13 June 2020, with the adversary assessing that it would be inimical to stage the attack with such additional firepower in town on said date. The visit was concluded successfully on 12 June 2020 and as of 0800 hours 13 June 2020, the Theatre Commander departed Monguno for Baga, with a halt at Cross Kauwa at about 1200 hours where he addressed the troops of the 401 Special Forces Brigade.

Barely 40 minutes of departure from Cross Kauwa, General Faruk Yahaya received information of the adversary's attack on Monguno. From the horizon, thick black smoke dotted the skyline. In a swift move, he ordered a detour to Monguno to provide support to Headquarters Sector 3 to repel the attack. Most pertinent was his decision to proceed to Monguno by 'cross-country' as opposed to the expected Main Supply Route Monguno-Cross Kauwa-Baga. This move was indeed significant as it enabled the team to gain surprise on the enemy, who had taken over 'Charlie 6 Gate' at Monguno, upon the team's arrival. Elements of the terrorists at Charlie 6 Gate were immediately neutralized by the team on arrival, and mopping up of the left-over terrorists was conducted with the Theatre Commander leading with sheer doggedness. That was indeed calmness and boldness personified from a 'first hand' perspective, with no own-troop casualties recorded.

Similarly, the Theatre Commander's convoy was ambushed by BHT in Mainok on 28 February 2021. Following the insurgents' change of tactics, which saw the destruction of critical national infrastructure such as the national electricity power lines, the terrorists damaged a pylon on the national grid in the Mainok general area in mid-2020. This resulted in a power outage in substantial parts of Borno State. Repair work has since commenced and is approaching completion in February 2021. The Theatre Commander had paid an on-the-spot visit to assess the repair work being executed by officials of the Power Holding Company of Nigeria on the fateful day. While returning to Maiduguri after the assessment visit, his convoy was ambushed, and in his usual manner, he rallied the troops to defeat the ambush with no casualty sustained on own troops. While the news filtered into the Army Headquarters, there was a lot of apprehension until the comprehensive situation report was received and Maj Gen F Yahaya, the Theatre Commander, was confirmed unhurt.

Synergy with other Components under his Command

Under General Yahaya's leadership, synergy among all components of the Theatre force was enhanced, resulting in enhanced Air-Land integration during engagements, among other things. The prompt response from the Air Task Force for close air support, ISR, and casualty evacuation, among others, provided the ground troops under his watch with the needed opportunity to further degrade the adversary in concert with their own artillery efforts. This also contributed immensely in enhancing troops' morale. Significant examples were the close air support provided to troops during the terrorist attack on Buni Gari on 18 April 2020, Monguno on 13 June 2020; and the decimation of the terrorists in large numbers in Kumshe on 6 September 2020, while occupying their former camp. The synergy between the ground forces and air component also increased the tempo of operations, with great results achieved under his watch.

The commencement of the relocation of the Maritime Component to Baga was undertaken under his watch, and this effort was finally realized in October 2021. It could be recalled that the Maritime Component had not deployed in Baga since it was dislodged in 2018, a feat, that has so far enhanced maritime presence in the Lake Chad area and complemented the Land forces' efforts at restoring normalcy in the general area. At the regional level, the Theatre under Major General Faruk Yahaya's watch deepened collaboration with the Multi-National Joint Task Force (MNJTF) in the Lake Chad Basin area leading to a series of successful combined operations.

In-Theatre Training, Logistics, and other Innovative Efforts

The passion for training to impart knowledge and drive home the belief that the best welfare for troops is training epitomized Major General Faruk Yahaya's tenure as the Theatre Commander, himself being a seasoned trainer. In-theatre training was wholly emphasized to improve the capacity of own troops. Emphasis was laid on ambush, counter/anti ambush drills to boost their fighting spirit. The Theatre also developed video clips on ambush and counter/anti ambush drills using its own troops' demonstrations, which were utilized as training materials across the Theatre.

Training cadres focused on practical lessons on First Aid, counter IED drills, route scanning and basic convoy drills, which conducted on a periodic basis. Furthermore, batched cadres on weapon handling were organized, particularly on the General Purpose Machine Gun, Machine Gun-1, and Self Propelled Gun-9 among others. A special focus was also given to improving the capacity of Un-armed Aerial Vehicles' handling and operations. Officers and soldiers were also trained as drone-pilots and organized into drone-teams to improve Nigerian troops surveillance capacity and battlefield awareness at lower levels, and this was extended to personnel of the Multi National Joint Task Force.

In order to improve logistic support in the Theatre, the Headquarters Theatre Command under the Theatre Commander's directive undertook salvage, repairs and refurbishment of arms, ammunition and vehicles. For instance, 7 Base Ammunition Depot Maiduguri, on the direction of the Theatre Headquarters salvaged and repaired 96 hitherto unserviceable Rocket 40 milimetre Rocket Propelled Gun-7 High Eexplosive Anti Tank by replacing the unserviceable propellant charges with serviceable ones removed from inert rounds of the same ammunition. In a similar vein, the Theatre carried out repairs on a variety of weapons and vehicles to reduce the effects of equipment casualties and sustain the tempo of operations.

The Theatre Headquarters also devised a system of identifying units with large quantities of unserviceable vehicles. This was to activate immediate intervention should the cost be beyond the capacity of such formation to bear, as part of efforts to boost vehicle holding in the Theatre. In this regard, several vehicles were repaired on a continuous basis and this greatly assisted to improve the overall mobility and lift capacity of the Theatre under Major General Yahaya's command. In addition to the logistics support provided, the Headquarters Theatre Command undertook various innovative measures to improve operational effectiveness across the Theatre. These were in the areas of Counter- Improvised Explosives Devices Equipment, Force Protection for Troops and Conversion of Soft Skin Vehicles to Armoured Fighting Vehicles. Some of these will be highlighted in this section.

The North East Nigeria Operations Theatre also witnessed some Research and Development Efforts under Major General Faruk Yahaya's watch. Because of the war effort in the Theatre and the need to preserve valuable national resources, Op LAFIYA DOLE, under his command, had to look inward to evolve home-grown technologies in military equipment. These include the local production of Mine Resistant Ambush Protected (MRAP) vehicles with materials sourced from within the Theatre, except for the bullet-resistant glasses, which were sourced from Kaduna. Additionally, Burnt and Beyond Economic Repairs Vehicule Blinde Leger (VBL) were reconstructed on new Buffalo Chasis and were immediately deployed in the Theatre. Furthermore, the conversion of gun trucks and tractors to "Armoured Gun Trucks All Terrain" was also carried out. In the same vein, 'Fire Eaters', which are metal sheets with armour plating, were made to provide local protection for troops while in harbour and in defensive positions. These could withstand 12.7milimetres (non-armour piercing) from

150 metres, which minimized the effects of the terrorists' small arms fire during encounters.

Under his supervision, the Theatre also created the Counter-IED Roller. Boko Haram's tactics often involved the use of IEDs to delay troops' advances and inflict maximum casualties. IEDs are also usually laid on supply routes to frustrate logistics supplies to troops. In order to counter this threat, the Theatre often deploys the Bozena Mine Clearing Vehicle to clear the routes of IEDs. However, Bozena tillers often caused damages to the routes, which leads to movement difficulty for vehicles. To overcome this disadvantage, the Theatre came up with the idea of attaching heavy rollers to the front of the Bozena in place of the tillers, which could be rolled over the IEDs to cause detonation. This proved effective as most of the IEDs laid by the terrorists were pressure triggered and the rollers had enough weight to activate such IEDs. The system was also flexible as the roller drums were detachable and damaged ones could easily be replaced.

Bravely Committed to Duty

Lt Gen Faruk Yahaya is bravely committed to duty. This was an account of Maj Gen IM Yusuf, his course mate. "This happened in 2020; I can't remember the exact date. I was at that time the Commander of MNJTF and Damasak came under attack. Actually, I had taken Maj Gen Ogunlade out for dinner; he had come to take over from me. We were out for dinner when I got the information that Damasak was under attack. This was past 8 PM, and the Commander actually called me to say that they were repelling, but these people are many, and his fear was that they may run out of ammunition. The attack was early in the night, and he desperately needed ammunition. So quickly, I told Maj Gen Ogunlade that I had to leave. I called our partners and spoke to them about replenishment at night. Can we resupply at night? And he said "Yes, if we have an ISR platform," so I said yes and that I would go with them. So I quickly called Maj Gen Faruk, who was then the Theatre Commander, and said, "I know our Air Force will not do this because of their own capability, but these guys are willing, so I am coming with the helicopter. Just get the ammunition ready, when I come, I will pick it up, and to give them confidence, we will do the resupply together with them." And you know before this people will come, start off and fly to Maiduguri, attack had been repelled, but the information was that they were on the outskirts, hoping to launch an attack in the morning, so that was when the resupply became even more compelling.

By the time I landed in Maiduguri, he was there and had brought the ammunition, so they quickly loaded and when we were about to go, he said he was going with me, I now said how "Force Commander, and Theatre Commander in one helicopter, I said no, I am going because these are foreigners - the pilot is an American and the other is a Ukrainian - is to give them confidence and be able to share the risks with them and all that. But the two of us cannot be. "And he said, if I am willing to be on that flight, then he will go; but if I am not going, then... So all efforts to convince him failed, and we both boarded. Because we carried ammunition, we couldn't carry any other person, it was only me and him in the helicopter, then the ammunition. By the time we took off, it was past 11 PM, and less than 15 minutes later, the aircraft developed problem.

Even he, I never told him about this part because I was wearing the earpiece and heard the conversation while he was not hearing. Something went wrong, a technical fault in the aircraft, so the pilot would not know his orientation, if he is banking, and the altimeter too went off, so he would not know the altitude. I just heard the pilot say, "Oh, this thing is off. He was communicating by saying I can't see it. What has happened." He said okay, he was going to turn the aircraft at exactly 180°, you know I am going this way, if I turn 180°, I am going the opposite direction. So, he should monitor and tell him when he is 180°, when he did 180°, we were heading back and he now said call the control tower. They actually declared an emergency. His hope was that when we turned back, at that altitude, we would be able to see the runway lights, and if he was able to see the runway light, if it was in the day time, it wouldn't be an emergency, but at night, when it was an emergency flight, it was impossible for you to land as those parameters were not working. And we started heading back, and they started calling; apparently as soon as we took off, the Control Tower just switched off the runway lights. So they kept on calling and all of a sudden, the runway lights came up and because I heard their conversation, I knew they also panicked. That was how we landed; this was around 12AM and then the next day, in the morning, we went to do this mission. So he still followed me on this mission." That sums up Gen Yahaya's level of commitment to duty, even at the cost of his own life. Not many people have such levels of dedication and commitment, especially in this clime.

Strategic Guidance to Subsequent Theatre Commanders

Upon his appointment as the Chief of Army Staff, Maj Gen Faruk Yahaya handed over to his Deputy Theatre Commander, Maj Gen FO Omoigui who supervised over the Theatre in an acting capacity from 28 May to 18 June 2021, before a new Theatre Commander assumed Command. The next Theatre Commander was Maj Gen CG Musa from 18 June 2021 until 28 January 2023 before handing over to Maj Gen IS Ali on 28 January 2023. As the Chief of Army Staff, Gen Faruk Yahaya continued to give strategic guidance and support to the Theatre Commanders. According to Maj Gen CG Musa, 'I was mandated to use the joint team, that I have, to restore peace in the North East specifically'. This was the strategic direction given to him by the Chief of Army Staff upon his appointment as the Theatre Commander. He is of the view that Gen Faruk Yahaya is goal oriented, and his focus is on achieving the objectives of the North East operation.

Generally we are talking about the Chief of Army Staff, frankly speaking, his posture, commitment, and style of leadership have actually made a lot of difference. Like I was telling you, when he came in at that time [as Theatre Commander], for the first three weeks, he didn't even know where the Theatre Headquarters was. He was taken and dumped into the Timbuktu Triangle. Orders and Counter-Orders were just coming in left, – right, and – centre. It wasn't good, but as you can see now, that is no longer there. He tells you to keep him updated with what you are doing and he looks at it; "yes what about this, we tell him no, this is what we are doing." And he visits regularly, he comes and we discuss and tell him these are some of the things that we are doing and the thing I like about him again is that he gives you an opportunity to talk. He listens, even if they bring an idea to him, and you feel differently about it, he says no, you are the one on ground. Then [in the past], people from Abuja would be the ones to call you and say you had to follow this road to that place; they were here, and all these things. Those things were creating a lot of problems, and then when you have Principal Staff Officers that want to show, "Oh we are with the Chief, we know better," all that is no longer there. They come to advice and listen to you, but the final decision is yours. That has really made our day, and the fact is that he is always willing and ready to provide what we need. Again, the good part of it is that he is a good individual, somebody who means well. There is no bitterness; he is not looking for faults, before now people want to hear all kinds of names, but he is not out for all those things. He is very simple, you will hardly ever hear him talk, but he wants the results to show and I think that is very critical and important. And now, junior ones are growing and seeing another kind of leadership. They don't have to come and insult you; on those days with your Two-Stars they can insult you by saying,

> You are stupid, and all those things." So he gives people that respect that you too will want to achieve, you don't want to let such a person down. Musa, 2023.

Non-Kinetic Approaches to CTCOIN Operations in Nigeria

Non-kinetic efforts are principal to CTCOIN particularly when fighting an ideologically based war. This is because kinetic efforts can only stabilise the crisis, but the permanent solution is non-kinetic i.e., good governance
(Omozoje, 2022)

Introduction

It has become a global truism that CTCOIN operations can hardly be successful when national resources are channelled solely into kinetic efforts. The contemporary experiences have shown that fighting non-conventional wars like CTCOIN requires, to a very large extent, non-kinetic approaches, which tend to address more of the root causes of conflicts or war. In a non-kinetic approach, countries depend mostly on soft power to plan several operations and activities that are usually civil-led and military-protected. Since 2013, the Federal Government of Nigeria (FGN) has employed CTCOIN strategies, which focused mainly on military containment, to provide security in the North East. Irabor in Kalambe (2019) observed that Op RESTORE ORDER (1, 2, and 3), the MNJTF, Op BOYONA, ZAMAN LAFIYA and Op LAFIYA DOLE were 98 per cent kinetic with remaining 2 per cent focused on non-kinetic quick impact projects to support the victims of the crisis in the theatre environment.

This situation necessitated the argument by Yusuf (2019) that there is need for a non-kinetic approach, which includes a bevy of non-coercive initiatives that focus on behavioural and infrastructural transformation, the diffusion of tension, and the provision of relief to communities affected by war, and the creation of an enabling environment for a speedy return to peace. As the CTCOIN operations became more intensive with increasingly complex emergencies that required more of non- of kinetic approach, the FGN activated its first official non kinetic approach to CTCOIN in the NE with the establishment of the Presidential Initiatives for the North East (PINE) in 2014. Subsequently, the Presidential Committee on Victim Support Fund (PCVSF) and Safe School Initiatives

(SSI) were later created in the same year by the administration of former President Goodluck Ebele Jonathan.

Since 2015, the FGN, under the leadership of President Muhammadu Buhari (GCFR), has initiated several other non-kinetic approaches such as the Presidential Committee on the North East Initiatives (PCNEI) Bama Initiatives (BI), the establishment of the North East Development Commission (NEDC), redesignations of the National Commission for Refugees, Migrants, and IDPs (NCFRMI) and the creation of the Federal Ministry of Humanitarian Affairs, Disaster Management, and Social Development (FMHSD). All these efforts are Civil-led and Military-protected and significantly leveraged soft power to record appreciable successes in countering terrorism and insurgency in the country. The second, and perhaps the most critical, component of the non-kinetic approaches is the Military-led and Civilian-targeted activities that have been initiated by the Armed Forces of Nigeria. Realising that CTCOIN should largely be non-kinetic, the DHQ and the services particularly the Nigerian Army, established the Department of Civil-Military Affairs to coordinate all non-kinetic operations in the theatre to complement the kinetic efforts in CTCOIN operations across the country. However, from 2021, the Nigerian Army under the leadership of Lt Gen Faruk Yahaya, has improved tremendously on its non-kinetic approaches, which have continued to yield more positive results in the CTCOIN operations. Thus, the prospects of non-kinetic approaches have become central to the overall discourse of CTCOIN operations in Nigeria.

Overview of the Civil-led Non-Kinetic Efforts of the Federal Government of Nigeria to CTCOIN

Nigeria has a long history of utilising non-kinetic approaches to finding lasting solutions to conflicts or war. The Nigerian Civil War, which broke out seven years after Nigeria's independence (1967-1971), presented a major instability that threatened the corporate existence of the country. With extensive use of hard power and prolonged hostilities, the war ended with a proclamation of "no victor, no vanquish" which ushered in the Reconciliation, Rehabilitation and Reconstruction known as the 3Rs Programme. The programme was essentially a non-kinetic approach to aid recovery from the civil war and promote unity in the country.

Regardless of its shortcomings however, the 3Rs programmes served as a soft power method of achieving what hard power couldn't by returning the country to stability (Abdullahi, 2021). The second major non-kinetic effort deployed by the FGN is the Presidential Amnesty Program (PAP) of 2009. Unlike the civil war experience, PAP was adopted after military campaigns against the Niger Delta militants failed to yield desired outcomes. The Nigerian government was compelled to re-strategize and entice the militants with the promise of amnesty, compensation and capacity building amongst other incentives. After the declaration of amnesty in 2009, the FGN embarked on many socio-economic development projects, environmental remediation, and youth empowerment programmes which in turn stabilized the region and increased oil production to above 2.2 million BPD from about 1 million BPD years earlier (Salihu and Yakubu, 2021).

Before the establishment of any special initiative or agency for the purpose of non- kinetic activities in the North-East and other parts of the country, the already existing government framework for emergency response, such as the National Emergency Management Agency (NEMA), the State Emergency Management Agencies (SEMAs), and the NCFRMI, were the first to be at the forefront of providing humanitarian assistance in the theatre. The role played by the Federal Government through NEMA and NCFRMI, the state governments, particularly in the cases of Borno, Adamawa and Yobe States was critical in the care for IDPs with the provision of accommodation, food, non-food materials, medical supplies and also in leading the advocacy for support in dealing with the insurgency and its effects both nationally and internationally (PCNI, 2016). In response to this advocacy, various Non- Governmental Organizations (NGOs) have also contributed in collaboration with Global Development Partners (GDPs) and the state governments to provide this much needed emergency relief to the victims of terrorism and insurgency while the kinetic activities of the CTCOIN operations are being carried on by the AFN (PCNI, 2016).

Interestingly, the first formal civil-led and military-protected non-kinetic initiative of the FGN in responding to the adverse effects of the activities of BHT was the PINE which was established in 2014. Deriving strengths from the Federal Ministry of Finance's Federal Initiative for the North East (FINE), the National Planning Commission's Special Planning Initiative for the North East (SPINE), and the originating platform from ONSA's

North East Economic Transformation Initiative (NEETI), the PINE's objectives were premised on the Marshal Plan for the revitalization of the economy of the North East (PCNI, 2016). Its mandate also included a short-term economic intervention programme which allows the Federal Government to leverage economic tools targeting the root causes of the insurgency, using the Soft Approach to Countering Terrorism Policy (SACTP) to address the underlying economic problems of the North-East. Also, in the same year, former President Goodluck Jonathan inaugurated a committee called the Victims Support Fund under the leadership of General T.Y Danjuma (Rtd.).

The VSF Committee set up the Nigeria Foundation for the Support of Victims of Terrorism as a private sector led initiative, which is the implementation arm of the Committee, with select members of the Committee as its Board. The Committee, at the official Fundraising Dinner on 31 July 2014, raised over 50 billion Naira in pledges, with over 20 billion Naira redeemed as of the end of 2016 (PCNI, 2016). Following the dwindling fortune of the education system in the North-East due to the activities of the BHT and the need for immediate intervention to secure the future of millions of children and youths in the region, the FGN, in collaboration with the UN Special Envoy for Global Education, and a coalition of Nigerian business leaders, established "The Safe Schools Initiative (SSI)" on 7 May 2014, during the World Economic Forum Africa (WEFA) held in Abuja. The objective of the SSI is to urgently protect hundreds of schools across the country, starting with schools in the North-East from future attacks and kidnappings. This announcement was followed by the inauguration of a Steering Committee for the initiative by former President Goodluck Jonathan on 9 July 2014 and the successful kick-off of the North East Schools Students Transfer Programme (NESSTP) (PCNI, 2016). It could be recalled that between 2009 and 2015, Boko Haram attacks in the North-East destroyed more than 910 schools and forced at least 1,500 to close. By the opening of 2016, an estimated 952,029 school-age children had fled the violence (Yusuf, 2019).

After the 2015 General Elections and the emergence of President Muhammadu Buhari, another North-East focused initiative called the Presidential Committee on the North East Initiatives (PCNI) was established in 2016 with a more robust mandate. The PCNI was to coordinate and manage the government approaches aimed at dealing with the issues of humanitarian aid, early recovery and resettlement, as well as the developmental challenges in a concerted attempt to tackle the root causes of the insurgency in the North-East region. The PCNI was also to serve as the overall coordinating body for the relevant activities of the VSF and the SSI, as well as all existing Federal Government structures involved in North-East interventions (PCNI, 2016). The PCNI was to also guide the planning activities of the State Governments and the Federal Government. Realising the magnitude of the devastating effects of the Boko Haram activities in the North-East and the long term socio-economic and stability plans required for the region to recover and return to its hitherto vibrant state, the FGN, through the NASS, enacted the North East Development Commission (NEDC) Act in 2017. Thus, the North-East Development Commission (NEDC) was established in 2017 as the focal organization charged with the responsibility to assess, coordinate, harmony and report on all intervention programs and initiatives by the Federal Government or any of its Ministries, Departments and Agencies (MDAs), states; and other development partners, and for the implementation of all programmes and initiatives in the North East states (NEDC, 2022).

As the number of victims of insecurity increased beyond those in the North-East, the FGN established the Federal Ministry of Humanitarian Affairs, Disaster Management, and Social Development (FMHDS) in 2019 as the overall coordinating ministry for all humanitarian activities in Nigeria (FMHDS, 2022). The FMHDS also serves as the parent ministry for some agencies that have direct bearing on the non-kinetic efforts of the FGN in the North-East and other parts of the country. These agencies include NEMA, NCFRMI, NEDC, the National Commission for Persons with Disabilities (NCPWD), and the National Agency for the Prohibition of Trafficking in Persons (NAPTIP). With the foregoing initiatives, the civil-led non-kinetic efforts of the FGN have contributed towards rebuilding the NE region of the Nigeria.

The Non-Kinetic Approaches of the Nigerian Army to CTCOIN

Since CTCOIN is a war that often takes place within the population, the competition between the military and the terrorists over the citizens' support becomes inevitable, because whichever side wins the hearts and minds of the people wins the war; hence, non-kinetic approaches are veritable tools in securing the loyalty and cooperation of the citizens towards achieving the end state of the mission (Yahaya, 2023).

The non-kinetic approach of the military to CTCOIN is derived largely from the principle of Military Operations Other Than War (MOOTW), which focuses on deterring war, conflict resolution, peacebuilding, and supporting civil authorities in response to domestic crises. In asymmetric warfare, where the enemies are hardly known and often revolve amidst the civil communities, winning the hearts and minds as well as the robust support of innocent civilians across society remain key to successful operations. This was why Yusuf (2019) observed that "if CTCOIN strategy focuses on gaining and maintaining public support through measures targeted at behavioural and development initiatives within the theatre, the end state of the operation could be achieved faster and more effectively." Realising this, the Defence Headquarters, the Nigerian Army, the Nigerian Navy, and the Nigerian Air Force established the Department of Civil-Military Relations, Civil-Military Affairs, and Civil-Military Cooperations, respectively. Each of these departments is principally engaged in non-kinetic activities, representing the soft power component of military operations in Nigeria. With the outbreak of insurgency and terrorism by the BHTG in 2009 and subsequently the Islamic State in West African Province (ISWAP), the Armed Forces of Nigeria (AFN) incorporated non-kinetic approaches to compliment the kinetic operations aimed at ending the crises.

Right from the onset of CTCOIN in 2009, non-kinetic efforts have been an integral part of the military operations by the AFN particularly the NA. However, these were so insignificant that they only constituted about 2 per cent of the operations (Irabor in Kalambe 2019). It was basically centred on providing minimal relief materials to the victims of insurgency in the theatre. With the change in the dynamics of the war due to the escalation of violence by the BHTG, the sporadic spread of its ideology among the youths in the North East, and the continuous increase in the number of unassessed areas for humanitarian activities, the NA established the Department of Civil-Military Affairs (DCMA) at its HQ in 2010. This was to formally institutionalise non-kinetic unit for the CTCOIN operations to complement its hard power operations not only in the NE but across the trouble spots in the country where the NA is conduction Internal Security Operations (ISOPS). This became expedient upon the realisation that winning the cooperation (hearts and minds) of the civil populace particularly the communities in the operation areas, is central to a successful asymmetric warfare that must be intelligence-led (Kangye, 2022).

The DCMA is headed by a 2-Star General who is referred to as the Chief of Civil- Military Affairs (CCMA). It has three directorates: Civil-Military Legal Desk, Information Management, and Psychological Warfare. A CMA Cells were also established in all divisions of the Nigerian Army and saddled with the task of interacting with and fostering Civil Military Cooperation (CIMIC) with the population in their Areas of Responsibility (AoR). In Op HADIN KAI (OPHK), the 7 and 8 Divisions of the Nigerian Army have been actively involved in the execution of humanitarian, behavioural, and developmental activities towards winning hearts and minds under the supervision of the Theatre Commander (TC). Thus, the DCMA at the Nigerian Army HQ is however responsible for coordination of the entire CIMIC activities and ensures that it contributes to the attainment of operational end states, win the loyalty of the population in theatres of operation, create a conducive atmosphere for healthy post-conflict reconciliation and enduring future relations (Yusuf, 2019; Kangye, 2022). Basically, the DCMA serves as the interface between the military and all civilian stakeholders. Through these directorates, the DCMA has continued to leverage the use of soft power to plan and execute numerous schemes and programmes as the non-kinetic component of the CTCOIN operations in the country.

The non-kinetic approaches of the military, in which the NA occupies a central position, could be categorised into 5 lines of efforts: Strategic Communications, CIMIC Projects, Deradicalisation Rehabilitation and Reintegration (DRR), Human Rights/International Humanitarian Law, and Non-Military Security Mechanism.

Strategic Communications

Leveraging Strategic Communications (StratCom) in all forms of warfare as a means of conveying information or indicators to an adversary or target audience in order to influence their reasoning or behaviour is variously referred to as Information Warfare, Influence Operations, Propaganda, Psychological Operations (PSYOPS) etc. (Yusuf, 2019). Fundamentally, the main objective of StratCom is to engage the perception of the target audience and explore opportunities to influence their thoughts, feelings, and behaviours. To this reality, the Nigerian Army established a Radio Station for the CTCOIN operations in the North-East, which is being used to sensitise the public on the ills of the insurgent activities and their strategy while highlighting government, the traditional institutions (Bulama), religious leaders and the Civilian Joint Task Force (CJTF) within the respective communities. StratCom in the North East theatre got a boost when 7 Division of the Nigerian Army established the PSYOPS Cell, which comprised professional military personnel and civilian stakeholders from the media and academia, especially sociologists, psychologists, and linguists. The Cell meets once every week to design, articulate and disseminate appropriate themes and messages aimed at undermining the recruitment base of the BHTG while encouraging defection/surrender of their members (Yusuf, 2019). According to Shaibu (2023), the PSYOPS Cell has, since 2017, produced five video documentary clips of counter-narratives, confessions and religious sermons in both local languages (Kanuri and Hausa) and Arabic, which have been disseminated to the public through various media outlets (Shaibu, 2023). This was buttressed by Abubakar and Oyesola (2023), who confirmed that the PSYOPS operations include the conversion of messages into leaflets and hand-bills in the above languages and dropping them at terrorist locations through air platforms. They also reported that Air flights are been provided for surrendered BHT members as well as rescued women and children in the theatre. Additionally, the DCMA has since 2018 been organising seminars and workshops with social media influencers, bloggers, and online journalists across the country for the purpose of countering fake news and soliciting their support for the military in the fight against terrorism and insurgency in Nigeria. Consequently, the military has recorded some milestones in this direction as the social media presence of the BHT and ISWAP has been seriously decimated and the counter-narratives of the PSYOPS have yielded good results. This is evidence when about 85,000 members and victims of BHT surrendered to the military within the last quarter of the year 2022.

Civil Military Cooperation Projects

The operating environment of CTCOIN is usually one in which local administration has been incapacitated, thereby making basic amenities of life such as shelter, water, food, school, and healthcare inot luxury items leaving the population in dire need of assistance. Others that are also critical not only to the socio-economic livelihood of the communities but to the mission, which include restoration of electricity and road and bridges repair, among others, automatically become of critical consideration of the military. This is because the military is often seen as the last government agency standing in such a situation. Consequently, the concept of Quick Impact Projects (QIPs) comes to the fore as an aspect of CIMIC. In the Nigerian context, the majority of the QIPs being executed by the military in the theatres are meant to alleviate the livelihood of the communities and the IDPs. For instance, since the commencement of CTCOIN operations, the Armed Forces of Nigeria particularly the Nigerian Army has carried out numerous QIPs at the strategic, operational and tactical levels of command (Yusuf, 2019).

At the strategic level, the COAS, through the DCMA, has executed several QIPs in all sectors within the Theatre such as the establishment of 2 Secondary Schools in Borno State. Some of the QIPs carried out at the operational and tactical levels include medical outreach and distribution of medical materials, hygiene and sanitation in Dikwa, Gwosa and Baga; immunization exercise and establishment of a clinic in Bama as well as free medical services to isolated communities such as Rann and Banki amongst others. Also, the provision of boreholes was done to provide access to portable water supply which was a serious challenge to many communities in the Theatre. Consequently, the Nigerian Army provided boreholes in Gulumba, Gana, Darajmel, Banki and Bita. On a large scale, the COAS initiated 50,000- litre capacity boreholes in IDP camps in Maiduguri and Dikwa amongst others. In the area of education, the military provided learning materials to pupils in several schools to encourage them to go to school in addition to providing security in the schools. Furthermore, the Task Force Brigade established and ran a primary school at the Government Secondary School IDP Camp Gwoza, where Nigerian Army officers and soldiers serve as teachers. Also, the 192 Battalion established a Secondary School in Gwoza Town and Islamic School at Housing Estate IDP Camp (Yusuf, 2019; Kwangyc, 2022).

One of the non-kinetic approaches of the Nigerian Army in the North-East which has enabled it to win the hearts and minds of the population, is road and bridge construction and trunk road repairs. The Nigerian Army constructed Bitta- Tokumbere-Camp Zero road. The Army has also provided several military class bridges and repaired several roads in the theatre such as Damboa-Sandia-Bulabulin and Maiduguri as well as Konduga-Bama-Pulka and Banki Junction to Banki (Yusuf, 2019).

Realising the efficacy of non-kinetic efforts in CTCOIN and other operations, the Nigerian Army has made it a policy whereby all Major

Generals now have the opportunity of planning and executing the most needed CIMIC project in their locales to win the hearts and minds of the citizens. Likewise, the communities can now make requests to the Nigerian Army for critical CIMIC project assistance. These are the changes we have introduced into our non-kinetic efforts which have continued to yield positive results (Yahaya, 2023).

The non-kinetic efforts of the Nigerian Army, however, witnessed a major transformation in 2021 when the COAS (Lt Gen Faruk Yahaya) re-strategized and recalibrated the operations of the DCMA and categorised interventions into 2, such as Essential Services and Chief of the Army Staff Special CIMIC Intervention Projects. The essential services include the construction of healthcare facilities, water projects-bole wholes and Dam as well as road and bridge construction, among others. For the COAS special CIMIC intervention projects, all the Major Generals in the Nigerian Army are given the opportunity of coming up with any CIMIC project a the cost range of 25million to 30million that could aid the Nigerian Army operations in various parts of the country. Through this, field Commanders are recording successes in winning the hearts and minds of the citizens in their operating communities as they have continued to support the troops with intelligence and public buy-in. One of such projects is the water project at Lasa in Borno State where the Nigerian Army constructed 60,000 litres capacity water Tank with 5 industrial bole wholes recharging it. Also, the Dam project in Fika is another example of such interventions. It has been reported that the Nigerian Army has to its credit more than 60 of such projects (Kangye, 2022).

According to Kangye (2022), the CCMA, 15 COAS special CIMIC projects are been executed every quarter, making it 60 in a year, regardless of other numerous projects that are being commissioned under the essential services category (Kangye, 2022). The foregoing has clearly shown that theArmed Forces of Nigeria particularly the Nigerian Army, upon the realisation that winning CTCOIN operations requires 80 per cent non-kinetic and 20 per cent kinetic, have fussed the two approaches as simultaneous activities that must be executed together to achieve the end state of the mission. These CIMIC projects, among many others that are ongoing, have assisted the military in forming an excellent relationship with the local communities in the theatre which has aided the successes recorded thus far in the CTCOIN operations.

Deradicalisation, Rehabilitation and Reintegration

The Deradicalisation, Rehabilitation and Reintegration (DRR) programme which is codenamed Op SAFE CORRIDOR is a critical component of the non-kinetic approaches to CTCOIN operations in Nigeria. The DRR programme came up as a result of several years of discussions within the Nigerian Government about how to encourage voluntary defections from members of the BHT. As early as 2013, four years into the insurgency, the authorities started to recognize that the kinetic response alone would be insufficient to dismantle the group (ICG, 2021). In September 2015, President Muhammadu Buhari set up a committee led by the Chief of the Defence Staff (CDS) with the support of the International Organisation for Migration (IOM) and other partners to develop, considered and adopted a strategic action plan for the De-radicalization, Rehabilitation and Reintegration (DRR) of willing and repentant members of the BHT. Consequently, in April 2016, the FGN established Op SAFE CORRIDOR as a military-led, multi-agency, non- kinetic and humanitarian operation with its facility located in Kwami LGA of Gombe State (Godwin, 2020). Thus, the Op SAFE CORRIDOR is a defectors programme for low-risk repentant Boko Haram combatants who were either captured in battle or voluntarily decide to hand in themselves. The programme aims to rehabilitate repentant Boko Haram militants and reintegrate them back into their respective communities as productive law-abiding citizens. The defecting members are to acquire vocational training, and access de-radicalisation, and civics programmes to become useful members of the Nigeria and Lake Chad Basin society upon release from the program (CDD, 2020).

The DRR process of the Op SAFE CORRIDOR commences with the voluntary repentant of a Boko Haram member who is subjected to vetting and cleared by the military and transferred to the Op SAFE CORRIDOR facility in Mallam Sidi community, Kwami LGA for the DRR programme. The DRR is a 52 weeks programme that involves psychospiritual, psychotherapy, counselling, recreational, and vocational training. The vocational training includes farming, woodwork and carpentry, barbing, and fashion designing, among others. Visitation by families and prominent personalities is part of the programme, to promote rehabilitation, build confidence and ensure smooth integration (Godwin, 2020). Thus far, Op SAFE CORRIDOR is yet to be a perfect institutional mechanism for DRR. It has, however, been serving the purpose for which it was hitherto created.

From 2016 to 2020 for instance, the programme hosted about 800 ex-Boko Haram members and graduated about 300 of them (Godwin, 2020); and from 2020 to 2022, the total number of fully de-radicalized ex-Boko Haram members has increased to 559 (The Cable, 2022).

Apart from the ex-Boko Haram members that are the primary focus of the Op SAFE CORRIDOR, the Operation has also extended its non-kinetic efforts to the host community to secure the people's maximum support and discourage the youth in the area from joining the terrorist group. To this effect, the Op SAFE CORRIDOR has conducted and executed some CIMIC projects and programmes across the Malam Sidi community. These include the employment of 45 locals into the service of the Op SAFE CORRIDOR, free medical outreach to more than 1500 people, including the aged, children, and pregnant women with the Op SAFE CORRIDOR's clinic serving as the only medical facility that treats not less than 15 locals on daily basis. Also, the Op SAFE CORRIDOR has delivered a functional borehole water project and donated mattresses to the Government Secondary School in the community (Shafa, 2020). These have, in no small measure created a bond between the Op SAFE CORRIDOR and the population as the people have continued to cooperate with and support the Op SAFE CORRIDOR's programmes.

Human Rights/International Humanitarian Law

Human rights observation is a critical component of any military operation which depicts the professionalism or otherwise of the armed forces. This was why the British COIN Doctrine maintains that:

> …as long as the military is seen to be legitimate, its actions are seen to benefit the population, and it acts with cultural sensitivity and in accordance with the law, the neutral population should support their presence and their activities to provide security and stabilization (British Army FM 2009: 3-11).

The Armed Forces of Nigeria recognise the fact that any unethical conduct by troops could be exploited by the criminal elements to discredit the military and woo the population into their folds. Because of its effect on the psyche of the population, the Nigerian Army in particular created the Human Rights Desk under the DCMA giving proof that respect for human rights is central in the conduct of Nigerian Army operations. To ensure compliance down the chain of command, the DCMA commissioned the 7 Division Human Rights Desk in Maiduguri in 2017 which has since been replicated in other Divisions. Consequently, the Nigerian Army has developed a Code of Conduct (CoC) and Rules of Engagement (RoE) that were distributed to troops to guide and regulate their conduct in operations. The aim of the Nigerian Army in these efforts is to serve and support the civil populace with dignity to gain and retain their cooperation and support. Of similar imperative is military compliance with the International Humanitarian Law (IHL). It is considered by the Armed Forces of Nigeria that it is a command responsibility to ensure troops' compliance with the IHL provisions (Yusuf, 2019).

Operating with the law will not only encourage public confidence and support, but will also ensure respect and support from the international community. Consequently, the Nigerian Army has been working with International Non-Governmental Organisations (INGOs) and the UN agencies to conduct periodic sensitization through seminars at Divisions and Brigades on the need for humane treatment of captured or surrendered members of the BHT, IWSAP and other criminal elements. The troops have so understood this and it has started reflecting in their conduct when dealing with the unarmed enemy. An example of this could be seen in the handling of 88 surrendered members of BHT by the Task Force Brigade in Gwoza between May 2017 and March 2018. According to Musa (2023), the Command is adhering strictly and professionally to the IHL. In his words, he asserted that:

> I think professionally, it has been very good. We have not had any serious professional misconduct. In the few ones we have had, we have standing court martials both at the Theatre and at the Divisions, so any personnel that commits an offence professionally goes through the process.
> (Musa, 2023).

Similarly, the General Court Martial sitting in HQ 7 Division of the Nigerian Army in Maiduguri sentenced 14 personnel found guilty of various offences relating to IHL violation between January 2017 and July 2019. Another classical example of professionalism in this regard is the handling of the clients at the Op SAFE CORRIDOR's facility at Mallam Sidi, where the surrendered members of the BHT are being treated with utmost respect and support while undergoing DRR processes.

The foregoing are practical demonstrations by the strategic military leadership to ensure that the Nigerian Army does not loose public confidence and support in the CTCOIN and other operations through personnel misconduct. In ensuring transparency in this regard, the Nigerian Army has been granting both local NGOs and INGOs like the International Committee on the Red Cross access to all detention facilities to evaluate the treatment of detainees and advice the military following IHL rules and procedures.

Non-Military Security Mechanism

The protection of the civil populace including the humanitarian workers, through non-military security mechanisms, in CTCOIN operations is foundational to winning the hearts and minds strategy. As asserted by Yusuf (2019), the civilian population remains the Centre of Gravity (CoG) for both the insurgents and the counterinsurgents, as they will continue to contest for the hearts and minds of the population to demonstrate their capacity to offer the best protection. Therefore, in protecting the civilians, the police, para-military agencies, CJTF, vigilante and neighbourhood watch, amongst others, have critical roles to play. Thus, the military has formed a synergy with these organisations in other to achieve the ultimate end state of the CTCOIN operations, which is the restoration of peace and stability within the theatres and the country at large. As evident in the theatre, the military is working together with these organisations as they have continued to evolve a non-military mechanism in ensuring security in the communities across the NE. This development became necessary to allow the military to concentrate on fighting the war, while civil policing can be ensured by these organisations. This has greatly enhanced civil policing and increased public confidence in the military on civilians' protection in the theatre.

Challenges of the Military-Lead Non-Kinetic Approaches to CTCOIN

Operating military-led non-kinetic approaches to counter terrorism and insurgency in Nigeria has not been without challenges. These include governance deficit, inadequate public awareness, military doctrine/training, funding CIMIC and a dearth of skilled manpower.

Governance Deficit

Before the outbreak of insurgency and terrorism in the North-East, the governance deficit was evident in many rural communities in the region. Some of the basic infrastructures that could signify the presence of government were either weak or absent in many places, thereby putting a huge burden on the military. Thus, the military is fighting BHT and ISWAP on the one hand, and doing government jobs on the other by constructing healthcare centres, building schools, constructing roads and bridges, as well as water and sanitation, among others. This situation of weak infrastructure has slowed down the kinetic operations of the military and inhibited it from recording successes in lesser time. According to Musa (2023), bad and untired roads that link many capital cities to the rural communities in the North-East have made it easier for the terrorists to plant IEDs on the roads with adverse consequences on the troops. He concluded by saying:

> As we were succeeding, our prayer is that the government, both state and federal, can come in and fix our roads. If they fix these roads, I can tell you that 60 per cent of our challenge is gone… From Maiduguri to Monguno is 145 KM, if the road is good, you are talking of one hour plus, in less than two hours you are there. But it takes you six hours because if you make mistake and step on one IED you are gone, especially if you are in a soft-skinned vehicle.
> So, that is our greatest challenge now. We have appealed and discussed severally, we have had promises and some contractors have come and they have awarded some of the roads, but they are yet to start. We now have the capacity to provide security for the contractors to come and fix the roads (Musa, 2023).

Apart from preventing the troops from moving faster during kinetic operations, the poor roads are also making non-kinetic efforts more difficult in the region. Thus, some infrastructures that ought to have been provided by the government, which could have eased the execution of non-kinetic operations were in deplorable states.

Inadequate Public Awareness

As it were, the public is yet to fully understand the role and duties of the military in a democratic system. In many rural communities, citizens have continued to see the military as a government, which is constitutionally assigned to provide good governance and socio-economic development; and are oblivious to the fact that the military is essentially established to defend the country, protect its people and facilitate CIMIC projects that could make the jobs easier and create bound between it and the communities of operation. Fundamentally, good governance and socio- economic development are the core responsibilities of the elected federal, state and local governments. More often, however, the military does hang in the balance of being seen as a protector and government at the same time. This perception often makes the communities see CIMIC projects as democratic dividends accrued from their elected governments instead of seeing them as a token of assistance from the military whose primary responsibility is to defence the country and protect the citizens. This often creates a dilemma in non-kinetic operations.

Military Doctrine/Training

Before 2009, the Armed Forces of Nigeria's doctrines were mainly kinetic operation oriented as virtually all the military training institutions had no specific non-kinetic operations in their curriculum. According to Omozoje (2022), non- kinetic is yet to be fully grounded in the Nigerian Army's doctrine although it has become a very important part of military operations in the country. As corollary, Ibrahim (2022) affirmed that non-kinetic approach is more of a strategic level. However, Commanders at the operational level also embark on some operations that are non-kinetic in nature to support the mission. He concluded that:

> Those of us in the teeth arms, let's say Infantry and Armour, feel that non-kinetic operations should be at the higher level while those of us at this operational level will just fight the battle. But it is not as if we are not letting the younger ones or the junior commanders know that there are some things, they need to do to also win the hearts and minds of the population. And that's why even when funds are been released to the commanders in the front, provisions are made for CIMIC activities

so that the Commander in the field could do boreholes, re-building of schools etc so he could win the hearts and minds of the people (Ibrahim, 2022).

The foregoing attests to the fact that there is a sound theoretical understanding of the non-kinetic approaches in the NA. However, the practical aspect of it has just been demonstrated with the CTCOIN operations against BHT and ISWAP. Consequently, the NA has continued to incorporate non-kinetic approaches into its doctrine which has enabled her training institutions to start reviewing their curricula in tandem with current realities with regard to non-kinetic approaches. As it is, the military personnel are just beginning to adjust to the fact that CTCOIN operations must be planned and executed with other security agencies and critical MDAs with particular reference to non-kinetic operations.

The Dearth of Skilled Manpower

Planning and executing non-kinetic operations require specialized skills to successfully pilot the process in a CTCOIN environment. Yusuf (2019) asserted that the skills set required is gotten from training in CIMIC, protection of civilians, gender mainstreaming, international humanitarian law and community relations amongst others. He further argued that there are very few personnel in the military who have acquired such specialisations currently. Using CIMIC Cell (G9) as an example, he concluded that most personnel deployed are not very proficient in the rudiments of winning hearts and minds. This needs to be improved upon as it inhibits ultimate success in the operations of the non-kinetic approach by the military.

Funding Civil-Military Cooperation

Civil-Military Cooperation (CIMIC) encompasses a spectrum of programmes and activities that are capital intensive. Citing an example from QIPs alone, Yusuf (2019) reported that inadequate funds constituted a major drawback towards the implementation of programmes and projects aimed at winning the hearts and minds in the theatre with minimal impact on the lives of host communities. With the assumption of Lt Gen Faruk Yahaya as COAS in 2021, the dynamics of CIMIC have changeed tremendously with the high increase in funding, advancement in needs assessment, planning, execution, monitoring and evaluation of projects and programmes

(Kangye, 2022). Consequently, the COAS has improved budgetary allocation to the DCMA down to formations and units thereby enabling them to execute more projects and programmes that are of high benefit to the host communities across the country and supportive of the mission's end state.

These challenges, amongst others, are militating against the military from fully leveraging non-kinetic approaches to CTCOIN. Although non-kinetic approaches hold a lot of prospects in tackling the causes of the crisis and winning the hearts and minds of the population, they can never be successfully planned and implemented without doing it along with the people. As the saying goes, "A man's head cannot be shaved in his absence". This has led to the realisation that CTCOIN is never a job for the military alone but that of the entire citizenry which requires a Whole of Society Approach (WOSA).

Towards a Whole of Society Approaches to CTCOIN

Globally, CTCOIN operations have continued to witness changes in approach, method and strategy which have expanded the stakeholders net to involve not only the military and government agencies but the whole gamut of society. The nature of asymmetric warfare has broken the barrier of government having the sole responsibility of providing security and created a critical role for the entire citizenry of the country; thereby entrenching a Whole of Society Approach (WOSA) not only for CTCOIN operations but national security in general. The WOSA to CTCOIN entails a robust combination of both kinetic and non-kinetic efforts and actors, not only to defeat the enemies of the State but also to unravel and address the root causes of the war. Thus, countries have now continued to apply 'Smart Power'which represents the blend of both hard and soft powers leveraging all the elements of national assets to ensure national security and development.

It is with this conviction that each of the five cardinal work streams (Forestall, Secure, Identify, Prepare and Implement) of Nigeria's National Counter Terrorism Strategy (NACTEST) 2016 were designed to incorporate WOSA (FGN, 2016). Consequently, CTCOIN operations in Nigeria are becoming more inclusive whereby both kinetic and non-kinetic approaches are been concurrently adopted. Before now and in 2015 particularly, the dynamics of the government's responses to terrorism and insurgency were changed from military affairs into a Whole of Government in Approach (WOGA) thereby incorporating more non-kinetic activities through many other Ministries Departments and Agencies (MDAs). However, Nigeria only recorded some appreciable successes in utilising both kinetic and non-kinetic approaches in CTCOIN operations through the WOGA which gave the need for the country to formally leverage a WOSA in this regard. The successful experiences of some countries around the world in CTCOIN operations have shown that hardly can a country succeed in tackling terrorism and insurgency without fighting along with the entire ecosystem of the citizenry, government and private institutions; and of cause, diplomatic collaboration with other countries and organisations of the world. This reality confirms the imperativeness of a WOSA which can be seen in the areas of citizens' buy-in and ownership, addressing the root causes of the conflict, enhancement of intelligence- led operations, military professionalism, socio-economic development, and sustainable peacebuilding as asserted by Irabo (2022). Therefore, citizens' buy-in and ownership which connote the belief in and acceptance of belonging in national actions by the citizens of a country is key in this regard. Thus, citizens' buy-in and ownership of CTCOIN operations are one of the projections of utilising a WOSA. Hitherto in Nigeria, the citizens did not see themselves being part of the CTCOIN operations, which they regarded as purely military affairs. Consequently, there were some setbacks in the fight at the initial stage of the operations. With the adoption of the WOGA and preferencing the non-kinetic approach, however, Nigerians have begun to accept that fighting terrorism and insurgency is everyone's business as it has been considered the constitutional responsibility of every citizen. Thus, advancement into a WOSA will ensure citizen buy-in and ownership of the CTCOIN operations in the country.

Of utmost importance is addressing the causes of insurgency and terrorism in Nigeria. In unravelling the root causes, many factors such as bad governance, parental neglect of children, defective Islamic education, and ungoverned spaces, amongst others, that are outside the purview of the military, were identified. Therefore, for CTCOIN to address the root causes of terrorism and insurgency, a WOSA is imperative. In winning the war, enhancement of the intelligent sector of the operation which means an increase in the availability of secret information that guides military actions must be ensured. The WOSA will avail Nigeria of this opportunity, given the centrality of the local communities in intelligence gathering. Thus, a WOSA that is citizens centred will assist a great deal in achieving intelligence-led CTCOIN operations in Nigeria. Furthermore, adoption of a WOSA will advance military professionalism, which has to do with the ethical behaviour of the armed forces in tandem with constitutional responsibilities. As earlier espoused, CTCOIN entails multiple actions and actors, of which the military is one. By utilising a WOSA, every actor and institution involved will be able to plan and implement their activities without overburdening the military with actions that are strictly outside its purview. Thus, the Armed Forces of Nigeria will be able to professionally execute operations in synergy with other components of the society when a WOSA is well utilised in countering terrorism and insurgency in Nigeria.

The WOSA to CTCOIN would boost socio-economic development not only in the North-East but the entire country. The socio-economic livelihoods of the terrorists and insurgents that affected communities and states would be accelerated through the simultaneous activities of all stakeholders as encompassed in a WOSA. While the Armed Forces of Nigeria are fully committed to clearing the terrorists and insurgents off the communities, the federal, state and local governments as well as community authorities and civil society organisations would be able to plan and implement socio-economic development projects and programmes in tandem with the overall vision of the WOSA to CTCOIN operations. Thus, stability and socio-economic prosperity could be jointly achieved. Sustainable peace entails enduring stability with the absence of violence and the presence of social justice. It is one of the cardinal objectives that are envisaged by CTCOIN, which is beyond kinetic operations. Of cause, the military has a key role to play in ensuring peace in the country, but it takes the whole of society to sustain it. Therefore, adopting a WOSA will not only lead to the attainment of peace in Nigeria but will also ensure its sustainability.

Conclusion

Embarking on CTCOIN operations without robust non-kinetic approaches has become impossible in Nigeria's national security pursuit. The initial kinetic responses of the FGN, through the Armed Forces of Nigeria, to the outbreak of insurgency and subsequent terrorism by the BHT in 2009 were trailed by shortcomings, as the military couldn't secure the needed support of the population. However, from 2013, the FGN and the military, particularly the Nigerian Army, were able to launch non-kinetic operations that later endeared the government and the troops to the people in the affected communities. The initiatives such as the PINE, PCVSF, SSI, PCNEI, BI, and NEDC were very laudable civil-led and military protected non-kinetic efforts of the FGN, which actually watered the ground for synergy between the people and the armed forces.

The establishment of DCMA by the Nigerian Army to basically carry out non- kinetic operations in the theatre provided avenues for winning the hearts and minds of the population to reinforce the kinetic operations. This cut across five streams of efforts such as StratCom, CIMIC Projects, DRR, Human Rights/IHL, and Non- military Security Mechanism that have continued to yield positive results for the Nigerian Army. Realising that the population is the CoG of CTCOIN, the Lt Gen Faruk Yahaya'sAdministration re-strategized and rejigged the DCMAby expanding its scope to directly take non-kinetic operations to every part of the country via the COAS, CIMIC Projects and Essential Services. Through these, the Nigerian Army has not just won the hearts and minds of the citizens in the North-East but the entire country, on account of which the successes recorded in the theatres, can be greatly attributed. This has indicated that, in Nigeria's pursuit of national security, the prospects of non-kinetic approaches are enormous, as they would not only assist the military against the enemies of the state but also help secure the buy-in of the population, thereby facilitating a WOSA to CTCOIN operations in Nigeria.

Section Four

CTCOIN: Operational and Strategic Thoughts

Lt Gen Faruk Yahaya
Chief of Army Staff in his office

Operational and Strategic Thoughts

Doctrine is the soul of Warfare
Sir Julian Corbett

The concept of fighting power clearly establishes the superiority of the conceptual component of fighting power over the physical and moral component in the conduct of operations. The conceptual component, which includes doctrines, principles of war, education, and the ability to learn and adapt, is indeed the soul of warfare as espoused by Sir Julian Corbett. The conceptual component is shaped by operational and strategic thoughts and enables a smaller force to defeat a larger force in battle. Doctrine particularly when linked with command philosophy is a force multiplier. It is therefore crucial to success in war. This is most pronounced at the military strategic level, as generalship is an intellectual endeavour that requires a thorough understanding of the nature and character of war in order to create a vision for success.

Lt Gen Faruk Yahaya's military success and the superiority of his command are based on deep knowledge and insight on the conduct of operations. This is underpinned by a combination of his intellectual knowledge, operational experience, and practical adaptability on the field. His military history background contributed to his development as an astute general with deep thoughts on the application and utility of force across all spectrums of warfare, particularly on CTCOIN operations. These include issues such as military leadership in CTCOIN, operational level tactics and maneuver, non-kinetic lines of operation, IEDs and draining of the swap. Others include the critical nature of logistics and communication, artillery, and emerging technology. The utility of intelligence and the primacy of politics are also covered. His thought also includes specific issues in the North East operations such as overarching cross-cutting themes, terrorism and geo-politics of the Sahel region, emerging initiatives, and sustainable solutions.

To understand his thoughts on the application of force at the operational and strategic levels in a CTCOIN campaign in general and the North-East Theatre in particular, we need to first understand the environmental setting of the North-East Nigeria.

This is considering that while CTCOIN theories may be universal, local and environmental conditions in the theatre of operations are critical to the application. This includes both the physical and human terrain. Thus, Lt Gen Faruk Yahaya's operational and strategic thoughts on CTCOIN operations in North-East Nigeria, the LCB and Sahel countries are shaped by the local and immediate environmental dynamics.

Environmental Setting of the North East

The North-East represents both a geographic and political region of Nigeria. It comprises six states; Adamawa, Bauchi, Borno, Gombe, Taraba and Yobe, with a total of about 284,646 square kilometers and an estimated population of about 26 million people (NBI 2016). Geographically, the North- East is the largest geopolitical zone and covers nearly one-third of Nigeria's total land mass. It is primarily divided between the semi-desert Sahel savanna and the tropical West Sudan savanna eco-regions. The region borders three countries: Chad, Niger, and Cameroun, which share ethnic, language, and cultural affiliations with each other, encouraging cross-border relationships and interactions. The region covers large swathes of Nigeria's borders with Cameroun, a significant part of the Niger Republic, and Chad at Lake Chad.

Borno, Adamawa, and Yobe States, the epicenters of the insurgency have a landmass of about 70,898; 36,917, and 45,502 square miles respectively. The three states have a total land area of about 152, 000 sq km, which represents about 16.34 per cent of the total land mass of Nigeria. This is quite a large area to cover with troops, which poses challenges to military operations as troops cannot effectively cover all the gaps. The landmasses of these states are characterized by seasonal streams as well as rocky and mountainous areas. However, the nature of the terrain supports seasonal operations for infantry, tanks, amphibious elements, and air operations. Two distinct characteristics of the environment are the terrain and climate.

Terrain

The northeastern terrain comprises open savannah forest and marshy areas. The ground is generally flat with mixed topography and clusters of vegetation cover, scattered cultivation, road networks, Lake Chad tributaries, and other water bodies. The undulating terrain, thick forestation, and islands afford threat elements sanctuary for camping, training, abduction of civilians, and concealment. Marshy conditions are prevalent at the riverbanks and shore of Lake Chad, which impede the vehicular movement of troops and the effectiveness of HE ammunition when fired. Most enclaves occupied by the BHT/ISWAP terrorists have thick all-year-round vegetation cover that provides concealment against air observation as well as water bodies that limit vehicle movement and effect HE ammo, especially during the rainy season. The terrain serves as an obstacle to troops movement, especially in areas of thick vegetation or water bodies, and bugs down vehicles with the presence of Unexploded Ordinances (UXOs) due to the soft ground. The need for troops to carry-out detailed terrain analysis before embarking on operations remains paramount in the North-East.

Detailed terrain analysis is critical and enables troops to coordinate maneouvre operations. For instance, during Operation RESCUE FINALE in the Sambisa Forest in December 2017, troops could not advance beyond NJIMIA to Camp Zairo and had to withdraw back to Bama. It was only after conducting a terrain analysis supported by an air recce that troops were able to discover the best route to assault Camp Zairo. Amphibious capable vehicles in water logged/marshy terrain and soft-skin vehicles or motorcycles in sandy terrain with dense vegetation are some of the decisions that can be reached after detailed study of the terrain is done. Therefore, it is necessary that emphasis be placed on terrain analysis prior to military operations, particularly CTCOIN operations through very difficult environments like the North-East. Decisions such as the use of run flat tyres on rough terrains, amphibious capable vehicles in water logged or marshy terrain, and soft-skin vehicles in sandy areas were innovations supported by terrain analysis.

Climate and Weather

The climate is characterized by the rainy season which lasts from June to September as well as the hot and dry season, from October to May, with temperatures as high as 40 degrees Celsius. The North-East also experiences the harmattan period between November and December.

Potiskum in Yobe State, for instance, is credited with recording the lowest ever temperature in Nigerian history with figures put at 2.8 degrees Celsius. However, the temperature range in March and April is between 30 and 33 degrees Celsius, and it is 31 in June, leading to dehydration in troops and overheating of vehicles. The North-East also experiences strong winds, with dust having adverse effects on aviation and equipment such as weapon stoppages due to the sandy condition. The weather, however, affords clear aerial and ground observation in January and limited aerial observation in April. Limited observation affects air and ground surveillance activities as well as air support from the NAF, which is detrimental to the overall success of operations such as intelligence gathering, air casualty evacuation and Air Interdiction are affected. It is therefore necessary for detailed weather analysis to be factored into operational plans to enhance success.

Weather analysis informs decision on timings for operations as well as the requirement to counter the effects of severe weather. Operations conducted in severe weather conditions without protective measures have been less successful due to the effects of such harsh conditions on troops. Making provisions for tools to clean weapons in wet, sandy/dusty conditions, provision of air-conditioned operational vehicles, a source of water during periods of high temperature/humidity, and the employment of listening posts during periods of poor visibility can be efficiently planned and employed only when detailed weather analysis has been done. Therefore, it is necessary for units and formations to factor weather analysis in operational planning.

Cultural Setting

Understanding the cultural setting in an area of operation is key to the successful conduct of operations. This is especially important in asymmetric warfare, without the knowledge of the local people, military operations make minimal progress, as the cooperation of the locals is difficult to achieve. Understanding the culture also helps win the hearts and minds of the people. The three core states of Borno, Yobe, and Adamawa in the North-East are inhibited by several ethnic groups. However, the major ethnic groups across the three states are the Kanuri, Shuwa Arab, and Margi. The local population in the North-East has ties with the BH/ISWAP terrorists, especially in Borno and Yobe states, which are predominantly Kanuri and Shuwa Arab. This impacts the ability of forces to maintain operational secrecy, isolate Internally Displaced Persons (IDPs), and acquire Human Intelligence (HUMINT) during operations.

The attendant effects of culture on ongoing CTCOIN operations include a lack of strong support from local communities, sustained terrorist recruitment and ease in obtaining information on troops activities. Locals can also be forced to collaborate with terrorists in their community due to a fear of being attacked. They can also be a ready source for the supply of logistics to terrorists, while sympathizers who are likely relatives of terrorists can be a ready source of information on troop's movements and activities. The situation in the Lake Chad Basin, where terrorists employ the services of locals for fishing businesses is instructive. It is therefore necessary for troops to study the cultures of communities and towns within the area of operations to aid success. Religion is also another part of culture. The majority of the population are Muslims as Borno State has 85 per cent Muslims and 7 percent Christian/traditionalists, while Yobe State has a 94.8 per cent Muslim population and a one percent Christian population, with 4.2 per cent of the population being traditionalists. Similarly, Adamawa State has 55 per cent of the population as Muslims, 30 per cent as Christians, and 15 per cent as traditionalists. Initially, the population in the North-East saw the activities of BH as being against Christians but this was short-lived as BHT targeted both Muslims, Christians and Traditionalists. Currently, efforts have been made to increase troops understanding of theater environments through theater specific training at Buni Yadi, Borno State. The recent successes in the North-East Theatre are linked to these efforts. Thus, to enhance proper assimilation in the theatre, cultural lessons are critical for troops prior to deployment to the North-East Theatre.

Socio-Economic Conditions

The socio-economic conditions in the North-East underpin the human terrain. In terms of comparative poverty, deprivation, and human development indices, the North-East has the worst poverty index, even within the context of Nigeria. According to World Bank and NBS data, the North-East poverty head count from 2004 to 2013 at the onset of the insurgency, remained particularly high at 47.6 per cent. Not unexpectedly the North-East was the only region to have registered an increase in the incidence of poverty from 45.56 per cent to 47.56 per cent over this period, as shown in figure 37. This was accompanied by a decrease in the number of its middle class and an increase in income inequality, as measured by the Gini coefficient over this period.

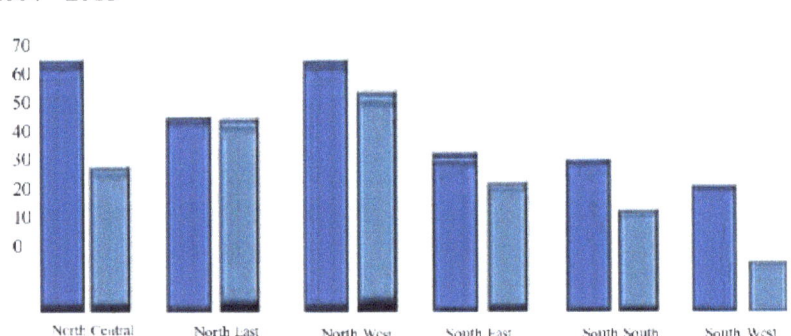

Figure 37: Changes in Poverty Headcount Ratio by Region 2004 - 2013

Source: World Bank calculations based on NLSS 2003–04 and GHS 2010–11, 2012–13

A number of recent evaluations confirm the North-East region as a deprived part of the Nigerian federation. According to the Oxford Poverty and Human Development Initiative (OPHDI, 2017), the North-East and North-West have the highest incidence of deprivation as measured by the Multidimensional Poverty Index (MPI) across various domains, with the most deprived state being Yobe with an MPI of 0.635. This is in stark contrast to the situation in the South-West, which has two of the least deprived States, Lagos and Osun, with MPIs of 0.035 and 0.043, respectively, as shown in Figure 38. The UNDP Nigeria/NBS computation also shows that the intensity of poverty is highest in Northern Nigeria, with the North-East at 44 per cent, just one percentage point below the North-West region where the intensity of poverty is 45 percent, and the South-West at 38 per cent.

Figure 38: Intensity of Poverty by Region

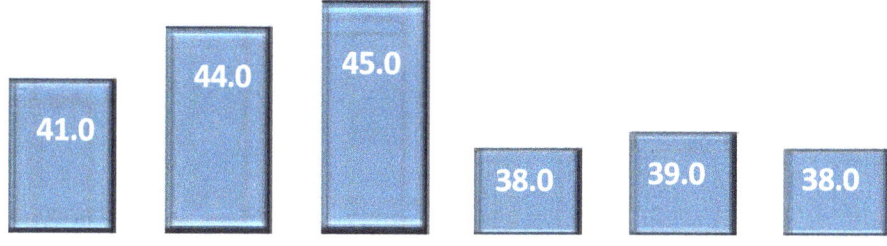

North Central   North East   North West   South East   South South   South West
Source: UNDP and NBS Computation, 2019.

The North-East region also lags behind other regions in terms of overall Human Development. The Human Development Index (HDI) is a summary measure of human progress that takes into consideration the average achievements in three basic dimensions of human development: a long and healthy life; access to knowledge and a decent standard of living across geographic areas and over time. The 2018 UNDP Nigeria/NBS computed HDI, at the state level, shows that Nigeria has an average HDI of 0.521. All the North-East states have HDI scores below the national average, ranging from a high of 0.4286 in Taraba to a low of 0.3238 in Bauchi, a figure less than half that of Lagos State at 0.6515. Cumulatively, the human terrain has shown that the above indices are causal factors that give rise to insurgency and demand urgent action on the security development nexus as part of the strategy to address the problem. These factors have historically been at the top of the list of conflict drivers, as seen in the North-East and areas like Sri Lanka, Somalia, and Colombia in their struggles against terrorism and insurgencies.

Leadership in CTCOIN Operations

Never tell people how to do things; tell them what to do, and they will surprise you with their ingenuity.
Gen George Patton

Leadership is conceptualized in various ways by scholars, leadership icons and several schools of thought. George Terry (1977) defined leadership as "the relationship in which one person, the leader, influences others to work together willingly on related tasks to attain that which the leader desires". The leader's desire is also known as his vision. There are different leadership styles, one of which is visionary leadership. This form of leadership involves leaders who recognize that the methods, steps, and processes of leadership are all obtained with and through people. Most great and successful leaders have aspects of vision ingrained in them. Outstanding leaders will always transform their visions into reality.

During a lecture by the COAS on his 'vision' for the Nigerian Army delivered at the Armed Forces Command and Staff College on 1 September 2021, he cited a quote by Roy Bennet on leadership that stated that "Good leaders have visions and inspire others to help them turn their vision into reality. Great leaders have visions, share visions, and inspire others to create their own." This and several other factors inspired Lt Gen Faruk Yahaya's vision for the Nigerian Army, which is "to have a professional Nigerian Army ready to accomplish assigned missions within a joint environment in the defence of Nigeria". The vision statement took cognisance of the current situation, efforts to be deployed, and projected an end state to be attained in line with his command philosophy designed to achieve the overall mandate of the Nigerian Army.

Military leadership is also known as command and is classified into three levels: strategic, operational, and tactical. CTCOIN is carried primarily at the tactical and operational levels of command. Junior leadership up to battalion level is classified as tactical level command or leadership, while brigade level up to Theatre Command is classified under operational level command or leadership. The success of CTCOIN operations hinges mainly on effective leadership at all levels, with junior leadership playing a key role. The need to operationalize the COAS Vision at the various levels of command informed its break down to 4 key strategic pillars: professionalism, readiness, administration, and cooperation.

The pillars of the vision provide a good insight into good leadership at both junior and operational levels. These include professionalism, indicating the requisite training and proper conduct of leaders at all levels. Readiness covers the effective use of available resources to achieve the Nigerian Army Mission. Administration provides for the wherewithal for the motivation of the fighting troops and cooperation entails the ability of commanders at all levels to work in synergy with sister services and other security agencies to achieve the common objective.

The IndianArmy which shares a lot of similarities with the Nigerian Army, considers junior leadership as its mainstay because they have, on many occasions, turned the tide against heavy odds owing to their superior training, high level of motivation, grit, and extreme sacrifice in CTCOIN operations. Junior leaders play a significant role in the resolution of this conflict as they, with their units, operate in close proximity to the insurgents and local population. It therefore implies that for operational leadership to succeed, there has to be a corresponding level of efficient junior leadership. Lt Gen Yahaya thus invested heavily to improve the professional competence of junior commanders through practical training and field exercises. The Chief of Training (Army), Maj Gen AB Ibrahim, noted the importance of joint training at tactical and operational levels with the introduction of joint final exercises by all Nigerian Army schools in Kontagora. This created the opportunity to test junior commanders across the wide spectrum of the Nigerian Army.

Command Philosophies of the COAS

The command philosophies of Lt Gen Yahaya supported the actualization of his vision which was instrumental to the great improvement in operational capability. These cardinal philosophies guided leadership at all levels. These include Command Style, prioritizing the Nigerian soldier, combat effectiveness, the acquisition of intelligence, and adequate mentorship. At the operational level, command style greatly influences the output from junior leaders. He believed that command should be participatory and inclusive, and creating a conducive working environment tha will improve overall productivity. Lagbaja (2023) attested to the mission-command-oriented style of leadership of the COAS, which has been instrumental to the success of 1 Division Kaduna in its assigned tasks. This is underpinned by the ability of the COAS to match tasks with the necessary resources. The Theatre Commander Op HADIN KAI, Maj Gen CG Musa, aptly summarized the COAS leadership style when he noted that the COAS had made things easier for his commanders. He gives them the freedom to command without unnecessary tension. In proving this freedom to command, he caters for every operational and administrative need of the commanders. He clearly demonstrated the tenets of mission command in words and deeds. The above philosophy is in line with the Mission Command principles, which speak to trust in subordinates who can plan, coordinate, and execute flexible yet disciplined decision making throughout complex operational environments, giving commanders the confidence to conduct decisive action boldly. Trust is the guiding principle and underpins the operational successes in the North-East. Hence, it is vital that operational level commanders allow freedom of initiative and action to junior leaders in order to create an enabling work environment for success in CTCOIN operations.

Mentoring as one of the cardinal philosophies of Lt Gen F Yahaya is believed to be key to improving the proficiency of present and future commanders. The success of CTCOIN operations depends on the good mentorship of junior level leaders by operational-level leadership. The capacity of the individual should therefore be considered in appointing operational level commanders because without it, the mentorship of junior leaders will suffer, which will affect the overall output of operations. Based on COAS's emphasis, relevant mentorship programmes were developed by all Nigerian Army Corps and schools to improve junior leadership mentoring. These include the invitation of accomplished service personnel to interact with students, lectures and other programmed activities leading to the development of a strong mentor-mentee relationship. This has supported the availability of military personnel (serving and retired) to share their personal and professional experience, as well as mentees who are willing and ready to receive and implement professional and personal advice. The outcome is mutual respect and increased professional competence, which have been instrumental to the success of the Nigerian Army in CTCOIN operations. To give a better perspective on leadership in CTCOIN operations, it is important to analyze various leadership models and determine how they could be employed to achieve results, especially in CTCOIN operations.

Types of Leadership Models

There are different leadership models that leaders or commanders may employ to get the best from their subordinates. There is no single model that could be described as the best, but a combination of some of these within the prevailing circumstances will help a commander achieve his objectives. Successful leaders come in different shapes and sizes. No two are alike, and no single leadership style is always the best. All leaders want to change the status quo, but they use different means. Some take the lead with their ideas, while others lead with their passion and conviction. Still others lead by demonstrating courage in the face of risks and the unknown, and some bring about change by serving others. In his leadership of the Nigerian Army, in both operations and peacetime, Lt Gen Yahaya applied a variety of these leadership models which have been in line with his vision and he achieved tremendous results. Therefore, it is necessary to share these models to guide present and future commanders.

Autocratic Leadership. Autocratic leadership styles are centered on the boss. In this type of leadership model, the leader holds all authority and responsibility. Such leaders make decisions on their own without consulting subordinates. They reach decisions, communicate them to subordinates, and expect prompt implementation. Autocratic work environment normally have little or no flexibility. Being autocratic by nature may not augur well between the operational and tactical levels of command. Tactical level input is required for success in CTCOIN operations; therefore, an autocratic commander stands the risk of isolation and sabotage thereby creating conditions for failure of his command. A commander being pushed to be autocratic in his leadership style may have along the line lost grip of certain aspects of his command and sees this method as a means of remaining relevant.

Democratic Leadership. Ademocratic leadership style does not necessarily imply wholesome freedom of action. In this leadership style, subordinates are involved in making decisions. Unlike autocratic, this leadership model is centered on subordinates' contributions. The democratic leader holds final responsibility for the outcome of the activities under their command, but he or she is known to delegate authority to subordinates. Commanders who try to be democratic in their leadership style needs to apply caution so that they do not delegate very critical aspects of their command that are crucial for success.

Transformational Leadership. Unlike other leadership styles, transformational leadership is all about initiating change in organizations, groups, oneself and others. Transformational leaders motivate others to do more than they originally intended and often even more than they thought possible. A commander who is transformational by nature is well appreciated by subordinate commanders and often get more results than expected. Such commanders go the extra mile to cater to the administrative and other needs of their subordinates, who in turn reward him with their loyalty and service.

Coaching Leadership. Coaching leadership involves teaching and supervising followers. Basically, in this kind of leadership, followers are helped to improve their skills. Coaching as a leadership style motivates, inspires, and encourages followers. This kind of leadership is akin to the adequate mentorship strand of the COAS command philosophy for improving the proficiency of present and future commanders. A commander who is a mentor is not only growing his command but also growing the NA for the future.

Charismatic Leadership. Charismatic leadership is defined by a leader who uses his communications skills, persuasiveness and charm to influence others. Charismatic leaders, given their ability to connect with people on a deep level, are especially valuable within organizations that are facing a crisis or struggling to move forward. In this leadership style, the charismatic leader manifests his or her revolutionary power. Charisma does not mean sheer behavioral change but actually involves a transformation of followers' values and beliefs. A commander would need to bring his charisma to bear when the tides of the operation in CTCOIN are not going as expected. His personality will be put to the test in such situations, and this is where charisma is needed to help turn the situation around.

Populist Leadership. Populist leadership style is otherwise known as crowd pleasers. This style of leadership tends to sway towards the sentiments of the followers more to please them than to offer real leadership values. Populist style of leadership has an expiry date, and the commander's real personality will be put to the test. While it is good to carry our subordinate commanders along in opinions and in decision making, commanders need to resist the urge to beat populist in nature, as it is easy for such subordinates to see through the hypocrisy in the intentions. Populism negates the principle of being firm and fair in command, as such leaders do not want to be seen as going against the interest of subordinates even when it is justified. Populist leaders only achieve temporary results, and such results cannot stand the test of time.

Visionary Leadership. This form of leadership involves leaders who recognize that the methods, steps, and processes of leadership are all obtained with and through people. Most great and successful leaders have aspects of vision in them. Outstanding leaders will always transform their visions into realities. The COAS, Vision for the Nigerian Army has been the guiding light for operational commanders down to tactical commanders. The application of the pillars of this vision has been the compass with which the NigerianArmy has marched successfully under the leadership of the COAS. A visionary leader must make available the means for his subordinates to achieve his vision. Thus, it includes the elements of mission command. The Nigerian Army, under Lt Gen Faruk Yahaya's leadership, strives to meet the necessary operational and administrative requirements for the actualization of COAS vision. This manifested itself in the tremendous results achieved in various CTCOIN operations and other engagements across the country. Similarly, the vision has guided the engagement of the Nigerian Army in external operations outside the country and helped to enhance professionalism.

The COAS, is an amalgam of coaching, transformational and visionary leadership. These inherent transformational and visionary attributes have underpinned the success of the Nigerian Army under his watch.

Troops Morale and the Protracted Nature of CTCOIN

In war, three-quarters depends on matters of character and morale; the balance of manpower and equipment comes only for the remaining quarter.
Napoleon Bonaparte

The protracted nature of CTCOIN and the challenges posed to the morale of troops present a test for leadership and command in CTCOIN operations. CTCOIN operations once commenced, extend over a protracted period of time due to their unpredictability and ever-changing dynamics. As such, these extended periods of engagement usually take their toll on the troops, thus affecting morale.

Several other factors affect the morale of soldiers in CTCOIN operations, which include losses in personnel and material, environmental conditions, including human and physical terrain conditions, and operational conditions, among others. The quote by Napoleon Bonaparte sums up the fact that adequate morale is a campaign-winning factor even in the face of shortcomings in equipment and other wherewithal. According to Lt Gen F Yahaya, morale constitutes all the elements that make the soldier perform better at his tasks and is a command responsibility.

Administration, as one of the pillars of COAS's vision, is aimed at catering for the well-being of all personnel, both in and out of combat. Sound administration is key to success in CTCOIN operations, and indeed in any other type of operation. Therefore, prioritizing the Nigerian soldier as one of COAS's command philosophies aims to provide the soldier with what he needs to operate effectively by ensuring welfare and administration are given attention to improve morale. The COAS made far-reaching efforts at improving the administration of personnel involved in CTCOIN operations across the country. According to the AHQ RSM, AWO Mohammed Sanusi, never have soldiers in the Theatre had their welfare so catered for. To cater for cases of over-stayed personnel especially in Op HADIN KAI, AHQ instituted a 3-year rotational policy such that no unit or personnel stayed in the operations beyond 3 years. Although some peculiar cases still existed where soldiers spent more than this period, these were handled on their individual merits. Akinjobi (2023) averred that the administration of personnel in the operational areas has been made simpler due to the COAS leadership style. Akintade (2023), who is the Chief of Logistics, also concurred with the view of Akinjobi. He emphasized that the level of logistic support deployed to the North-East is unprecedented in the history of the Nigerian Army. Also, AHQ ensured that the operations were not starved of funds, including allowances, while commanders, who deprived their personnel of any allowances or benefits during the operations were sanctioned within the ambits of the law.

Other novel administrative policies were introduced, such as a definite pass policy that enabled personnel at determined intervals to proceed on pass to go and see their families and loved ones. This was also enhanced by the introduction of welfare flights in conjunction with the Nigerian Air Force. Troops who were scheduled to pass were airlifted to either Abuja or Lagos depending on their final destinations. In the mid-life of the current insurgency in the Northeast around 2014, troops' morale was affected by inadequate equipment. In some particular cases, almost whole units declined to take part in operations due to inadequate small arms, personal protection gears and other equipment necessary for combat.

The situation has increasingly improved with the introduction of several new pieces of equipment to the operations, which have helped to turn the tide in favour of the Nigerian Army. The Nigerian Army increased its equipment procurement. Omozoje (2023) stated that, the Nigerian Army has not had it this good within the last 25 years in terms of equipment procurement. There is a great synergy between logistics and administration, which is manifesting in huge operational successes. The most notable is from the China North Industries Group Corporation Limited (NORINCO), with a contract worth US $152 million for VT-4 main battle tanks, ST1 light tanks, SH-5 self-propelled 105mm howitzers, Typhoon MRAPs, Spartan armoured personnel carriers, armoured guard booths, and buffalo vehicles, among others. By mid-2022, in Op HADIN KAI, AHQ inducted 129 AFVs, 75 gun trucks and combat supplies in support of offensive Op LAKE SANITY and Op DESERT SANITY. The influx of new equipment raised troops morale and led to a massive surrender of Boko Haram terrorists and their families, while many others migrated out of the region. The provision of protective gear for personnel such as bullet proof jackets and helmets, among other kit needs has been given priority. Adequate kitting is a huge source of morale for personnel, and knowing they have a level of first line protection gives them more impetus to fight.

Winning the Hearts and Minds

The successes recorded in CTCOIN in the North-East were also due to various non kinetic operations undertaken by the Nigerian Army. This was usually employed with the kinetic approach in what is called the "carrot and stick" approach leading to a large influx of terrorists and their families surrendering in droves. CTCOIN is a protracted operation, and there will be a need to address the root causes of the problem. Salihu (2023) noted that as of January 2023, over 80,000 terrorists and their families had surrendered to own troops. Op SAFE CORRIDOR was formed in 2015 as an avenue for the surrender of terrorist elements who wanted to give up fighting, especially innocent persons who were taken hostage by the terrorists and others caught in the crisis. Op SAFE CORRIDOR provided opportunity for safe passage of this group of persons by holding them in designated holding areas and deradicalizing them, then teaching different vocations before re-integrating them into society. AHQ under the COAS leadership reinforced the synergy between the respective CTCOIN operations and Op SAFE CORRIDOR to cater for the influx of surrendered terrorists.

Winning the hearts and minds of the general populace is critical as the center of gravity in most insurgencies is the population. The Chief of Civil Military Affairs, Maj Gen M Kangye (2023), stated that the battle between insurgents and the state is therefore a tug-of-war for the loyalty and support of the population. A successful counterinsurgency strategy requires winning the population away from insurgents by drawing on a mixture of kinetic and non-kinetic actions. Therefore, people's engagement is key to winning hearts and minds for CTCOIN. Commanders at all levels were made to continually engage with the local population through traditional leaders, opinion leaders, and other persons of influence to help change the narratives already implanted in the populace by the terrorists. Quick impact projects and specific image-building activities such as the provision of water across communities especially in the Northeast, the restoration of damaged roads and bridges, support for the educational systems, and the provision of general security were used by Nigerian Army troops under COAS leadership to win the populace's support, which underpinned operational success.

In the final analysis, leadership is a three-way concept involving a leader and the subjects with an objective as the destination. Without these three necessary elements, leadership does not exist. A good leader therefore determines the destination of his leadership encapsulated in his vision, which must be made clear to his subjects with whom he works hand in hand to achieve the set goals. As a result, the COAS outlined his vision, which was the direction he wanted the Nigerian Army to take in order to achieve the assigned mandate, as soon as he was appointed. The vision was further broken down into pillars, which were guidelines to achieving it.

The vision applied to all sections and endeavours of the Nigerian Army and to a very extent, guided how the business of soldiering is carried out under his leadership.

There are several ways to approach the subject of leadership. A combination of some of these methods is necessary to achieve given mandates. No form of leadership is adjudged the best, but that which achieves the desired results will, in such circumstances, stand out. In complex situations like CTCOIN operations, a commander has to be dynamic enough to combine the right forms of leadership when the occasion demands.

CTCOIN operations are quite complex because of the close proximity of the enemy to population centres. Therefore, good leadership at both the tactical and operational levels is very necessary. The COAS Vision served to guide operational commanders on how to lead at the operational level and then cascade the same guidelines down to the tactical commanders, who are in closer proximity to the troops, the enemy, and the populace. This form of relationship contributed immensely to the Nigerian Army's successes on CTCOIN operations. Leadership is therefore a function of the leader and the subjects working together to achieve a common purpose.

Operational Level Tactics and Manoeuvre in CTCOIN

Commanders at every level must therefore act with audacity, dash, and determination, seizing the initiative and thus subordinating their opponents will to their own.
Marshal Tukhachevskii

Tactics and Manoeuvre are critical in the conduct of operations and are battle-winning factors if well applied both in conventional and asymmetric operations. Tactics in CTCOIN differ greatly from conventional warfare. In CTCOIN, conflicts are hybrid, include asymmetric threats, and are more likely to occur in complex terrain. The forces will have to fight dispersed and in depth. They must be capable of retaining mobility, have a high level of organic lethality to compensate for the difficulties with establishing mutual support, and be prepared to fight intermingled with regular and irregular enemy forces, as operational penetration will be inevitable. The British Army came to the above realisation during Op PANTHER'S CLAW, a British-led military operation in the War in Afghanistan in Helmand Province in southernAfghanistan. It aimed to secure various canals and river crossings to establish a permanent International Security Assistance Force (ISAF) presence in the area. Helmand Province was the most difficult for coalition forces as it had the highest concentration of Taliban.

In the North-East, which was the Nigerian Army's first major experience with protracted CTCOIN operation, shifting from conventional to asymmetric tactics posed a problem. This was compounded by the peculiar nature of the region, with large swathes of difficult terrain and insurgents that were part of the population. The difficulties in holding several fronts simultaneously led to the adoption of the Super Camp concept. The Super Camp tactic was defensive in nature and emphasised the concentration of superior force at designated areas from which limited offensive actions were carried out. The Super Camp tactics left many villages and towns vulnerable to insurgents' attacks and gave the insurgents more freedom of action. The Super Camp Tactic was in tune with the Responsive Offensive Doctrine (ROD), which was the doctrine hitherto embraced by the NA. It was more reactive than proactive.

It therefore became obvious that the Nigerian Army was faced with an urgent need to rethink its counter insurgency approach and to evolve new strategies and tactics that would facilitate the expeditious attainment of the strategic and tactical goals of her counter terrorism and counter insurgency efforts in the North-East. This eventually led to the evolution of the Mobile Strike Team (MST) concept to complement the Conventional Warfare approach. As anticipated, this asymmetric warfare concept devised by the Army Headquarters and adopted by the Theatre Command Op LAFIYA DOLE, proved highly successful in swiftly overrunning most of the existing Boko Haram Camps, especially within Northern Borno up to the fringes of Lake Chad, and recapturing areas that were hitherto under their occupation. However, owing to certain inherent challenges that characterised this war fighting strategy, the Army Headquarters once again saw an overarching need to rethink and revamp its counter insurgency strategy and tactics. This is with a view to evolving a more potent and enduring approach that would lead to an expeditious destruction of the remnants of Boko Haram and ISWAP terrorists. It was meant to bring about a swifter end to the menace of terrorism and insurgency in Nigeria. Accordingly, this critical need was subjected to extensive brainstorming sessions that eventually gave birth to the evolution of the Army Super Camp (ASC) concept.

ASCs refer to permanently manned and well-protected Main Operating Bases (MOBs), from which forces are projected to the insurgents' enclaves and hideouts or to their routes and crossing points. Consequently, ASCs are large camps that contain both fighting troops and the logistics elements required to sustain their operations. The camps are properly sited with adequate space for the logistics elements to dump the combat supplies needed to support the troops as they embark on diverse missions and tasks, including long-range patrols, raids, and ambushes, as well as fighting patrols.. Additionally, the camps are equally large enough to permit continuous In-theatre training activities aimed at further sharpening the troops' capacity to effectively dominate the area. This is to deny the terrorists freedom of action and equally seek and destroy them within their hideouts in order to bring about a speedy and favourable end to the menace of terrorism in Nigeria.

It is pertinent to note that, as part of the ASC Concept, all the communities and towns such as Gubio, Magumeri, Kareto, Gajigana, Gajiram, and Mairari, among others, from where static deployments were collapsed to form the Super Camps were designated as Response Areas (RAs). Other larger towns with a sizeable population and government presence are designated Strong

Response Areas (SRAs). At each of the RAs and SRAs, potent, sizeable, and well-equipped mobile troops are deployed on a 24-hour basis to mount road blocks, conduct clearing and fighting patrols, cordon and search or raid operations, and lay ambushes as may be necessitated by the prevailing threats to each of the specific RAs in order to rid them of Boko Haram activities. The Super Camp concept envisaged more potent, better manned, and better equipped forces deployed to locations or communities on wheels and on a 24-hour basis to ensure they are better patrolled and protected than when they had static deployments. To this end, adequate guidelines were issued to formations/units in order to facilitate the effective conduct of the activities at the respective ASCs.

The Army Super Camp concept has the inherent advantages of concentration of forces, and convergence of logistics within a large camp with opportunities to project forces to the insurgents' enclaves or to the various Response Areas while still holding such camps in strength. Other advantages include enhanced logistics support for troops, effective dispensing of Petroleum Oil and Lubricants to vehicles, centralized repair and maintenance of vehicles and other equipment, and quality feeding for troops. The concept also confers opportunities to concentrate troops for in-theatre training, refitting of vehicles and equipment, and effective administration of troops across the Theatre. Also, the Super Camps afforded the opportunities to project short, medium and long-range patrols, raids, ambushes and clearance operations to insurgents' hideouts and crossing points as expected in an asymmetric warfare environment. However, these strategies did not bring about the expeditious defeat of the insurgency and the restoration of peace and stability across the entire North-East as originally expected.

The Nigerian Army Doctrine 2022 introduced the Proactive Responsive Doctrine (PRD) which emphasized hitting the enemy's centres of gravity before it conceived actions towards Nigerian Army troops. Proactive Responsive Doctrine' dictates that the Nigerian Army always maintains the posture of being proactive rather than reactive and offensive in seeking out the adversary. There was also a redirection from the Manoeuvrist Approach to Warfare (MAW) to the Manoeuvrist Approach (MA), to reflect and encompass the spectrum of both war and Military Operations Other Than War (MOOTW) currently undertaken by the Nigerian Army. The PRD Doctrine saw the dismantling of Super Camps and the setting up of Forward Operational Bases (FOBs). The FOBs are highly mobile, well equipped and highly lethal units. This change in tactics from the Army Super-Camp Concept to Forward Operating Bases in combination with synergy from the

Nigerian Air Force underpinned the immense victories recorded by the Nigerian Army especially in the Northeast.

The implication of the PRD doctrine and the attendant use of FOBs were more effective in engagements with adversaries and underpin current operational successes. This is considering that the concept of FOB was already in the Nigerian Army TTP and only required minor adjustments to succeed. The change to the use of FOB is instrumental to the degrading and current efforts to defeat BHT and ISWAP in the North-East. The successes recorded are such that normalcy has resumed in greater parts of Borno State, thus creating a shift of activities to the North-West, that is gradually becoming the epicenter of CTCOIN operations as opposed to the North-East. The PRD posture of the Nigerian Army is equally achieving successes for the Nigerian Army in the Northwest. According to Akinjobi (2023), the introduction of FOBs is instrumental to the current success achieved in the CTCOIN operations. This is considering the general and tactical understanding of the use of FOB by troops. This is unlike the ASC concept, something that a lot of personnel did not come across until they were deployed in the field and so to a lot of people, it was confusing. This contributed to the change from the ASC concept to the FOB concept in the North-East.

Improvised Explosive Devices

IEDs have dealt more casualties to personnel than direct confrontation with insurgents in the North-East. In 2017 alone, about 100 personnel were killed by IEDs. Also, some of the commanding officers lost in OPLD were killed by IEDs. Between 2015 and 2020, the Nigerian Army made concerted efforts to rid the theater of IEDs by investing in CIED resources, including the use of IED detectors and sniffer dogs. These achieved a measure of success but did not properly ensure force protection as BHT and ISWAP kept changing their methods of employment. The employment of IED by terrorists is a global phenomenon and a challenge to military forces. The US witnessed an average of 30 IED attacks per day during OP IRAQI FREEDOM. The US CENTCOM, through the Joint Improvised Explosive Device Defeat Task Force (JIEDD TF), developed adaptive tactics and material solutions to CIEDs, leading to the introduction of MRAPs into the operation and Tactical Explosive Detection Dogs (TEDD) which significantly reduced IED-related incidences. Pakistan also had its fair share of IED attacks on its personnel in its CT COIN operations. Every IED incident is carefully catalogued and displayed on a model at the National Counter Terrorism Centre in Kharian, Pakistan, explaining the circumstances leading to such attacks and the measures taken. This serves to provide lessons learned for troops embarking on CTCOIN operations in order to reduce such incidences.

The operational level tactics in the North-East took cognisance of the IED threat and the improved capability of BHT and ISWAP to deploy IEDs. BHT's capability in the making of IEDs has been on the increase since 2009, when it started its asymmetric warfare against the Nigerian state aimed at establishing their caliphate in northern Nigeria. Following the activities of troops of ORO in 2012, BH retreated into deep enclaves and adapted the use of IEDs to prevent troops from reaching their enclaves. The troops deployed their limited C-IED capability in the form of a few Nigerian Army Engineer (NAE) personnel trained in Second World War demining techniques. The NAE produced the frequency jammer as a C-IED measure to defeat the effect of the remotely detonated IEDs, but the terrorists countered such efforts with pressure plate IED (U. Ladan, personal communication, 1 May 2021). During the ORO, the insurgents appeared to recognise the importance of IEDs to their overall objectives and made efforts to develop their technical capacity and material sourcing. The Nigerian Army identified IED as one of the main thrusts of insurgent asymmetric operations but a holistic strategy to develop C-IED capability was lacking. At the joint operations level in the theatre, no distinct provision for C-IED interagency collaboration exists.

Although the Nigerian Army has some C-IED capability, the technical infrastructure for effective C-IED measures remains limited, making it difficult to decisively curtail the threat of IEDs in the North-East. While the limited response persisted, BHTs introduced anti-lift and multiple initiation points emplaced IEDs in an effort to remain two steps ahead of the Nigerian Army C-IED efforts. Efforts are ongoing to improve C-IED capability through engagement with the German Technical Assistance Group (GTAG), the British Military Assistance Training Team (BMATT), and Americans through the USARA C-IED training provided to the Nigerian Army along with C-IED equipment (US Embassy, 2019). The training was aimed at improving the capacity of EOD personnel. In spite of this effort, the attrition rate among EOD personnel in the C-IED measures in the North-East has been on the increase (M.N.B. Mamman, personal communication, 25 April 2021), thereby raising a serious doubt on the adequacy of human capacity of the EOD personnel for C-IED measures.

Inadequate technical equipment and infrastructure hampered the ability of the Nigerian Army engineering unit tasked with countering IED threats, despite the efforts of the FGN over the years through investment in technical infrastructure. According to Adeosun (2020), between 2015 and 2017, the FGN procured MRAP vehicles to provide adequate protection for troops against IEDs attacks. Other C- IEDs include the Bozena 5 and the Amtrac 400. Local production of indigenous C-IED equipment (Kadiri, 2021) includes the EZUGWU MRAP, the ODE rechargeable blasting device, and the IED crusher. According to Ochai (2021), the use of the existing technical infrastructure successfully neutralized 213, 434, and 547 IEDs in Op LAFIYA DOLE in 2018, 2019, and 2020 respectively, preventing loss of lives and property.

Despite the successes recorded against IED attacks using locally made equipment, Oladimeji rated the state of technical infrastructure as inadequate considering the danger BHT IED attacks posed and considering that the majority of the equipment found effective is Hand Held Metal Detectors (HHMD). The HHMD are primarily used by the NAE in detecting IEDs in the North-East and other theaters of operation. Some of the metal detectors come from partner countries and are fourth- generation models procured by the Nigerian Army. Attempts were also made to produce HHMD locally. The most notable and successful is the individual effort of MWO Usmania Ladan, who has produced several versions of the device that are being used in the North-East and elsewhere. The major problem with HHMDs is that they slow down the movement of advancing troops due to the need to manually scan every inch of tracks, a situation that has underscored the need for a vehicular borne IED detector. These delay would also need to be factored into operational tactics and manoeuvres.

Vehicular-mounted mine detectors with sensors fitted in their front have been successfully developed in some countries. The Nigerian Army R&D team could work on congregating a number of the HHMD sensors to create a vehicle-mounted IED detector. This could be installed on a skid steer loader with the necessary ballistic reinforcements to protect the crew. This is necessary to speed up the pace of advancing troops in IED-infested areas of operations. Efforts are ongoing by NAE, CED, and NASDC to carryout reverse engineering and modification of the existing HHMD in order to develop vehicle-mounted C-IED equipment.

The use of IED awareness as part of the solution to the problems have been prioritised. The Nigerian Army has made efforts to increase IED awareness through the infusion of C-IED training in all training schools and for troops on pre-induction training. In addition to the awareness about IEDs, the emphasis is on the development of technical skills and optimization of Research and Development efforts to enhance local production of C-IED equipment.

Draining the Swamp in CTCOIN

Defeating insurgents and terrorist may require the temporary relocation of villages to provide the desire operational conditions for success "Draining the Swamp" involves the forced relocation or elimination of the civilian population to expose the terrorists or insurgents. In other words, relocation deprives the aforementioned of the support, cover, and resources of the local population. This is typically targeted at the limited demographic area that supports the insurgency.

Draining the swamp tactics have been employed in other climes like in addressing the Rohingya crisis in Myanmar. Ethnic Rohingyas were relocated from their traditional homes to refugee camps in order to expose separatist rebels suspected of cohabiting with them. This enabled Myammar to force freedom of action against the rebels. The downside of such methods of counterinsurgency is that their severity may provoke increased resistance from the targeted population. In contemporary times, concerns about public opinion and international law can rule out counterinsurgency campaigns using this tactic.

In the North-East, draining the swamp was partially tried in Jakana and Beneshek, among others. Akinjobi (2023) noted that draining the swamp in CTCOIN will have to be a strategic decision as the Army cannot do it alone. Having the buy-in of the strategic political leadership is critical. Also, the utility is higher when all lines of operations are working in sync.

Similarly, in the NW theatre of operation, due to the incessant banditry attacks along Road Kaduna-Abuja, the Kaduna State Governor, Mallam Nasir El-Rufai, in May 2022 proposed the relocation and possible demolition of Katari, Rijana, and Akilibu villages, which were recurring targets in most bandit attacks along the corridor. The proposal was vehemently opposed by traditional leaders of the three communities, who absolved their subjects of complicity in the spate of attacks emanating from the area. Although these communities were not cleared, the threat served as a warning to them not to collaborate with criminals, and where possible, to report any infiltration of their communities by criminal elements. With concerted efforts by troops, the situation along the Kaduna-Abuja corridor has greatly improved.

Draining the swamp could be carried out with sufficient evidence that the continued existence of the community is aiding the activities of the criminal elements in CTCOIN. But this should be carried out after due process has been followed due to the expected outcry by both the inhabitants and external interest groups. After the attack on Kuje Prison in July 2022 and subsequent ambush of Gds Bde troops in Bwari, villages and camps around Abuja that were sufficiently identified to host the bandits were immediately cleared, with some of the bandits being eliminated. Therefore, draining the swamp can lead to success in CTCOIN with careful planning and coordination.

Logistics Support in CTCOIN Operations

Logistics is critical to the successful employment of tactics and manoeuvre in all spheres of operations. The ability to supply and sustain an army is the difference between a professional army and a well-organized militia. This assertion is particularly relevant to CTCOIN, where the concept of logistics support differs from that of conventional warfare. The PULL logistics concept (supply based on demand) generally utilized in conventional warfare is not very suitable for CTCOIN operations. In CTCOIN, logistics units and other logistic providers are expected to adapt to the fluid nature of asymmetric warfare by performing similar functions as available in conventional operations. The imperative of an ever-changing security situation in the absence of delineated a FEBA in a CTCOIN environment poses an increased challenge to logisticians in planning the logistics support. Accordingly, logistic units must be ready to provide logistic support to highly lethal, fluid, and highly mobile combat teams operating simultaneously at different locations, including support for humanitarian operations. Such logistics support must be robust and be required to span across clearly identified and defined logistics lines of operations (LLOs) visualized and articulated by the logistics commander. Logistic units will be required to maintain robust logistics support in CTCOIN until conditions stabilize and civilian organizations can assume those duties.

The uniqueness of the CTCOIN environment requires logisticians to seek distribution efficiencies wherever possible. Logisticians must strive to eliminate backtracking and unnecessary distribution traffic. Because of the diverse requirements for logistics support in CTCOIN, logisticians are expected to be involved in the entire operational planning process, including the execution, stabilization, and consolidation phases of the operation. Accordingly, the PUSH concept of logistics is thus recommended for CTCOIN operations. In adopting the PUSH concept, logistics modulation is applied where composite modules or teams are detached to mobile elements of combat forces involved in several concurrent operations in the AO. Because of the complex logistic requirements and conditions under which CTCOIN operations are conducted, commanders must ensure a careful logistic planning including a detailed Logistics Preparation of the Battlefield prior to the conduct of any operation. This is the dominant contemporary view of logistics support for CTCOIN operations.

The US Army aptly demonstrated efficient logistics support during its War Against Terror in Afghanistan from 2001-2021. Its logistics prowess was demonstrated through its capacity to deploy troops from the USA to commence operations in any theatre across the world in 48 hours and to sufficiently sustain the force. This feat is largely achievable through the availability of sufficient platforms and the rigorous training of its logistics personnel as a result of constant funding. Thus, the US Army effectively utilized a combination of the PUSH-PULL logistics support concept, leveraging its manufacturing capacity and potential to speedily move materiel, to support its combat troops in an asymmetric environment.

The Nigerian Army is currently involved in CTCOIN operations in the North-East and North West. These operations involve huge logistics requirements which are sometimes impeded by logistics constraints. The Nigerian Army CSS corps are largely organized for conventional logistics support, which could make its support for highly mobile and decentralized CTCOIN operations a challenging endeavour. Some efforts have been made to introduce the PUSH concept of logistics support with the modularisation of logistics in OPHK, for instance. These efforts include the establishment of the office of the TLCC and logistics bases in addition to the conventional logistics support architecture. However, these efforts are not institutionalized and cascaded to unit and combat teams' level. Additionally, snippets of actions in this regard are not codified, and this has resulted in the ineffective application of lessons learned. Hence, the culture and mentality of conventional logistics support systems still hold sway in the various theatres of operations despite the fact that the Nigerian Army is involved in CTCOIN operations demanding highly mobile combat teams. Consequently, the Nigerian Army has codified the best practices from past logistics commanders in the various theatres of operation to be adopted as logistics best practices for a CTCOIN within Nigerian Army operational theatres. Additionally, the curricula of CSS training schools are also being reviewed to reflect logistics best practices in line with contemporary national security realities. The Nigerian Army's CSS exercises are also being modified to reflect a balance of conventional and asymmetric warfare.

The current model of providing logistics in the field involves paying commanders to source their needs on a unit basis. A drawback of this method is that logistics are not standardized across units or formations as their methods may differ with attendant consequences. The new thinking includes the use of vetted and trusted local suppliers controlled at higher levels of command as part of the logistics system. They could be integrated into the operation for the provision of logistics, as it may be difficult to set up a definite supply chain in a fluid CTCOIN operation. This is to ensure that commanders in the field do not spend ample time directly making purchases at the detriment to operational planning and execution.

Communications Support in CTCOIN Operations

The successful execution of military operations depends on robust communications support which enables commanders to convey plans, directives, and orders in the management of operations. The ancient Chinese General, Chang Yu, captured the kernel of support for communications in his remark that, "When masses of troops are employed, certainly they are widely separated, and ears are not able to hear acutely nor eyes see clearly. Therefore, officers and men are ordered to advance or retreat by observing flags and banners and to move or stop by the signals of bells and drums.

Thus, the valiant does not advance alone, and the coward does not flee". This gives credence to the assertion that no military force can successfully prosecute operations in the absence of reliable communications support.

The importance of communications in warfare has played out in several military operations. At the onset of Op IRAQI FREEDOM in 2003, communications technology support was one of the major factors that influenced the planning and conduct of operations. As General Colin Powell espoused, "efficient communications during the armed conflict in Iraq increased the pace of operations, improved the decision-making process and synchronized the various capabilities of the fighting force". The importance of communications is also playing out profoundly in the ongoing Russia-Ukraine War.

The current global security environment is dominated by a myriad of asymmetric threats ranging from transnational and sub-national terrorism and insurgency, armed banditry, subversive secessionist regimes, and militancy, among others. As a result of these threats, militaries are compelled to conduct CTCOIN operations in an increasingly complex, dynamic, and multi-agency environment, as seen in the North-East theatre of operations.

Peculiarities of Communications in CTCOIN Operations

As the CTCOIN environment is complex, dynamic and dominated by multiple stakeholders, including military and non-military elements, it is crucial to understand the peculiarities that are pertinent for the provision of effective communications support in CTCOIN operations. Some of these peculiarities include poor infrastructure, a resource-intensive nature, difficulty of integration, compatibility and multiplicity of platforms.

CTCOIN operations are often carried out in areas that are generally underdeveloped, rural, and have poor infrastructure. In these areas, roads are usually few, making the movement of construction and maintenance stores difficult. Additionally, telecommunications infrastructure in these areas is not often well developed or may not exist at all. Even where the infrastructure exists, it is often destroyed by the insurgents as part of a calculated campaign of terror against the local populace, as witnessed in North-East Nigeria. All these issues make it difficult to leverage existing infrastructure to provide communications support to troops in CTCOIN operations.

Communications planning in conventional operations usually follows the chain of command, with communications resources allocated in accordance with the grouping of subordinate formations. However, most engagements in CTCOIN operations are undertaken by small teams of troops operating from widely dispersed bases, which make communication resources intensive in nature. These troops carry out constant mobile operations such as patrols, raids, and ambushes in order to dominate their AORs. Oftentimes, theatre-wide communications networks are established, linking all bases and mobile elements to provide a coherent operational picture for commanders. However, this places huge demands on communications equipment and personnel, thus making communications support in CTCOIN operations daunting.

As CTCOIN forces become more involved in several CIMIC activities in order to win the hearts and minds of the local populace, military components are more likely to find themselves operating in a multi-agency environment. As Lt Gen Robert Caslen, the former Commander of the US Army Combined Arms Centre, noted, "the dynamic, complex, and uncertain CTCOIN operating environment will test the mental agility, adaptability, and cooperative nature of the nation's civilian and military personnel as never before. The consequence is that the operational environment would comprise multiple communications platforms that require integration. The overarching purpose of such integration is for commanders to exercise hitch-free command and control over the joint force as well as seamless communications across the military and civilian elements operating in the environment.

The multiplicity of platforms is peculiar to most CTCOIN theatre of operations. The contemporary CTCOIN environment is proliferated with platforms that support various types of communication systems. There is now an assortment of voice, data, and multimedia communications platforms, which introduce complexities into communications support. Additionally, the manning, operation and maintenance of multiple communications platforms require numerous coordinating activities to knit the disparate platforms into an integrated whole in the battlespace. This is a key characteristic of deploying legacy Combat Net Radios (CNRs) as the primary means of communication, as they tend to create interoperability glitches for the fighting forces. Synthesizing these platforms into a converged system for interoperability requires extensive expertise and experience, as well as meticulous planning of communications support in COIN operations. Also, the creation of communication synergy between land and air components will largely enhance operational efficiency.

Communications Support in Operation HADIN KAI

The communications architecture in JTF North-East Op HADIN KAI has evolved over the years in a quest to ensure effective communication. Salient features of this architecture include changes in organizational structure, a layered communications strategy, the use of remote collaboration tools and the increased use of Commercial- of-the-Shelf (COTS) equipment. At the beginning of operations against the BHTs, communications support was provided by a signals squadron that was part of the 21 Brigade, then based in Maiduguri. However, as the force structure in the theatre expanded in line with operational requirements, the signals element evolved to the present organizational structure of 3 signals brigades, providing communications support to the 3 sectors of JTF NE Op HADIN KAI.

A layered communications strategy is employed to achieve robust, seamless, and secure communications support in Op HADIN KAI. In this regard, HF CNRs in the base, manpack, and vehicular configurations are used as the primary means of communication. This is complemented with Land Mobile Radio (LMR) systems deployed principally along major Main Supply Routes, as well as an array of satellite-based radios and phones. In line with the strategy, communications support is engineered to ensure that every troops location or mobile team has a minimum of three means of communications. This layered approach ensures redundancy, thus reducing to the barest minimum communications problems in the Op HADIN KAI Theatre. The layered strategy is instrumental to the operational successes recorded in the North-East.

The use of remote collaboration tools has been most beneficial to ongoing operations. As part of innovations for the strategic management of Nigerian Army operations, AHQ authorized the establishment of the Nigerian Army Video Teleconferencing Operations Network (NAVTON). The network enables the Chief of Army Staff to virtually interact with formation commanders and their staff during operations briefs and other virtual conferences. NAVTON currently links the AHQ Operations Centre with all divisional headquarters and some key JTF headquarters via Virtual Private Network (VPN) connections. The signals commanders at the various

NAVTON nodes manage the infrastructure deployed at their formations.

While NAVTON is a Nigerian Army platform, the Theatre Commander, JTF North- East Op HADIN KAI, also utilizes the platform to conduct regular briefs with his sector commanders. This has led to a marked improvement in the exercise of the functions of command, control, and coordination in Op HADIN KAI.

The use of COTS equipment is necessary in contemporary operations considering the high cost of military grade CNRs in the provision of communications support to troops. Accordingly, considering the substantial quantity of communications equipment required in CTCOIN operations, the continued dependency on military grade CNRs became unsustainable. To address this, NAS has increasingly relied on COTS equipment for its communications needs as these are cheaper, more readily available, and easier to maintain. This is also in line with global trends; a recent example is the use of Starlink commercial satellites by the Ukrainian military. Starlink satellite communication is a global satellite internet and communication infrastructure provided by over 1200 satellites deployed by SPACE X, a company owned by Elon Musk. The services are just about to be rolled out and are potentially capable of solving many internet and communication difficulties due to the location of the satellites close to earth. The Nigerian Army could partner with SPACE X to secure frequencies for military communication and take advantage of the various services the company offers, which include data, voice, and satellite telephony, among others. Thus, a plethora of COTS communications equipment are currently deployed in Op HADIN KAI, including LMR infrastructure and various satellite communications devices. These have played a key role in ensuring robust and seamless communications in Op HADIN KAI have been instrumental to operational successes.

In the final analysis, one of the greatest challenges faced by military commanders is that of communications. The ability to transmit information, orders, and intelligence efficiently and timely from one location to another in a battlespace is recognized as key to success in both conventional and CTCOIN operations. Communication planning in CTCOIN operations is usually challenging as the environment is complex and dynamic, with multiple stakeholders operating in it. Accordingly, communications planners need to take into account some peculiarities inherent in operating in such an environment, including poor infrastructure, its resource-intensive nature, integration, and multiplicity of platforms.

The communications support for JTF North-East Op HADIN KAI has evolved over the years. Salient features of this include changes in organizational structure and the employment of a layered communications strategy. Others are the use of the NAVTON for remote collaboration and the increased use of COTS equipment. All these have translated to robust and seamless communications support, with the attendant positive impact on operations.

Fire Support in CTCOIN Operations

The quality of a decision is like the well-timed swoop of a falcon which enables it to strike and destroy its victim.
Sun Tzu

Fire support refers to the collective and coordinated use of indirect-fire weapons, armed aircraft, and other lethal and non-lethal means in support of a battle plan. Fire support includes mortars, field artillery, naval gunfire, air defense artillery in secondary mission, and fire delivered from armed drones. Fire support in CTCOIN is a very crucial campaign winning factor and requires more precision and promptness in decision than in conventional warfare. This is so aptly captured by Sun Tzu in his book "On War".

Fire support has been very key to our operational successes in our CTCOIN operations. The Nigerian Army has over the years developed its organic fire support capabilities and tailored them to suit the peculiarities of CTCOIN operations. Some of these include organic infantry fire support from mortars, artillery fire support, and armoured fire support. The robust cooperation between the Nigerian Army and the Nigerian Air Force, coupled with our dynamic force structure at the theatres of operations, led to the integration of air fire support into our operational plans. The mantra of jointness from the Defence Headquarters to the various services contributed to the efficient fire support the Nigerian Army under my leadership enjoyed from the Nigerian Air Force. The integration of modern technology in warfare also saw the inclusion of armed drones in our fire support plans, leading to the Nigerian Army acquiring state-of-the-art armed drones that have been able to deliver precision strikes to the adversaries.

Air Power and Army Aviation in CTCOIN

Counter insurgency emphasizes population-centred methods to achieve objectives and also win hearts and minds. However, conventional warfare focuses on the need for firepower, maneuver, and associated tactics. Airpower is a campaign- winning factor in CTCOIN, but the population-centred nature requires the controlled nature of air support.

The Nigerian Air Force as it is presently constituted is more suited for conventional warfare, as CTCOIN is best executed with close air support organic to the land forces. The Super Tucano is the best weapon in the arsenal of the Nigerian Air Force for COIN operations. Notwithstanding, the Nigerian Air Force has been able to adapt most of its platforms to CTCOIN roles.

In the words of Lt Gen Faruk Yahaya "In the spirit of jointness and cooperation and in keeping my vision alive, my leadership of the Nigerian Army has witnessed unprecedented cooperation with the other services, especially the Nigerian Air Force, who have been a reliable partner in our CTCOIN operations". The restructuring of the Theatre Command of the Joint Task Force (Op ZAMAN LAFIYA) by DHQ and the appointment of component commanders from the sister services under the Theatre Commander helped increase the availability of fire support from the Nigerian Air Force. Despite the unrelenting efforts of the Nigerian Air Force, the experiences of our CTCOIN dictate that the Nigerian Army needs to have its own organic close air support capability. An Army Aviation Command comprising light attack aircraft, medium-range attack helicopters, light transporters, and ISR capability from unmanned aerial vehicles will greatly complement any ground force involved in CTCOIN operations. Air power for CTCOIN will require a mix of Army Aviation for close air support for ground forces and the air force for strategic targets.

The Pakistan Army Aviation Corps is an integral fighting force of the Pakistan Army. It has historically been involved in combat missions in support of CTCOIN in Afghanistan, Somalia, Sierra Leone, and some other nations, as well as COIN operations within Pakistan. The Army Aviation has also been involved in non- combat missions like search and rescue after earthquakes in Kashmir in 2005 and cyclone disasters in Bangladesh in 1991. Some equipment of the Pakistan Army Aviation Corps includes helicopter gunships, light attack helicopters, transport helicopters, light transporters, surveillance aircrafts and training aircrafts.

A model of an army aviation unit was deployed in Nigeria between 2014 and 2015 by technical partners who provided assistance with huge success in the fight against insurgency during that period. Equipment deployed included 6 light attack helicopters, two helicopter gunships, two Mi-8 medium transport helicopters, one Diamond surveillance aircraft and one

Caravan surveillance aircraft. This aviation unit provided adequate close air support to 3 Division covering Adamawa State, while the NigerianAir Force provided strategic air interdiction of long-range targets. This unit was also on call to 7 Div covering Borno and Yobe States, providing them with ISR support and sometimes fire support. Since then, the idea of an Army Aviation Command has been emphasised but not much has been done beyondits establishment of aviation units and minimal development of aviation infrastructures like hangars. Under my leadership, I have furthered this dream by having discussions with aviation manufacturers like Airbus on the production of air assets to fulfil this dream. Pilots have also been trained on various platforms, although the acquisition of these platforms is at very advanced stages. I am quite optimistic that when the army aviation comes on stream, air power support for the Nigerian Army will be greatly enhanced.

Use of Artillery in CTCOIN

The artillery is suitably deployed to support ground troops over long ranges and against enemy forward of troops locations. Counter insurgency emphasizes population-centred methods to achieve objectives and also win hearts and minds. However, conventional warfare focuses on the need for firepower, maneuver, and associated tactics. It therefore leaves one with the question of what the roles of artillery are in CTCOIN operations.

In Iraq, some US Army artillery units were taken off the gunline and become military police units, transportation units, and infantry maneuver forces because of a lack of missions for the field artillery in COIN operations. There were assumptions that the artillery causes too much collateral damage on the battlefield and, in some cases, will hinder COIN operations. In order for the artillery to be successful, this mindset had to be changed through the development of better, smarter, and more accurate types of munitions available for employment in the theater. The artillery community developed the new GPS (global position system) GMLRS (guided multiple-launch rocket system) round and successfully fired it in Iraq while fighting the insurgency, achieving outstanding results.

The same situations apply to the artillery in CTCOIN ops in Nigeria. The nature of the terrain and disposition of the enemy make artillery fire a potential source of collateral damage. Therefore, for the artillery to remain relevant in CTCOIN ops, it must invest in smart equipment and munitions that are capable of delivering pin-point hits on the enemy. The current guns and howitzers and the recent Multi-Barrel Rocket Launchers (MBRLs) in the artillery inventory cannot be effectively employed against insurgents in city centres and populated areas except in isolated engagements However, insurgents in the theatres of operation have been driven away from population areas, making it easier for the artillery to engage them without fear of collateral damage. The artillery has successfully engaged concentrated terrorist areas in the North-East, such as the Sambisa Forest and Timbuktu Triangle, and the Mandara Mountains along the borders with Cameroun, with high degrees of success. The Nigerian Army Artillery has been efficient in supporting the Nigerian Army in CTCOIN as a result of the immense support given to it. The artillery weapons are in a constant state of functionality due to extensive repairs and regular servicing carried out on them. As Chief of Army Staff, "I made it a point of duty to regularly visit gun locations to encourage the men and see how they employ their weapons. I envision that the artillery corps will gradually acquire guns that are more compact, produce even better results, and have the capabilities to be infused with modern technologies for better efficiency. This will help with coordination with other fire support systems in the theatres of operations".

Use of Drones in CT COIN Operations

Armed Drones deliver precise firepower to bear on the enemy and could be a huge force multiplier in CTCOIN ops. Their accuracy on targets reduces concerns about collateral damage in these operations, some of which are carried out in populated areas. Armed drones are expensive and are used for High Valued Targets (HVTs), but if well employed, they could be worth the investment. The use of an armed drone in Afghanistan to kill Al Qaeda leader Ayman al-Zawahiri is quite instructive. Similarly, the extensive use of drones in the Russia-Ukraine crisis to deliver pin-point targets is another attestation of the relevance of this technology in target acquisition in populated areas. Drones have been used to disrupt military convoys and damage entire warships.

Drones have also been used effectively to direct artillery fire during the Russia-Ukraine crisis. This synergy could also be used to make the artillery more relevant in CTCOIN because it will reduce the level of collateral damage the weapons can inflict on populated areas. The Nigerian Army is currently building up its UAV Command with the acquisition of 12 units of unarmed Aerosonde military-grade UAVs with ranges of over 200 kms. The Nigerian Army has already acquired the Bayraktar TB2, a Turkish-manufactured drone currently being used in Ukraine, while pilot and other operator trainings on the equipment were carried out in Turkey. The armed drones are already being put to effective use with all infrastructures in place, including launch pads and hangers.

Introducing of drones into the theatres of operations in Nigeria, especially the North-East has added to the firepower of the Nigerian Army and largely changed the dynamics of operations. The NA UAV Command has been so organized to ensure that drones are available to support the Infantry for ISTAR purposes, artillery for fire direction and Intelligence for ISR purposes, as well as other arms for various other missions. The future of drone technology as a means of fire support in the Nigerian Army will involve the incorporation of satellite technology with already embedded technology in the drones to synchronize with other fire support elements for greater efficiency.

Fire Support Coordination

The best output from fire support systems is derived from effective coordination of the respective fire support elements. A Fire Support Coordination Centre (FSCC) is a necessity in every major operation. The JTF (Op ZAMAN LAFIYA) has a FSCC commanded by a Brig Gen and is responsible for the acquisition of targets for the various fire support systems in the theatre. The FSCC ensures judicious use of the firepower available to achieve the best results. The FSCC coordinates air, artillery, mortars and armed drone fires for various operation commanders.

Fire support coordination has been crucial to our successes in CTCOIN operations. This enabled the appropriate selection of targets for the Nigerian Air Force, which was quite effective in eliminating large gatherings of insurgents or movements of insurgents. Based on credible intelligence, the Nigerian Air Force was severally involved in the North-East, the North Central, and the North-West in targeting several terrorist leaders. The artillery has been useful in dispersing the gathering of the insurgents and in targeting their logistics supplies and the introduction of the armed drones compounded the problems of the insurgents. The drones have been delivering precise strikes on selected targets within the theatres.

My future view of fire coordination in our theatres of operations is one that takes advantage of emerging technologies for better coordination. The US Army is currently using space sensors to help its artillery see and shoot well beyond their current capability. The Army taps into orbiting satellites to help guns on the ground hit long-range targets. This is made possible because the guns on the ground are modern and possess the necessary technologies to enable communication with the satellites. In the ongoing Russia/Ukraine crisis, there is extensive use of satellite technology to control fires from artillery, drones, and other fire support systems.

The Nigerian Army has numerous possibilities to enhance fire support coordination using similar capabilities. Our current satellites, controlled by NIGCOMSAT, do not possess adequate military capabilities, so resorting to commercial satellites could help us achieve our objectives. Nigeria is currently covered by the Starlink satellite communication satellites provided by Space X and is one of the first African countries to be linked to these earth-orbiting satellites. Space X has over 1200 constellation satellites in orbit that provide varying capabilities. With an upgrade of our equipment, satellite communication from Space X could be used to help coordinate our fire support in our CTCOIN operations. The Defence Space Administration (DSA) could research further on these possibilities.

Fire support coordination is not complete without a communication plan. There must be seamless communication between the coordination centre and the supporting elements on the one hand, and between the centre and the supported troops on the other hand. To this end, we have made extensive efforts to improve our communication equipment for troops on the ground and also air-to-ground communication to enable fighting troops to direct aircraft and other weapons fire accurately and efficiently.

Fire support is a very decisive element of CTCOIN operations due to the complex nature of such operations because, in many cases, the enemy is in close proximity to population centres. While there is a requirement to bring down supporting fire on the adversary in support of ground troops, utmost care needs to be taken to avoid collateral damage in the process due to the nature of these supporting weapons. In CTCOIN, supporting fire is provided by the Air Force, artillery, infantry support weapons, armour, and more recently, armed drones. Each of these fire support elements has its own unique characteristics and types of targets they are used against. In our CTCOIN operations, air support has been used to disrupt insurgents' movements and convoys, engage their gatherings, and target their leadership. Artillery fire support has been used over long ranges to hit the adversary's logistics and other key targets. The recent introduction of armed drones has changed the dynamics of fire support. The technology involved with armed drones enables them to deliver more precise hits on the adversary with devastating effects.

Fire support is not effective without central coordination. In our theatres of operation, the FSCC has been established to better coordinate the effects of the various fire support systems. In today's world of improving technology, fire support coordination is enhanced with satellite technology, and this is the level I envision for our fire support coordination. This also includes robust communication between ground troops and the supporting fire establishments. It is my belief that fire support in our CTCOIN operations will be more effective as the Nigerian Army embraces emerging technologies and applies them appropriately.

Utility of Intelligence in Operations

Nothing is more worthy of the attention of a good general than to endeavor to penetrate the designs of the enemy.
Niccolo Machiavelli

The vision laid down by Lt Gen Faruk Yahaya, CFR, as COAS demanded that he expressly state his command philosophy, which served as guides to subordinate commanders, one of these guides is the acquisition of intelligence, which revolves around leveraging information and communication systems to obtain intelligence, conduct counter-intelligence and conduct deception measures to achieve success, which is in sync with the view of *Niccolo Machiavelli* on the value of intelligence in operations. Intelligence is a driver for activities both in operations and in peace- time. Intelligence remains key to the Nigerian Army's success in different operations, which informs the need to invest heavily in intelligence systems.

The COAS command philosophy on acquisition of intelligence is not just about procurement of intelligence systems but of activities in the whole gamut of intelligence operations, which include the entire intelligence cycle of direction, collection, processing, and dissemination. Furthermore, the counterintelligence efforts directed at the enemy's intelligence activities also need to be taken into consideration, as our intelligence will be whittled down if we do not consider what the enemy is doing. Finally, other elements of intelligence operations were considered, which include deception operations, information operations using the wide array of media spaces.

Acquisition of intelligence is an expensive but quite rewarding venture, and the Chief of Army Staff has left no stone unturned, or costs spared in enabling the Nigerian Army Intelligence Corps (NAIC) to perform optimally. Advancements in technology and the expansion of the frontiers of information systems demanded that the NAIC and other security agencies upgrade their equipment and processes to meet up with this growth. It is noteworthy that the NAIC is currently in tune with contemporary intelligence agencies and has thus contributed to our overall successes.

Intelligence in CTCOIN Operations

The NA's multiple engagements on many fronts demand that intelligence be given a front row in our mission plans. CTCOIN is a largely intelligence-led type of operation due to the close proximity of the enemy to population centres, civil population and other forms of soft targets. It is also difficult to distinguish friend from foe when the enemy comes from the civilian population and, in some cases lives with them. This therefore makes the use of intelligence in CTCOIN operations quite complex. An array of intelligence resources is available for employment to ensure the success of CTCOIN Operations. These include, HUMINT, Communication Intelligence (COMMINT) or Signal Intelligence (SIGINT), technical intelligence, and ISR platforms, among others.

Human Intelligence

HUMINT remains the traditional method of intelligence acquisition. Despite the advancements in technology, this source of intelligence remains very relevant and needs to be continually developed. The killing of Osama Bin Laden and Ayman al-Zawahiri, two key Al-Qaeda leaders by US forces brought to light the role of HUMINT in CTCOIN. Despite the sophistication of US Intelligence resources, human sources were very critical in providing the needed information, which was used along with other technological resources to home-in on their respective locations before strikes were carried out. The placing of bounties on the heads of terror leaders is an indication that HUMINT is necessary in the execution of CTCOIN Operations.

In the North-East and indeed other theatres of operation, HUMINT has played dual roles of aiding own troops attacks on insurgents and also preventing insurgents' ambushes against own troops. Several terrorist leaders and key fighters have been neutralized as a result of HUMINT efforts. NA efforts in declaring several terrorists wanted with bounty placed on them have continued to yield results. HUMINT has been instrumental in the conduct of offensives deep into the terrorists' enclaves. This resulted in the neutralization of some key terrorist commanders among other terrorists in Garin Ba'Abba, Parisu and Njimiya within Sambisa Forest. One of such operations resulted in the neutralization of Abu Asiya, a notorious terrorist Comd in Parisu on 12 September 2022 by troops working in collaboration with hybrid forces. It therefore implies that the NAIC should make the cultivation of a wide range of HUMINT resources a priority.

Communication Intelligence

COMMINT is a reliable force enabler in CTCOIN, particularly in intercepting terrorist plans before, during, and after operations. COMMINT is employed by advanced armies to track terrorists, especially their leaders. The US forces used COMMINT to track the communications of aides to Osama Bin Laden in Pakistan, which led them to his hideout in Abbottabad, where he was taken out. Similarly, India relied greatly on communication intercepts to the monitor activities of terrorists within the country and at its border with Pakistan which were used to prevent attacks by terrorists and also to launch attacks on them. Using the legal intercept tools of ONSA, communication intercepts of terrorists were used extensively between 2014 and 2015 in the Northeast with huge results. The successes made the terrorists resort to use of satellite communication by their leaders. With the subsequent acquisition of satellite communications intercepts, the terrorists had to the resort to traditional means of passing vital information. Communication interception demands diligent analysis to achieve results and requires training.

The NAIC is taking advantage of technological advances to enhance its combat intelligence capabilities. The Corp currently has substantial communication intercept capabilities, which have proven useful in our CTCOIN operations for the identification and tracking of terrorist leaders and key commanders. These capabilities need to be sustained and possibly expanded due to their huge potential. COMMINT has been involved in CTCOIN operations in the area of terrorists' communication intercepts as well as the geolocation of terrorists, their collaborators, and logistics suppliers for subsequent arrest. Thus far, over 27 terrorists' communications intercepts have been recorded in December 2022 alone. These sustained efforts have contributed positively to the Theatres' operational successes. Some achievements associated with COMMINT in ongoing CTCOIN operations include; the sustained interception of terrorists' communications, which generally provided insight into the terrorists' likely intentions. This served as an early warning to troops about an impending untoward action by the terrorists. Consequently, such information was timely analyzed and disseminated to supporting units and formations in order to remain vigilant.

Identification and arrest of terrorists/collaborators/logistics suppliers was also possible through COMMINT. The activities of terrorists' logistics suppliers and collaborators remained a major cause for concern within CTCOIN operations. In this regard, sustained terrorists' communication intercepts were deployed with a view to identifying and arresting the terrorists as well as their logistics suppliers and collaborators. This also enabled the blockade of terrorists' logistics nodes to deny the terrorists access to the much-needed logistics to further their cause. This was attributable to the sustained deployment of COMMINT in monitoring the movement of terrorists' logistics as well as supply routes.

CTCOIN operations in the North-East have continued to witness the surrender of terrorists in droves. This surrendering process was largely impacted by the use of COMMINT, as voice recordings are usually sent periodically to the terrorists in the forests. This convinced a lot of the terrorists to surrender as observed in the mass surrender of terrorists and their families. As at 8 April 2023, 93,900 terrorists and their families had surrendered to the Nigerian Army in major CTCOIN areas of operations. The surrender of repentant terrorists was not devoid of hitches. One of such issues was the growing concern over some repentant terrorists providing information to their cohorts in the forests. Through sustained communications intercepts, such accomplices were identified and apprehended. Similarly, there was the discovery of errant soldiers with questionable loyalty. The errant soldiers were eventually arrested and arraigned for court-martial. The potential for the use of COMMINT is endless and will need to be encouraged in CTCOIN operations. The emphasis on the upgrade of COMMINT equipment and capacity building for NAIC personnel remains paramount.

Intelligence Surveillance and Reconnaissance Assets

Intelligence, Surveillance and Reconnaissance (ISR) assets are one of the most reliable sources of intelligence in CTCOIN ops and are critical for success. ISR assets are products of technological advancements in intelligence gathering and are great force multipliers in today's military operations. ISR assets with their reach and capabilities have helped to give a better intelligence picture of our contemporary areas of conflict.

With the acquisition of aerosonde tactical drones for the NA, the intelligence picture of the battlespace of our CTCOIN ops will become clearer if well applied and will underpin future success.

The NAIC did not have its organic military-grade ISR capability. It relied on the ISR platforms of allied partners who left the theatre in 2018 and thereafter, those of the Nigerian Air Force, in line with the need for synergy with other arms and services. Recently, the Nigerian Army acquired 12 Aerosonde tactical drones from the US which were its first military-grade drones and efforts are in top gear to immediately launch them into operations. Further acquisition of similar platforms has been concluded and with these platforms, the intelligence picture of the battlespace of CTCOIN ops will become clearer if well applied. A strong synergy between the Nigerian Army UAV Command and the NAIC in the deployment of the UAVs to maximize their benefits is highly desirable and critical. The sighting and neutralization of over 80 terrorists in Arina in Marte LGA, Borno State, on 14 December 2022, as well as the timely conveyance of intelligence on terrorists' convergence and movement as acquired by the Nigerian Army UAVs (WATCHKEEPER) are a few instances of the capability provided by the newly inducted ISR platforms. Considering that asymmetric operations are intelligence- led and intelligence underpins success, the Nigerian Army will need to invest more in ISR capabilities.

Information Operations in CTCOIN

Closely related is the fundamental role of Information operations (Info Ops) in CTCOIN operations. Information operations refer to the integrated employment, during military operations, of information-related capabilities in concert with other lines of operation to influence, disrupt, corrupt, or usurp the decision-making of adversaries and potential adversaries while protecting our own. Info Ops is an intelligence-related operation where the information involved needs to be processed and its effects on both friendly and enemy forces are carefully evaluated before they are disseminated.

CTCOIN operations in the North-East have shown that information operations are a combat multiplier because terrorists win or lose depending on how much they can imprint a perception of lethality (hence the terror in terrorism) upon a population, in order to influence the government. Terror groups have embraced modern communications technologies that spread their message exponentially more effectively than anything seen previously. Some have created their own media conglomerates to professionally produce original media. The importance of media operations to terrorism was highlighted by the late Al-Qaeda leader, Ayman al- Zawahiri, when he said in 2005 that "We are in a battle and half of this battle, is taking place on the media. We are in a media battle for the hearts and minds of our ummah". This underscores the relevance of Info Ops in CTCOIN Operations.

Global terrorist groups such as Al Qaeda and ISIS have embraced the extensive use of social media handles and mainstream media to propagate their ideologies to win over and transmit their ideologies to the uninformed population. These media operations are also adopted by our home grown terrorist groups who have formed alliances with these global groups. It is therefore not surprising to see the Boko Haram Group and ISWAP engage in media operations akin to those of Al Qaeda or ISIS, as applicable. Boko Haram and ISWAP have adopted the templates of their global partners to propagate fear and spread propaganda through extensive use of the media. Media platforms such as the AMAQ and the Telegram social media handle have been heavily utilized by both JAS/ISWAP to disseminate video and audio propaganda messages. The 2 December 2022, videos of supposed ISWAP terrorists pledging allegiance to the new ISIS caliphate are instructive in this regard.

Info Ops by the Nigerian Army have been targeted primarily at reacting to contents put out by the terrorist groups, thereby giving the latter an edge in the information warfare. These have been achieved through media briefings or releases and, more recently, the use of the Nigerian Army Cyber Warfare Command to track and neutralize contents in the online media with terrorist tendencies. There was inadequate concerted effort to upscale information operations to the enemy's Centre of Gravity (CoG), which in CTCOIN includes the population, their beliefs, political support, among other intangible CoGs.

In realization of the above, the Chief of Army Staff sanctioned the upscaling of information operations in Nigerian Army CTCOIN operations. This involved a synergy between the NAIC, the Signal Corps, and the DAPR. The NAIC created contents for the Information Operations due to its specialty in psychological operations. The Signal Corps provided the platform for communicating the contents while the

DAPR took responsibility for dissemination. Info Ops Centres were established at Theatre headquarters with the above constitution for the coordination of Information Operations tailored to the specifics of that operation. Several parleys with media organizations, the designing and distribution of psyops leaflets, media broadcasts in different languages, deliberate key leader engagements within communities of interest, and other CIMIC and CIMIR duties have been employed to bridge the gap between the Nigerian Army and the citizenry. This has largely enhanced the perception and public support received by the Nigerian Army especially with regards to the provision of timely information necessary for actionable intelligence across the various theatres of operation.

The Future of Intelligence Operations in CTCOIN

Intelligence is a force multiplier for any military operation, and its employment is therefore a necessity. Advancements in intelligence are accompanied by revolutions in technology and several other endeavours. It is therefore desirable that intelligence in Nigerian Army, operations should move in line with advancements in technology and other essentials involved in the intelligence craft. Investment in emerging technologies such as ISR platforms will increase the intelligence-gathering capability of the Intelligence Corps. Additionally, combat is being heavily influenced by space technology and any emerging intelligence organization must key into this new realm of combat to remain relevant. The NAIC therefore needs to expand its frontiers of intelligence gathering to this realm by keying into existing space technology institutions like the National Space Research and Development Agency (NASRDA) and Nigerian Communication Satellite Company (NIGCOMSAT). This can be achieved through proper synergy with the Defence Space Administration (DSA), the Defence organization saddled with satellite technology.

The proactive exploitation of HUMINT will put the NAIC on the initiative rather than just being reactive. This is in tandem with the Proactive Response Doctrine (PRD), which the Nigerian Army has adopted in the NigerianArmy Doctrine (NAD) 2022. Proactive intelligence exploitation will largely help the Nigerian Army achieve the PRD as it will give the troops in operation the initiative against the adversary. There is no doubt that extensive deployment of HUMINT is expensive, but no cost should be spared in obtaining adequate intelligence as the effects of adversary action on troops morale and efficiency are more costly.

The adversary is equally trained and has its own intelligence processes running simultaneously in the theatre. Therefore, the NAIC of the future will need to step up its counter-intelligence efforts targeted at the roots of the enemy's intelligence activities. This is equally in line with the PRD of the Nigerian Army, which is aimed at making the enemy react to its own actions rather than the other way round. The role of artificial intelligence as a key enabler in gathering and analyzing intelligence on an adversary's forces will need to remain in view. Military grade intelligence platforms, capable of withstanding cyber-attacks, endowed with autonomous learning and analysis capabilities, and equipped with sensors or interfaces in both the physical world and cyber-space, are required.

Finally, the acquisition of intelligence, being one of the Chief of Army Staff's cardinal philosophies, buttresses the importance he placed on intelligence in the conduct of operations, especially CTCOIN. Beyond the acquisition of intelligence, the Chief of Army Staff placed emphasis on the full aspects of intelligence operations, which include counterintelligence and information operations among others. CTCOIN being quite a complex operation requires that the enemy and the population be taken into consideration as it is a people centered conflict. The NAIC has been positioned to execute these aspects of intelligence operations in support of the Nigerian Army in CTCOIN operations.

Intelligence capacity has been boosted with the acquisition of ISR assets by the Nigerian Army and it is believed that if well exploited, it will yield the desired benefits. The field of COMMINT has equally boosted Nigerian Army operations. Within its available resources, the NAIC has made giant strides in this field, with significant results in CTCOIN and other operations. The extensive use of the media, especially social media, by terrorists to propagate their ideologies to the population informed the need for Nigerian Army forces to upscale their information operations capability. Some visible efforts have been made in this direction, but there is still some work to be done in order to win the hearts and minds of the populace, who in most cases are the center of gravity for terrorist groups that need their support to continue to propagate their unwholesome activities.

The highlighted aspect of intelligence operations informs the need to improve the Nigerian Army's capacity in these areas. Therefore, the Chief of Army Staff's desire for the future of intelligence for the Nigerian Army is the full exploitation of technology to enhance intelligence acquisition, the upscale of human intelligence operations, and efficient engagement in counterintelligence and information operations to give Nigerian Army troops a continual advantage over the enemy.

Primacy of Politics in CTCOIN

War is an extension of politics by other means
Carl Von Clauswitz

The primacy of politics in CTCOIN describes the important place of politics in the crisis leading to CTCOIN operations. The political variable describes the distribution of responsibility and power at all levels of government. Since an insurgency is fundamentally a struggle for political power, the political environment in the country is critical. This demands that attention be paid not just to the formal political system (such as political parties and elected officials) but also to informal political systems (such as tribes, ethnic groups, and other centers of power). Long-term success in COIN is ultimately based on political efforts; all counterinsurgents must focus on the political impact of their actions. Therefore, tactical leaders may be expected to broker local political solutions. According to Clausewitz, war is an extension of politics by other means. For politics, aims are the ends, and war is the means, and the means can never be conceived without the ends. CTCOIN Operations are therefore military responses to political decisions thus, commanders need to know the political environment of each crisis. If the aim is not kept in sight, such operations can become political burdens for the military and the nation in general.

CTCOIN operations elsewhere in the world lend credence to the primacy of politics. In Op IRAQI FREEDOM and Op ENDURING FREEDOM, the US Army's involvement in Afghanistan achieved limited strategic success over time because it had become a political, social, and financial burden on the government, which ultimately impacted negatively on US national security. It achieved military successes but did not achieve the political objective of defeating global terrorism. The political dimension of any crisis must be well understood by commanders who must ensure their troops act within the confines of the overall objective. In the North-East, a series of military objectives have been achieved. However, it is important to clearly align with the political objectives, as the inability to achieve them will leave a political burden on the system, which will diminish military achievements. Key dynamics in the North-East, which include regional and international support, humanitarian issues, the security development nexus, and issues of rule of law, require political and strategic guidance and solution, while military lines of operation provide the enabling conditions for success.

Cross - cutting Themes in the North East Theatre

There are cross-cutting themes in the CTCOIN operations that need to be examined. These are the politics of international and regional support, humanitarian situations, the security-development nexus, and issues of rule of law and justice.

International and Regional Support

The fight against terrorism is a global enterprise, and fortunately, some consensus seems to be emerging on the issue. Many countries have pledged to support Nigeria's efforts at CTCOIN, but the responses have been mixed. This underscores the importance of international cooperation in countering terrorism and violent extremism. The threats of terrorism and violent extremism rapidly emerge, disaggregate, and re-emerge and therefore demand increased bilateral and multilateral synergy to address them. While pledges of support have been received from countries like the USA, UK, Germany, and France, not much has been achieved on the ground. Activities of BHT and ISWAP have dominated US congressional actions on Nigeria in recent years, leading to the designation of the group as a Foreign Terrorist Organization (FTO) and some members as Specially Designated Global Terrorists (SDGT), including Abubakar Shekau, condemnation of Boko Haram's attacks on civilian targets, expressions of support for the Nigerian people, and the US development of a regional strategy to address the threat posed by Boko Haram.

The US military's assistance for regional efforts to counter Boko Haram has been channeled primarily through engagement with Nigeria's neighbours: Cameroon, Chad, and Niger. The sale of 12 Super Tucano A-29 aircraft and accompanying ammunition is noteworthy. The US also pledged support to enhance aerial surveillance of BHT areas of operation in the North-East and to provide information to the armed forces. This has been going on in a limited manner and not in real time. Counterterrorism assistance to Nigeria from Western countries, has however been constrained by allegations of human rights violations. This has compelled the armed forces to look inwards while diversifying their sources of equipment supply to deal with the insurgency. As they say, necessity is the mother of invention, and the Armed Forces are now engaged in serious research and development leading to local production. One of these is the manufacture of a mine resistant armed vehicle (MRAP) christened Ezugwu by the Defence Industries Corporation of Nigeria (DICON).

Humanitarian Issues

The humanitarian crisis in the North-East region is far from over, and the humanitarian-peace nexus needs to be interrogated. The situation is complex and monumental, with more than two million people displaced, tens of thousands killed in the last decade alone, and the destruction of basic economic and social infrastructure that will take a long time to rebuild. The insurgency has caused multi- dimensional crises in health, education, food security, shelter, water, hygiene and the totality of productive livelihoods. Quite clearly, the humanitarian situation in the North-East challenges the ability to stabilize the security situation and here in lies the value of interrogating the humanitarian-development-peace nexus. Can peace and security be achieved without effectively addressing humanitarian situation? Addressing the humanitarian issues requires vertical and horizontal partnerships built around accountable institutions and skilled, motivated and committed human capital. It requires institutional capacities founded on functional systems and reliable infrastructure. For instance, since mid-2015, under the supervision of the Borno State Government and NGOs, over 500,000 IDPs have been relocated from Maiduguri to Gubio, Damasak, Gamboru Ngala, Rann and other settlements in Borno State. Similar relocations of IDPs and other refugees have been conducted in Yobe and Adamawa States. This confirms a clear understanding of the importance of addressing the human terrain challenge as a means of enhancing security.

Security and other essential support are provided by the Nigerian Army to IDPs that were recently relocated to the affected areas. These include the deployment of military equipment to clear farms and the provision of security in farms, the rebuilding of houses to facilitate returns, and the restoration of economic activities with the involvement of the Borno State Government, UNICEF, and other INGOs. The Nigerian Army provided the enabling environment for over 126 international humanitarian NGOs to operate and also provided escorts for their activities in unstable and inaccessible areas. Troops also administer polio vaccines as part of routine patrols in areas considered inaccessible by government health agencies. While the Nigerian Army's humanitarian efforts are meant to win hearts and minds, they are more importantly a route to achieving sustainable peace and security. However, a flip side of the humanitarian-peace nexus is the conflict of interest of humanitarian actors, as they claim to operate on the basis of the principle of neutrality. It is imperative that all actors and stakeholders work in synergy to address the humanitarian crisis as prerequisite to stabilising the security situation.

Security-Development Nexus

The idea of an interlocking relationship between security and development has been codified through the concept of the security-development nexus. The two previously distinct policy areas are now increasingly overlapping in terms of the actors and agencies engaged and the policy prescriptions advocated. Thus, the framework of the 'security–development nexus' is a critical means of addressing the current situation in the North-East. The difficulties in the North-East are due to the inability to fully calibrate the interconnectedness and direct correlation of the two significant criteria for established peace: security and development. These two criteria create a catch-22 situation: there is no development without security and vice versa. So the nexus between security and development should help define strategies, policies and programming in the North-East. This means that at policy and operational levels, the linkages between security and development should be taken into account. Policies combining security and development would assist in winning the hearts and minds of local populations; their use would boost economic development and thus counter radicalism and terrorism; as such, societal development is a key driver to sustainable peace and security. There is growing evidence of linkages between the emergence of violent extremism and conditions of economic deprivation, bad governance and conflict. Issues such as governance, access to decision-making, levels of social exclusion, relative deprivation and marginalisation, as well as political opportunity, all play a role.

The link between socio-economic conditions and manifestations of violent extremism as seen in the North-East and other places demands close attention, particularly in the North-East as regards youth unemployment and governance issues at local levels and declining socio-economic indicators. Drivers and causes of radicalization in the North-East can be found on multiple levels and include a sense of grievance and discrimination in the lack of development, governance issues, the presence of an extreme ideology, and local support networks for extremism. Youth unemployment is high. Individual and group grievances such as poverty, unemployment, illiteracy, corruption, discrimination, and political or economic marginalization are used as mobilizing instruments, while the pull factors are the benefits of joining groups like BHT. These benefits include the sense of belonging and the group's ideology, which emphasizes that it is possible to change society through violent action instead of enduring the frustrations of a dysfunctional process. According to the RAND Counter-Insurgency Study Group "the quicker a government is in providing services to the population, the greater is the ability to undermine popular support for insurgents and the more likely the propensity to defeat insurgency". The Nigerian Army conducts quick impact projects and community-based services such as medical outreach in line with this but what is required is far beyond what the Nigerian Army can do. The Federal Government's reconstruction initiatives such as the Presidential Initiative for the North-East (PINE) and the North-East Development Commission, are highly commendable and have the potential to address some of the underlying issues. However, reconstruction efforts through PINE and other initiatives have to keep up with the security imperatives. While there is rebuilding of schools and houses and provision of agricultural items like fertilizer to encourage IDPs to return to their homes, development initiatives involving the entire economic and social system will bring about enduring stability in the region.

Rule of Law and Justice

Rule of law and justice issues are important in the conduct of CTCOIN operations. It is linked to the politics of international collaboration, civil society agitation and matters dealing with the freedom and rights of groups and individuals in affected communities. International actors such as Amnesty International have continuously accused the military of human rights abuses sometimes even without hearing the Nigerian Army side of the story. Some of the accusations against the troops are detention without trial, dragnet arrest, sexual and gender based violence etc. While the Nigerian Army cannot completely deny that a few infractions occurred and offenders were punished, there is no widespread abuse as claimed. The Nigerian Army has set up human rights desks at all levels and introduced rights education to the training of troops to inculcate the importance of observing Rules of Engagement (ROE). Troops operate under a code of conduct and ROE to ensure maximum restraint in dealing with members of the public, for which the Nigerian Army has received commendable feedback.

Furthermore, the Nigerian Army has been engaging in dialogue with some NGOs like the ICRC, Human Rights Watch, and some UN agencies to address and respond to concerns of human rights violations. Unsubstantiated allegations by NGO's and civil society actors, however, remain a major distraction in the performance of stability tasks in the North-East region. Increased collaboration between the Nigerian Army, NGOs, and civil society groups is required to enhance the rule of law and sustainable peace and development.

Terrorism and Security Geo-Politics in the Sahel Region

The Sahel stretches from the Atlantic Ocean eastwards through Northern Senegal, Southern Mauritania, Mali, Burkina Faso, Southern Niger, Northeast Nigeria, Northcentral Chad, and the Sudan. It is a 500km belt of land below the Sahara Desert that includes the Lake Chad Basin nations, namely Niger, Chad, Nigeria, and Cameroun. Other nations in the Sahel region include Burkina Faso, The Gambia, Guinea, Mali, Senegal, Sudan, and Mauritania. The spread of terrorism and violent extremism, transnational organized crime, and illicit cross-border trafficking in drugs, arms, and people, as well as a lack of good governance, put the Sahel in regional and global focus.

The Sahel and the entire West African region in particular are suffering from the debilitating impact of the threat of terrorism and violent extremism. While the threat posed by terrorist groups in the Lake Chad region is said to be abating, there are concerns about growing and persisting terrorist footprints in parts of Mali and Burkina Faso. Instability has also been a recurring theme in these regions, with their underlying dynamics growing increasingly complex. The coups d'état in Burkina Faso, Guinea, and Mali over the past two and a half years are key issues. Also, the withdrawal of Op BARKHANE on the one hand, the strengthening of anti-French collaboration in Algeria and Mali, and different perspectives on US and EU interventions present other contexts. The region's structural conflict drivers are weak governance and under-development remains an issue. These developments have implications for national security of Nigeria and other bordering countries.

The 2 main 'jihadist' coalitions operating across Sahelian countries are the Jama'a Nasrat ul-Islam wa al-Muslimin (JNIM), an Al-Qaeda affiliate based in Mali that also operates in Burkina Faso and Niger, and the Islamic State in the Greater Sahara (ISGS). Both groups are now essentially competing for the control of different areas, specifically the tri-border region between Burkina Faso, Mali, and Niger. Limited military capabilities in the area provided the opportunity for ISGS to significantly launch series of lethal attacks along the southern Malian borders in March 2022. Other terrorist groups within the Sahel include the Boko Haram terrorist group, which has over the years metamorphosed into 2 factions; the Jama'atu Ahlis Sunna Lidda'adati wal-Jihad (JAS) and the Islamic State of West Africa (ISWAP). Most of these groups capitalise on governance challenges and the presence of large swathes of ungoverned spaces within the Sahel to expand their areas of influence.

Governance issues within the Sahelian nations have been an underlining factor in the recent surge of terrorism across the region. The recent spate of coups in Mali, Burkina Faso, and Guinea underpin the situations. Similarly, diplomatic and political friction between the Sahelian countries, including the G5 Sahel (a regional, intergovernmental organisation between Sahelian countries), resulted in the withdrawal of Mali from the organization on 15 May 2022. This was due to the denial of Mali the opportunity to lead the rotating presidency by other members of the group namely Chad, Niger, Mauritania, and Burkina Faso. The counter-terrorism response from the G5 nations was thus undermined by the diplomatic and political faceoff between members states. Other regional bodies, such as the Multinational Joint Task Force (MNJTF), were also formed to enhance security and address governmental issues among the nations of the Lake Chad Basin.

Operation BARKHANE

Op BARKHANE, which was set up in August 2014 at the peak of the terrorist insurgency in Mali, had at its inception about 5,500 French troops deployed in Burkina Faso, Chad, Mali, and Niger. In the mist of relatively slow progress in the CTCOIN, in August 2022, the force was expelled by the military junta in Mali Compelling the French to relocate the headquarter to Chad. The operation was later terminated in November 2022. The end of Op BARKHANE led to more direct engagement with the national armies by French Forces. Thus, the French did not necessarily withdraw their entire force from the sub-region; French officers still occupy key military positions in MINUSMA. Similarly, Russia through WAGNER engagement with the military junta in Mali is growing.

G-5 SAHEL

The G5 – Sahel midwifed by the French and sponsored by the EU was established in 2013 with Mauritania, Chad, Niger, Burkina Faso, and Mali as members to counter terrorism threats in their parts of the Sahel. The Coalition suffered the same fate as Op BARKHANE in Mali leading to their relocation to Ndjamena Chad with Burkina Faso, Chad, Mauritania, and Niger as current members. Despite the relocation, internal politics and mutual distrust have undermined the groups' capabilities. Key issues include allegations of marginalization by some member states in group activities, particularly infrastructural development by the EU.

A meeting of the G5 Ministers of Defence was held on 11 January 2023, to deliberate on the future of the Coalition, the outcome of which will determine further strategic direction. Nevertheless, the G-5 SAHEL without Mali, which was the epicenter of the coalition, would be a hard decision to make by the member states with potential to affect future outcomes, particularly as regards counter terrorism and counter insurgency operations.

Underlying Threat Factors

Cross-border activities by various non-state actors along the nation's porous borders pose a major national threat. Nigeria shares about 4,047 km land borders with neighbouring countries: Benin Republic to the West (773km), Niger to the North (1,497 km), Chad to the North-East (87 km through the islets of the Lake Chad) and Cameroon to the East (1,690km) along with a maritime border of 853 km. These areas are porous and not adequately policed. Consequently, the activities of criminal networks engaged in smuggling, trafficking in humans and illicit drugs, and the proliferation of small arms and light weapons are pronounced across Nigeria's international borders. These activities have been exacerbated by the crises in Libya, Mali, Chad, the Central African Republic, and Sudan among others.

Additionally, the Boko Haram Terrorists (BHT) activities along the Niger-Chad-Cameroonian borders epitomize the threat posed by our unsecured borders. However, it is worth mentioning that the Federal Government of Nigeria is evolving best practices in border management to enhance territorial integrity. Some of the measures adopted are the launch of the Migration Information and Data Analysis System (MIDAS) by the Nigeria Immigration Service in conjunction with the International Organization for Migration (IOM) to enable the government to better understand mobility patterns through its statistical information. This is to ensure that people crossing Nigerian borders do not pose threats to national and international security. This is in addition to the launch of the 5-year NIS Border Management Strategy (2019-2023). This is to ensure transparency, reduce corruption, disrupt the activities of smugglers, and protect the wellbeing of citizens and the dignity of human rights by ensuring they are not manipulated by unscrupulous human traffickers, as well as disrupt the activities of smuggling. It is worth noting that the Nigerian Army is fully involved in Op SWIFT RESPONSE, in conjunction with the Nigeria Customs Service (NCS), which is aimed at checking the unwholesome activities of smugglers whose criminal activities have impacted negatively on the nation's economy in the face of dwindling resources. Successes have been recorded, but the challenge remains.

Second, is Transnational Organized Crimes such as financial flow and money-laundering, drug and human trafficking, and the proliferation of Small Arms and Light Weapons (SALWs) have a direct impact on Nigeria's national security. Illicit financial flows and other crimes remain a major concern as they are increasingly linked to terrorism. This is in spite of the determined efforts of relevant institutions saddled with the responsibility of protecting the economy and its financial institutions and systems from misuse or abuse.

The proliferation of SALWs is a global phenomenon arising from the spread of conflicts. It is estimated that over 70 per cent of the 8 to 10 million illegal weapons in West Africa are domiciled in Nigeria and in the hands of non-state actors and criminal groups. This is not unconnected with past and on-going conflicts in West and North African countries, such as Liberia, Sierra Leone, Cote d'Ivoire, Mali, and Libya. The proliferation of SALWs aids non-state actors such as the BHT and bandits, while undermining the monopoly of state-owned instruments of coercion. These illicit arms stoke up violent conflicts, armed banditry, kidnapping, cattle rustling, militancy, violent agitations by dissident groups such as the proscribed IPOB, and insurgency/terrorism experienced in Nigeria. The Nigerian Army has been conducting several operations and exercises to combat this trend in aid of civil authority. Some of the exercise include Exercise ATILOGWU UDO, GOLDEN DAWN, PYTHON DANCE, CROCODILE SMILE, and AYEM AKPATUMA; joint operation, Op HADARIN DAJI; and Operation THUNDER STRIKE.

Third is an environmental threat, which is a major driver of conflicts across the country and in the Sahel. The threats stem from population explosion, unplanned human settlements, periodic environmentally-induced human conflicts, as well as environmental disasters caused by natural and human factors. Climate change is key, with the associated global warming and environmental degradation having immense consequences on the livelihoods and well-being of the people. Desertification in the North as well as erosion and floods in the South threaten food security and other economic losses. Additionally, desert encroachment is partly responsible for the loss of grazing reserves and the obliteration of grazing routes, which is directly linked to pastoralists-farmers conflicts. For instance, Lake Chad has shrunk from about 25,000 square kilometers in 1964 to less than 2,000 square kilometers. This has forced pastoralists to drift southward in search of pastures and water for their cattle. The forced migration sometimes results in the destruction of farmlands along the cattle routes, eventually leading to clashes between pastoralists and farmers. A good example of the Nigerian Army's contribution towards mitigating environmental threats is the establishment of Disaster Response Units across the country to support the civil authority during periods of disasters arising from environmental challenges.

The last is terrorism and violent extremism as Nigeria has been grappling with terrorism and violent extremism in the past 10 years due to the Boko Haram insurgency. While BHT has been splintered into 2 factions with the emergence of the Islamic State West Africa Province (ISWAP) in 2015, the complexity of the threats still persists. This is in consonance with the rise of global terrorism as a strategic threat with a significant increase of its logistical, financial and operational capabilities. The overall objective of the insurgents is to create an Islamic caliphate in the North-East Region in order to control large swaths of territory, with Nigeria being the springboard of its West African caliphate. It is worth emphasizing that the activities of the terrorists have largely been degraded by the combined efforts of the Armed Forces of Nigeria and other security agencies as well as the MNJTF. However, there are still concerns that these terrorist groups remain a threat given their wide reach, their collaboration, and the alliances they formed with other extremist groups operating within the Sahel region. The potential use of disruptive and emerging technologies remains a key concern considering the growing advances in this field and the possible attack on the critical National Information Infrastructure (CNII). The threats emanating from the insurgents include, among others, mass displacement and migration, creation of a large number of Internally Displaced Persons (IDPs), undermining governance and the rule of law, national cohesion, and economic activities. Others include destruction of infrastructure and human rights violations. The defeat of ISIS in Syria has the potential to strengthen linkages between foreign-based terror cells and terror groups in the North-East. Realizing the nature of the threats, a whole-society approach in collaboration with our contiguous neighbours and international partners is the best bet.

Emerging and Enduring Initiatives

The Sahel and West African Region in particular is still host to some CTCOIN coalitions and groupings, despite some setbacks. These include the Element Francais Au Sahel, Accra Initiative, the MNJTF in Ndjamena, the Joint Planning Committee in Tamaraset, the French Forces in Senegal, and the Re-organized French Forces in the Sahel. These forces are discussed subsequently:

Elements Francaise Au SAHEL

The closure of Op BAKHANE by the French authorities, which was perceived as an end to French engagements with the Sahel countries, assumed a new dimension with the establishment of Element Francais Au Sahel. It is a new initiative by the French that aims to maintain elements of the French force in their respective locations in Burkina Faso, Chad, Mauritania, and Niger to continue engagement with national authorities on bilateral basis. This new strategy seeks to eliminate the negative attitude towards BARKHANE and remain relevant in the political and military space in the sub-region.

Accra Initiatve

The Accra Initiative is a coalition initiated by Ghana in 2017 which currently has Benin, Burkina Faso, Côte d'Ivoire, Ghana, Niger and Togo as members. It was set up to prevent the spillover of terrorism from the Sahel and address transnational organised crime by enhancing security cooperation. Nigeria, the UK, the UN, and the EU have also shown support for the coalition. In November 2022, Heads of States and Government of Accra Initiative countries committed to mobilizing resources to make the Multinational Joint Task Force of the Accra Initiative (MNJTF/AI) operational as soon as possible. In addition to its concerns about the expanding terrorism threat, Ghana is also at the forefront of renewed UN engagement on maritime security in the Gulf of Guinea because of the risk of links between terrorist and pirate groups.

Multinational Joint Task Force

The MNJTF, an effort of the Lake Chad Basin Commission (LCBC) nations, namely; Cameroon, Chad, Niger, and Nigeria, to pool resources to address threats of terrorism in the four countries, has made appreciable progress. This is considering that the MNJTF has troops deployed along the borders as sectors, and these components form the fulcrum of the CTCOIN in the Lake Chad Basin.

The MNJTF was mandated "to create a safe and secure environment in areas affected by Boko Haram activities, restore state authority, and facilitate humanitarian assistance within the Lake Chad Basin (Nwolise 2017). The forces strength pledge by TCC on 30 July 2015 is as follows:

Fig 39. Summary of Forces Pledged to the Multinational Joint Task Force by the Troops Contributing Countries.

Serial	Country/Sectors	Headquarters Location	Pledge Strength	Remarks
(a)	(b)	(c)	(d)	(e)
1.	Benin-MNJTF Garrison	N'Djamena	150	Co-located with Headquarters MNJTF
2.	Cameroon-Sector 1	Mora	2,250	
3.	Chad-Sector 2	Baga Sola	3,000	
4.	Nigeria-Sector 3	Monguno	3,250	Initially at Baga
5.	Niger-Sector	Diffa	2,000	
	Total		10,650	

The security situation in the LCB is a combination of terrorism and criminal activities, which together undermine the liberties and livelihood of the people of the Lake Chad region. The Year 2020 Global Terrorism Index Report ranks 4 of the Lake Chad Basin countries (Chad, Cameroon, Niger, and Nigeria) are among the 10 least secure countries in sub-Saharan Africa. This is due to the security threats in the region, which manifest in the form of direct attacks on civilian communities by terrorists, abductions, sexual exploitation, and enslavement within the Lake Chad region.

Currently, there are 3 active groups within the Lake Chad Basin that broke out of or are affiliated with Boko Haram. These include the Islamic State in West Africa Province (ISWAP), Jama'atu Ahlis Sunnah (JAS), popularly known as the Shekau faction, and the Bakura faction. Although the manifestation of their activities is distinct to some extent, there are areas where they share similar modes of operation (Yusuf 2023). The resilience demonstrated by the various groups despite the counterinsurgency efforts in the Lake Chad Basin could be attributed to their ability to exploit ungoverned spaces both within the basin and across the Sahel. The groups continue to use the old smuggling and trading routes across the Sahel to import arms and mercenaries to sustain their activities. The terrorists also use these ungoverned spaces to obtain financial support from their international collaborators, particularly the Islamic State (IS), which is ISWAP's major benefactor.

Despite the success recorded by MNJTF, it has faced challenges. The absence of a robust security framework at the Secretariat of the

Commission has created a serious vacuum in the decision-making process at the strategic level of the Force. This vacuum is occasionally filled by the decisions of the Meeting of Ministers of Defence or the Summit of Heads of State of Troops Contributing Countries. Funding of the MNJTF is another contending issue that needs further interrogation. The gap in the funding of the force mainly emanates from the complexities in its support and management structures. The ambiguous command and control structure and the apparent unwillingness of the troops-contributing Countries to fully cede command to the Force is another issue (Africa Report No. 291, 2020). Thus, the Force Commander exercises only limited operational control of the Force, as the troops are only available to the Force for specific MNJTF operations and thereafter revert to their respective national operations.

At the operational level, differences in Tactics, Techniques, and Procedures (TTPs) amongst the countries pose another significant challenge to the Force (Yusuf 2023).

During the conduct of major operations such as Operations AMNI FAKAT and YANCIN TAFKI, these differences amongst the countries manifested from the planning phase up to the execution of the operations. For instance, whereas the tactical procedures of the Nigerian military are basically similar to those of the UK military, those of Cameroon and Niger are similar to those of the French military with slight adaptations. Perhaps the most difficult operational challenge confronting the Force is the lack of appropriate C-IED equipment. IEDs have remained the single greatest threat on the main supply routes within the theatre and have accounted for about 60 per cent of military casualties and 70 per cent of civilian casualties from January 2019 to October 2020 (MNJTF Report to EU, 2020). The dearth of amphibious platforms is also a challenge and undermines the ability of troops to enter the Lake Chad Islands, where BHT and ISWA have established major strongholds (Yusuf 2023). Prominent amongst these islands are Tumbun Fulani, Tumbun Rago, Madayi, Doro Lelewa, Tchoukoutalia and several other enclaves around the Darak Islands.

Despite the challenging and contending issues, the MNJTF had successfully conducted a major operation which helped stabilize the security situation. These include Op GAMAAIKI, conducted from June to October 2016 to liberate the areas captured by BHT along the River Komadougou-Yobe, as well as the areas stretching from Damasak to Bosso via Malam Fatori up to the Lake Chad Islands. Op RAWAN KADA, which was executed from January to June 2017, was geared towards consolidating the gains of Op GAMA AIKI. Op AMNI FAKAT was a ground and air campaign conducted from March to July 2018 to clear areas held by terrorists up to the Lake Islands. Following the success of these operations, Op YANCIN TAKFI was launched in January 2019. Unlike the previous MNJTF operations, which were time-based, YANCIN TAKFI was designed to continue until the terrorists were flushed out, with provisions for routine review to ensure it remained effective. The successes recorded so far by the MNJTF imply that it has the potential to significantly contribute to sustainable peace and development in the LBC.

There are other national operations such as Emergence IV in Cameroon, JTF OP HADIN KAI in Nigeria, and elements of the G5 Sahel in Chad that are also deployed near the Lake Chad Basin. The HQ MNJTF interacts with the national operations through the sectors. This is through periodic offensive operations, in members' states based on the threat situation. However, the effectiveness of the MNJTF has been undermined over priority setting, reluctance by member states to cede command to the force itself, and funding and procurement delays. A successful response to militancy in Lake Chad will depend not only on the joint force but also on whether states can improve conditions and inspire more trust among residents of affected areas. Despite the challenges, Op LAKE SANITY was a testament to the level of cooperation among the MNJTF nations despite challenges of fundings, platforms, and manpower.

External Support and Relations among Actors

Relations between the Sahel countries and other external factors, including France, the EU, the US, and Russia have been a source of concern. The engagement of Russia's Wagner group by Mali is an issue, while Algeria, which has been a major stakeholder in the peace process in Mali abhors French interventions in the country. It has expressed concerns that they money paid to Wagner for the security of the solid mineral areas could better be used for empowerment in agriculture to provide jobs for the youths involved in the conflict.

In December 2022, Ghana criticised Burkina Faso for allocating a gold mine to the Wagner Group as a form of payment. Also, German forces, which have been involved in both the EU training mission and MINUSMA in Mali, decided that they would pull out due to Mali's ties with the Wagner Group, starting in the Second Quarter of 2023. Similarly, Cote d'Ivoire and the UK announced in November 2022 that they would withdraw from MINUSMA amidst repeated interference by Malian authorities.

The EU is a major funding partner for the MNJTF and G5–Sahel and has also indicated interest in contributing to the Accra Initiative. The involvement of the EU in the funding of these CTCOIN coalitions is such that any temporary cuts in funding could have a significant impact on the functioning of the coalition. For instance, the EU provides monthly POL for MNJTF sectors, training support, and the maintenance of the MNJTF HQ and its staff. In 2022, the funds for this support were not released to the MNJTF until September due to challenges emanating from the Russia–Ukraine Crisis. The MNJTF resorted to borrowing until the EU fund was eventually released. The EU intervention also includes assistance in the provision of communication and intelligence support like radios, night vision equipment, drones, and an ISR platform to the MNJTF. However, EU assistance to the G-5 Sahel has been dwindling in the past few years, which has left much more to state funding of the operation. This situation raises question as to the EU's capacity to sustain the MNJTF funding for any reasonable period of time.

The situation in the Sahel created new opportunities for international competitors to increase their influence within the Sahel. External partners, including Turkish and Russian actors, are active in the Sahel, providing varied forms of assistance, including military and border security support. This includes the presence within the region of military contractors such as the Wagner Company and the influence it has on the relationship between Mali and European actors, including the French. This, some scholars and practitioners believe, signals a general reshaping of political control and international equilibria within the G-5 region. This may lead Sahel nations to re-negotiate their military and political cooperation with external partners.

The slow progress in tackling the terrorist threats has raised questions regarding the full commitment and motives of some of the external partners towards the defeat of terrorism in the Sahel region of West Africa in general. The promotion of humanitarianism and geo-political considerations remain possible motives apart from the defeat of terrorism and insurgency.

Implications for Nigeria

Nigeria remains a strategic stakeholder in the fight against terrorism in Africa due to geo-political considerations and the impact of domestic terrorism and their affiliation with a global terror group, the Islamic State of Syria (ISIS), on Nigeria. The historic links between Mali-based Al-Qaeda groups and Boko Haram, as well as the southward drift of terrorist groups like the Islamic State in the Greater Sahel and the Jama'at Nasr-al Islam wal Muslimin into Burkina Faso are another emerging threat to Nigeria. Amid the manifestations of these terrorist groups in the region, the political situation in Mali, Burkina Faso, and Chad has hampered the consolidation of effects against the terrorist threats. It is in this light that the dynamics within the CTCOIN coalitions remain a critical factor in the region if much progress is to be made in tackling the terrorism threat. As it stands, the MNJTF remains the most effective coalition in the sub-region despite funding challenges.

While the MNJTF has made enormous progress, the effectiveness of the force has been hampered by a lack of resources to sustain operations for long periods. Thus, given the waning financial status of the EU, an alternative source of funding for the CTCOIN coalition would need to be established. This is considering that the MNJTF is the backbone of the LCBC countries, regional strategic CTCOIN effort and would need to be strengthened for an enduring CTCOIN effort in the sub-region.

The situation in the Sahel has socio-economic, humanitarian, security, and environmental implications for Nigeria. The Sahel produces huge challenges as the effects of terrorist groups have led to a major disruption of the socio-economic livelihood of the people of the North-East and the Lake Chad region. These include the destruction of educational institutions, health facilities, and the prevention of farming, fishing, and business ventures. This has negatively affected the national security of Nigeria and other countries, as well as the wellbeing of the citizenry. The threats in the Sahel region have also affected the humanitarian situation in Nigeria especially in the North-East region. According to the UNHCR, the activities of BHT have resulted in the displacement of over 2.5 million people including over 300,000 refugees, while over 10 million people remain at risk of food insecurity. Threats within the Sahel also impact Nigeria's national security due to porous borders and the proliferation of small arms and light weapons. The instability within the Sahel has also resulted in the movement of illegal migrants into the country, leading to an increase in banditry, and outright attacks on vulnerable communities. Environmental issues of climate change within the Sahel, especially along the Lake Chad Region, are also of note. Issues of desertification and the recent over flooding of River Kamodugu – Yobe led to the destruction of farmlands, livestock, and means of livelihood within communities in Yobe, Borno, and Jigawa States.

Sustainable Solutions

Whole of Society Approach

Security and humanitarian challenges underpin the quest to fully defeat BHTs and ISWAP in the North-East. The multiple links between terrorism and development imperatives in the North-East demand it. The Organization for Economic Co- operation and Development (OECD) acknowledges that development does have an important role to play in helping to deprive terrorists of popular support and addressing the conditions that terrorist leaders feed on and exploit. Development and security operations must go hand in hand and this is best achieved through a whole of government and whole-of-society approach.

The military, MDAs, the media, civil society, religious leaders, and academia all have crucial roles to play. Additionally, Nigerians must continue to take ownership of the counter terrorism operations by providing public support to motivate the soldiers and demonstrate legitimacy. Government presence through development activities in the liberated areas to win hearts and minds, shore up public support, and degrade the terrorist support bases would need to be maintained and enhanced. Sustained progress has been made in the North-East but more is still required to completely defeat the threat. A whole-of-government approach would ensure that the intertwined objectives of development, good governance, and security are achieved. Linked to the whole of government approach is also the need for a whole of society approach through the mobilization of the entire society in support of government efforts toward defeating terrorism and insurgency in Nigeria.

An Inclusive Governance Process and Socio Economic Development

Addressing the conditions conducive to the spread of terrorism in the North-East are crucial to defeating and eliminating the emergence and spread of violent extremism and insurgency. The most important facet of CTCOIN operations in the North- East should be the provision of socio-economic alternatives to the groups at risk of violence (the youth) and the delivery of governance, which is at the core of the security-development nexus. The establishment of the NEDC gives ample opportunity to integrate the economies of the North-East region through a transportation network, communication facilities, and agricultural value chains that will kick start economic growth and development. This will require increased coordination of the activities of all North-East specific initiatives: PCNI, the Victim Support Fund, NEDC, and all the activities of the state governments in the region.

Investing in human capital and the empowerment of youth, women, and girls is also necessary, as development is not all about economic growth but reorientation of social systems. Thus, issues of inclusion and access to decision-making are important. The education system will need to be redesigned to increase accessibility to basic and higher education, likewise, improvement of healthcare delivery as a way of improving human capital that will drive development in the future while denying BHT radicalization and recruitment grounds now. Ultimately, socio- economic development should address the root causes of the insurgency, such as lack of rural development and poverty.

The importance of building and strengthening democratic institutions even in the face of insurgency cannot be overstated. The development of democratic structures and institutions, which supports free and fair elections, aids in the defeat of terrorism and insurgency by bolstering governance. Conventional wisdom seems to hold that authoritarian regimes could be better equipped to fight insurgencies due to unity of command, but in the long term, democratic systems are more effective in managing the tensions generated by internal conflict and also bringing disparate groups on board. State authorities should ensure that local government institutions thrive in situ rather that relocating to, and operating from state capitals, as currently happens. Efforts would need to be intensified to strengthen government presence and structures in local governments areas in the North-East.

Credible Border and Military Presence

The Nigerian Army and the AFN would need to continue to maintain a credible military presence in the North-East while border agencies enhance security at the international borders. This will deny BHT freedom of action and facilitate good governance. A credible military presence will also ensure open and free economic activities on Lake Chad. The Lake Chad remains vital for fishing, farming, transportation of goods, and other economic activities as it grants access to the wider Sahel and Central Africa Sub-region, which are vital for economic growth.

A credible military presence will counter smuggling and the proliferation of SALW, a causal factor in the insurgency and enabler for BHT/ISWAP, and other criminal elements. BHT's lifeline remains the porous border connecting Nigeria with Cameroon, Chad, and the Niger Republics, which it exploits to smuggle weapons, other logistics, and for sanctuary. Extensive border security will reduce the proliferation of SALW and illegal entry and exit. This will be based on the deployment of technology for effective ISR and surveillance drones to cover large swathes of land that cannot be covered by security agencies. LCBC and Sahel countries would need to enhance the capacities of border management agencies and possibly identify border communities as key stakeholders in border management while also dominating the under/ungoverned spaces in their territories. This will also include the re-appraisal of extant sub-regional and regional border protocols to strengthen their provisions and ensure their effective implementation. The ability to maintain a credible military presence will depend on a continuous military capability upgrade, capacity building for troops, boots on the ground and improvements in troops' welfare. These areas are priorities and will continue to receive attention. A program that will allow the Nigerian Army to effectively project force through improved fire and maneuver with the introduction of Nigerian Army Aviation

Sustainbable International Collaborations

The CTCOIN operations in the North-East require international collaboration, humanitarian support, environmental preservation, security cooperation and economic development. The re-intensification of engagement with regional and strategic partners to mobilize resources to address these issues and defeat terrorism is critical. Acknowledging that security and development are linked in addressing terrorism is an important first step in designing effective strategies for regional and international collaboration in the North-East. Linking international collaboration thematically and operationally is critical in addressing the agenda for peace, sustainable development and security measures. Security collaboration with neighbouring countries through platforms such as the MNJTF remains important for border security to address the influx of weapons, the movement of preachers with extremist ideologies, and other criminal groups.

Neighbouring countries play significant roles in internal conflicts. An insurgency is unlikely to be defeated if it retains external financial or manpower resources. For instance, in Sri Lanka, the government maintained constant diplomatic and political contacts with the Indian government, providing assurances that India's strategic interest in Sri Lanka would be protected and that the grievances of the ordinary Tamils would be addressed. This outreach increased regional support, leading to victory. The MNJTF involving Nigeria, Niger, Chad, Cameroon, and Benin remains a critical part of the framework to defeat BHT and ISWAP. It is in the self-interest of Nigeria's neighbours to key into Nigeria's efforts to effectively defeat BHT and ISWAP to restore sustainable peace and development.

Similarly, the security situation in the Sahel thus demands the need for a more sustainable strategy of building consensus among the countries in the region. International bodies and nations including the EU, AU, ECOWAS and the USA would need to holistically support both national and regional efforts aimed at tackling the security threats and challenges bedevilling the region. Identifying and addressing the drivers of instability within the Sahel region remains paramount for socioeconomic sustainability of its people. Issues of poor governance, unsecured borders, and climate change among others must be effectively tackled in collaboration with international organizations to addressing the threat factors within the region.

The capacity of the MNJTF could be further enhanced through deeper cooperation with the LCBC nations and its foreign partners. Areas such as funding, provision of military platforms and manpower by the TCC would largely enhance the combat capacity and effectiveness of the MNJTF. According to General Agwai, despite Nigeria's internationally acclaimed contributions to global peace, it still has problems accessing its military needs and requirements and getting the needed international support to speedily defeat terrorism and insurgency. International support remains critical in defeating terrorism in Nigeria and the greater Sahel Region. The sub-region will need to evolve policies that can address the root of terrorism and insurgency through establishing principles to enhance synergies within LCBC and Sahel countries. Nigeria's foreign policy as always, will need to continue to prioritize regional security and development.

Developing Credible Narratives and De-Radicalization Measures

The development of counter narratives will assist in shaping perceptions and deconstruction of misinformation in support of CTCOIN operations in the North- East. Existing counter narratives would need to be improved upon by mapping the theatre landscape and the message carried to the local populace including BHTs/ ISWAP elements. This is to discourage the population from supporting the terrorists. Defeating the ideologies and re-conceptualizing the philosophy upon which BHT is built remains critical. The Nigerian Army FM radio station in Borno State and various psyops operations are being used and have contributed to the huge success recorded in degrading BHT/ISWAP.

Similarly, more efforts are required in counter-radicalization and de-radicalization measures. While Op SAFE CORRIDOR, with its main focus of encouraging all repentant BHTs to surrender and undergo the de-radicalization process, has achieved some level of success, more work needs to be done. Communities will also need to be prepared to receive returnees associated with Boko Haram.

Section Five

The Nigerian Army of the Future

Lt Gen F Yahaya
Chief of Army Staff

Lt Gen F Yahaya, Chief of Army Staff and the PSOs at the commissioning ceremony of the Nigerian Army Heritage and Future Centre, Giri, Abuja.

Vision and Strategic Posturing

Three days after the appointment of Lt Gen F Yahaya as the 22nd Chief of Army Staff (COAS) on 27 May 2021, he unveiled his vision for the Nigerian Army. This was promptly followed by a mission statement. According to Brigadier General Mohammed Yerima, the Director Army Public Relations at the time, in the Punch Newspaper of 30 March 2021, the COAS made these solemn statements of commitment, strategic foresight, and insight when he addressed the senior leadership of the Nigerian Army, which included Principal Staff Officers and Field Commanders at Army Headquarters.

The exercise of *visioning and missioning* by and for the Nigerian Army is in keeping with international best practices in the leadership of corporate bodies in various fields of human endeavour, including the armed forces. Etymologically, both the words vision and mission have roots in religion. In HadeethEnc (2022), Abu Qatadah reported Prophet Muhammed (PBUH) as saying: *A good vision is from Allah, and a bad dream is from Satan*. Indeed, on the SerachTruth.com platform (2022), the word "vision" is reported to be used 53 times in 47 verses in the English translation of the Quran by Abdullah Yusuf Ali. Furthermore, mission possesses a missionary character or the compulsion to spread the truth and beneficence of Islam. Similarly, in Christianity, vision depicts a sacred encounter that results in a view of the future or specific advice on how to approach a situation. This explains the profuse use of the word *vision* in 73 verses in 23 books of the Holy Bible. Just like in Islam, the concept of mission is rooted in Biblical truths and signifies *purposeful movement or being sent from one place to another for a purpose*.

From its divine origin, visioning found strong footing in the military. No wonder the great Generals of antiquity had surreal visions. For instance, Scipio Africanus (c 250BC), one of the greatest soldiers of the ancient world, had a vision to *contemplate the heavens in order to act rightly on earth*. This awesome vision inspired the creation of a new army that defeated Hannibal in the Second Punic War and asserted Rome's supremacy in Spain, Africa, and the Hellenistic East. Secondly, according to the update by Bawden in the Britannica (2022), Genghis Khan, the Great Mongolian warrior-ruler (1162-1227), had a provocative and overtly bellicose vision *to turn the cultivated fields of northern China into grazing lands for his horses.* This tradition of far-sighted military aspirations and visioning is manifest to this day in warfighting and Generalship.

From martial applications, the art of visioning has however spread to other human endeavours such as politics, business and education. In politics, Gaius Octavius Thurinus better known as Augustus, one of the greatest Roman Emperors of all time, had a political vision *"that the sun is going to shine on all regions of the Roman Empire, bringing peace and prosperity to all regions"*. In more contemporary times, and in the heat of the cold war in the 1960s, the United States of America (USA) had a vision to "promote leadership and demonstrate the technological advances of a free and democratic society". This vision drove the USA to the first moon landing by Neil Armstrong and Edwin 'Buzz' Aldrin on 20 July 1969. Closely associated with vision statements are mission statements. Different mission statements abound across the world and in different eras of human existence. These mission statements range from the arcane to the pragmatic: for TED, a nonpartisan and non-profit organisation in the USA, the mission is simply "to spread ideas"; for Nike, an American based multinational sportswear company, it is to "bring inspiration and innovation to every athlete in the world"; and for Sweetgreen, an American fast-food restaurant chain, the mission is "to inspire healthier communities by connecting people to real food".

From the foregoing, a vision statement is a short but punchy description of a nation's or an organisation's corporate aspirations and the wider impact it aims to create in the future. It identifies where the nation or organisation intends to be in the future or where it should be to best meet the needs of its stakeholders. Vision depicts a shared understanding of the nature and purpose of the organisation and uses this understanding to move the organisation to greater heights. It is akin to determining the destiny of an organisation but not as an idyllic wish but as a destination to work for. According to Yahaya (2022), "a vision provides a road map for attaining the desired objectives of an organisation". Typically, a vision statement defines the dream and long-term goals, while a mission statement describes what the organisation does, who it serves, and what makes it unique in terms of its existence and justification. The latter typically answers the questions, "what is an organisation going to do" and "how will it do it"?

Vision and mission statements underline the commitments of an organization and are often undergirded by a statement of core values, which highlight fundamental principles and philosophical ideals. The latter are used to inform and guide the decisions and behavior of the employees and signal to external stakeholders what's important to the organization. Core values shape corporate culture and establish standards of conduct against which actions and decisions can be assessed. A values statement is often memorable, actionable, and timeless, but the actual format for codifying them is varied. The values statement could simply be a list of core values, a phrasing of values into short inspiring statements, or a brief explanation of the values. The incontrovertible truth about vision, mission, and values statements is that they convey the purpose, direction, and underlying principles of the organization, respectively. When developed in a thoughtful and deliberate manner, these statements can serve as powerful tools that provide the organization with meaningful guidance, especially during times of rapid change. Consequently, taking the time to craft relevant mission, vision and value statements is imperative and should be done with utmost care.

Vision, mission, and values collectively serve as the foundation for the development of an organization's Strategic Plan, which will, among other things, show the ways and means of achieving the ends of the organization's vision statement. In practice, the process of creating corporate vision, mission and value statements requires certain structured steps, as postulated by Lotich (2019). These structured steps are shown in hierarchical order in Figure 40 below:

Figure 40: Corporate Steps to Developing Vision

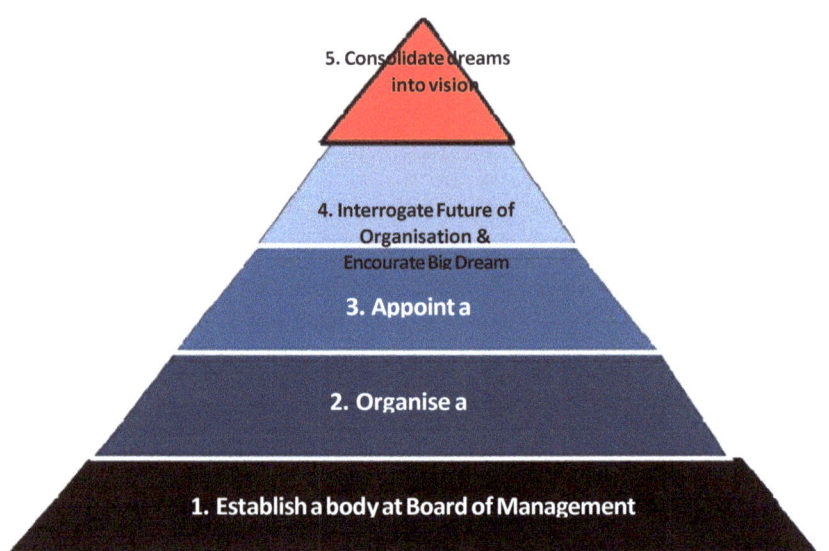

Figure 2: Value Chain of Activities to Assess a Vision Statement as postulated by Lotich (2019)

The first step is to establish a body at the board or top management level with the purpose of fashioning a vision. In the alternative, there could be an assemblage of an advisory team made up of internal experts and perhaps external consultants. The second is that these bodies may meet in a retreat or a small conference set up specifically for that purpose to brainstorm on the vision or mission. Thirdly, team facilitator, who would drive the visioning sessions without unduly influencing their outcomes may be appointed. Next, the team is to be encouraged to dream BIG on critical questions relating to the organisation, such as its overall long-term goals and the environmental threats and opportunities. Finally, ideas on a preliminary vision from the brainstorming sessions are shared, interrogated, and harmonised to form a vision statement. This process may be repeated for mission statements.

Values, vision, and mission statements are closely related and are thus easy to conflate, but there are some subtle differences. Also related are the derived corporate objectives. The similarities and dissimilarities between the terms in terms of the attributes of time, purpose, and audience are shown in Fig 41 below.

Fig 41: Differences and Similarities of Values, Vision, Mission, and Objectives

Serial	Attributes	Strategic Statements			
		Values	Vision	Mission	Objectives
(a)	(b)	(c)	(d)	(e)	(f)
1.	Time	Often set at inception and timeless	Longsighted, outlook. Change at major points of inflexion.	More frequent based on contemporary Situation	Most frequent depending on current challenges
2.	Purpose	Guidance, cohesion, and commitment.	Gives the "why" for futuristic goals	Gives the "what" and "how" to get to visionary goals	Specific targets in furtherance of the vision and mission
3.	Audience	Internal and external	Employees and other stakeholders	Public, customers, and employee policies	Employees and internal organs

The most significant difference between these statements is the timeframe. Values are often determined at inception and are timeless. A vision is longsighted, focusing on the distant future, while a mission is more frequent and outlines things the organization is doing to reach the defined visionary goals. Objectives are most frequent and respond to current challenges. In terms of purpose, values provide internal guidance, team cohesion, and commitment, as well as external trust. A vision focuses on "why" the organization has chosen its futuristic goals, while mission describes more of the "what" and "how" to get to there. Objectives give Specific, Measurable, Achievable, Relevant and Timebound (SMART) targets in furtherance of the vision. Thirdly, values are for internal and external audiences, while vision is typically more focused on employees and other stakeholders to help drive the organization's work for the future. The mission is "public facing", primarily geared towards consumers, although it can also be designed to drive company policies for employees and offer a sense of cohesiveness for decision making; and lastly, strategic objectives are for internal organs and employees.

After the vision and mission statements have been made and adopted for a considerable time, it makes good sense and is best practice to assess their impact. This can be done systematically, as shown in the figure below:

Figure 42: Value Chain of Activities to Assess a Vision Statement

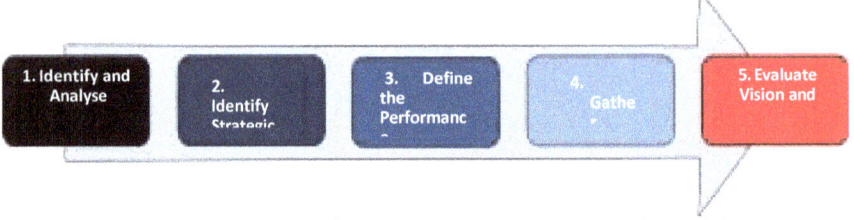

Firstly, identify key words and/or phrases in the vision and/or mission statements and interrogate these words and/or phrases to get a deeper understanding of their meanings. This may require some form of engagement with the author(s) or custodian(s). Secondly, identify the strategic objectives derived from the vision and/or mission statements; thirdly, define Performance Measurement Indicators (PMIs) that show progress towards the vision and/or mission statement. These must be SMART; fourthly, gather data on the PMIs; Lastly, consolidate the data generated and evaluate the progress of the vision and/or mission statement, as well as their general impact.

The art of vision-making, and strategic prepositioning has become best practices in Nigeria's corporate culture. For instance, Mainstream Energy Solutions Limited has a vision *"to be the recognised performance leader of the electric power industry in Nigeria and beyond"*. Its mission is *"to generate and deliver electricity in a safe, reliable, efficient, and most environmentally friendly manner"* These statements are undergirded by the core values of: teamwork, responsibility, innovation, integrity, and passion. Secondly, MTN Nigeria, a foremost communications services provider in Nigeria has a vision *"to lead the delivery of a bold new digital world to our customers"*. Its mission is *"to make our customers' lives a lot brighter"*. As a global brand, MTN subsists on its core values of leadership, integrity, relationships, innovation, and a can-do attitude. It prides itself on its ability to make the seemingly impossible possible, connecting people with friends, family, and opportunities and enriching lives through its products and services.

The vision of Julius Berger is "to be Nigeria's most dynamic construction company", and its mission statements are "to seize the opportunity for both the company and the nation, to work with dedication, to maintain the trust of clients and to operate with a holistic approach and a solutions-driven mindset". Its core values are: integrity; innovation; partnerships; and reliability. Julius Berger has lived up to its vision, as it is now unarguably the foremost construction company in Nigeria. The vision of SSL Cloud HRMS, an information technology company in Nigeria, wants to become the choice provider of IT solutions that help organisations and businesses manage and improve their productivity within Nigeria, Africa and the world". Its mission is "to help customers discover excellence as we deliver on the promise of our vision and our promises to our customers". Its core values are: integrity, teamwork, client-drivenness; as well as creativity and innovation. Lastly, Konga, an online trading company, has the multiple vision "to be a powerful force for the economic growth of Africa, to connect Africans with each other and the rest of the world through technology and commerce, and to be a company that employees, customers, and the society are proud of and depend on". Its mission is "to be the engine of commerce and trade in Africa" and its core values are: customers; hard work; honour and integrity; teamwork and sacrifice; passion as well as constant evolution".

From this small cross-section of companies in the energy, communications, construction, computing, and online trading industries in Nigeria, it is clear that vision, mission, and value statements are: inspiring, relevant, focused on the fundamentals of the companies, and quite significantly, enduring. Indeed, these statements do not change very often. However, the same cannot be said of vision and mission statements in the various arms of the Armed Forces of Nigeria (AFN), largely due to the high turnover of Service Chiefs who are the Commanders and Chief Executive Officers of the Services. Consequently, since 2010, the Nigerian Air Force, the Nigerian Navy, and the Nigerian Army have published several vision and mission statements.

Starting with the Nigerian Air Force (NAF), which is the youngest of the 3 Services, Air Marshal Alex Sabundu Badeh, the 18th Chief of the Air Staff (CAS) from 4 October 2012 to 16 January 2014, had a vision to *"transform the NAF into a self-reliant and highly professional fighting force through the application of innovative technology in fulfilment of national defence and security objectives"*. He was succeeded by Air Marshal Adesola Nunayon Amosu, the 19th CAS, who served from 16 January 2014, to 13 July 2015 during the peak of the Boko Haram insurgency. He had a vision *"to consolidate the transformation of the NAF by employing innovative approaches with a focus on joint capabilities and consideration for credible international partnership"*. Next was Air Marshal Sadiq Baba Abubakar, the 20th CAS from 13 July 2015, to 26 January 2021, who had a vision *"to reposition the NAF into a highly professional and disciplined force through capacity building initiatives for effective, efficient, and timely employment of airpower in response to Nigeria's national security imperatives"*. This was backed by a mission to *"ensure the integrity of the airspace by gaining and maintaining control of the air while retaining a credible capacity to fulfil other airpower tasks demanded by national defence and security imperatives"*. Finally, Air Marshal Isiaka Oladayo Amao, the 21st CAS was appointed on 26 January 2021, and has a vision *"to enhance and sustain critical airpower capabilities required for joint force employment in pursuit of national security imperatives"*.

In the Nigerian Navy (NN), Vice Admiral Ola Saad Ibrahim the 19th Chief of the Naval Staff (CNS) from 8 September 2010, to 4 October 2012, had a vision *"to emplace a Navy that is adequately motivated and capable of effectively combatting the security challenges in Nigeria's maritime domain and in the West African subregion to enhance the wellbeing of the Nigerian people"*. This was backed by a mission that *"the NN shall discharge its constitutional roles and assign tasks in a professional and responsible manner, consistent with global best practices for the defence and protection of Nigeria's territorial integrity"*. He was succeeded by Vice Admiral Dele Joseph Ezeoba, the 20th CNS, from 4 October 2012, to 16 January 2014. Admiral Ezeoba initiated the CNS Strategic Guidance series, which encapsulated a vision *"to emplace a robust and combat-ready Navy that is capable of effectively combatting the security challenges in Nigeria's maritime domain, including the Gulf of Guinea, for Nigeria's economic prosperity and national development"*. He backed this with a mission *"to discharge its constitutional roles and assigned tasks in a professional and efficient manner, consistent with global best practices for the defence and protection of Nigeria's territorial integrity"*.

Next was Vice Admiral Usman Oyibe Jibrin, the 21st CNS who served between 16 January 2014 and 13 July 2015. He had a vision *"to emplace a well-trained, equipped, maintained, organised, and highly motivated naval force capable of being employed singly and with other arms of service in the defence of*

Nigeria's maritime environment, other troubled spots, and the Gulf of Guinea for sustained economic prosperity". This was followed with a mission statement: *"to consistently and professionally deploy a well-trained, organised and highly motivated naval force capable of effectively and efficiently discharging constitutional roles and assigned tasks for the defence and economic prosperity of the Federal Republic of Nigeria"*. Vice Admiral Ibok-Ete Ekwe Ibas, the 22nd CNS, served from 13 July 2015, to 26 January 2021. He had a vision *"to develop a credible naval power in fulfilment of the NN's constitutional roles towards enhancing national prosperity and security"* and a mission *"to deploy a naval force that is well trained, organised, and highly motivated to discharge its constitutional roles professionally and efficiently for the defence of Nigeria in ensuring her economic prosperity"*. Finally, Vice Admiral Awwal Zubairu Gambo, the 23rd CNS, who was appointed on 26 January 2021, has a vision *"to leverage on all factors of national location, technology, training, teamwork, and synergy to re-energise the NN and enhance her as a motivated and ready naval force in the discharge of its constitutional mandate and other assigned tasks in fulfilment of national security objectives."* The accompanying mission is *"to optimise the deployment of the NN in the performance of her constitutional roles and the undertaking of assigned tasks while promptly responding with commensurate actions to the emerging national security challenges"*.

Comparatively, the Nigerian Army had fewer interventions. Lt Gen Onyeabor Azubuike Ihejirika, the 18th COAS between September 2010 and January 2014, had a vision *"to transform the Nigerian Army into a force better able to meet contemporary challenges"*. He was succeeded by Lt Gen Kenneth Tobia Minimah, the 19th COAS between 2014 and 2015, who had a vision *"to optimize the capacity of the Nigerian Army to deal with the national and global security challenges"*. Next was Lt Gen Tukur Yusuf Buratai, the 20th COAS between 2015 and 2021. He had a vision *"to have a professionally responsive Nigerian Army in the discharge of its constitutional roles"*. The late Lt Gen Ibrahim Attahiru was the 21st COAS between 25 January and 21 May 2021, He had a vision *"to have a Nigerian Army that is repositioned to professionally defeat adversaries in a joint environment"*.

A significant feature of the Armed Forces of Nigeria is that more often than not, the formulation of the vision and associated mission statements does not follow the structured steps suggested by Lotich (2019). Rather, they capture the profound experiences, objective view, and service-oriented perspectives of the Service Chiefs on the aspirations and opportunities as well as the threats and challenges of national security provision. This was the case with General Faruk Yahaya, the 22nd Chief of Army Staff. According to Musa (2023), the Theatre Commander Operation HADIN KAI, the COAS vision "draws from his profound experience and deep understanding of the contemporary challenges of the Nigerian Army and the need for fundamental re-engineering of the system to meet national security aspirations". At a lecture in Jaji, Yahaya himself stated that *"based on my experience garnered over three decades of meritorious service in command, staff, and instructional capacities, I have conceived an ideal Nigerian Army that I seek to build. This is the outcome of a thorough assessment of the existing Nigerian Army's capabilities vis-à-vis the challenges and expectations for current as well as future operations. The issues that have informed my perception are inadequate equipment holding, manpower deficiency and proficiency, low morale, as well as the need for better synergy. I intend to superintend over a Nigerian Army that will have flexibility, capacity, and capability to operate under all conditions in collaboration with other Services and agencies. Hence, I envision having a robust, agile, and adaptable force capable of defending the nation from all internal and external threats of conventional, asymmetric or hybrid nature. This is a constitutional imperative, which I am determined to accomplish in line with the provisions of our oath of allegiance"*.

Predicated on these perceptions, Yahaya (2021) declared that "my vision for the Nigerian Army is *to have a Professional Nigerian Army Ready to Accomplish Assigned Missions within a Joint Environment in Defence of Nigeria*". In furtherance of this vision, the mission is *"to command the Nigerian Army to win all land battles in defence of the territorial integrity of Nigeria, protect her national interest, and accomplish assigned tasks in aid of civil authority among other responsibilities"*. These strategic statements are promoted against the background of the Nigerian Army's core values of loyalty, selfless service, courage, discipline, integrity, and respect for others. The vision evolved from a fundamental gap analysis made by the COAS. These gaps include: discerning shortfalls in professionalism arising from extended and extensive operational commitments across the nation; uncertainties in the state of military readiness; manifest problems in the administration of combat forces; and a lack of synergy between the Services as well as between the Services and other security agencies. Consequently, they informed the articulation of the four command pillars of professionalism, readiness, administration, and cooperation upon which the vision is hinged.

The four pillars, namely professionalism, readiness, administration, and cooperation, are conceptually espoused in furtherance of the vision. Firstly, Huntington (1957), defines the characteristics of military professionalism as expertise, responsibility, and corporateness. These qualities drive the military to apply knowledge, skills, and aptitudes in a responsible manner while showing unmatched distinctiveness. The military typically shows specialized knowledge in the management of violence and maintains a monopoly in its application and advancement. According to Yahaya (2022), "professionalism entails the capacity to execute all operations and activities in line with established military, national and international best practices. It embodies the application of excellent military skills and competencies, high ethical standards, and reasonable motivation". Military expertise requires realistic capacity building to meet the changes of the contemporary security environment. On corporateness, Huntington further argues that military professionalism differentiates military personnel from other specialists. Clearly, civilian engineers, pilots, drivers, and mechanics are professionally like their military counterparts but vocationally and environmentally different. This distinctness and corporateness are evident in the mutually binding relationships between military personnel in the course of their duties. Yahaya (2023) believes that to ensure professionalism, the Nigerian Army must return to the tenets of basic soldiering and strict adherence to its traditions, customs, and ethics. It must uphold regimentation while implementing an effective welfare system as well as sanction and reward systems.

Secondly, the United States Department of Defence defines Force Readiness as *"the ability of military forces to fight and meet assigned missions"*, while the US Army states the four elements of readiness as manning, training, equipment, and leadership development. To Yahaya (2022), force readiness is the ability to properly man and operate available equipment by Nigerian Army troops in furtherance of mission objectives. Ofoche (2022), the Chief of Transformation and Innovation (COTI) reiterated this philosophy when he intoned that" readiness can only be achieved by well-trained and administered troops who are in a high state of morale to discharge assigned missions". Clearly, the combat readiness of Nigerian Army troops is vital to the success of all operations. Thus, the roadmap to readiness would entail improved training, optimal resourcing, innovation, firm leadership, and pro-activeness. It is important that adequate platforms and equipment are procured to facilitate the effective performance of assigned roles. These values are to be accompanied by an improved maintenance system to ensure operational efficiency and effectiveness. Furthermore, research and development are required to regenerate new platforms, equipment, and methodologies.

Thirdly, Military Administration involves managing military personnel, their training, and operations, as well as the provision of logistics, welfare, and other services in furtherance of their assigned tasks. In many ways, military administration serves the same role as public administration in the civil society. Yahaya (2022) stated that sound military administration is essential to operational effectiveness and high morale. It consists of all tangible and intangible efforts aimed at putting troops in the best state of mind to discharge their duties effectively. It engenders the right attitude and frame of mind that are prerequisites for organisational sustainability and mission accomplishment. As a result, it is critical to ensure good troop administration at all levels of command. This will include the prioritization of personnel welfare, promotion of merit, celebration of gallantry, honouring heroes, and supporting military families. Significantly, Omozoje (2022), the Chief of Policy and Plans, emphasized that rewards and sanctions need to be administered diligently and fairly to ensure that those deserving of accolades are recognized while those who go contrary to expectations are punished in line with extant rules and regulations.

Fourthly, cooperation covers interoperability, integration, and synergy with other Services and security agencies. It requires adaptable Tactics, Techniques and Procedures, flexible mind set, and the acquisition of platforms to operate seamlessly in a joint environment. Cooperation in working relationships with stakeholders is an essential factor for success in military operations. Synergy at all levels and a cordial working relationship with stakeholders are critical to fulfilling collective defence goals. All existing gaps in inter-Service and interagency relationships need to be bridged through a robust joint, interagency, and intergovernmental framework configured to confront current security challenges. Clearly, the Nigerian Army's leadership philosophy emphasizes jointness in all national security endeavours.

After more than 20 months of implementing the vision statement by General Faruk Yahaya "*to have a Professional Nigerian Army Ready to Accomplish Assigned Missions within a Joint Environment in the Defence of Nigeria*", it is important to systematically interrogate its impact. Basically, the vision reveals certain unmistakeable key words and phrases. These are professionalism, readiness, joint environment, assigned missions, and defence of Nigeria, which are exactly or generally co-terminus with the four pillars supporting the vision as depicted in Figure 43 below:

Figure 43: Elements of the COAS Vision and its Four Pillars

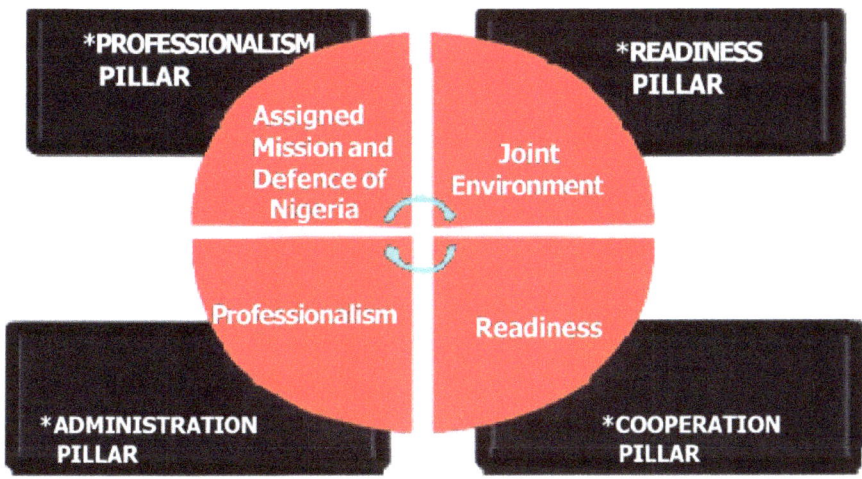

In particular, the Joint Environment referred to in the vision is a subset of the Cooperation pillar, while the Administration pillar covers the administration of personnel, capabilities, operations, logistics, welfare, and morale in furtherance of assigned tasks and the overall defence of Nigeria. To meet its constitutional mandate and oath of allegiance, the Nigerian Army is working steadfastly to fulfil its vision and mission statements. However, questions arise as to the quality of the implementation of the vision. A pragmatic way of assessing the progress made and perhaps, the inherent challenges is to interrogate the success or otherwise of the accompanying pillars. This is more so as, according to Omozoje (2022), "the Nigerian Army applies an outcome-based approach in assessing the performance of its critical functions". In line with this approach, the performance of the pillars is examined in lieu of the COAS vision.

In terms of Military Professionalism, the Nigerian Army is promoting capabilities such as: the organisation of forces and the planning, execution, and direction of operational activities. These include the science and art of war as well as both organizational and administrative skills. The Nigerian Army is currently being repositioned to conduct protracted land operations independently or jointly with other Services and security agencies. Additionally, it is undergoing restructuring and reorientation aimed at inculcating a mind-set to employ diverse capabilities in the conduct of joint operations in any terrain within Nigeria. As part of efforts to checkmate terrorism, insurgency, banditry, and other criminal activities, according to Ibrahim (2022), the Chief of Training (Army), "the Nigerian Army has adopted a new doctrine and concept of war fighting that involves offensive, robust, and highly mobile strike teams". This concept evolved from the lessons learned from past experiences where elements of the Nigerian Army sat in defence and inadvertently surrendered the initiative to the adversary. Aggressive and concerted force projection into criminal enclaves supported by other Services and agencies has changed the attitude and morale of troops to conduct more effective combat operations. Relatedly, Nigerian Army recently stepped-up intelligence and psychological operations against criminal elements. In particular, the capacity of the Intelligence Corps has been improved to carry out influence and psychological operations against armed groups across the nation. These non-kinetic efforts contributed to the surrender of numerous BHT operatives. Indeed, according to Onyeuko (2022), in one week in August 2022 alone, a total of 280 Boko Haram terrorists surrendered along with 1475 family members. These non-kinetic efforts have proven to be viable force multipliers to reduce the adversary's potentials for propaganda, indoctrination, and recruitment.

Furthermore, Military Professionalism requires obeisance to civil authority and the rule of law. This responsibility drives the public good of common defence. Each step up in the hierarchy of the military profession demands more responsibility because the personnel are required to make important decisions and deliver critical actions. In view of the coordinating role of Senior Non-Commissioned Officers (SNCOs), especially Regimental Sergeant Majors (RSM), in the chain of command and their overall impact on military professionalism, the Nigerian Army embarked on measures to restore their value so as to sustain regimentation and promote responsibility. These measures include promoting their career advancement, welfare, status, and prestige. Some of these measures include the provision of befitting houses, Hilux vehicles, kitting, and special grants to RSMs. The immediate impact of these measures is huge. RSMs are now being seen fittingly as able and proud leaders of the body of soldiers in the Nigerian Army. Soldiers now aspire to be RSMs. On a general note, the Nigerian Army has also set up a Department of Personnel Management (DPM) for soldiers, like the department of Military Secretary for officers. This Department is responsible for the personnel forecasting of soldiers in the Nigerian Army, career planning, career growth and development, professional advancement and expertise, promotions, morale, responsibility, and self-actualization of soldiers.

The continuous promotion of personnel responsibility and service corporateness is typified by the activities of the Department of Civil Military Affairs (DCMA). According to Kangye (2022), the Chief of Civil Military Affairs, in the past one year alone, the DCMA, buoyed by the COAS vision, has conducted various programmes to improve both personnel responsibility and foster corporateness. Some of these programmes include: sensitization workshops and seminars on Human Rights, International Humanitarian Law (IHL), Rules of Engagement (RoEs), and Nigerian Army policies on social media handling; COAS, special Civil Military Cooperation (CIMIC) intervention schemes, and the Quick Impact Projects (QIP); Quarterly Media Chat, Weekly Civil Military Hour on Armed Forces Radio, and the Shield Programme of Radio Nigeria. On the whole, military professionalism has received an enormous boost since 2021. This has enabled Nigerian Army personnel to proudly identify with the colours of the Service and the assigned missions in furtherance of national defence and security.

On Force Readiness, the Nigerian Army is actively promoting the quartet of manpower, equipment, training, and leadership development. First and foremost, Army Headquarters has set up a committee to review its Order of Battle (ORBAT), which is the basis for organisation, structure, and manning in the Service. In the meantime, the Nigerian Army has intensified its recruitment drive to facilitate force regeneration and renewal in light of current and future security challenges. Indeed, data from the Army Headquarters shows that a total of 23,870 soldiers were recruited between 2021 and 2023, comprising 5,100 of the 81 Regular Recruitment Intake (RRI), 6130 of 82 RRI, 6220 of 83 RRI, and 6420 of 84 RRI. Also, a total of 726 officers were commissioned in the period comprising Regular Combatant Commission (RCC), Short Service Commission (SSC), Direct Short Service Commission (DSSC) and Concessional Commission (CC).

These intakes decidedly indicate an expansion in the personnel strength of the Nigerian Army.

In the area of equipment, Akintade (2022), the Chief of Logistics (Army), stated that the Nigerian Army is promoting availability, sufficiency, adequacy, accessibility and operability. With full support from the Ministry of Defence, it has continued to modernize and expand its inventory with the acquisition of new platforms, vehicles, and equipment. These include: Armoured Personnel Carriers; armoured tanks; self-propelled artillery weapon systems; Shacman trucks; assorted weapons such as NSV and anti-air guns; Mine Resistant Ambush Protected vehicles; and auxiliary vehicles such as cranes and bulldozers. There are advanced plans to acquire UnmannedAerial Vehicles (UAVs) for Intelligence Surveillance and Reconnaissance, early warning, and situational awareness. In addition to platforms, vehicles, arms, and equipment, the Nigerian Army has embarked on an unprecedented and large- scale procurement of about 42 million 7.62 mm rounds. To ensure the sustainability of these capabilities, a planned maintenance system comprising preventive, corrective, predictive and restorative maintenance in units, theatres, and depots is being implemented.

Planned logistics management has seen the implementation of routine, special, and contingent logistics provision. For example, personnel are routinely fully kitted with uniforms, accoutrements, and combat gear before and after operations; fuel, particularly diesel depots abandoned years ago, have been reactivated; Meals- Ready-to-Eat and both night vision equipment and wet- weather capabilities are now available. The Nigerian Army normally conducts field exercises with nominal logistics inputs. A unique innovation in October 2022, was the conduct of a full- fledged logistics exercise, controlled by the Nigerian Army College of Logistics, for 2 weeks with nominal tactical inputs. The goal was to reinforce the criticality of logistics in operations and to promote both its effectiveness and efficiency.

While embarking on these capacity-building programmes, the Nigerian Army is also building on the legacies of past COAS, by strengthening Research and Development (R&D) activities to develop indigenous capacity in the manufacture and production of military hardware and software. The recent conversion of a TAF Truck into a crane that can lift a 25-ton vehicle typifies this attitude. The R&D philosophy to develop homegrown production capability is manifest in ongoing collaborations with the Defence Research and Development Bureau (DRDB) for the local production of weapons. Indeed, good progress has been recorded in the development of a 12.7mm Anti-Aircraft gun and the Rocket-Propelled Grenade RPG-7 Launchers. According to the Akintade (2022), 80 percent of the operational problems of the Nigerian Army had been logistical. However, recent developments have made logistics management quite manageable. Reflecting on the level of logistics preparations for Op DESERT SANITY, he stated that the Nigerian Army has never had it so good. Indeed, frontline units are now assured of at least 60 percent of the Table of Equipment (TOE) on transportation vehicles. On the whole, effective logistics provision is now routine.

A common military quote from General Erwin Rommel is that "the best form of welfare for the troops is first-rate training, for this saves unnecessary casualties". This is in line with the equally common military saying that "the best equipment is only as good as the man behind it". Accordingly, at the Second Senior Command and Leadership Seminar hosted by Headquarters 1 Division Kaduna in 2021, Yahaya reiterated the resolve to reposition the Nigerian Army to conduct operations more effectively through training to improve the capacity of personnel to confront the security challenges bedevilling Nigeria. In line with this commitment and the imperative of training, the Department of Training is mandated to coordinate and functionally oversee all training activities in the Nigerian Army. It is the pivot of training directives and instructions regarding training. It has taken it upon itself to promote: physical and mental fitness; standard of training, professional competences in a joint environment, combat readiness, as well as manpower and capacity development. Consequently, Ibrahim (2022), the Chief of Training (Army), stated that the Department is making a concerted and continuous effort to train and motivate troops to complement equipment procurement. These training programmes include: regimental training, unit training, professional training, specialist training, train-the- trainer programmes, equipment type training, staff training, leadership training, tactical, operational, and strategic level training.

In particular, the Nigerian Army has embarked on a basic soldiering course for young soldiers after Depot Zaria named Exercise SHINING STAR as well as a Basic Battle Course and environment-specific combat training that are conducted in Division Training Schools. In-Barracks Training is routinely conducted in all units. However, in preparation for operational deployments in the North-East, Pre-Deployment Training is conducted at the Nigerian Army School of Infantry (NASI), while In-Theatre and Acclimatization trainings are conducted at Nigerian Army Special Forces School (NASFS) Buni Yadi. For Peace Support Operations, mission-specific Pre-Deployment Training is conducted at the Martin Luther Agwai International Leadership and Peacekeeping Centre (MLAILPKC) in Jaji.

Apart from training carried out in Nigerian Army Schools locally, the Nigerian Army is collaborating with some friendly nations and foreign partners on specific skills development training. For example, KEAALTUM from Israel is conducting Advanced Infantry Battle Inoculation Training for young soldiers titled Exercise RESTORE HOPE in Training Centre Kachia. BMATT is conducting advanced infantry training for 4 SF Comd and 81 Division nicknamed Exercise PROJECT STINGER at NASME Makurdi, while the Office of Security Cooperation at the USA Embassy is conducting an advanced infantry training package titled Exercise FAST BOLT for the 103 and 174 Battalions. Furthermore, the Indian Army Mobile Training Team is conducting Train-the-Trainer packages for selected instructors at NASI and NASFS.

For officers, the NigerianArmy has commenced a special training course nicknamed Exercise COMPETENT OFFICER at 20 Battalion Serti for fresh graduates from the NDA. This is followed by a compulsory Infantry Young Officers Course (YOC) for all subalterns, regardless of their chosen arms or services. After graduation, the YOC officers attend professional courses in their various arms and services. In the rank of captain, officers attend the Junior Leadership and Staff Officers course at Jaji, and upon promotion to the rank of major, they attend the Senior Leadership and Staff Officers course also in Jaji. In the rank of lieutenant colonel attend the War Course, and in the rank of Colonel, they attend the Strategic Management and Policy Studies course. A recent innovation is that Direct Regular Commission (DRC) officers now undergo promotion examinations and attend the graduated leadership course. In addition to all of these, Field Training Exercises have now been extended from 3-4 days to 10-14 days.

These diverse but uniquely consolidative training programmes are conducted both in-country and in friendly nations abroad. They are geared for available systems and, in accordance with the wisdom that *"militaries prepare today for tomorrow's wars"*, also geared for anticipated weapons systems such as the Nigerian Army Air Wing and the Panchito Unmanned Aerial Systems (UAS), which are prepositioned for situational awareness across

theatres of operations and ungoverned spaces used as criminal sanctuaries.
To build survival instincts, endurance, personal management, decision-making, esprit-de-corps and leadership skills, the Nigerian Army conducts inter formation competitions such as the Obstacle Crossing Competition, the Orienteering and Adventure Championship, Combat Cross Country Competition, and Nigerian Army Small Arms Competition, to name a few. To improve leadership potentials, the Department of Training, in conjunction with the Nigerian Army Resource Centre, is organizing Leadership Awareness Development Courses in various Divisions Areas of Responsibility (AORs) to sharpen leadership skills. The leadership and sense of responsibility of NigerianArmy officers have been boosted by the leadership style of the COAS to set lofty goals, establish work teams, cause significant empowerment, devolve decision-making authority to subordinates and show trust. This style has also promoted the Mission Command Philosophy of decentralized execution of operations through mission-type orders that emphasize trust, initiative, judgement, and creativity of the on-scene Commander. The sum total of manning, equipment, training, and leadership is that the Nigerian Army is now, relative to the recent past, more ready to deliver on its missions and mandate. The renewed vigour in the Nigerian Army, separately and in association with other Services and agencies to combat terrorism, insurgency, criminality, and illegalities across the nation has caused an immediate review and initiation of a number of kinetic efforts. These include: reorganization and renaming of Op HADIN KAI in the North East; merging of Op HADARIN DAJI in the North West with 8 Division Sokoto; merging of Op SAFE HAVEN with 3 Division Jos; initiation of Op SHINING STAR in 1 Division Kaduna AOR; resurgence of the operations against IPOB and the ESN in the South East by 82 Division Enugu. Military administration in the Nigerian Army is focused on optimally managing the force, particularly in the areas of command and control, training, logistics, welfare, and other services in furtherance of their assigned operational tasks. First and foremost, the COAS has adopted a Mission Command philosophy in managing the command and control of fighting forces. According to Ofoche (2022), this empowers commanders to independently exercise judgement and exploit the human element in operations, emphasizing trust, initiative, force of will, and creativity. Secondly, for some time, two critical issues that had bogged down the administration of Nigerian Army forces in theatre were troop rotation and

troop movement. Infrequent rotation of units and troops meant that some fighting men overstayed in the operational theatre for up to 5 and 6 years, while others kept being moved in and out of theatre for even longer periods. This caused combat fatigue and was quite demoralizing. Additionally, troop movement in and out of theatre was conducted by road. This also applied to troops on pass.

To resolve the challenge of troop, overstay and combat fatigue, the Nigerian Army has initiated and implemented a comprehensive troop rotation plan. Operational units are assigned colours and stationed outside the Theatre AOR. New recruits are deployed to Colour units where they are constantly trained and readied for operation. Rotated troops come through the Colour units for administration before being deployed to training schools and other units depending on service exigencies. Additionally, to resolve the challenge of troop movement, the Nigerian Army, in conjunction with the Nigerian Air Force, commenced the airlifting of off duty troops on 9 August 2021 with the maiden Charlie 130 flight for troops in Op HADIN KAI from and to the operations area. This unique programme is to address the problems of distance, travel time, risk of road traffic accidents, fatigue, and other associated challenges. This is considered a key element of sound administration and a motivating force for operational success. The rotation plan is envisioned to ensure rotation circles of at least 12 to 18 months. These two issues typify the renewed commitment to military administration in the Nigerian Army.

A major perennial problem of personnel administration in the Nigerian Army is accommodation, which has for so long eluded the Service. As a prelude to solving the problem, the Nigerian Army has concluded a comprehensive survey and data collection on personnel accommodations. These include the number and typology of accommodation holdings in barracks and other facilities; the geographical mapping of such information; detailed information on the number, typology, and spread of accommodation requirements and current gaps; as well as the projected manning schemes and future accommodation gaps. This information is required to plan barracks development, troop deployment, and personnel postings.

A lot of work has been done on the Cooperation pillar. In matters of training, sister Services and agencies are nominated for Nigerian Army training courses and capstone exercises in the Army War College Nigeria are conducted jointly. In the instance of joint task forces, cooperation is being driven in the areas of force structure, representation, command and control, and communications. Firstly, the organization of some existing task forces across all theatres of operations was restructured. The erstwhile Op LAFIYA DOLE has been reorganised into a Joint Task Force (JTF) with integral land, maritime, and air components and designated Op HADIN KAI (OPHK). Now at the JTF OPHK, there are Land Component, Maritime Component, and Air Component Commanders who are all answerable to one authority, the Theatre Commander. Furthermore, key elements of these components and personnel from other agencies are represented at the JTF Headquarters. It would be recalled that, in the past, there were multiple operations with overlapping responsibilities within the same AOR, while some units had multiple authorities or "multi-hatted", which negatively impacted command and control during operations. These problems have now been addressed, and both the manpower and platforms of various components are now under the unified command of the Theatre Commander who can now assign missions to the component commanders depending on their comparative environmental and functional advantages.

A significant element in the operations in the North East is the newfound collaboration between land and air components of the Task Force. Akinjobi (2022) stated that driven by the COAS vision, the Nigerian Army has cemented a fantastic operational relationship with other Services and agencies, particularly the Nigerian Air Force. This collaboration has resulted in the joint coordination of Close Air Support, tactical bombings, troop insertions, tactical air lifts, and evacuations. Significantly, ground to air communications have also improved. The goal of interoperability has not been reached but surely the newfound cooperation and collaboration with the Services and agencies will drive the dynamic towards this ideal.

It is important to note that banditry in the North-West and North Central is being curtailed as a result of steps taken in conjunction with other Services and agencies to ensure the situation in the affected areas is brought under control. Indeed, simultaneous operations have been initiated across the contiguous states of Katsina, Sokoto, Zamfara, Niger, and Kaduna to contain bandits within these states, prevent them from relocating to other states prior to final determination. Also, Op SHINING STAR is targeting all bandits' hideouts in the forested areas, and 82 Division is incapacitating both the IPOB and ESN and limiting their freedom to conduct criminal activities.

According to Bennet (2022), *"good leaders have visions and inspire others to help them turn those visions into reality. Great leaders have visions, share visions, and inspire others to create their own."* In line with this truism, the COAS vision has permeated all the departments, formations, and units of the Nigerian Army. For instance, the DCMA has bought into the COAS vision and envisions its role in it to "enhance the credibility and integrity of the Nigerian Army as an agent, protector, and defender of community and national interest through proactive Civil Military Relations and CIMIC engagements in line with the COAS vision". From this Departmental perspective, the DCMA has articulated specific objectives and a Plan of Action to achieving them in furtherance of the COAS vision.

Generally, the momentum set by the vision has resulted in overall improvements in the Nigerian Army, occasioned by the enactment of policies in various areas. These policies include the Nigerian Army Equipment Maintenance Policy, the Nigerian Army Policy for the Employment of UAS/UAVs, the Nigerian Army Energy Management Policy, the Nigerian Army Accommodation Policy, and the Nigerian Army Policy on Research and Development. The vision thus shows an appreciable internal drawdown and top-bottom diffusion.

Externally, the COAS vision shows qualities of both backward integration and forward alignment. In terms of backward integration, it incorporates critical elements of defence management and organization in the National Defence Policy (NDP) 2017 to promote vigorous and active strategic responses in furtherance of the national defence policy objectives. These defence policy objectives include: the establishment and maintenance of a strong, professional, people-oriented and well- equipped armed forces capable of responding to internal and external threats and contributing to national development, as well as support for the creation of an enabling environment for self-reliance in the production of military equipment and supplies. Indeed, the backward integration of national defence policy objectives in the COAS vision is in line with the typical understanding of backward design as a process of setting goals before determining the methodologies for attaining them.

The COAS vision is also uniquely forward-looking. Indeed, the four pillars of the COAS vision are seemingly prescient. One year after the launch of the vision, the AFN launched the Armed Forces of Nigeria National Military Strategy (NMS) 2022 in furtherance of the NDP 2017. The force management enablers defined in the NMS 2022 are: Joint and Integrated Efforts; High State of Readiness; Adaptability; and Task Organized Forces. By the same reasoning, the inherent capabilities envisioned in the

COAS vision are coincident with some of the expressly stated desired capabilities of NMS 2022. These include: early warning; special operations forces; interoperability; sustainability; force projection; force protection; joint training; development of equipment and skill capabilities; development of a cohesive joint force; development of operational concepts; as well as patriotic and highly motivated troops. Clearly, the four pillars of the COAS vision seem to have foreseen the strategic direction of the NMS 2022 one year before it was enunciated.

Professionalism is a lot better in the Nigerian Army now. Appointments are made based on pedigree and competence without undue regard to place of origin, tribe, or religion. Bassey (2022), the General Officer Commanding, 8 Division, headquartered in Sokoto, emphasized this when he stated that: "I am Efik from Cross River State in the South-South. I am Christian and do not speak Hausa. I was called up one day by the COAS and appointed to command the 8 Division, which oversees security in Sokoto State, the home state of the COAS, the seat of the Sultan of Sokoto, the head of the Moslem ummah in Nigeria, as well as Katsina, the home state of President Muhammadu Buhari". He stated proudly that "whenever the President is at home in Daura, Katsina State, it is my great honour to protect him". To Bassey, the aphorism "to whom much is given, much is expected" rings very true. From a professional position of leadership, the command is led and administered professionally. Improved professionalism is also evident in the conduct of in-theatre forces. Commanders now command operations without fear of unfounded recriminations and distractive self-righteous finger-pointing. Operational targets are given and accompanied by the provision of personnel, equipment, and logistics requirements. This has caused Commanders and units to perform with greater freedom of action and with better operational outcomes. On the rare occasions when they suffer losses, Administrative Authorities now show concern, first and foremost, for the dead and injured before equipment.

The various theatres of operation have keyed into the COAS vision in terms of force readiness. This typically takes the form of specialized sector and environment specific operational training for in-theatre forces, in addition to broad based training with international and local NGOs. According to Shaibu (2023), the General Officer Commanding 7 Division, these trainings include functional awareness on International Humanitarian Law (IHL) and sexual exploitation. Other areas of force readiness include increasing the force's strength, balancing the force, and gross expansion in equipment holdings. For instance, to emphasize the expanded capabilities, the force now has ISR assets that give situational awareness even for forces on the move and at night, which enables deliberate operations and improved force protection.

Force administration has taken a progressive turn in the North-East theatre of operations. Personnel enjoy more leaves now, and land forces are rotated regularly to prevent combat fatigue. A major initiative is that both rotating forces and individuals on pass are airlifted from Maiduguri to Abuja or Lagos for onward journeys to their destinations. The same arrangement is made for reporting troops and personnel. Musa (2023), the Theatre Commander Ops HADIN KAI thanked the COAS for this groundbreaking initiative and emphasized the great impact of these airlifts on the sense of belonging of troops, personnel morale, commitment, and the will to fight.

There are significant developments to report on force cooperation. Gone are the days when undue interservice competition and even rivalries undermined operational effectiveness. A clear case in point is the level of coordination, collaboration, and synergy that now exists between the land and air forces as well as between land and naval forces. According to Oyesola (2023), the Air Component Commander of Ops HADIN KAI, the directive by the COAS to the Land Component to station their newly acquired Unmanned Aerial Vehicles (UAVs) under the control of the Air Component underscores the new mindset and paradigm shift in the relationship between land and air forces. Also, drones of the Land Component are deployed for Intelligence Surveillance and Reconnaissance (ISR) missions, and the results are applied for joint operations planning and application. The most remarkable aspect of the newfound cooperation is the synchronization of air operations with land operations for better operational outcomes. In terms of cooperation, Yeldin (2023), the Maritime Component Commander, recalled the entrance of the Nigerian Navy in the North-East theatre of operations with the Belarus-trained Special Forces, which basically conducted land-based operations in association with Land Component forces. However, with the establishment of the Naval Base at Baga, naval forces now operate jointly with Amphibious Forces of the Land Component to deny the adversary freedom of movement on Lake Chad and adjoining waterways. This has particularly denied the adversary use of the waterways for logistics movement. According to Musa (2023), cooperation is extended to other agencies, the media, traditional leaders, religious leaders, and even non-governmental organisations such as motor unions.

In particular, components from the Department of State Services (DSS), National Security and Civil Defence Corps (NSCDC), and National Immigration Services (NIS) highlighted improved communication, adequate representation in the force structure, regular consultation, joint operations planning, functionally sectorized tasking, common reporting protocols, a sense of belonging, and an unmistakable sense of professional appreciation. Bawa (2023), the NSCDC Component Commander recalls that the new sense of cooperation has caused the extension of the initiatives on force administration to all the integral agencies and Amadi (2023), representing the DSS Coordinator, puts it succinctly that, in terms of cooperation, "all the components are administered as one entity".

In sum, the implementation of the COAS vision and mission statement has caused gross improvements in the four important pillars of professionalism, force readiness, military administration, and cooperation. The overall result of the concerted efforts to attain the vision is diverse but has been decidedly impactful in deterring, containing, countering, and neutralizing violent elements and groups of national insecurity in Nigeria. This is much in keeping with the National Security Strategy 2019 vision "to make Nigeria a secure, safe, just, peaceful, prosperous, and strong nation". Going forward, and in view of the economic realities, the Nigerian Army may strongly consider: cost-effective homegrown mechanisms in combatting insecurity; deliberate capacity building of the Nigeria Police Force (NPF) and other security first responders; systematic devolution of certain responsibilities; application of whole-of-society paradigms for security provision; and the revolutionary integration of human initiatives and creativity with technology.

Final Thoughts

There is every likelihood that national security threats to many nations will continue to grow in spread, sophistication, and intensity. This postulation could be attributed to the multifarious political, economic, developmental, and other factors that continue to spawn conflicts around the world. In the last year, the world has witnessed a debilitating conflict in Ukraine that has greatly affected nearly every part of the world. Similarly, adverse climatic conditions, including large-scale flooding and wildfires have underlined the fact that global warming is real and could pose national security threats in the immediate, medium, and long terms. While large scale organized terrorism such as that undertaken by ISIS may have been defeated in the Middle East, major parts of the Sahel and indeed sub-Saharan Africa remain firmly in the grip of terrorist/jihadist groups. The foregoing implies that nations must continue to build their militaries and other national security tools to be able to ward off threats to the well-being of their citizens and global peace and security in general.

Nigeria has its fair share of growing security threats, with the major one being organized terrorism, which started in the Northeast of the country and gradually mutated into several other forms of threats. These include banditry, kidnapping for ransom, and wanton attacks on public infrastructure among other unwholesome acts. The Nigerian Army is a key tool for tackling national security challenges in the country. In its nearly 160 years of existence, the Nigerian Army has proven to be an indispensable force to promote the security, growth, and development of Nigeria. The roles of the Nigerian Army are clearly spelled out in the 1999 Constitution of the FRN (as amended). To effectively perform this role, the Nigerian Army must ensure it remains competitive by envisioning and developing the required capacities and capabilities to meet present and future threats. Some of the key areas the Nigerian Army must continually develop include doctrine, organization, training, leadership, infrastructure and facilities, material and acquisition, technology, and policy, among others. There is no gainsaying the fact that the Nigerian Army cannot accomplish its future missions and roles in isolation but must seek collaboration and partnership through jointness and cooperation with other agencies and multinational and intergovernmental organizations. Responding to the aforementioned growing threats has stretched the Nigerian Army in terms of manpower and equipment, leading to a multiplicity of operations across the entire landscape of the country. In anticipation of a future of sustained threat climate and even emerging threat, the Nigerian Army will need to reposition itself to respond effectively to these challenges.

In recognition of the imperative to consolidate on current development and chart the future of the NA, the COAS established the NAHFC at Giri, Abuja. The NAHFC was established on 16 December 2022 and operationalized on 19 January 2023. The mission statement of the NAFHC is "to serve as a research organization for the Nigerian Army through the formulation and development of policy frameworks". This includes; continuous forecasting for the NigerianArmy's strategic objectives within acceptable time frames, institutionalising and mainstreaming novel solutions to tactical, operational, admininstrative, and logistical challenges facing the Nigerian Army, providing strategic inputs for future plans and continuous modernization of the Nigerian Army, and conducting independent analysis to develop policy formulation for the Nigerian Army. Others include analysis of the impact of global, regional, transnational and national security issues on the Nigerian Army, maintaining a key strategic issues list for the Nigerian Army, providing valuable research to Nigerian Army leadership and many more. The establishment of NAHFC puts the future of the Nigerian Army in safe hands particularly as regards matching future capabilities with current and future threats.

The anticipated areas of restructuring will include the application of technology in all facets of operation, force posture and structure, human resources, and training, among others.

Application of Technology in All Facets

Military technology includes a range of weapons, equipment, structures, and vehicles used specifically for the purpose of warfare. It includes the knowledge required to build such technology, employ it in combat, to repair and replenish it. Technology may may be required in warfare may be divided into five categories. Offensive weapons, aimed at harming the enemy, and defensive weapons to ward off enemy offensives. Transportation technology moves personnel and equipment; communications coordinate the movements of forces, and sensors detect forces both friendly and hostile and guide weaponry.

The Nigerian Army is striving to keep with emerging technologies in warfare. Most advanced armies are currently at the Fourth Generation Warfare (4GW) stage, where there is less emphasis on the use of men, weapons systems have become more advanced and computerized, and communications on the battlefield have greatly advanced and are in real time. 4GW has been characterized by the use of technologies such as Unmanned Aerial Vehicles (UAVs), armed drones, artillery weapons systems, missile defence systems controlled by satellite, and other emerging technologies. The Russia/Ukraine crisis has witnessed a prolific display of 4GW technologies. However, some advanced militaries are already researching Fifth Generation Warfare (5GW), which will be characterized by the use of robotics and artificial intelligence to execute warfare. The Nigerian Army is in the advanced stages of meeting up with certain stages of 4GW, such as the acquisition of UAVs and armed drones, investment in satellite communication technology, and computerized weapons systems.

The Nigerian Army is to a great extent reliant on imports for its equipment and technologies. The future of the Nigerian Army depends on investment in Research and Development (R&D) to contribute to the development of a military industrial complex (MIC) where weapons and equipment could be produced tailored to its needs. The Nigerian Army could partner with academia and further existing partnerships with private organisations to improve its R&D capabilities, leading to self-sustenance in some aspects of equipment production. A nation cannot be fully reliant on itself for its military equipment needs, but the Nigerian Army needs to identify long-term partners to collaborate with on equipment supplies and the transfer of technology.

Force Posture and Structure

The Nigerian Army ORBAT 2016 clearly spells out the desired force posture and structure of the Nigerian Army which is currently structured into 8 fighting divisions. It is also structured along the line of Corps which consists of combat arms, combat services, and combat support services, all of which support the divisions. Despite this structure, there is an uneven spread of forces across the country in response to the myriad of threats emanating from around the country. ORBAT 2016 proposed the establishment of additional brigades and units to cover certain observed gaps. Therefore, the full implementation of ORBAT 2016 would ensure the Nigerian Army achieves the desired spread in the country in the future.

The threat climate in the country and future projections indicate that the Nigerian Army will continually be engaged in various forms of internal security operations and CT COIN. For better efficiency, decentralized commands may be necessary. Therefore, reducing the lines of communication between AHQ and the forward troops may be necessary. This could be achieved by creating regional operational commands by grouping divisions into commands that make it easier for the COAS to have an overview of the entire areas of operations across the country. Therefore, the 8 divisions could be grouped into 4 regional operational commands for better efficiency and control. To achieve the above, some amendments to the Nigerian Army ORBAT 2016 will be necessary to cater for this increased requirement for manpower.

A re-invigorated force structure needs to have the complement of a full fighting force. The Army should be able to carry out extended independent operations before calling for support from sister services. In this way, the Nigerian Army should have elements of organic air support, which are already being conceptualized by the development of Nigerian Army Aviation. When fully developed and evenly spread to support all the commands across the country, the Nigerian Army would be capable of independently taking on limited threats before calling for the support of the Nigerian Air Force. An effective special force will also complement the efforts of the Nigerian Army going forward due to the nature of existing and future threats. Special Forces are not an all-comers affair but should be well selected, properly trained and adequately equipped. There is a need to continually review our special forces set up to conform to best practices that can be suited to the nature of threats facing us as a nation. Finally reviewing the force posture and structure will be incomplete without aligning our equipment needs to the nature of threats. I have begun re-equipping the Nigerian Army in line with contemporary threats across all the combat arms and combat support arms and gradually moving away from conventional warfare. If this process is sustained, the Nigerian Army will be able to better tackle its emerging threats.

Human Resources Size of the Nigerian Army and Training

The Nigerian Army has an established strength of over 300,000, comprising about 10 per cent officers and 90 per cent soldiers. However, the current strength is below 50 per cent of its establishment. The current manpower situation cannot ensure the full implementation of the existing Nigerian Army ORBAT 2016. This situation would be aggravated with the proposed expansion of the NA into regional commands. The proposal to create regional operational commands could see to the establishment of associated training depots for the recruitment of more personnel to cater for this anticipated manpower increase.

The Nigerian Army under my leadership has placed a premium on training. Therefore, we have improved training systems, which have helped improve professionalism. Some of these are the immense support given to TRADOC and other Nigerian Army training outfits and schools. Some novel efforts include advanced infantry training for soldiers graduated from the Depot Nigerian Army, known as Ex RESTORE HOPE, which prepares them for deployment to existing theatres of operations around the country. Also, foreign training in specific areas of expertise has been intensified. There is no army that can succeed without the requisite training, and this should therefore be a recipe for the future success of the Nigerian Army. A future increase in strength will inform the need for expansion of training institutions across the Nigerian Army. This should be consistent with the proposed expansion in structure. Currently, division training schools exist but need to be expanded to full battle schools so that divisions can be self-dependent to a large extent on trained personnel. The proposed expansion to regional operations commands should also see the establishment of training centres in each command. There will also be a need for further review of training doctrine to emphasise jointness and enhance synergy with other services. The experiences learned from CTCOIN in the last 13 years will serve as a catalyst to the kind of training that will impact on our army if we have to do better in the future.

Conclusion

Leadership cannot be complete without a vision that will transcend into the future. This is the foundation I intend to lay and the legacy I am leaving behind. I have highlighted our challenges and exhaustively analysed our modest efforts to tackle them. Taking cognizance of existing and future threats, it was necessary to make projections into the future and visualize how the Nigerian Army will need to posture itself to confront the emerging scenarios. The fast-rising pace of technological development dictates that the military should equally develop itself in the area of military technology.

The Nigerian Army is doing its best in this regard as it is updating its equipment and weaponry to align with these technological advancements. It is also improving its R&D capability to build up its equipment production capability. The nature of future threats also demands that the Nigerian Army review its force posture in terms of structure and organisation to effectively cover the entire threat landscape across the country. This will also be in tandem with equipment restructuring to ensure that its commands have the requisite fighting capabilities. Furthermore, there is a need for the Nigerian Army to meet up in strength to cater for its anticipated force structure. The current combat efficiency on manpower is inadequate to meet these projections.

Therefore, a planned increase in manpower is inevitable to put more boots on the ground in anticipation of the creation of new formations across the entire country. Such a manpower increase must also be complemented with proper training, which will lead to the creation of training outfits along with the proposed formations. Proper training is a legacy to be bequeathed to the Nigerian Army in anticipation of future challenges.

REFLECTIONS

Nigeria has tackled the challenge of terrorism and insurgency in the North East for over a decade. Government's main effort at Counter Terrorism and Counter Insurgency (CTCOIN) had been kinetic measures spearheaded by the Armed Forces of Nigeria in concert with other security agencies and non-kinetic measures by other government agencies. One of the contending variables, amongst others, for the success of CTCOIN Operations in the North East and other operations had been the issue of inter-service and inter-agency collaboration and cooperation. Since March 2021, the CTCOIN operations in the North East and other operations across the nation have enjoyed significant impetus to cooperation and jointness. I have always believed that the mindset of collective approach to problem solving is pivotal to achieving operational objectives. In this wise, Services are to bring their skills and competences to the joint environment for mission accomplishments. The realization and conviction of the Chief of Army Staff, Lieutenant General Faruk Yahaya on the imperatives of this orientation is a value that smoothened the paradigm shift. The aggregate of the philosophy of jointness is profoundly manifest in our successes in the North East. Indeed Faruk's joint credential is impeccable.

It is on this note that I salute the COAS on this biography titled "Lieutenant General Faruk Yahaya: Counter Terrorism and Counter Insurgency Theory meets Practice". I therefore align with this publication and indeed support it. More importantly, I use this opportunity to put on record my appreciation of the immense effort of Lieutenant General Faruk Yahaya in the nation's fight against terrorism and insurgency in all ramifications. This treatise captures the deep personality of its accomplished subject, the essential principles that go into his operational and strategic planning; the administration of men under his military command and the remarkable outcomes of his military exploits, particularly in the North East. As such, the book should be acceptable to a discerning local and international reading public, in addition to being an important input to policy making.

General LEO Irabor
Chief of Defence Staff
Federal Republic of Nigeria

Effective leadership is an essential part of military service which every military commander strives to symbolize. For this reason, every commissioned officer is engrained with multiple leadership styles and skills for effective service delivery. Over time, the military has advanced from using the authoritarian leadership approach to a more effective combination of transformational, participatory and servant leadership styles, which is exactly what the 22nd Chief of Army Staff, Lt Gen Faruk Yahaya embodies. A leader who has been able to integrate these three leadership styles that have made him outstanding. A man whom I have defined as a product of destiny considering the different phenomenal leaps he attained as a leader at different stages of his career.

Starting our journey in the NDA History Class of 1985, he began to exhibit these leadership styles which convinced us to unanimously elect him as Course Senior throughout our academic years. In the same vein, in our final year the entire Army class of 37 Regular Course unanimously elected him to preside as Course Senior while holding the appointment of Company Senior Under Officer in Mogadishu Battalion. It was quite obvious to us then as it is now that he was highly respected by both superiors and subordinates largely due to his unique leadership attributes. As Gen Omar Bradley noted, "no commander can become a strategist until he first knows his men. Far from being a handicap to command, compassion is the measure of it. Unless one values the lives of his soldiers and is tormented by their ordeals, he is unfit for command." This is indeed true of Lt Gen Faruk Yahaya's leadership style which is people-centred.

His time as the Military Secretary (Army) gave him ample opportunity to know which officer was best suited for what task. As COAS, he ensured that all the necessary logistics at his disposal were deployed to the theatre. He is a strong adherent of the mission-command philosophy. He selects the right person for the task, provides the wherewithal to execute the task, and gives him the freedom of action to execute the task. This has proven very effective in the Counter Insurgency operations in the North East and other parts of the country.

Lt Gen Faruk is a man who, in my opinion, exemplifies firmness, fairness, and integrity. He is a man of principle who stood by his resolve to do the right thing, irrespective of whose oars are gored. Additionally, his simplicity is worthy of emulation. Even as a senior officer, he would occasionally drive himself to visit colleagues without his security details or aide de camp. He always wore simple white fabric, which never changed even after he clinched the highest seat in the Nigerian Army. Truly, Lt Gen Faruk Yahaya has been destined to lead the Nigerian Army, and I believe that our dear country will continue to tap into his potential for a long time.

Maj Gen IM YUSUF
Commandant Nigerian Defence Academy

I have had the pleasure and honour of observing and engaging Lt Gen Faruk Yahaya for over 38 years. First as a course mate, and now as his Chief of Policy and Plans. Lt Gen Faruk Yahaya is a Soldier's General with a penchant for following the rules, staying within accepted norms, and regulations and telling the truth to power in his usual jovial manner. His vision statement as COAS looked at having a professional Nigerian Army anchored on jointness and cooperation with other agencies of government. The Air Force and the Navy thus remain fundamental parts of our operations. This has yielded positive results for the Army under his watch and underpins his joint credentials.

Lt Gen Faruk Yahaya has changed the trajectory of the Nigerian Army, placing it on a steady, upward path to greatness and achieving its mandate of securing the nation. He brings a steadied and incisive approach to addressing National Security issues, revealing a thorough knowledge of the local dynamics at play often couched under "We are all from here". This has translated to the general perception that there is much improvement in security within the North East of Nigeria and indeed the entire country. This is because under his leadership, the Army is focused on getting results. The troops are better conditioned for battle, and the required operational platforms and logistics support are provided. The whole idea of his leadership is to have an army that can serve the nation professionally. He has achieved that within the short period of his tenure as COAS.

He has made efforts to ensure that the Nigerian Army has the home-grown capability to produce many of its platforms. The morale across the Army is also very high, and the reason is simple: his sound administration of men. The confidence is high within the Army and has led to an increased operational tempo, which accounts for the unprecedented number of terrorists that surrendered under his watch as COAS. The combat degradation and near defeat of the BHT/ISWAP in the North East Nigeria and Lake Chad Border areas underscore his astute leadership of the Nigerian Army and the professional competence of the Force under his watch.

Maj Gen AB OMOZOJE
Chief of Policy and Plans Nigerian Army

Muhammadu Buhari, President, Commander in Chief of the Armed Forces of the Federal Republic of Nigeria (L) and Lt Gen F Yahaya, Chief of Army Staff (R)

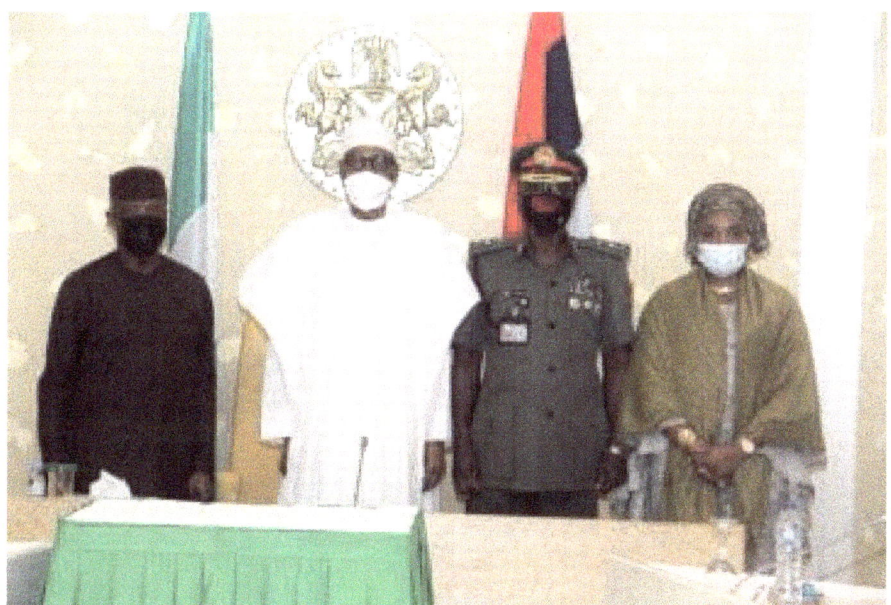

Muhammadu Buhari, President, Commander in Chief of the Armed Forces of the Federal Republic of Nigeria, Prof Yemi Osinbajo, Vice President, Lt Gen F Yahaya, Chief of Army Staff and Hajia Salamatu Yahaya, wife of the Chief of Army Staff

President, Commander in Chief of the Armed Forces of the Federal Republic of Nigeria and the Vice President, decorating the Chief of Army Staff with his new rank while the wife, Hajia Salamatu Yahaya watches

Maj Gen Bashir Salihi Magashi (rtd), Minister of Defence, General LEO Irabor, Chief of Defence Staff, and Lt Gen F Yahaya, Chief of Army Staff in the Minister's office

General LEO Irabor, Chief of Defence Staff (L) and Lt Gen F Yahaya, Chief of Army Staff (R)

Pictorials

Muhammadu Buhari, President, Commander in Chief of the Armed Forces of the Federal Republic of Nigeria (R) presenting Award of CFR to Lt Gen F Yahaya, Chief of Army Staff

Service Chiefs from L-R: V Adm AZ Gambo - CNS, Gen LEO Irabor - CDS, Lt Gen F Yahava - COAS and Air Mshl IO Amao - CAS

Lt Gen F Yahaya, Chief of Army Staff (centre) with Commanders and PSOs in North East Theatre

Lt Gen F Yahaya, Chief of Army Staff (L) with Maj Gen AB Omozoje, Chief of Policy and Plans (R)

Pictorials

Lt Gen F Yahaya, Chief of Army Staff (R) and Maj Gen IM Yusuf, Commandant, Nigerian Defence Academy (L)

Lt Gen F Yahaya, Chief of Army Staff (L) and Maj Gen SO Olabanji, Commander TRADOC NA (R)

Lt Gen F Yahaya, Chief of Army Staff (centre) with some of his course mates and Acting CO, 37 NDA Demo Battalion

Lt Gen F Yahaya, Chief of Army Staff (centre), Maj Gen OT Akinjobi, Chief of Operations and Maj Gen CG Musa, Theatre Commander, Operation HADIN KAI

Pictorials

Rt Hon. Aminu Tambuwal, Governor of Sokoto State and Lt Gen F Yahaya, Chief of Army Staff

Prof Babagana Zulum, Governor of Borno State and Lt Gen F Yahaya, Chief of Army Staff

Senator Hope Uzodinma, Governor of Imo State, Lt Gen F Yahaya, Chief of Army Staff and His Royal Highness, Eze Samuel Ohiri, Eze Imo

Lt Gen F Yahaya, Chief of Army Staff and Sir Sa'ad Abubukar, Sultan of Sokoto

Oba Rilwan Akinolu, Oba of Lagos and Lt Gen F Yahaya, Chief of Army Staff

Lt Gen F Yahaya, Chief of Army Staff and HRH Alhaji Ahmadu Aliyu Ogga Onawo, Andoma of Doma

Cameronian Defence Attache (R) on courtesy visit to Chief of Army Staff (L)

Maj Gen David Baldman, Adjutant General of California National Guard (L) on courtesy call to Chief of Army Staff (R) on 7 Dec 21

Pictorials

Lt Gen F Yahaya, Chief of Army Staff with Amina Mohammed, UN Deputy Secretary General and her delegation during a courtesy visit

Lt Gen F Yahaya, Chief of Army Staff with some NGO representatives when he was the Theatre Commander, Operation LAFIYA DOLE

Lt Gen F Yahaya, Chief of Army Staff with some senior officers on 16 October 2021 during First CDS OSMA Sahel Military Games for Peace and Solidarity Abuja 2021

Lt Gen F Yahaya, Chief of Army Staff with students of Fatima College of Nursing, Sifawa, Sokoto State

Pictorials

Lt Gen F Yahaya, Chief of Army Staff and Hajia Salamatu Faruk Yahaya, President Nigerian Army Officers' Wives Association (NAOWA)

Lt Gen F Yahaya, Chief of Army Staff and Hajia Salamatu Faruk Yahaya, President NAOWA and Some other NAOWA Executives during COAS Annual Conference 2021 in Abuja

Lt Gen F Yahaya, Chief of Army Staff and Prof Babagana Zulum, Governor of Borno State serving food to troops at 7 Division Hospital complex

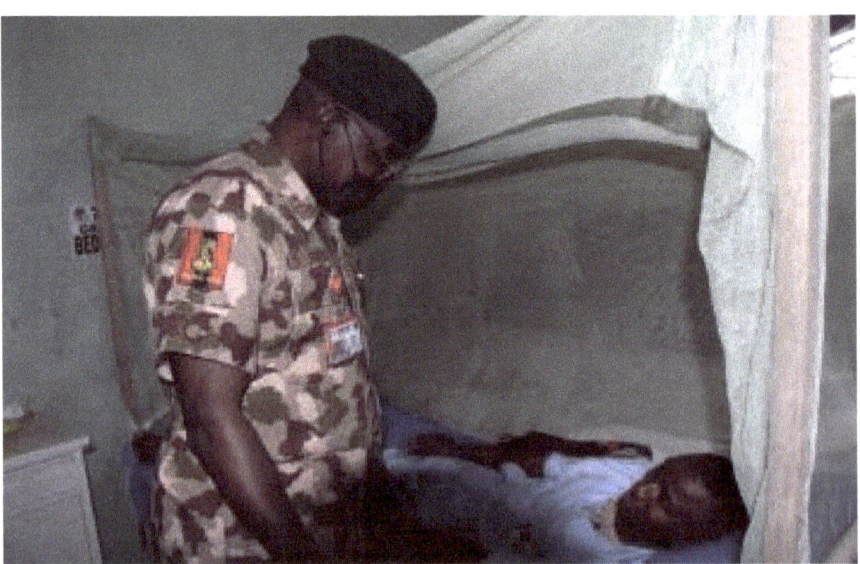

Lt Gen F Yahaya, Chief of Army Staff visits an injured soldier receiving treatment at 7 Division Hospital in Maimalari Cantonment, Maiduguri, Borno State.

Pictorials

Lt Gen F Yahaya, Chief of Army Staff addressing some officers in the field when he was Theatre Commander, Operation LAFIA DOLE

Lt Gen F Yahaya, Chief of Army Staff with some troops in the North East as Theatre Commander

Lt Gen F Yahaya, Chief of Army Staff and wife, Hajia Salamatu Faruk Yahaya, after receiving his national honour as Commander of the Order of the Federal Republic (CFR)

Lt Gen F Yahaya, Chief of Army Staff and family

Pictorials

Lt Gen F Yahaya, Chief of Army Staff and his only brother, Alhaji Abubakar Yahaya

Lt Gen F Yahaya, Chief of Army Staff, his wife Hajiya Salamatu Yahaya and son, Al-Ameen

Lt Gen F Yahaya, Chief of Army Staff with some Sifawa community leaders, Sokoto State

Notes on the Contributors

Maj Gen EV Onumajuru is the current Chief of Army Special Services and Programmes, Nigerian Army. He was a former Director of Administration, Defence Intelligence Agency, and also Deputy Commandant/Director of Studies at the National Defence College, Nigeria. Maj Gen Onumajuru was the Chairman of this Project Team. He contributed to Leadership Grooming and Selection, Commanding the North East Theatre, Operational and Strategic Thoughts on the Conduct of CTCOIN, as well as the Final Thoughts on the Future of the NA.

Brig Gen N Ashinze is the current Director of Psychological Operations at the Army Headquarters Department of Civil Military Affairs. He was formerly of the Land Forces Simulation Centre, Nigeria and Nigerian Army School of Infantry. Brig Gen Ashinze contributed to the Operational and Strategic Thoughts on the Conduct of CTCOIN as well as the Final Thoughts.

Brig Gen OO Obolo is the current Director of Coordination and a member of the Faculty at the National Defence College Nigeria. Brig Gen Obolo was the Secretary of the Project Team. He contributed the Evolution of CTCOIN operations in the North East Nigeria. He also contributed to Leadership Grooming and Selection, Commanding the North East Theatre and the Final Thoughts.

Cdre Amatare Kpou (rtd) is currently the Coordinator, Admiralty University of Nigeria. He was a former Director of Naval Education, Director of Academic Research and Analytical Support, and Director of Curriculum and Programme Development after being a Directing Staff at the National Defence College, Nigeria. Cdre Kpou contributed Imprints of Leadership as well as Vision and Strategic Posturing.

Prof Freedom C Onuoha is with the Department of Political Science, University of Nigeria, Nsukka. He is the Coordinator of the Security, Violence, and Conflict Research Group at the University. He contributed Factors and Actors of Insecurity in Nigeria: Manifestations and Impacts as well as Terrorism and Insurgency in Nigeria.

Prof Usman A Tar is the current Dean of the Faculty of Arts and Social Sciences at the Nigerian Defence Academy (NDA). He is also a Distinguished Endowed Chair of Defence and Security Studies at the NDA. Prof Tar contributed the Precedence, Origin, and Dynamics of Insecurity in Nigeria: Theoretical and Empirical Notes.

Dr Adam Abdullahi is a Senior Research Fellow and the current Head of the Department of Defence and Security Studies at the Centre for Strategic Research and Studies, National Defence College, Nigeria. Dr Abdullahi contributed the Non-Kinetic Approaches to CTCOIN Operations in Nigeria.

Dr Abubakar B Sifawa is a Senior Research Fellow at the Nigerian Army Resource Centre. He was of the Usman Dan Fodio University, Sokoto. Dr AB Sifawa contributed to the Imprints of Leadership.

Dr Chinedu S Udeh is a Directing Staff and Member of Faculty at the National Defence College Nigeria. Dr CS Udeh contributed Huffing and Puffing for Tough Times: Military Training in the Nigerian Defence Academy and a Life of Service to the Nation and Humanity.

Fig 44: Lt Gen F Yahaya, Chief of Army Staff and the Editorial Team

References

Abbass, I.M., (2012), "No Retreat No Surrender: Conflict for Survival between Fulani Pastoralists and Farmers in Northern Nigeria." European Scientific Journal, 8 (1).

Abdulkadir, A., (2012). Dead hostages: Didaqimkill Mcmanusand Lamolinara? *Citizen Platform.*

Abdullahi, A., (2022) .*Internally Displaced Personsand National Security in Nigeria: The NCFRMI in Perspective.* NDC Course 29 Participant Research Project Submitted to the National Defence College Abuja, Nigeria.

Adamolekun, T., (1999) Religious Freedom and Tolerance: catalyst for stability and Development in a Demonstration in a Democratic Nigeria' in Nigeria Journal for Curriculum and instruction, vol. 8 No. 33.

Adamu, A. (1990), "Redefining West African Security", Paper Presented at the Seminar on Global Changes and Challenges to Sub-Regional Maritime Security. NIIA, Lagos, December

Addeh, E. (2023). OPEC confirms Nigeria's 1.3 million bpd February Crude Oil Output. Thisday Online 15 March 2023.

Ademola, A. (2021). The growing threat of armed banditry in north-west Nigeria. *STRIFE.*https://www.strifeblog.org/2021/01/08/the-growing-threat-of-armed- banditry-in-north-west-nigeria/

Adegbami, A., (2013). Insecurity: A threat to human existence and economic development in Nigeria. *Public Policy and Administration Research*, 3(6), 8-13.

Adedigba, A. (2022). Children's day: As insecurity rages, Nigerian children are in the line offire.*Humangle,*https://humanglemedia.com/childrens-day-as-insecurity-rages-nigerian-children-are-in-the-line-of-fire/

Adepegba, A., (2021,May20). 127 south-south, south-east cop skilled; 25 stations razed–report. *Punch.* https://punchng-com.cdn.ampproject.org/c/s/ punchng.com/127-ssouth-seast-cops-killed-25-stations-razed-report/?amp

Adegoke, N., (2015). Youth unemployment and security challenges in Nigeria., Asian Journal of Humanities and Social Studies, 3(1),13-22.

Adejoh, S., (2019) Terrorism, Sexuality and Sexual Violence in North-Eastern Nigeria: A Psychosexual Analysis. Covenant Journal of Business and Social Sciences (CJBSS) Vol. 10,(2).p76-87.

Adejoh, S. and Anya, R.N (2021) Environment and Security Nexus in West Africa and the Sahel Region. Journal of Contemporary International Relations and Diplomacy. Vol. 2, No. 1, pp.228-246

Adejoh, S and Onuh, E.M (2017) Religionand the Nigerian State: antithesis and synthesis. HUMASS: McUJournal of Humanities, Management, Applied and Social Sciences Vol. 1 No. 1 pp.I41-158

Adejoh, S and Ukhammi, E (2021) Defence Economics and National Security Challenges in Nigeria. Zamfara Journal of Development, Vol. 2 (2) (2021).pp. 57-72.

Adeleke Adegbami (2013). Insecurity: A Threat to Human Existence and Economic Development in Nigeria.

Adeola, G.L .& Oluyemi, F. (2012).The Political and Security Implications of Cross Adibe, J. (2019,November14). How Boko Haram went from a peaceful Islamic sect to one of the world's deadliest terrorists in a decade. Quartz,https://qz.com/africa/1748873/boko-harams-10-year-reign-in-nigeria-has-been-devastating ADF Staff (2018). Battling book haram: Nigerian and regional effort shelped turn the tide against the insurgent group. *Africa Defence Forum*,11(1),8-15.

AFP, (2021). Nigeria jihadist in fighting kills scores in Lake Chad. https:// www.france24.com/en/live-news/20210928-nigeria-jihadist-infighting-kills-scores-in-lake- chadAjani,J.,&Edeh,S .(2013,February24).Abductionofforeigners:Securityforcescloseinonkidnappers.*Vanguard.*

Agusto&Co., (2022,May5). The economics of insecurity: Nigeria's roughpatch. https://www.agusto.com/publications/the-economics-of-insecurity-nigerias- rough-patch/

Ahmed, I.L., & Sulaiman, A. (2022,June29). The socio-economic effects of insecurity in Nigeria. https://dailynigerian.com/the-socio-economic-effects

Akanji, O. (2009). The politics of combating domestic terrorism in Nigeria. In W. Okumu & A. Botha, (Eds.), *Domestic terrorism in Africa: defining, addressing and understanding its impact on human security*. Pretoria: InstituteforSecurityStudies,p.60.

Akpobibibo, O., (2003). Confronting the Human Security Dilemma-Towards Building Akubor, E.O. (2017), "Climate Change, Migration and Conflict: A Historical Survey of People of Northern Nigeria and their Neighbors from the period of Mega Chad. " Localities, 7:9–

Akwara, A.F., Awara, N.F., Enwuchoia, J., Adekunle, M. and Udaw, J.E. (2013). Unemployment and Poverty: Implication for National Security and GoodGovernance in Nigeria. International Journal of Public Administration (IJPAMR), Vol. 2, No. 1, October, 2013

Albert, I.O (2018) Nigeria's Security Challenges in Historical Perspective in Ayodeji, O, Olutayo A.,Abimbola, A and Saheed, A (ed) Security

Challenges and Management in Modern Nigeria, UK: Cambridge Scholars Publishing

Ajaja, T. (2022, December 3). How unemployment, poverty rubbish fight against in security (III). *Punch*, https://punchng.com/how-unemployment-poverty- rubbish-fight-against-insecurity-iii

Andrew, C. and Kennedy, M. (2003). Root Causes of Human Insecurity in A New SecurityParadigm:TheCambridgeSecuritySeminar,UniversityofCambridge,UK Akintade, OB, 2022, Chief of Logistics Army, Interview by the Team, Abuja, October14.

Amadi, S, 2023, Representing Akhun, S, Department of State Services (DSS) Component Commander, Operation HADIN KAI, Interview by the Team, Maiduguri, 7 January.

Army Headquarters (AHQ)2020. "Report of the Committee to articulate the NA position on OPLDCIED Plan, AHQ, Abuja, May 2020.

Anka, Y. (2021). Banditry: Spotlight in leaders who turn against one another. *Humangle*. https://humangle.ng/banditry-spotlighting-gang-leaders-who-turn- against-one-another/

Assessment of Nigeria's Response to Threat of Improvised Explosive Device (IEDs)in Northeast Nigeriahttps://papers.ssrn.com/sol3/papers.cfm?abstract_id=3773899

Asadu, C. (2019). Chatham House: $582bn stolen from Nigeria since independence. The Cable, https://www.thecable.ng/chatham-house-582bn-stolen-from- nigeria-since-independence

Ayitogo, N., (2022). Insecurity: Armed persons kill 65 Nigerian police officers, 85 soldiers in first half 2022. *Premium Times*.https://www.premiumtimesng.com/ news/headlines/545989-insecurity-armed-persons-kill-65-nigerian-police- officers-85-soldiers-in-first-half-2022.html

Ayodeji, O, Olutayo A., Abimbola, A and Saheed, A (2018) Security Challenges and Management in Modern Nigeria, UK: Cambridge Scholars Publishing

Benjamin R add. The Tragedy of Afghanistan is one of Ambition, not Action.https://www.resetdoc.org/story/the-tragedy-of-afghanistan is one-of-ambition-not- action/

Brigadier PS Mann, SM, VSM (Rtd). Conduct of Junior Leaders in Counter Insurgency Operations A Decisive Factor. https://usiofindia.org /publication/

usi-journal/conduct-of-junior-leaders-in-counter-insurgency-operations-a-decisive-factor/

Bwari attack; soldiers raid Abuja forests, arrests terrorists, destroy bandit scamps, seize weapons, others https://www.sunnewsonline.com/bwari-attack-soldiers- raid-abuja-forests-arrests-terrorists-destroy-bandits-camps-seize-weapons- others/

Bawden, C.R., entry in Britannica, Gengh is Khan, Mongo Ruler, last updated 18 October 2022

Bennet, R., (2022) Quotein Good reads at www.goodreads.com assessed 3 November 2022

Berkowitz, L. (1989). Frustration-aggression hypothesis: Examination and reformulation. Psychological Bulletin, 106 (1), 59–73.doi:10.1037/0033-2909.106.1.59

Berkowitz, L. (1989). Frustration-aggression hypothesis: Examination and reformulation. Psychological Bulletin, 106 (1), 59–73.doi:10.1037/0033-2909.106.1.59

Boulding, K.E. (1956). General systemstheory: The skeleton of science. Management Science, 2(3), 197–208.doi:10.1287/mnsc.2.3.197

Breuer, J., & Elson, M. (2016). The frustration–aggression hypothesis according to Berkowitz (1989).Figshare.doi:10.6084/m9.figshare.4224270.v2

Beland, D. (2005). The Political Construction of Collective Insecurity: From Moral Panic to Blame Avoidance and Organized Irresponsibility, Center for European Studies Working Paper Series 126.

Border Migration between Nigeria and Her Francophone Neighbours, Internal Journal of social Science Tomorrow, Vol. 1, No. 3.

Burton, J., (1997), Violence Experienced: The Source of Conflict, Violence and Crime and Their Prevention, New York: Manchester University Press

BBC News, (2015). Who are Nigeria's boko haram islamists? http://www.bbc.com/ news/world-africa-13809501

Blair, D. (2015). Boko Haram is now amini-IslamicState, withitsownterritory.*Telegraph*.http://www.telegraph.co.uk/news/worldnews/africaandindianocean/nigeria/11337722/Boko-Haram-is-now-a- mini-Islamic-State-with-its-own-territory.html

Bala Usman, Y. (1979). *Studies in the History of Sokoto Caliphate: the Sokoto Seminar paper, Department of History, Ahmadu Bello University.*

Bukarti, A.B., (2022). Democracy under threat: why the security risks to Nigeria's 2023 elections must not be overlooked. London: Tony Blair Institute for Global Change.

Canada: Immigration and Refugee Board of Canada, (1999,November8). Nigeria: Societal and government reaction to cultactivities. https://www.refworld.org/ docid/3ae6ad530.html

Chime, V. (2022). Insight: How security situation in south-east degenerated in one year. *The Cable*, https://www.thecable.ng/insight-how-security-situation-in- south-east-degenerated-in-one-year/amp

Center for Democracy. (2020). Stakeholders' Dialogue on Government Approaches to Managing Defecting Violent Extremists. A Policy Brief, Abuja, CDD.

Commission NorthEast Development.(2022,1025). *About Us*. Retrieved from https://nedc.gov.ng/about-us/

Charles T. (n.d.). *Great Man Theory*. Classman, B. (2008). *Caring (Character Counts) (The six Pillars of Character).Bearing Books*.

Caslen R. (2022,1026). *"Forging a Comprehensive Approach to Counter in surgency Operations"*.https://cco.ndu.edu/Portals/96/Documents/prism/ prism_2-3/Prism_3-14_Caslen-Louden.pdf,

CEIC Report https://www.ceicdata.com/en/indicator/nigeria/crude-oil-production Cronin, A.K. (2004). Behindthecurve: Globalization and international terrorism,*International Security*, 27(3),30–58.

Dayo, B. (n.d.). How "Japa" became the Nigerian buzzword for emigration.Okayafrica,https://www.okayafrica.com/emigration-in-nigeria-japa/

Dada, P., (2021) .Insecurity increases number of orphans, widows in Nigeria—Osinbajo. *Punch*,https://punchng.com/insecurity-increases-number-of- orphans-widows-in-nigeria-osinbajo/

Daily Trust, (2022).75% of Nigeria's budget lost to corruption–forensicexperts.https://dailytrust.com/75-of-nigerias-budget-lost-to-corruption-forensic-experts/ Denoeux, G. & Carter, L (2009), Guidetothedriversofextremism.US:UnitedStates Agencyfor International Development.

Department of Defense (2001). *Dictionaryofmilitary and associated terms*. Joint Publication 1-02 Washington, D.C.

Developing Countries: An Overview. In P.Keefor & N. Loayza (eds). Terrorism, Economic Development and Political Openness. Cambridge; Cambridge University Press

DoD Dictionary version .(2008).url:http://www.dtic.mil/doctrine/jel/doddict/

Dollard, J. ,Miller, N.E. ,Doob, L.W., Mowrer, O.H., & Sears, R.R. (1939). Frustration and aggression. New Haven, CT: Yale University Press

Duerksen, M. (2021). Nigeria's diverse security threats. *ACSS Spotlight.* https:// africacenter.org/spotlight/nigeria-diverse-security-threats/

Duyile cited in Adamu, Yusuf M (2007), "Print and Broadcast Media in Northern Nigeria" www.kanoonline.com

Eme O.I. and Anyadike, N (2013) SECURITY CHALLENGES AND SECURITY VOTES IN NIGERIA, 2008-2013, Kuwait Chapter of Arabian Journal of Business and Management Review, Vol. 2, no. 8. 10-32

Ekekwe, N. (2022). Why most Nigerians remain poor despite Nigeria earning$742billionin 21 years from oil.Tekedia,https://www.tekedia.com/ why-most- nigerians-remain-poor-despite-nigeria-earning-742-billion-in-21-years-from-oil/

European Commission's Expert Groupon Violent Radicalisation. (2008). *Radicalisation processes leading to acts of terrorism.* A Concise Report submitted to the European Commission, 15 May, p.6.

France24, (2020). Jihadists in northeast Nigeria execute five abducted humanitarian workers.https://www.france24.com/en/20200722-jihadists-northeastern- nigeria-execute-abducted-humanitarian-workers-islamic-state

FederalGovernmentofNigeria.(2016).*NationalCouterTerrorismStrategy..AbujaONSA.* Federal Ministry of Humanitarian Affairs. (2022,1019). *About the Ministry.*Retrieved from https://www.fmhds.gov.ng/about-fmhds/

Freedman, L (1998) "International Security: Changing Targets; Foreign Policy, 110:48- 63.

Garuba, (Ed); International Peace and Security: The Nigerian Contribution. Lagos, Gabumo press.

Gaffey,C.(2016).Bokoharamsplinterswithisisoverchildsuicidebombers:USgeneral.*Newsweek.*http ://europe.newsweek.com/boko-haram-splinters-isis-over-child-suicide-bombers- us-general-473004

Galvin, John R., "What's the Matter with BeingaS trategist?" Parameters, Winter 2010.

General of the Army Douglas MacArthur, (1933), Annual Report of the Chief of Staff of the United States Army

George, L. (2019). Oil theft cost Nigeria 22 million barrels in first half—NNPC.*Reuters.*https://af.reuters.com/article/idAFKCN1VK1NT-OZATP

Godwin, A. (2020). Operation Safe Corridor: A Global Non-Kinetic Model. Nigerian Defence Magazine, First Edition, Abuja, DHQ. 19-25.

Group International Crisis. (2021) *An Exit from Boko Haram? Assessing Nigeria's Operation Safe Corridor*. Brussel, ICG.

Godwin, A. (2021). Cultists behead disbanded vigilante leader in Rivers, severe body Port Harcourt. *Guardian*. https://guardian.ng/news/cultists-behead- disbanded-vigilante-leader-in-rivers-severe-body/

Global Security.org, (n.d). Islamic State West Africa Province (ISWAP). https:// www.globalsecurity.org/military/world/para/iswap.htm

Greer, J (2018), "Training: The Foundation for Success in Combat" The Heritage Foundation, www.heritage.org/military

Gurr, T. 1970. Why Men Rebel. Centre of International Studies. Princeton University Press .NewJersey

Huntington, S., (1957). The Soldier and the State: The Theory and Politics of Civil- Military Relations, Belknap Press.

Harbison F., (1973),. "Pattonand Military Leadership", Definition of Leadership, New York: Oxford University Press, .P2. Cited in Yahaya F. ,Military Strategic Leadership: My Perspective, being COAS Lecture delivered to Nigerian Air Force War College Course 8/2022.

Hammes, T. X. (2005). Why study small wars? *Small Wars Journal*, 1.

Harris-Hogan, S., Barrelle, K., & Zammit, A. (2016). What is countering violent extremism? *Exploring CVE policy and practice in Australia, Behavioural Sciences of Terrorism and Political Aggression*, 8 (1), 6-24.

Hanafi, A. (2021). How we killed 10 girls for fortification rituals, attacked Imo prison, police stations ESN commander.*Punch*,https://punchng.com/ how-we- killed-10-girls-for-fortification-rituals-attacked-imo-prison-police-stations-esn- commander/

Haruna, A. (2022). More unattended children join Borno IDP camps but provision saren't enough.Humangle,https://humanglemedia.com/more-unattended- children-join-borno-idp-camps-but-provisions-arent-enough/

Hassan, I. (2018). From Boko to Biafa: How insecurity willaffect Nigeria'selections.*AfricanArgument*.https://africanarguments.org/ 2018/12/boko-biafra-nigeria-insecurity-2019-elections/

HistoricalSurveyofPeopleofNorthernNigeriaandtheirNeighborsfromtheperiodo f MegaChad."Localities,7:9–https//.www.army.mil,ng.2023.

Hill, M. (2009). *The Spread of Islam in West Africa: Containment, Mixingan Reform from Eight to Twentieth Century, Standard Programon International and Cross-CulturalEducation.*

HumanRightsWatch,14March,(2014),http://www.hrw.org/news/2014/03/14/nigeria- boko-haram-attacks-cause-humanitarian-crisis

Idris, H. (2016,September11). Shekau Vs Barnawi: The battle for boko haram's soul .*Daily Trust*.http://www.dailytrust.com.ng/news/news/shekau-vs- barnawi-the-battle-for-boko-haram-s-soul/162159.html

Igbuzor, O. (2011). Peace and Security Education: A Critical Factor for Sustainable Peace and National Development, International Journal of Peace and Development Studies Vol.2(1),1-7,January

Ighodalo A., (2012). Electioncrisis, liberal democracy and national security in Nigeria's Fourth Republic. British Journal of Arts and Social Sciences, 10 (11), 163- 174

Ikejiaku, B. (2009). The Concept' Poverty' Towards Understanding intheContextofDevelopingCountries'PovertyquaPoverty':Withsome ComparativeEvidenceon

Ike-Muonso, M (2021) A history of insecurity in Nigeria. https://www.businessamlive.com/a-history-of-insecurity-in-nigeria/

Imobighe, T.A (1990)" Doctrine for and Threats to Internal Security" in A. E Ekoko and M.A

Vogt (Eds) Nigerian Defence Policy: Issues and Problems, Lagos: Malt House PressIroanusi,Q.(2022).Nigerianswantnextpresidenttoprioritisesecurity.PremiumTimes,https://www.premiumtimesng.com/news/headlines/565498-2023-nigerians-want-next-president-to-prioritise-security.html

Isamotu, I. (2022).80%ofmilitarypersonnelperformingpolicedutiesin36states–CDS.DailyTrust,https://dailytrust.com/80-of-military-personnel-performing- police-duties-in-36-states-cds/

Irabor, LEO. (2022). *Counter Terrorism and Counter Insurgency: Utilising the Whole of Society Approach*. Abuja, DHQ.

Institute for Economics and Peace. (2015). *Globalterrorism index 2015: Measuring and understanding the impact of terrorism*. Brussels, IEP.

Johnson, R. (2013) .*A Maninthe Making:Strategies to Help Your Son Succeed in Life"*.

Kissinger H. Leadership: Six Studies in World Strategy, New York, Penguin Press, 2022, p. 416.

Kalambe. (2019). *Non-Kinetic Efforts in Counter Insurgency Operations in the North Eas t Region of Nigeria*. NDC Course 27 Participant Research Project Submitted to the National Defence College Abuja, Nigeria.

Kankara, A.I. (2010). "Forestsas Catalyst for Industrial Growth: Their Distribution and Disappearances in Katsina State http://www.taskarmammanshata.blogspot.com.

Koontz, H., O'donnell, C. and Weihrich, H. (1986) Essentials of Management. 4th Edition, McGraw Hill International, Singapore.

Lai, Cand Huili, S (2017). Systems Theory. John Wiley & Sons, Inc.

Leach, B. (2021). *Born Leaders versus Made Leaders, Are Leaders Bornor Trained? 15 Min Read..*

Liman, H.M. (2022,). Secondary School classmate of Faruk Yahaya, Interview by the Team, Sokoto.

Lubabatu, H. (2022). Eldersister of Faruk Yahaya. Interview by the Team, Sifawa. Lobe, J. (2012,June21). Nigeria: Three boko haram leader sput on US terrorism list. *Inter Press Service*.http://www.ipsnews.net/2012/06/nigeria-three-boko-haram-leaders-put-on-u-s-terrorism-list/

Mahmood, O. (2016). Faction friction: Rebranded boko haram threatens west Africa.*HIS Jane's Intelligence Review*, 28 (1),29.

Makama, Z. (2022, December 12). Clash of terrorists: Boko Haram element stake to their heels as ISWAP fighters storm camp in Samb is a. *Zagazola.org*, https://zagazola.org/index.php/breaking-news-edit/clash-of-terrorists-boko-haram-elements-take-to-their-heels-as-iswap-fighters-storm-camp-in-sambisa Mamu, T. (2012,June2). Another islamic sect emerges…to counter boko haram. *Desertherald*.http://desertherald.com/?p =1526#more

Mneimneh, H. (2009). Takfirism, critical threats.https://www.criticalthreats.org/ analysis/takfirism

Moore, R.S. (2007). *The basis of counter insurgency*. Joint Urban Operations Office, US Joint Forces Command.

Maina, J. (2022). *"The Russian Invasion show show Digital Technologie shave become Involved in All Aspects of War"*, The Conversation, Online Academic Journal,. Retricvcdfromhttps://theconversation.com/the-russian- invasion-shows-how-digital-technologies have become-involved-in-

Maddern, S. (2021). *Melting Pot Theory, Wiley Online Library, DOI:10.1002/ 9781444351071.wbeghm359.*

Mark, B. and Crawford, Y (2002), Beyond State Crisis (Washington DC: Woodrow Wilson Center Press, 2002)

Maslow, A. (1970) Motivation and Personality. Harper & Row Publishers Inc., New York.

Miller, N.E., Sears, R.R., Mowrer, O.H., Doob, L.W.,& Dollard, J. (1941). I. The frustration-aggression hypothesis. Psychological Review, 48(4),337–342.doi:10.1037/h0055861

Mala Babs (1984)' Religious Pluralism in Nigeria: The way out and Factors Favouring it' in Oseni, 2:1 and Mala B. (Ed) Religion, Peace and Unity in Nigeria. Ibadan: NASR.

McNamara, R. (1968), The Essence of Security, London: Harper and Row. Sustainable Peace in Nigeria's Delta, A presentation at the ceremony in honour of Ms Ibiba Don Pedro, the Winner of the 2003 CNN African Journalist of the Year Award at the Lambeth Town Council Building, London, Saturday 18 October.

Manual, B.A. (2009). Countering Insurgency. London, MOD.

Millett, Allan R., Williamson Murray, and Kenneth H. Watman. "The Effectiveness of Military Organizations." International Security 11, no.1 (1986):3771. https:/ /doi.org/10.2307/2538875.https://www.oxfordreference.com

Nigeria A2Z, https://www.nigeriaa2z.com/2009/12/19/agwai-bows-out-of-the- military/accessed14January2023.

Naku, D. (2022,7 March). Kidnapper snow harvest, sell victims' organs–Rivers survivor. Punch, https://punchng.com/kidnappers-now-harvest-sell-victims- organs-rivers-survivor/

National Bureau of Statistics, (2022). *Nigeria multi dimensional poverty index:* Abuja, NBS

Nextier SPD.(2018). Wild, wildnorth-west. *Nextier SPD Policy Weekly*, 1(15),1-2. Nextier SPD. (2021,November5). Addressing secession agitations. Nextier SPD.https://nextierspd.com/addressing-secession-agitations/

Nick Reynolds. Learning Tactical and Operational Combat Lessons for High-End Warfighting from Counter insurgency.https://www.tandfonline.com/ doi/abs/ 10.1080/03071847.2019.1700686?journalCode=rusi20

Nigerian Army Doctrine 2022. The Role of Field Artillery in Counterinsurgency Operations.https://apps.dtic.mil/sti/pdfs/ADA463835.pdf

Nigerian Defence Academy "Our History" www.nda.edu.ng

Non-Kinetic/Counterinsurgency Operations A Study in Command. https:// info.publicintelligence.net/USMC-NonKineticCOIN.pdf

Njoku, L., & Ogugbuaja, C. (2021,May1). Inside story of arson, killings as unknown gunmen terrorise Southeast.*Guardian.* https://guardian.ng/saturday-magazine/cover/inside-story-of-arson-killings-as-unknown-gunmen-terrorise-southeast/

Nwangwu, C., Onuoha, F.C., Nwosu, B., & Ezeibe, C.(2020).The political economy of Biafra separatism and post-war Igbonationalism in Nigeria. *African Affairs*, 119(477),526-551.

Nwaogu, N.R., Weli, V., & Mbee, M.D. (2019). Analysis of effectiveness of amnesty program as a response tool in containment of the impact of" cult related "activities in Niger delta region. *As in Research Journal of Arts & Social Sciences*, 9(4),1-16.

Nasi, J. (2020). Ansaru militant group claims responsibility for the attack on Yobe emir. *The Cable*. https://www.thecable.ng/militant-group-claims-responsibility- for-attack-on-yobe-emir

New Architecture for Regional Security in Africa: Perspectives on Counter- Terrorism and Counter-Insurgency in the Lake Chad Basin. Lexington Books, Lanham, impress.

Nwabufo, F. (2016). DSS' captures'Al-Barnawi's' deputy', Danhajiya. *The Cable*. https://www.thecable.ng/iran-iraq-behind-shiia-sect-says-dss-official

Obi, C., (1997). "Oil, Environmental Conflict and National Security in Nigeria: Ramifications of Ecology–Security Nexus for Subregional Peace, Arms Control, Disarmament, and InternationalSecurity,"OccasionalPaper, <https://

Oche,M.(2022,71).TheGuardianNewspaper.

Ochoche,S.A(1997)"Changing Concept of International Peace and Security" in Chris A.

Odeniyi,S. (2022,August2). 7,222 killed,3,823abductedinsevenmonths–Report.Punch,https://punchng.com/7222-killed-3823-abducted-in-seven-months-report/

Odita, S. (2020). We were recruited in Mosques, trained in Libya–Suspected terrorists confess", *Guardian*.https://guardian.ng/news/we-were-recruited-in-mosques- trained-in-libya-suspected-terrorists-confess/amp/

Ogbodo A (2017). Open Letterto Tukur Buratai in The People's Soldier: A Collection of Articles on Lt Gen Tukur Yusuf Buratai, compiled by Sam Odemni, Kuru, National Institute Press, p.147.

Ogbeche, C. (2016,November23). 14cops, 21 others nabbed for robbery, kidnapping.Blueprint, https://www.blueprint.ng/14-cops-21-others-nabbed-for-robbery- kidnapping/

Ogune, M. (2021, March 26). Herder-farmer crisis displaces over 300,000 Nigerians. https://guardian.ng/news/herder-farmer-crisis-displaces-over-300000-nigerians/

Ogunleye, G.O., Adewale, O.S.,Alese B.K. and Ogunde, A.O. (2011). A Computer- Based Security Framework for Crime Prevention in Nigeria, A Paper presented at the 10th international conference of the Nigeria computer society held from July 25th-29th

Ojeme, V.& Odiniya,R.(2013,June19). Nigeria has over 1,499 illegal entry routesinterior minister. *Vanguard*,http://www.vanguardngr.com/2013/06/nigeria-has- over-1499-illegal-entry-routes-interior-minister

Ojewale, O. & OnuohaF.C.(2022,May3).Violence in Nigeria's south-east demands a holistic response. ISS Today, https://issafrica.org/iss-today/violence-in- nigerias-south-east-demands-a-holistic-response

Okafor, T. (2021,September 27). Insecurity costs Nigeria $40.6bn worth of investments in 1 year. Businessday, https://businessday.ng/business-economy/ article/insecurity-costs-nigeria-40-6bn-worth-of-investments-in-1-year/

Okoli A.C., & Atelhe, G.A. (2014). Nomads Against Natives: A Political Ecology of Herder/Farmer Conflicts in Nasarawa state, Nigeria. American Journal of Contemporary Research, 4(2), 76–88.

Okoli, A.C. (2016). Petroleum Pipeline Vandalism and National Security in Nigeria, 2001–2012. Ph.D. thesis submitted to the School of Post-graduate Studies, Nigerian Defence Academy, Kaduna (August).

Okoli, A.C. and Atelhe, G.A., (2014) Nomad saga instnatives: Apolitical ecology of herder/farmer conflicts in Nasarawa State, Nigeria. American International Journal of Contemporary Research, 4(2),76–88,

Olawoyin, K.W., Akinrinde, O.O., & Irabor, P.O. (2021). The multinational joint task force and Nigerian counter-terrorism operations in the lake Chad region. *The Copernicus Journal of Political Studies, 1,119.*

Olugbode, M. (2020, May 25). Military killed 1,015 boko haram terrorists in two months, says Buratai. *Thisday*.https://www.thisdaylive.com/index.php/2020/05/25/military-killed-1015-boko-haram-terrorists-in-two-months-says-buratai/ Onuoha, F.C. (2010). The Islamist challenge: Nigeria's boko haram crisis explained.

African Security Review,19(2),54-67.

Onuoha, F.C. (2013) .*Jama'atu Ansarul Musilimina FiBiladisSudan: Nigeria's evolving terrorist group*. AlJazeera Centre for Studies.

Onuoha, F.C. (2020). Dilemma of Voluntary Surrender to State Security Forces by Boko Haram Recruits in Nigeria, *African Journal of Terrorism and Insurgency Research (AJoTIR)*,1(1),199-218.

ONSA, (2014). *The National Counter-Terrorism Strategy (NACTEST)*. Abuja: ONSA,

ONSA, (2019).*National Security Strategy*. Abuja: ONSA.

Owete, F. (2017, July 29). ANALYSIS: How Nigerian military repeatedly claimed it killed Boko Haram leader, Abubakar Shekau. *Premium Times*, https://www.premiumtimesng.com/news/headlines/238515-analysis-nigerian-military- repeatedly-claimed-killed-boko-haram-leader-abubakar-shekau.html

Omonobi, K. (2022,May13). Army nabs 3 soldiers over sale of missing ammunition to bandits.Vanguard,https://www.vanguardngr.com/2022/0 5/army-nabs-3- soldiers-over-sale-of-missing-ammunition-to-bandits/

Onuoha, F.C.(2021,July21).Nigeria's ambitious new maritime security project must avoid old traps. The Conversation, https://theconversation.c om/nigerias-ambitious-new-maritime-security-project-must-avoid-old-traps-163989

Onuoha, F.C & Akogwu J.C (2022a). Armednon-state actors in Nigeria
And challenges of peace building in a fragile state.In Bakut, B.T., Gwaza, P.A., Okafor, G.I., and Ikelionwu, N.I (eds.). *Towards sustainable peace and security in Nigeria* (Abuja:Institute for Peace and Conflict Resolution, 2022). pp. 130-161.

Onuoha, F.C & Akogwu J.C (2022b). From terrorism to banditry: Mass abductions of school children in Nigeria. *ConflictTrends*,(1):37-45.

Onuoha F.C, Iroezumuo, E.B and Onuoha, A.R. (2022). Policing oil theft in Nigeria's Niger Delta region. In Usman A. Tarand Dawud M. Dawud. (eds.) *Policing criminality and insurgency in africa: perspective sonth echanging wave of law enforcement*. (US: Rowman & Littlefield, 2022). pp.251-271.

Onuoha F.C., Okafor J.C., & Femi-Adedayo O.O. (2021. "Nigeria: Militancy, insurgency and the proliferation of small arms and light weapon", in Tar U.A., Onwurah C.P. (eds) *The Palgrave handbook of small arms and conflicts in Africa*. (London: Palgrave Macmillan, 2021), pp.777-802

Onuoha, F.C. & Okolie-Osemene, J. (2019). The evolving threat of kidnapping for ransom in Nigeria. in Oshita O., AlumonaI., Onuoha F.C (eds) *Internal security management in Nigeria: Perspectives, challenges and lessons*. Singapore: Palgrave Macmillan.

Onuoha, F.C. & Oyewole, S. (2018). Anatomy of Boko Haram: The rise and decline of a violent group in Nigeria. AlJazeera Centre for Studies.

O'Neill, B.E. (1990) *Insurgency & terrorism: Inside modern revolutionary warfare*. Brassey, p.13.

Orhero, A.J (2020) Human Security: The Key to Enduring National Security In Nigeria, Journal of Public Administration, Financeand Law. Issue 17/ (470- 484)

Orji, S. (2019, May 15). Nigeria farmers form vigilante groups to confront bandits. *Aljazeera,* https://www.aljazeera.com/indepth/features/nigeria-farmers-form- vigilante-groups-confront-bandits-190514064544456.html

Osaghae, E.E. (2011). The Crippled Giant: Nigeria since Independence. London: Hurst

Osinowo A Aetal. Iconic Soldierand peacemaker: A Biography of Martin Luther Agwai, Lagos: May University Press Limited for National Defence College, 2019, p.197.

Oyero, K. (2022,January5). Finally, F G declares bandits as terrorists. *Punch*, https://punchng.com/breaking-finally-fg-declares-bandits-as-terrorists/

Ozoigbo, B.I (2019) Insecurity in Nigeria: Genesis, Consequences and Panacea.

European Journal of Social Science Studies, Vol. 4, Issue 4.

Peterside, D. (2021,May10) The scourge of ritual killings in Nigeria. *Premium Times,* https://www.premiumtimesng.com/opinion/460583-the-scourge-of-ritual- killings-in-nigeria-by-dakuku-peterside.html

Peskowitz, A. Information Operations on the Counterinsurgency Battlefield. https://smallwarsjournal.com/jrnl/art/information-operations-on-the- counterinsurgency-battlefield.

Pratt, S. (2010).What is the difference between counter-insurgency and counter- terrorism?",E-International Relations, 2010, http://www.e-ir.info/2010/12/20/ the-european-union-power-and-ethical-goals/

Presidential Committee of North East Initiative. (2016). *Rebuilding the North East: The Buhari Plan. VolumeI, Emergency Humanitarian Assistance Social Stabilization and Protection Early Recovery, Initiatives Strategies and Implementation Frameworks. Maidi.*

Reider ,B.J. (2014,October28). External Support to Insurgencies. https://smallwarsjournal.com/jrnl/art/external-support-to-insurgencies.

Rotberg, R. & Campbell, J. (2021,May7). Nigeria is a failed state: The first step to restoring stability and security is recognizing that the government has lost control. https://foreignpolicy.com/2021/05/27/nigeria-is-a-failed-state/

Robert R. (2003) State Failure and State Weakness in a Time of Terror (Washington D.C.: Brookings Institution Press 2003);

Robert R. (2004) When States Fail: Causes and Consequences (Princeton: Princeton University Press, 2004);

Robert, I.R (2016) Failed States, Collapsed States, Rosemary I. Okolie-Osemene (2019) A Historical Perspective of Nigeria's Internal Security Since 1999. nbook: Internal Security Management in Nigeria (pp.69- 82).

Sampson, I.T. and Onuoha, F.C. (2011). 'Forcing the Horse to Drinkor Making it Realise its Thirst'? Understanding the Enactment of Anti-Terrorism Legislation (ATL) in Nigeria, Perspective on Terrorism, Vol. 5, No. 3-4.

Sandler, T.&W. Enders. 2008. Economic Consequences of Terrorism in Developing and Sadiq, L. (2021, October 6). How terrorists who declared cease fire on abductions gunneddown' 30 bandits' in Kaduna, *Daily Trust*. https://dailytrust.com/how-terrorists-who-declared-ceasefire-on-abductions-gunned- down-30-bandits-in-kaduna.

Sadiq, L., & Yaba, M.I. (2022, May 6). Ansaru in massive recruitment in Kaduna, distributes' Sallah Gifts', *Daily Trust*. https://dailytrust.com/ansaru-in-massive- recruitment-in-kaduna-distributes-sallah-gifts

Sahara Reporters. (2021, June 26). Boko Haram, ISWA Preunite to work together in new video, appoint Al-khuraishias' Leadero fall Muslims. http://saharareporters.com/2021/06/26/boko-haram-iswap-reunite-work-together- new-video-appoint-al-khuraishi-leader-all-muslims

Salkida, A. (2021,May21). What Shekau's death means for security in Nigeria, Lake Chad. Hum Angle, https://humanglemedia.com/what-shekaus-death- means-for-security-in-nigeria-lake-chad/

Sampson, IT, & Onuoha, FC, (2011). Forcing the Horseto Drinkor Making it Realizeits Thirst'? Understanding the Enactment of Anti-Terrorism Legislation (ATL) in Nigeria. *Perspectives on Terrorism*, 5(3-4),33-49.

Samuel, M. (2019,July 10). Economics of terrorism in Lake Chad Basin. *ISS Today*.https://issafrica.org/amp/iss-today/economics-of-terrorism-in-lake-chad-basin Sasu, D.D. (2022, June 28). Terrorism in Nigeria-statistics & facts,statista.https://www.statista.com/topics/7396/terrorism-in-nigeria/#dossierKeyfigures Shuaib, S. (2012, June 3). New group emerges, vows to avenge killing of Muslims.*Leadership*.

Simon, J.D. (1994). *The terrorist trap*, Bloomington, in, USA: Indiana University Press. Terrorism Research. Differences between Terrorism and Insurgency" http://www.terrorism-research.com/insurgency/

Sabiu, M. (2021, April 13).30,000 bandits setup 100 camps in the north. Tribune. https://tribuneonlineng.com/30000-bandits-set-up-100-camps-in-the-north/

Sanni, K. (2022). Nigeria records drop in sea robberies, piracy attacks– Report. *Premium Times*, https://www.premiumtimesng.com/news/top-news/544222-nigeria-records-drop-in-sea-robberies-piracy-attacks-report.html

SBM Intelligence (2020) 'The economics of the kidnap industry in Nigeria, Lagos. https://www.sbmintel.com/wp- content/uploads /2020/05/202005_Nigeria- Kidnap.pdf

SBM Intelligence (2022) 'The economics of Nigeria's kidnap industry,Lagos.https://www.sbmintel.com/wp- content/uploads /2022/08/202208_The-economics-of- Nigerias-kidnap-industry.pdf

Stakeholder Democracy Network (2020). *A proposed model for disarmament, demobilisation, rehabilitation, and reintegration of cult gang members in the Niger Delta*. Port Harcourt: SDN.

Sifawa, A. (2014). *Sifawainthe History of the 19th Century of Hausaland, Centre of Islamic Studies, Usmanu Danfodiyo University*.

Shehu Mohammed. (2022). *Chairman Bodinga LGA, personal communication*, 12 December.

Salihu Mand Yakubu, Y. (2021). Beyond the Battlefields, Non-Militarized Approach and Management of Armed Conflict in Nigeria: Takeaways from Operation Safe Corridor. African Journal of Peace and Conflict Studies, Vol. 10 No1,

frican Journal of Peace and Conflict Studies, 123-145.

Shafa BM. (2021). The Strategic Objective of Operation Safe Corridor is Being Achieved. Nigerian Defence Magazine, First Edition, Abuja, DHQ. *Nigerian Defence Magazine*, 71-76.

Trimingham, S. (1962). *History of IslaminWestAfrica.NewYork: Oxford University Press*.

The Cable. (2022,1023).*559ex-Boko Haram Fighters Graduate from FG's Rehabilitation Programme*. Retrievedfromhttps://www.thecable.ng/559-ex-boko-haram-fighters-graduate-from-fgs-rehabilitation-programme

The Jihadi Websites Monitoring Group, (2010).Periodic a review, March (2).

The US Joint Publications. (2014,October24). Counterterrorism. http://www.jcs.mil/ Portals/36/Documents/Doctrine/pubs/jp3_26.pdf

Tar U.A (2020) Introduction: The Frontiers of Small Arms Proliferation and Conflicts in Africain U.A. Tarand C.P. Onwurah (eds.), The Palgrave Hand book of Small Arms and Conflicts in Africa, https://doi.org/10.1007/978-3-030-62183- 4_2

Tar U. A and Adejoh, S. (2017) Military Alliance and Counter Terrorism in Sub Saharan Africa: Multinational Joint Task Force in perspectives. Covenant Journal of Politics and International affairs Vol. 5. N0. 2, pp1-12.

Tar, A.U and Adejoh, S (2021) The Theoretical Parameter for the Proliferation and Regulation of Small Arms and Light Weapons in Africain Tar, A. U and Onwurah, C.P (eds) Palgrave Handbook of Small Arms and Conflicts in Africa. Switzerland: Palgrave Macmillan

Tar, U.A and Safana, Y.I (2021) Forests, Ungoverned Spaces and the Challenge of Small Arms and Light Weapons Proliferation in Africa Tar, A.U and Onwurah,

C.P (eds) Palgrave Handbook of Small Arms and Conflicts in Africa. Switzerland: Palgrave Macmillan.

Tar, U.A. (2009) The Politics of Neoliberal Democracy in Africa: Stateand Civil Society in Nigeria. London/NewYork: I.B.Tauris.

Tar, U.A. and Shettima, A.B. (2010) Endangered Democracy? The Struggle over Secularism and its Implications for Politics and Democracy in Nigeria. Uppsala: Nordisk a Afrika institutet.

Tyoden, S.G. (2005). "Stateand Security in Nigeria's Fourth Republic". Iin A.T Ganaand Y.B

Tacticsin Counterinsurgency. https://irp.fas.org/doddir/army/fmi3-24-2.pdf Teaching the Intelligence Process: The Killing of Bin Laden as a Case Studyhttps://digitalcommons.usf.edu/cgi/viewcontent.cgi?article=1304&context=jss Terror attacks in Jammu: Cellphone intercepts link militants to Pakistan, say top officials. https://www.hindustantimes.com/india-news/terror-attacks-in-jammu-cell-phone-intercepts-link-militants-to-pakistan-say-top-officials/story- H9atG0cowDHS2hs47cSdcI.html

The Bin-Laden Operation: Tapping Human Intelligence https://worldview.stratfor.com/article/bin-laden-operation-tapping-human-intelligence

Tutu: The Slow Genocide Against the Rohingya.https://www.newsweek.com/tutu-low-genocide-against-rohingya-337104

US Drone Strike Kills al-Qaida Leaderin Kabul https://www.defense.gov/News/News-/us-drone-strike-kills-al-qaida-leader-in- kabul/

Ukraine conflict: How are drones being use https://www.bbc.com/news/world- 62225830 Omelle (Eds), Democratic RebirthinNigeria.vol1,1999-2003.Abuja:AFRIGOV.

United Nations Environment Programme, (2013), Annual Report. https://reliefweb.int/sites/reliefweb.int/files/resources/P%202013% 20Annual%20Report- 2014UNEP%20AR%202013-LR.pdf.

UNODC, (n.d). Nigeria, EU, UNOD Crenew commitment saga in stterrorism, unveil a follow- on project. UNODC, https://www.unodc .org/nigeria/en/nigeria—eu—unodc-renew-commitments-against-terrorism—unveil-a-follow-on-project.html

United States Department of Defence (2001). Joint Publication 1-02. Department of Defence Dictionary of Military and Associated Terms.

Uduu, O. (2022). In 2021, internal conflict accounted for 94% of displaced persons in Nigeria. Dataphyte, https://www.dataphyte.com/latest-reports/in-2021- internal-conflict-accounted-for-94-of-displaced-persons-in-nigeria/

US Army Doctrine for Command. (2022). *Control, Communications, and Computer(C4) Systems Support to Joint Operations, 1995accessed26October.* https://www.hsdl.org/?view&did=3768,

US Army Joint Military Operations Historical. (2022,1026). https://www.jcs.mil/Portals/36/Documents/History/Monographs/JMO.pdf,accessed26Oct22.von Bertalanffy, L. (1951). General system theory; A new approach to unity of science. .Problems of general system theory. Human Biology, 23(4),302–312

WFP, (2022) .Hunger Hotspots: 4 countries face famine, UN report warns. https:// www.wfp.org/stories/hunger-hotspots-4-countries-face-famine-un-report- warns

World Bank Group, (2015) *North-East Nigeria Recovery and Peace Building Assessment: Synthesis Report.* Abuja: World Bank.

Ward law, Grant (1982). *Political Terrorism: Theory, Tactics and Counter- Measures* .London: Cambridge University Press.

Warner ,J., & Matfess, H. (2017). BokoHaram's operational profile in suicide bombings. In exploding stereotypes: the unexpected operational and demographic characteristics of Boko Haram's suicide bombers (pp.6–28). Combatting Terrorism Centre at West Point.

Weak States: Causes and Indicators. https://www.brookings.edu/wp-content/uploads/ 2016/07/statefailureandstateweaknessinatimeofterror_chapter.pdf

World Peace Foundation (n.d.) United Nations Missionin Sierra Leone (UNAMIL) Brief. African Politics, African Peace.

www.nairaland.com

Yusuf, I. (2019). *Winning the Hearts and Minds in Counter insurgency Operations: Operation Lafia Dolein Perspective. Abuja, NA Archive.*

Yahaya, F., (2021). My Vision, Lecture at the Armed Forces Command and Staff College Jaji,

Yahaya, F., (2022). COAS Vision, being a lecture presented at the Army War College Nigeria.

Yahaya, F., (2023) Interview with the Chief of Army Staff, held in February 2023

Zartman, W (1995) Collapsed States: The Disintegration and Restoration of Legitimate Authority (Boulder: Lynne Rienner)

Zenn, J. (2019). The return of Al-Qaeda's faction in Nigeria: What's going on in Zamfara? *Terrorism Monitor*, 17 (6),https://jamestown.org/program/the- return-of-al-qaedas-faction-in-nigeria-whats-going-on-in-zamfara/

Wesley K Clark, Concept of Modern Warfare, Oxford University Press, 2001, p. 20.

Personal Communication

Adamu,Y.S. Nigerian Immigration Service (NIS) Component Commander, Operation HADIN KAI, Interview by the Team in Maiduguri on 7 January 2023

Alhaji Abubakar Yahaya, Permanent Secretary, Sokoto Civil Service and elder brother of Lt Gen Faruk Yahaya, personal communication in Sokoto 12 December 2022.

Alhaji Haliru Mohammed Sifawa, Chief Imam of Sifawa, personal communication 11 December 2022.

Alhaji Sule Magaji.(2022).*childhood friend of COAS personal communication,12 December.*

Alhaji Shehu Samaila Suleiman, Galadima Rabah and secondary school mate of Lt Gen F Yahaya personal communication on 13 December 2022.

Alhaji Shehu Mohammed, Chairman, Bodinga LGA, Sokoto State, personal communication on 12 December 2022.

Alhaji Sule Magagi, Business man and Lt Gen F Yahaya childhood friend, personal communication 12 December 2022.

Alhaji Muhammad Buhari T, District Head of Sifawa, personal communication in Sifawa Sokoto State on 12 December 2022.

Alhaji Yusuf Barde, former Headmaster in Sifawa, personal communication on 11 December 2022

Alhaji Ibrahim Gidado, former Commissioner of Information, Sokoto State and secondary school mate of Lt Gen F Yahaya, personal communication 12 December 2022.

Fatima, H, eldersister of Faruk Yahaya, Interview by theTeam,Safawa. 2022.

Gidado. I. Secondary School classmate of Faruk Yahaya, Interview by the Team, Sokoto.

Mallam Aliyu Modi, Primary School classmate of Lt Gen F Yahaya, personal communication on 12 December 2022.Maj Gen AB Omozoje, Chief of Policy and Plans, Army Headquarters and NDA course mate of Lt Gen F Yahaya personal communication on 18 October 2022.

Maj Gen OA Akintade, Chief of Logistics, Army Headquarters and NDA course mate of Lt Gen F Yahaya, personal communication on 18 October 2022.

Maj Gen IM Yusuf, Commandant Nigerian Defence Academy and NDA course mate of Lt Gen F Yahaya personal communication 10 January 2023.

Maj Gen UU Bassey, former General Officer Commanding, 8 Division, Nigerian Army Sokoto, personal communication on 12 December 2022.

Maj Gen Lagbaja TA. *GOC 1 Div Kaduna, personal communication on 10 January 2023.*

Maj Gen AB Omozoje, 15 January 2023. Maj Gen MS Yusuf, 4 January 2023.

Maj Gen CG Musa, 20 January 2023. Maj Gen OT Akinjobi, 17 January 2023. Maj Gen M Kangye, 8 January 2023.

Malam, A.M. *COA Sprimary schoolmate, Personal Communication on 12 December* 2022.

Suleiman, S.S. Secondary School classmate of Faruk Yahaya, Interview by the Team, Sokoto 2022.

Yusuf Barde, *Head Teacher Primary School Sifawa 11 December* 2022.

Index

A

Abbe, Godwin, 95
Abdullahi, Adam, 25, 26, 27, 36, 40, 191, 241, 396, 397
Accra Initiative, 325, 326, 330
Action Against Hunger, 164
Adebayo, Adeyinka, 50
Ademulegun, Samuel A, 50
Adeniyi, Olusegun, 220
Adeosun, LO, 194, 205, 286
African Union Mission in Sudan, 175
Agwai, Martin Luther, 92, 96, 336, 410
Akintade, OA, 58, 277, 354, 355, 399, 416
Al Qaeda, 162, 188, 300, 310
Al Yaqut Media Center, 162
Al-Barnawi, Abu Musab, 159, 160, 162, 163, 164
Alkalawa, 18, 19
Amotekun, 126
Ansaru, 131, 151, 152, 159, 160, 161, 162, 163, 168, 407, 411
Armoured Personnel Carriers, 65, 354
Ashinze, N, 395
Attahiru, I, 98, 195, 209, 210, 347
Azazi, OA, 93

B

B Stabilini, 161
Barebaris of Borno, 17
Bassey, Wellington, 50, 53, 361, 416
Biafra Day, 134
Biafran Liberation Council, 134
Black Axe, 138
Black Brazier, 138

Boko Haram, 64, 65, 89, 96, 97, 98, 115, 119, 121, 124, 125, 126, 130, 131, 145, 146, 151, 152, 153, 156, 157, 158, 159, 160, 163, 165, 166, 167, 168, 169, 170, 171, 176, 177, 178, 179, 180, 181, 182, 183, 184, 185, 186, 187, 188, 191, 196, 197, 198, 201, 202, 203, 204, 206, 207, 208, 210, 217, 219, 222, 223, 224, 225, 226, 230, 234, 242, 243, 249, 250, 278, 282, 283, 310, 316, 321, 323, 325, 326, 327, 331, 336, 346, 352, 398, 400, 403, 405, 408, 409, 411, 412, 414
Bonaparte, Napoleon, 17, 277
Borno State, 17, 88, 98, 159, 164, 165, 176, 177, 180, 182, 185, 196, 199, 203, 228, 229, 231, 247, 248, 267, 284, 309, 317, 336, 383
British Special Boat Squad, 161
BudgitIT, 166
Buratai, TY, 93, 96, 97, 98, 195, 196, 230, 347, 407, 408

C

Carlyle, Thomas, 17
Chad Basin countries, 327
Chibok, 159, 191, 192, 215, 229
Civilian Joint Task Force, 200, 246
Civil-Military Affairs, 240, 244
Civil-Military Cooperations, 244
College of Nursing Sciences, 74
Combat Cross Country Competition, 357
Combat Net Radios, 292
Corbett, Julian, 263
Corruption Perception Index, 111
Counter-Terrorism Strategy, 126
Countering Violent Extremism, 167
Crocodile Smile, 324
Cross-border activities, 322
Crowe, Bill, 91

CTCOIN, 90, 152, 153, 166, 167, 168, 169, 171, 172, 173, 175, 181, 184, 187, 198, 200, 203, 204, 239, 240, 241, 243, 244, 245, 246, 247, 248, 249, 252, 255, 256, 257, 258, 259, 263, 264, 265, 267, 271, 272, 273, 274, 275, 276, 277, 278, 279, 280, 281, 284, 285, 287, 288, 289, 290, 291, 292, 294, 297, 298, 299, 300, 301, 302, 303, 306, 307, 308, 309, 310, 311, 312, 315, 316, 319, 322, 325, 326, 330, 331, 333, 335, 336, 370, 395, 396
Cyber Warfare Command, 94, 310

D

Dapchi, 164
Daughters of Jezebel, 138
Defence Industries Corporation of Nigeria, 317
Defence Research and Development Bureau, 94, 354
Defence Space Administration, 94, 127, 302, 311
Department of Civil-Military Relations, 244
Department of State Services, 151, 363, 399
Dikko, AM, 195, 196
Direct Short Service Commission, 353

E

Eastern Security Network, 134
Ebube-Agu, 126
ECOMOG, 83, 175
Effiong,, Philip, 50
El-Rufai, Nasir, 287
Ethan, OT, 187
Ezeoba, Dele Joseph, 346

F

Fatima Yahaya Foundation, 61, 72, 76, 77

Federal Ministry of Humanitarian Affairs, Disaster Management, and Social Development, 240, 243
Fifth Generation Warfare, 367
Fire Support Coordination Centre, 301
Fodiyo, Uthman ibn, 18, 19, 20, 21, 25, 26, 38, 45, 46
Force Readiness, 349, 353
Foreign Terrorist Organization, 316
Fourth Generation Warfare, 367
Fulfulde, 162

G

G5 – Sahel, 322
Gambo, Awwal Zubairu, 347
Gandhi, Mahatma, 17, 77
Gaskiya Ta fi Kwabo, 51
Giuliani, Rudolph, 175
Global Development Partners, 241
Global Islamic Media Front, 162
Global Peace Index, 165
Global Terrorism Index, 123, 327
Gowon, Yakubu, 37
Grand Commander of the Order of the Federal Republic, 69
Greenlanders, 138
Gulf of Guinea, 140, 326, 346, 347
Gwoza Hills, 183

H

Hadith, 27, 158
Hajiya Fatima Yahaya Foundation, 44, 72, 73, 74, 77
Hand Held Metal Detectors, 286
Harmattan, 23
Hitler, Adolf, 51
Holy Qur'an, 27
Human Development Index, 111, 269

I

Ibas, Ibok-Ete Ekwe, 347

Ihejirika, AO, 187, 347
Ijaw/ Itsekiri crisis, 85
Improvised Explosive Devices, 64, 97, 284
Indigenous Peoples of Biafra, 114
Infantry Corps, 56, 57, 207
Internal Security Operations, 129, 178, 244
Internally Displaced Persons, 125, 228, 267, 325
International Organisation for Migration, 249
Ironsi, Aguiyi, 50, 113
Islamic Jihad, 17, 18, 25
Islamic State of Syria, 331
Islamic State West African Province, 131, 152

J

Japa, 146, 401
Jibrin, Usman Oyibe, 346
Jonathan, Goodluck, 96, 152, 182, 187, 240, 242

K

Kanem Bornu Empire, 17
Kebbi Kingdom, 18
Kontagora, 37, 272
Kpou, Amatare, 395
Kuje Prison, 288
Kwara State, 36

L

Lake Chad Basin, 96, 126, 165, 175, 176, 226, 232, 249, 267, 320, 321, 326, 327, 329, 407, 411
Lincoln, Abraham, 17
Locust Beans, 24
Logistics Preparation of the Battlefield, 289

M

Maimalari, Hassan, 199
Mandara Mountains, 184, 210, 211, 214, 300
Manoeuvrist Approach to Warfare, 283
Migration Information and Data Analysis System, 323
Mijinyawa, Liman Muhammadu, 26, 28, 29, 33
Military Operations Other Than War, 244, 283
Minimah, Kenneth Tobia, 347
Mogadishu Battalion, 81
Mothercat Construction Company, 162
Movement for the Actualization of the Sovereign State of Biafra, 113, 134
Movement for the Emancipation of the Niger Delta, 137
Movement for the Survival of the Ogoni People, 137
Multinational Joint Task Force, 96, 126, 175, 214, 321, 326, 327, 412

N

National Commission for Persons with Disabilities, 243
National Commission for Refugees, Migrants, and IDPs, 240
National Correctional Service, 228
National Cyber Security Policy, 126
National Defence College, Abuja, 87, 395, 396, 397, 404, 410
National Directorate of Employment, 120
National Drug Law Enforcement Agency, 228
National Emergency Management Agency, 241
National Security and Civil Defence Corps, 363
National Space Research and Development Agency, 127, 311

Niger Delta, 64, 65, 85, 110, 112, 113, 115, 116, 119, 126, 130, 136, 137, 138, 139, 144, 241, 409, 412
Niger Delta Avengers, 137
Niger Delta Peoples Volunteer Forces, 137
Nigeria Customs Service, 209, 323
Nigeria Immigration Service, 209, 323
Nigerian Air Force, 50, 65, 88, 90, 94, 134, 164, 165, 177, 180, 198, 199, 205, 206, 211, 244, 278, 295, 297, 298, 301, 309, 345, 358, 359, 368, 403
Nigerian Army Depot, Zaria, 51
Nigerian Army Distinguished Service Star, 69
Nigerian Army Infantry Corps, 56
Nigerian Army Intelligence Corps, 305
Nigerian Army Resource Centre, 220, 357, 396
Nigerian Army Special Forces School, 197, 356
Nigerian Army Video Teleconferencing Operations Network, 293
Nigerian Civil War, 240
Nigerian Defence Academy, 41, 53, 381, 396, 406, 408, 416
Non-Military Security Mechanism, 245, 252
Non-State Armed Groups, 129
North East Development Commission, 240, 243
North East Schools Students Transfer Programme, 242

O

Obolo, OO, 395
Obstacle Crossing Competition, 357
Office of the National Security Adviser, 149, 151
Ogoni Clean Up Initiative, 65
Ombatse Militia Group, 182
Omoigui, FO, 236
Omozoje, AB, 58, 239, 415, 416

Onumajuru, EV, 395
Onuoha, Freedom C, 119, 131, 134, 136, 137, 140, 141, 144, 145, 151, 154, 157, 160, 165, 168, 171, 395, 407, 408, 409, 411
Op BOYONA, 168, 176, 181, 182, 183, 184, 185, 186, 187, 188, 239
Operation Thunder Strike, 324
Operation HADIN KAI, 209, 293, 348, 399, 415
Operation Safe Corridor, 171, 402, 403, 412
Organization for Economic Co-operation and Development, 332
Orienteering and Adventure Championship, 357

P

Passing Out Parade, 55
Patton, George, 79, 271
Peace Support Operations, 63, 86, 196, 356
Petroleum Industry Act, 65
Pink Ladies, 138
Presidential Amnesty Program, 241
Presidential Committee on the North East Initiatives, 240, 242
Proactive Responsive Doctrine, 283
Python Dance, 324

Q

Queen of the Battle, 56

R

Reconciliation, Rehabilitation and Reconstruction, 240
Regular Combatant Commission, 56, 62, 353
Rini, Tari Usman, 41
Royal Military Forces Training College, 49

S

Safe Schools Initiative, 242
Sahel countries, 264, 326, 329, 336, 337
Salafist Jihadism, 157
Sambisa Forest, 115, 170, 181, 183, 185, 192, 196, 200, 201, 202, 210, 211, 214, 223, 226, 265, 300, 306
Service Support Arms, 57
Shekau, Abubakar, 157, 159, 179, 316
Shodeinde, Ralph A, 50
Sifawa, 17, 18, 19, 20, 21, 22, 23, 24, 25, 26, 27, 28, 33, 35, 36, 37, 41, 42, 45, 46, 47, 51, 61, 71, 72, 74, 76, 81, 394, 405, 412, 415, 416
Sifawa, Abubakar B, 396
Sisters of Darkness, 138
Small Arms and Light Weapons, 117, 323, 413
Soft Approach to Countering Terrorism Policy, 242
Sokoto Caliphate, 18, 25, 32, 33, 44, 45, 400
Southern Nigeria, 37
SPACE X,, 294
Special Anti-Cult Squads, 139
State Emergency Management Agencies, 241
Subscriber Identification Module (SIM) cards, 141
Super Camp, 97, 208, 219, 281, 282, 283

T

Tactics, Techniques, and Procedures, 328
Tafsir, 27
Tar, Usman A, 115, 117, 118, 122, 126, 396, 409, 412, 413
Terrorism Prevention Act of Nigeria, 153
Timbuktu Triangle, 217, 218, 219, 221, 222, 223, 224, 225, 226, 236, 300

Transnational Organized Crimes, 323
Tzu, Sun, 92, 297

U

Udeh, Chinedu S, 396
Unexploded Ordinances, 265
Ungoverned spaces, 114, 118, 257, 321, 327, 334, 357
United Nations Office on Drugs and Crime, 167
University of Calabar, 96
University of Sokoto, 41, 47, 52, 53
Unknown Gunmen, 135, 136, 406
Unmanned Aerial Vehicles, 354

V

Violent Non-State Actors, 119

W

Wagner Company, 330
Warri, Delta State, 84
White Angels, 138
Whole of Government in Approach, 257
Whole of Society Approach, 256, 332, 404

Y

Yu, Chang, 290

Z

Zabarmari, 165
ZAMAN LAFIYA, 168, 176, 187, 188, 190, 191, 192, 193, 194, 195, 239, 298, 301
Zulum, Babagana, 98, 383

www.ingramcontent.com/pod-product-compliance
Lightning Source LLC
Chambersburg PA
CBHW040318300426
44111CB00022B/2940